Land Reform in China and North Vietnam

Edwin E. Moise

Land Reform in China and North Vietnam

Consolidating the Revolution at the Village Level

The University of North Carolina Press · Chapel Hill · London

Library of Congress Cataloging in Publication Data

Moise, Edwin E., 1946–
Land reform in China and North Vietnam.

Bibliography: p.
Includes index.
1. Land reform—China. 2. Land reform—Vietnam—
(Democratic Republic) I. Title.
HD1333.C6M64   1983   333.3'1'51   82-15900
ISBN 0-8078-1547-0

To my father,
who more than any other person
has shaped my conception of history
and historical scholarship

Contents

Tables

Figures

Abbreviations

CB	*Current Background* (U.S. Consulate, Hong Kong)
CCP	Chinese Communist Party
DRV	Democratic Republic of Vietnam
FBIS	U.S. Foreign Broadcast Information Service *Daily Report: (Area Editions): Far East*
FYI	*For Your Information: Yenan Broadcasts* (Shanghai: United States Information Service)
GAC	Government Administration Council (equivalent to Cabinet)
GVN	Government of Vietnam (State of Vietnam 1949–55; Republic of Vietnam 1955–75)
ha.	hectare (1 ha. = 2.47 acres)
ICC	International Control Commission
ICP	Indochinese Communist Party
MAC	Military and Administrative Committee
NCNA	New China News Agency
PLA	People's Liberation Army
PRC	People's Republic of China
SCMP	*Survey of the China Mainland Press* (U.S. Consulate, Hong Kong)
VNA	Vietnamese National Army (later ARVN)

Preface

My main concern in this study is land reform in China from 1947 to 1953 and in Vietnam from 1953 to 1957, but before covering these matters in detail I have had to summarize the development of Chinese land policy up to 1947; this summary forms an indispensable background to what comes after. Those of my readers who are already familiar with the literature of land reform in China may find little that is new to them up to about the middle of Chapter 3; I must ask them to bear with me.

I have in general given Chinese names and terms here in the *pinyin* system of romanization. There are, however, a few names of people and places for which some other spelling is both firmly fixed in the minds of most English-speaking readers and different enough from the *pinyin* spelling for the *pinyin* to be confusing or at least distracting. I have therefore used the traditional spellings of Peking, Canton, Taipei, Hong Kong, and Chiang Kai-shek. I have also, of course, used the traditional spellings in references to published works which used them. I regret the existence of unavoidable inconsistencies, as when statements by Mao Zedong are footnoted to Mao Tse-tung, *Selected Works*.

I would like to express my gratitude to Mieczyslaw Maneli, formerly of the International Commission for Supervision and Control in Vietnam, who found time at some inconvenience to himself to talk to me. David Marr lent me his notes of discussions he had in Vietnam in 1975. The U.S. Foreign Broadcast Information Service not only granted me permission to use and cite the materials I wanted, but responded with extraordinary speed to my initial request when time was valuable to me. I would also like to thank all those who have read this study, or portions of it, and given useful comments: Norma Diamond, Albert Feuerwerker, Grigorii Sukharchuk, Tanaka Kyoko, Ezra Vogel, John Whitmore, Ernest Young, my father Edwin Moise, my wife Rebecca Zerby Byrne Moise, and several anonymous referees. I am in debt to many librarians, notably Ma Wei-yi, John Musgrave, and Wan Wei-ying of the University of Michigan, Charles Bryant of Yale, A. Kohar Rony and several others whose names I never learned at the Library of Congress, and Myra Armistead, Steve Johnson, Nancy Keffler, Dale Simmons, Ruth Taylor, Marian Withington, and others at the Clemson University Library.

I was supported by a National Defense Foreign Language Fellowship, an Augustus Hendelman Fellowship, and a fellowship from the Center for Chinese Studies of the University of Michigan (using funds originally provided by the Ford Foundation) for part of the time I was preparing this study.

I would like to thank the following publishers for permission to reproduce copyrighted material:

Excerpts from William Hinton, *Fanshen: A Documentary of Revolution in a Chinese*

Village (Copyright © 1966 by William Hinton), reprinted by permission of Monthly Review Press.

Excerpt from Mieczyslaw Maneli, *War of the Vanquished* (Harper & Row, 1971), reprinted by permission of Harper & Row.

Excerpts from Isabel Crook and David Crook, *Revolution in a Chinese Village: Ten Mile Inn* (Routledge & Kegan Paul, 1959), and from Isabel Crook and David Crook, *The First Years of Yangyi Commune* (Routledge & Kegan Paul, 1966), reprinted by permission of Routledge & Kegan Paul, Ltd.

Excerpt from Douglas Pike, *Viet Cong: The Organization and Techniques of the National Liberation Front of South Vietnam* (M.I.T. Press, 1966), reprinted by permission of The M.I.T. Press.

Excerpt from Suzanne Pepper, *Civil War in China: The Political Struggle, 1945– 1949* (University of California Press, 1978), reprinted by permission of The University of California Press.

Excerpt from Edgar Snow, *Red Star over China* (Random House, 1938; Grove Press, 1973), reprinted by permission of Lois Wheeler Snow.

Harvard University Press has informed me that under the doctrine of "fair use" I did not need its formal permission to use two short excerpts from Ezra Vogel, *Canton under Communism: Programs and Politics in a Provincial Capital* (Harvard University Press, 1969). I would like to thank the Press, nonetheless.

I have incorporated in this book, in altered form, portions of two articles:

Edwin E. Moise, "Land Reform and Land Reform Errors in North Vietnam," *Pacific Affairs* (Spring 1976), reprinted by permission of *Pacific Affairs*.

Edwin E. Moise, "'Class-ism' in North Vietnam: 1953–1956," in William S. Turley, ed., *Vietnamese Communism in Comparative Perspective* (Westview Press, 1980), reprinted by permission of Westview Press.

I bear sole responsibility not only for all statements of fact and opinion made herein but also for any mistranslations where sources in languages other than English are cited.

Land Reform in China and North Vietnam

1

Introduction

Successful revolutionaries, once they are in power, must decide how to govern. In a country such as twentieth-century China or Vietnam, there are three major possibilities:

1. The new rulers may fit themselves into the patterns of the old regime, making few fundamental changes. Many low-level functionaries of the old administration will keep their positions and will continue to rule the villages much as they did before. This is what happened to China under Yuan Shikai (Yuan Shih-k'ai) and then Chiang Kai-shek and to South Vietnam under successive regimes, several of them claiming to be "revolutionary," in Saigon. It also happened under the Communists, briefly and in limited areas, in both China and Vietnam.

2. The new government may carry out what is usually called a "nationalist" program, asserting itself against foreign powers and autonomous satrapies within the country, and pushing modernization and economic development. This program will substantially alter the socioeconomic structure of the country, making most of the population both richer and more secure, but it will not necessarily narrow the gap between rich and poor. This is what the Meiji Restoration did in Japan and what anti-Communist "nationalists" promised but never managed to accomplish in Vietnam and China.

3. The third possibility is a real social revolution, in which the poor are mobilized to overthrow the basic structure of society in favor of a new and presumably more egalitarian order. There need not be any conflict between the social revolution and the "nationalist" revolution. Most Communists would argue that, in the long run, the two revolutions cannot be separated; that in a nation made up mostly of poor peasants, it is only by giving the poor a real stake in the revolution that revolutionary leaders can acquire enough support to attain nationalist goals. The Chinese and Vietnamese Communist parties can find considerable evidence for this assertion. While carrying out major social reforms, they have mobilized immense numbers of peasants to work for nationalist goals. It would be very hard to argue that the nationalist goals could have been better accomplished if the social reforms had been omitted.

Still, there can be many short-term conflicts between the goals of egalitarian reform and those of nationalism or simple administrative efficiency. Almost any specific task can be accomplished faster

3

if all energies are focused on that task. Mobilizing the peasants to destroy the traditional elite in the villages and to root out elements sympathetic to that elite from the revolutionary organizations themselves may produce long-term benefits. But at the same time it can distract attention from immediate problems of administration and agricultural production. In the Chinese and Vietnamese revolutions, therefore, people who sincerely believed in egalitarian reforms sometimes felt obliged to put them off for months (land reform in China often came to a halt during the seasons when the peasants most needed to be in the fields), or even years (both China and Vietnam postponed land reform to concentrate on resistance to foreign invaders).

There are, of course, conflicts between individuals and groups within Communist parties over how much social reform should be carried out and how quickly. During the land reform, disagreements at the top levels of the Chinese and Vietnamese parties were seldom extreme. Changes in policy were more often based on shifts in the views of the leadership as a whole, or on changing circumstances, than on shifts from the dominance of one group of leaders to the dominance of another. But at lower levels there was usually a broad range of views, from leftist zealots determined to level economic inequalities at once, regardless of consequences, to landlords who had infiltrated the Party in order to preserve their power and privileges. At any given time, Communist leaders were likely to be dealing with both leftist and rightist deviations by local cadres.

The most important stage of the social revolution, in both China and Vietnam, was land reform. This movement involved much more than taking land from the landlords and giving it to the poor; it was directed against all the sources from which the old rural elite drew its power. In the economic sphere these included not only land but also draft animals, grain stocks, agricultural tools, and money. In some areas usury was a more serious problem than tenancy. The landlords' power was also bolstered by their control of key social and political organizations: village administrations, clan organizations, religious bodies, and occasionally local branches of the Communist Party. The goal of the land reform was not only to take away the land and other wealth of the landlords but to cut them off from the psychological and organizational bases of their power and to destroy their prestige, so that they would lose all influence over the peasants. This meant that it was dependent on the genuine participation of the peasants in a way that is not true of most land-reform programs in non-Communist countries, which begin and end with the transfer of land ownership. The peasants were supposed to take the land from its former owners themselves, rather than get it as a gift from the government. Du Runsheng (Tu Jun-sheng), a senior CCP spokesman on land reform, said in 1950:

Land reform is a revolution which reforms the social system, a whole series of political, economic, and cultural revolutions, destroying the old and establishing the new, with division of the land as the central element. Division of the land is a result the peasant masses attain through political and economic struggle; it is a result of peasant dictatorship; it is "the land returning to its original owners"; it is the peasants seizing the landlords' land by revolutionary methods. [1]

Revolutionary leaders in China and Vietnam, although following the Russian pattern of distributing land to the peasants in private smallholdings before moving toward the eventual goal of collectivization, were able to use this pattern to greater advantage. In the Russian Revolution, the peasants took over landlord land in a very disorganized fashion, starting in the summer of 1917. This probably could not have occurred if the Bolshevik Party had not first weakened and then overthrown Kerensky and the Provisional Government. But in most areas land distribution was not carried out directly by the Bolshevik Party; the peasants undertook it themselves, taking advantage of the climate the Bolsheviks had created. In some areas land distribution was even led by members of the Social Revolutionary Party, traditionally a more peasant-oriented party than the Bolsheviks. The Bolsheviks therefore did not get full credit from the peasants for the land reform. The policies that seemed to the peasants to be specifically Bolshevik policies were the confiscatory taxes necessitated by the civil war of 1918–20, and later the Stalinist collectivization.

In China and North Vietnam, land reform was carried out under clear Communist leadership. It was an opportunity for the Communists both to win the gratitude of the poor and to develop a political structure in the villages, recruiting cadres from among the peasants. In many areas of both China and Vietnam, the land reform and associated campaigns provided the first real contact between the Communist parties and the peasants, which helps to explain why relations between the Party and the peasants have been better in these countries than in the Soviet Union. Collectivization in particular proved far easier in China and Vietnam.

The techniques of land reform took a long time to develop. When elements of the Chinese Communist Party first began establishing rural guerrilla bases in the late 1920s, they had no clear ideas about how to mobilize the poor against the rich. By the early 1930s, they had evolved a very radical land reform policy, which was applied in the Jiangxi (Kiangsi) Soviet and other areas. The radical policy being carried out in the Soviet Union at this time probably had a considerable influence.

In the mid 1930s, the CCP decided to compromise on the class struggle in order to form a united front against the Japanese invasion of China. From 1937 until 1945 policies toward the

---

1. *Nanfang ribao* (Canton), 10 December 1950, p. 3.

landlords varied considerably but were for the most part moderate. After Japan was defeated, the civil war between the CCP and the Guomindang (Kuomintang) government resumed. War was accompanied by a renewed land reform, which was radical but not so much so as that of the Jiangxi period. Most of North and Northeast China had been covered by the time the war ended in 1949. The remainder of the country, except for some ethnic minority areas, underwent land reform between 1950 and 1953 under policies less radical than those of either the Jiangxi period or the late 1940s.

The Vietnamese Communist Party[2] first acquired control of large areas of Vietnam late in World War II. For most of the 1940s it was too preoccupied with struggles against the Japanese and then the French to do much against the landlords. Around 1950, as the Party gained ground in its struggle for independence from France, egalitarian reform policies starting with rent reduction became practical. Emphasis on class struggle increased after the passage of a formal land-reform law (very similar to Chinese laws) in 1953 and the end of the war against France in 1954. By late 1955 and early 1956, wild excesses were being committed in the name of class struggle; a campaign to correct the resulting errors lasted from late 1956 to early 1958.

The Vietnamese land-reform law was clearly based on Chinese models, although there were some modifications. This imitation was possible because the economic and political situations of the two countries had a surprising amount in common, at least on the surface, at the time of their revolutions.

Both China and Vietnam were relatively poor agricultural societies with high population densities, deficient in land and capital. In many areas, hunger was the normal condition of life. An unexpected disaster, natural or man-made, could bring devastating famine. There was considerable inequality, without any formal class system to stabilize social and economic status. Both upward and downward mobility could occur, although in Vietnam the communal landholding system had some stabilizing effect. Land was scarce, and its control was crucial to political and economic power. This pattern is in contrast to the traditional situation in most of mainland Southeast Asia outside Vietnam, where land had been plentiful, and until quite recently the key to power had been control of the labor that could put this land under cultivation.

The predominant pattern in China and North Vietnam—the situation with which the land reform was designed to deal—was one of farms operated by individual families and of private land ownership moderately concentrated. The potential beneficiaries of land reform were mostly peasant families which already operated small farms,

---

2. From 1930 to 1945, the Indochinese Communist Party; from 1945 to 1951, no formal name (referred to by euphemisms like "the Organization"); from 1951 to 1976, the Vietnam Lao Dong (Workers') Party; from 1976, the Vietnamese Communist Party.

but either did not own the land they worked or did not have enough land. The potential victims included a few very large landlords, but most were people of rather moderate wealth—medium and small landlords, rich peasants, and perhaps well-to-do middle peasants. Land-reform planners had to deal with questions such as: How to draw the line, among these people of moderate wealth, between those who should have their land taken and those who should not? How to ensure that people who were not rich enough to have land taken from them, but not poor enough to be given more land, would side with the poor rather than the rich, or at least remain neutral? How to undermine the authority and prestige of landowners who lived in the villages where they owned land, knew their tenants, and had ruled the villages for as long as anyone could remember?

There were areas of China and North Vietnam with patterns other than that just described, but the variations seldom created exceptional difficulties for the land reform. Most of them actually made it simpler. Where plantation agriculture had used techniques of large-scale production that would have been difficult to maintain if the plantations had been split into smallholdings, the government took them over and ran them as state farms. Where all the land had been owned by a few extremely wealthy landlords (likely to be absentees), it could be taken from them much more easily than from a large number of small landlords, and with less worry about borderline cases.[3] Where considerable amounts of land had been held communally or by clan organizations, it was distributed to the poor like landlord land; the difficulties of undermining the authority and prestige of the former managers of such land were about the same as if they had been its owners. The serious problems of land reform—the problems with which this book will primarily be concerned—were the problems of the typical areas, where the land was owned by individual families, worked by individual families, and moderately concentrated.[4]

Both China and Vietnam had long traditions of administrative government. The emperors had tried actually to rule their countries through formal civil service systems. There was supposed to be a uniform administration over the whole of these countries, even if it was a very superficial administration by the standards of the modern nation state. This was strikingly different from the more common pattern in societies at this economic level, which is for the central government to have little role in administration except in the immediate vicinity of the capital. Strong central administration was less of a break with the past in China and Vietnam than it

---

3. For further comments see Chapter 13.

4. Note that this pattern was less typical of South Vietnam than it was of North Vietnam; there was a great deal of communal land around Hue, and private landholdings southwest of Saigon were highly concentrated.

would have been in most of Southeast Asia. Nevertheless, it went much further than its traditional prototypes. A great variety of decisions formerly made by individuals had become government matters in both China and Vietnam by 1960. The central governments had more control over provincial officials, and these officials had more control over the population. (These facts are linked; the traditional regimes would not have dared to trust their own officials with so much power.) The mass population, in turn, had far more control over both the composition and the behavior of local administrations than it had had before the revolution. There was greater political integration and more communication at all levels. This required the recruitment and training of a new local elite that could be trusted to serve the interests both of the central government and of the mass population far more reliably than the old elite. In most villages, land reform was the most important stage of the process by which the old elite was destroyed and the new one created.

In both China and Vietnam, the revolutions that carried out land reform were also nationalist revolutions in a direct and immediate sense; they had to fight off foreign invasions. Many people from the exploiting classes therefore supported these revolutions, at least for a time. Revolutionary leaders had to balance the danger of weakening the nationalist struggle by alienating such supporters against the danger of weakening the class struggle by accepting them. What made the problem especially embarrassing was that, in both countries, the logic of the rural situation called for the initiation of radical class struggle at a time when the Party was still trying to present a moderate face to urban populations. The compromises that resulted did not produce optimal results in either cities or countryside.

In both countries, land redistribution was carried out in the context of revolutionary mass mobilization. Peasant organizations with considerable power were set up in the villages to implement the reform. These village organizations carried out complex programs, which made allowances for various special cases and at least tried to approach what revolutionary leaders regarded as an optimal distribution of land. Such tasks would have been beyond the administrative capacity of a government trying to carry out land reform simply as an administrative process, imposed and supervised from outside the villages. Thus if we examine the Japanese land reform of the late 1940s, we will find that although it was extremely radical in its redistributive goals, it was also relatively crude. It did not distinguish between people who rented out land because they were rich and could not be bothered to cultivate it themselves, and those who owned a small amount of land, which they were for some reason unable to cultivate and which they therefore rented out. An attempt to make such a distinction would have provided a loophole for massive evasion of the law, and no political base for the land reform, capable of blocking such evasion, had been established within the villages.

Japan likewise did not try to distribute land on an equal basis; almost all land simply went to whoever had been the tenant on 23 November 1945. A proposal for distribution of land among the poor on a more equal basis had been rejected; Ronald Dore comments that it would have led "to appalling difficulties of execution."[5] Government officials supported by mass mobilization were able to carry out quite sophisticated programs in China and Vietnam.

The central concern of this book will be the extremely complex relationship between policymaking by Communist leaders and actual events in the villages. I shall try to demonstrate four main points:

1. Land reform is not a natural outgrowth of village life. Peasants, left to themselves, do not think in the patterns required for a campaign of the type carried out in China and North Vietnam. Therefore, the program in those countries had to be initiated by a revolutionary leadership outside the villages.

2. However, it could not be something simply imposed from the outside. Participation by local peasants had to be genuine and enthusiastic. This meant that the peasants, or at least a significant fraction of them, had not only to accept policies introduced from the outside, but to understand the rationale of those policies well enough to apply them creatively.

3. When Communist leaders tried to persuade peasants to support land reform, they were not engaged in some Machiavellian scheme. They were genuinely convinced that the program would benefit the peasants. Land reform was not something into which the peasants had to be sucked by lies and deception. On the contrary, it worked best if Communist leaders were candid about their policies and intentions, and, for the most part, they were indeed quite candid.

4. For Communist leaders to establish a sound connection between their policymaking and actual events in the villages was extremely difficult. A senior Party leader, even if he were of peasant origin, would have interests, attitudes, and assumptions different from those of the bulk of the peasants. Most historians have noted the obvious fact that the Communist leaders were much closer to the peasants than most anti-Communist leaders. But to be closer to the peasants than Chiang Kai-shek, or closer than Bao Dai, did not necessarily bring one close enough. In a number of cases the gulf between Party leaders and village society remained so large that it would be legitimate to say that the leaders responsible for village affairs simply did not know what they were doing. They might be so vague in their thinking that base-level cadres did not have adequate guidance, or their thinking might be based on a total misunderstanding of the actual situation in the villages.

It is the last of these points that most clearly differentiates this book from the existing literature on land reform. People who write about revolutions, whether they are Western scholars or actual

---

5. Dore, *Land Reform in Japan*, p. 140.

Communist leaders, try to do so in such a fashion as to make the events comprehensible. This usually leads them to describe policies as responses to problems. A certain situation existed, and the Party devised certain policies as responses to that situation. Many authors write as if the Party can be presumed always to have foreseen the final results of its policies. Those who do not take such an attitude generally assume at least that the policies carried out in the villages were carried out because central leaders, knowing the situation, thought they would produce a favorable result. Such a picture ignores the turmoil and chaos of a society in revolution. This book presents three major case studies of land reform—northern China, 1946–48; southern China, 1949–53; and North Vietnam, 1953–56. In only one of these (the second) did Communist leaders have either a communications system that could provide adequate information about village affairs, or the opportunity to sit down and analyze the available data calmly, decide what needed to be done, and instruct base-level cadres to do it. In the other two cases, the ultimate goals of land reform might be clear enough, but the mechanisms by which specific policies were formed and transmitted were sorely deficient.

The Logic of Land Reform

One can reasonably say that it was inevitable that the Communists in China and Vietnam would distribute land to the peasants. The necessity of winning poor-peasant support for revolutionary wars, the desirability of destroying a potentially hostile landlord class, and Marxist doctrines of class struggle all pointed to a need for some drastic reform, and neither the Chinese nor the Vietnamese Communist parties developed the administrative capacity to carry out collectivization early enough to consider it as an alternative to smallholder redistribution. Was this inevitable development to be regretted? The stated goals of land reform were to redistribute wealth and power from the traditional rural elite to the peasants and to recruit a new group of rural leaders who would ally themselves with revolutionary leaders at the national level as well as with the peasant masses from among whom they had come. It can reasonably be argued that these goals were desirable, that they could be attained by the means used in land reform, and that in the areas where the land reform was properly conducted the results were well worth the cost.

   To judge the value of land reform from an economic viewpoint, we must consider both the immediate effect on peasant levels of living and the long-range effect on the productivity and growth potential of the economy. The immediate effect of a substantial equalization in levels of wealth was to lift a large portion of the peasantry out of a state of poverty so extreme that actual starvation had been a serious threat to them. This was a matter of such importance, from a moral standpoint, that it would have been

justified even if it had involved a slight decrease in the productivity of the economy as a whole. In fact it did not do so; the new
order was economically more efficient than the old.

It has sometimes been suggested that egalitarian redistribution of
wealth impairs economic growth. The arguments that have been
made against land reform include the following:

1. Concentrations of wealth are necessary to produce the investment that leads to growth. This certainly does not apply to China
and Vietnam, where the traditional rural elites had not put much of
their wealth into productive investments in either the rural or the
urban sectors.

2. The redistribution, attacking the richest elements in the
countryside, will in the process attack the most productive farmers. This was at least a minor problem in most of China and North
Vietnam, and it was a really serious problem in many areas.
However, land-reform authorities tried to minimize the damage by
concentrating their attack on those of the rich who made no significant contribution to production. The owner of a conspicuously
large amount of land was treated better if he hired laborers to
work it and provided active management and capital than if he
simply rented it out; he was treated better still if he worked the
land by his own labor and that of his family.

3. Collective ownership reduces the incentive for individuals to
work hard and to take proper care of capital goods; "everyone's
property is nobody's property." This argument is, strictly speaking, an objection not to the land reforms analyzed in this book,
which redistributed land and goods as private property, but to the
collectivization that followed several years later. However, it is
relevant here because the land reform had been intended all along
to be a step toward collectivization.

4. The foregoing problem leads to another. When the land was
distributed to the peasants, they knew that there would be a later
stage in which private smallholdings would be gathered into
cooperatives. In China there had at first been plans to allow smallholdings to persist for a considerable period; as late as 1955 Mao
Zedong (Mao Tse-tung) cited 1960 as the target date for getting all
peasants into semisocialist cooperatives.[6] But the schedule was
speeded up and most peasants were actually in fully socialist
cooperatives before the end of 1956. The Democratic Republic of
Vietnam had probably planned from the beginning to make a similarly rapid transition to cooperatives. The expectation of imminent
collectivization must have reduced significantly the incentive for
the peasants to invest in improving their land. The same thing
definitely happened for a shorter period at the time of land

---

6. Mao Tse-tung, *Selected Works,* 5:202–3. Estimates that the
CCP had originally planned for the transition to cooperatives to
last fifteen to eighteen years may refer to the time necessary to
reach fully socialist cooperatives.

reform, when some people who knew or suspected that their property was about to be confiscated neglected it.

There were, then, significant sources of inefficiency in the postreform economy, and its growth rate has not always been satisfactory. But the performance of prerevolutionary agriculture had been still worse, and the reasons are not hard to find. The capital that might have been used to increase agricultural production had been heavily concentrated in the hands of a landlord class that had rather little direct involvement in production, and the level of cooperation between the landlords and the peasants who actually worked the land had been quite poor. A landlord who invested to improve the land could not always be sure he would be able to collect an increased rent from his tenants as a result. On the other hand, a tenant who improved the land could not be sure that the landlord would *not* be able to raise the rent. The tenants were too poor to pay for good farm tools, and it was not obviously in the landlord's interest to pay for them.[7] This problem was even more important than it might appear at first sight, since in both China and Vietnam food was a factor of production. A large portion of the peasants were sufficiently malnourished to impair noticeably their capacity for physical labor. When the land reform leveled inequalities of wealth, it raised the average nutritional level of the rural population and thus made a significant contribution to productive capacity.

It might be objected that most of China and Vietnam were sufficiently overpopulated so that an increase in the amount of labor applied to the land would not have had any value. This objection arises, however, from a confusion between the concepts of population surplus and labor surplus. In an automobile factory, or on an American dairy farm, there is a certain amount of work that needs to be done, and one can compute with considerable precision the number of people necessary to do it. But on a peasant farm

---

7. Cheung, *The Theory of Share Tenancy*, especially chaps. 2 and 4, argues that sharecropping does not lead to economic inefficiency. However, quite aside from the fact that he deals only with the question of how efficiently wealth is used once a decision has been made to use it in production (in other words, he does not consider the possibility that a landlord might use for luxury consumption wealth that a poor peasant would have invested in buying a plow), he assumes that there will be nearly perfect coordination between landlords and peasants. If a landlord owns money or capital goods for which a peasant has a constructive use, it is assumed that they will have no difficulty reaching an agreement acceptable to both, allowing this capital to be put to its most efficient use, and it is further assumed that each party can be reasonably sure the other will keep the letter and spirit of the agreement. The real state of class relations, in prerevolutionary China and Vietnam, was quite different.

growing rice, there is almost always one more task to be performed, which will raise production a little bit.[8] The field can be weeded four times instead of three during the growing season, the rice can be transplanted twice instead of once, fish can be raised in the field during the period when it is flooded, and so on. If one extra person is added to the farm to perform these tasks, the increase in production may not pay for the cost of feeding the new mouth; this is what we mean when we say that China and Vietnam are overpopulated. But if the people already on the farm can be enabled to do these extra tasks themselves, production will rise; this is what some Chinese have meant when they said in recent years that China has a labor shortage.

The landlords owned: land, which was often used inefficiently because of the tensions in the landlord-tenant relationship; grain, which they hoarded for long periods before releasing it for use and which occasionally rotted if they miscalculated and hoarded it too long; and money, which was often hoarded for even longer periods. We may discount some of the extremes of Communist propaganda, ranging up to the claim that the landlords were opposed to increases in agricultural production, but it is plain that the desire of the landlords to increase production was not strong enough to make them devote their resources to that goal. Shifting wealth to the peasants enabled them to feed themselves better and to buy the farm tools and so on that they were in a position to use directly[9] (incidentally expanding the market for urban industries, an important consideration).

Given that collectivization was to occur, land reform was a necessary intermediate step. The Chinese and Vietnamese Communists, although they used some coercion in collectivization, did not wish and could not afford to use massive force, as Stalin had in the Soviet Union. To the greatest extent possible, they wanted the agricultural producers' cooperatives to be voluntary associations of peasants who had been persuaded that they could enjoy a higher level of living as cooperative members than as individual smallholders. This would have been quite impossible if great inequalities of landholdings had still persisted at the time of collectivization. No rich peasant or well-to-do middle peasant could have been persuaded that his fortunes would be improved by joining with landless or almost landless poor peasants in a cooperative, unless the well-to-do were given so much control of the cooperative that the poor became in effect their hired hands. But once land reform had reduced inequalities of land ownership, the various components

---

8. Geertz, *Agricultural Involution*, pp. 35–36.

9. Beneficial effects of this type have sometimes been exaggerated, as when *Nanfang ribao* of 28 December 1950, p. 3, boasted of how many draft animals the peasants were buying in a village that had just finished land reform. The fallacy becomes apparent if we ask who was selling.

of the rural population could join together on something like an equal basis. Not all middle peasants believed Communist claims that the efficiency of large-scale production would make them better off joining in cooperatives with poor peasants who, after land reform, still had slightly less land and tools than they did, but at least these claims were not a joke.

It might be suggested that the revolution could have acted to eliminate the inefficiencies of the old economy without confiscation, by permitting and encouraging the landlords to use their wealth more productively and by mediating between the landlords and peasants to protect the interests of both and to reduce conflict. Thus, if a landlord were to put up the money to buy a new plow for a tenant, the government could both guarantee that the land-lord would be repaid at a profit, and protect the tenant from the kinds of usurious interest rates and devious financial manipulations that had in the past often made a loan from a landlord the prelude to a major disaster for a peasant. Similarly, the government could have guaranteed that whoever made significant improvements in a piece of rented land—landlord or tenant—would enjoy the full fruits of his investment. Such policies might have led to significant increases in production without the need for egalitarian redistribution.

There would, unfortunately, have been several disadvantages to that program. First, it could not have been perfectly effective; no government can monitor all the details of a private economy. Second, to the extent that it worked it would have done so quite gradually, and to leave the peasants in a state of extreme poverty for another decade or two was morally unacceptable to the Communist leadership. Third, it would have placed the Communists in the position of acting as guarantors of the property rights of the rich, and indeed as more vigorous and effective guarantors than the reactionary regimes before the revolution had ever been. So grotesque a betrayal of the ideals for which the revolution had been fought would probably have led to a total collapse of the morale of the rural cadres, leaving the government without the capacity to carry out the program.

The land reform was necessary from an economic viewpoint, then, whether we consider it as an end in itself, or as a preliminary to collectivization. The CCP itself now regrets that it went as far as it did in collectivization; the recent expansion of private plots and the more extreme forms of the household-responsibility system have in effect restored the family farm as a significant component of the rural economy. However, even if the CCP were to decide someday that individual farming is in general superior to collective operation, that would not undermine the justification for land reform. The prerevolutionary economic system had been less efficient than either the smallholder system created by land reform or the collective agriculture that ensued a few years later.

Redistribution of power and prestige was a much more complex process than redistribution of land and was more likely to go

seriously astray. On the whole, however, the political effects of
land reform were beneficial. The land reform did not lead to a
fully democratic system and could not have been expected to do
so; a great deal of the power that had formerly been held by the
landlords and rich peasants ended up in the hands of the Communist Party. However, a significant amount of power really was
transferred to the middle and poor peasants; the claims of such a
transfer were not simply a rhetorical cloak for the transfer of
power to the Communist Party.

Some Crucial Problems

Four major categories of people carried out land reform in China
and Vietnam: Communist Party leaders at the national level, the
cadres who actually went into the villages, the peasants who were
recruited as village leaders and activists during the campaign, and
the broad mass of peasants, who did not become village leaders,
but whose support and participation was still necessary if the
campaign were to succeed. Only rarely could there be full agreement between people on these four levels. The revolution had
overturned the previous social, economic, and political structure,
and it had destroyed many of the familiar reference points by
which people had judged the limits of the possible and the desirable. Land reform promised to destroy some of the remaining ones.
It would be absurd to expect, even assuming the highest levels of
intelligence and goodwill, that people of widely different backgrounds, with different viewpoints, would reach a uniform judgment of tricky questions under such confusing conditions.
Communist leaders had to remain calm while facing the facts that
the cadres going out to the countryside might not understand or
agree with all of the policies they were supposed to be implementing, and that many peasants either doubted the desirability of land
reform or had their own ideas about how it should be carried out.
The latter problem especially raised a conflict between the needs of
central leadership and peasant spontaneity. The peasants had to be
a genuine force in the land reform. If land-reform cadres from
outside a village made all the real decisions and peasants merely
carried them out, the psychological impact of the reform would be
reduced. Also, outside cadres would not know enough about the
village to be capable of running everything properly themselves.
On the other hand, it was necessary to make sure the reform
followed the policies laid down for it. Some land-reform cadres saw
an insoluble contradiction here: the peasants would not follow
government policies unless there were representatives of the
government standing over them, telling them what to do at every
point.[10] Their superiors felt that the land-reform policy was

10. Editorial, *Changjiang ribao* (Hankou), 26 December 1950,

sufficiently in accord with the wishes and needs of the peasants so that if the peasants were properly taught, they would see that the policy was in their interest and would follow it with only a moderate amount of supervision.

There were times and places at which the land reform came close to the ideal model; public meetings of the broad mass of the peasants made important decisions on class demarcation and on the confiscation of land and other wealth, using approximately the criteria laid down by the official land-reform policy. In some other places the land-reform cadres did not know how to teach the peasants about government policies, did not have the time to do so, or simply did not trust the peasants, and therefore they did everything themselves. The peasants became essentially passive, and sometimes even disapproving, spectators.

Between these extremes there were some interesting intermediate cases. Decisions might be made, not by the mass population of a village, but by a small group of peasant activists, who had been trained and helped by land-reform cadres from outside the village. The success of this procedure depended on how well the activists had been chosen and on whether the inactive majority of the peasants at least approved of the decisions being taken. There were also cases in which large numbers of peasants were participating in land reform, but their actions clearly were not spontaneous. Thus we are told about the events of a single day, which represented the climax of land reform for one village on the outskirts of Canton. First, about two thousand peasants gathered for an outdoor meeting. A particularly hated landlord was brought before them, and there was much shouting of slogans and accusations. He tried to deny his crimes, but after the peasants had detailed his various misdeeds, he had to confess. The next landlord was then brought forward, and so on, until eighteen landlords had confessed their crimes and handed over their land deeds. The peasants then scattered to the homes of the landlords, confiscating what they found there and searching out concealed property. They brought such of the confiscated property as was movable back to the meeting ground before sunset.[11] For all of this to have been accomplished so quickly and smoothly, every step must have been planned beforehand; one wonders whether even the landlords may not have been made to rehearse their roles. Still, it would be unwise to dismiss this morality play as an empty sham. Peasants who could not have written the script for such an affair themselves may still have participated with genuine enthusiasm after someone else had written one. Also, a considerable part of the script would in fact have been written by the peasants who enacted it; many of the people who made planned denunciations of the landlords' crimes at the mass meeting would have been repeating speeches that they

reprinted in *Nanfang ribao*, 3 January 1951, p. 3.

11. *Nanfang ribao*, 18 December 1950, p. 2.

had originally made spontaneously in group discussion sessions during the preceding weeks.

This book should convey a sense of how land reform developed over time, both locally and at the national level. Within each village, the landlords and rich peasants started out in firm control. The poor peasants resented this situation more actively in some areas than in others, but hardly anywhere were they prepared, psychologically or organizationally, to rise up and overthrow the old order. Communist cadres had to chip away at the power of the old elite, while building up peasant organizations. There were many false starts in these tasks; the landlords and rich peasants infiltrated peasant organizations, and even after those poor peasants who were promoted to leadership positions got over the initial problem of inexperience, some of them turned out to be corrupt or tyrannical. Most villages ended up with the old elite virtually destroyed, and a new leadership recruited from and satisfactory to the mass of the peasantry, but attainment of these goals had not been quick or simple. Each village had to go through one reform after another, each one cutting down the power of the old rural elite a little further, giving the peasants a little more political training, and checking up on the peasant leaders who had been promoted in previous stages.

At the national level, it took many years for the Communist leaders to get over their tendency to revolutionary dogmatism. When the revolution began, the leaders (many of whom were urban men) had a very limited understanding of village conditions and no experience with the problems of transforming rural society. They had little to guide them in policy formation except for their revolutionary convictions, which were fervent but vague. In general, if there were a dispute over policy, leaders would not be able to choose between policies on their merits, because the information that might have formed the basis for a rational discussion was not available. In order to avoid lapsing into paralysis through inability to be sure that any policy was the correct one, a leader would pick a policy (often on the basis that it showed the greatest revolutionary zeal), convince himself that the rational arguments for that policy were much better than they actually were, and decide that those who disagreed were probably suffering from a lack of class spirit if not outright counterrevolutionary sentiments. The upshot was often very radical policies and a paranoid exaggeration of landlord influence both within and outside the Party. If someone tried to argue that the landlords were not strong enough at a particular time and place to threaten the revolution seriously, not only was the argument likely to be rejected, but the person making it might be added to the list of possible agents or dupes of the landlords within the Party.

As time went by, both discussions of land-reform policy within the Party and the policies themselves became more rational. Although the argument that a given policy was best because it showed a proper revolutionary attitude by no means disappeared, it was increasingly supplemented by the argument that a given policy had been demonstrated to produce good results. Leaders became able to deal more calmly both with opposition to land reform at the village level and with Party members who criticized particular policies. They became more willing to try persuading opponents that the policies being criticized would in practice produce good results, both because prolonged trial and error had produced policies more defensible under this standard and because the facts on which such a discussion could be based had become more readily available. The temptation to charge opponents with lack of loyalty to the revolution, and to choose extreme policies in order to display one's own zeal, declined as years of struggle and indoctrination created a general atmosphere of confidence; most Party members trusted their comrades and expected their comrades to trust them. As the revolutionary movement grew stronger, it could afford to be more tolerant of opposition. In particular, when counterrevolutionary infiltrators within the Party no longer posed a threat to one's own life, one would be less tempted to take hasty action in regard to a comrade whose behavior seemed suspicious. The result was that policy became less self-consciously radical, and it came to be recognized that in some areas extremes of class struggle might be inexpedient, or might be unnecessary because of the weakness of the "feudal forces." Discussion of policy became more concerned with the concrete situation and the actual results of this or that policy than with the maintenance of revolutionary purity.

This is not to say that the Communists were abandoning their radical goals over time. In China, the calming process described above involved the sacrifice of so few of these goals that when Mao Zedong looked back at it from the perspective of the Cultural Revolution, he did not seem very displeased. What was happening was that the revolutionaries were learning how to carry out radical goals in a more efficient manner. It was still necessary to get rid of the landlords, but if low-level cadres suggested that the job could be done better in a given village if it were delayed for six months, the leaders were willing to listen. If they decided that the delay was not in fact justified, they would explain this to the cadres. Cadres who still refused to proceed might have to be punished, but even then the leadership could remain reasonably calm.

In the early stages of the revolution, land policy oscillated between periods of a united front, when class struggles were heavily restricted (1924–27 and 1937–41 in China, 1941–52 in Vietnam), and periods of extreme class struggle. During the extreme periods, many people, some of them probably motivated by a desire to prove to themselves and the world that their behavior in the moderate period did not mean that they were not real revolutionaries, became so preoccupied with not showing lenience to any enemy of the revolution that they attacked many people who were in no sense enemies. When such paranoia was abandoned, the class struggle became stronger rather than weaker. Before the land reform was finished in China, it appears to have achieved the Communist dream of combining redness with expertise. The much shorter history of land reform in Vietnam did not allow such a prolonged and clear evolution; the period of radical paranoia lasted until the end of the land reform proper. However, if we include the correction of errors that followed, a pattern of moderation very similar to that in China becomes apparent.

It should be apparent by this time that a land reform of the type under consideration is an extraordinarily complex process. Among the major questions that did not have obvious answers were: (a) Should the Party try to establish complete economic equality in the countryside, taking land from everyone who owned even a little more than the average amount? If not—if it allowed some people to continue owning more than the average amount—where should it draw the line? (b) How harshly should it treat those from whom land was being taken? Should it leave them with as much land as the average holding for the area in which they lived, or should it cut them down to below the average level, perhaps strip them of all their land, as punishment for past exploitation? Should it take from them forms of wealth other than land? Should it kill some large fraction of them? (c) What attitude should the Party take toward individuals from the old rural elite who seemed willing to abandon their allegiance to their former class and join the Communist Party?

Terminology

In order to convey the flavor of the period and of the original documents, I have tried to discuss land reform in the terms the Communists themselves used. This choice of language has introduced many Communist value judgments into the text. Some of these have been embodied in the words used; thus I refer to "liberated areas," and when I say "landlord," I mean a person who fits the Communist definition of a landlord. Some have appeared in statements or comments; when I have described Communist policies as misguided, or downright disastrous, this means that the policies were ineffective or counterproductive in the accomplishment of Communist goals. There are problems with this approach. The most important is that Communist terminology made the boundaries between classes seem more clear-cut than they actually were; in particular, it did not include the landlords as part of "the people," the moral community. A properly trained land-reform cadre felt that the landlords and peasants were fundamentally hostile groups, that the peasants owed nothing to the landlords, and that it was a delusion to expect the landlords to think they owed anything to the peasants. In some villages this was a good reflection of the actual state of class relations, but in others the relationship between rich and poor had been more complex, and Communist terminology did not match the perceptions of either landlords or peasants. The problems posed by the use of Communist terminology are, however, very small compared with the difficulty of conducting a meaningful discussion of land reform in any other terminology. I have tried to describe what happened in the land reform as accurately as possible; on the basis of these facts my readers can form their own value judgments, some of which may be sharply different from those of the Communists. But I have assumed that my readers will also want to know why the Communists did what they did, how they looked at their situation, what they were trying to accomplish, and whether they did indeed accomplish it. An attempt to use phraseology not embodying Communist values would have interfered with my effort to convey this information.

The Communist analysis of rural class structure was fairly complex and it changed over time, but the main outlines were as follows:

The main criterion for deciding class status was *exploitation*: an economic[12] relationship in which one person is able to obtain wealth that has been created by another person's labor. In the rural economy, the most important forms of exploitation were the renting of land, the hiring of labor to work land, and usury. Although the Communists hoped in the long run to abolish exploitation, they did not regard it as such a hideous sin that any person who engaged in it had to be treated as an enemy, so they did not feel the need to invent some euphemism to be used when the exploiter was a person of whom they approved.

The *poor peasants* and *agricultural laborers* formed a majority of the rural population. They were massively exploited as tenants, hired laborers, and recipients of high-interest loans. In this study the term *laborer* will refer only to agricultural laborers.

The *middle peasants* neither exploited others nor were exploited to any large extent. Most of them owned their own land, although some rented land from other people. Some of them (especially *well-to-do middle peasants*) exploited others to a small extent, usually by hiring laborers, but occasionally by renting out land.

The *rich peasants* exploited others to a substantial extent, especially by hiring laborers, but they still did major agricultural labor themselves. Those who rented out more than half their land

---

12. The qualifier "economic" removes certain social and political relationships from the category of exploitation. Thus when a peasant couple grows grain, the portion eaten by their children or taken by the tax collectors of the People's Government is not considered to represent exploitation. There were sometimes difficult borderline cases when the Communists suspected that a relationship that appeared to be social was actually economic and qualified as exploitation. Thus they believed that some young men who were in theory adopted sons were de facto hired laborers being exploited by their "foster parents."

were called *rich peasants of a semi-landlord character.*

The *landlords* were rich enough to avoid doing major agricultural labor; they lived by other people's labor. Defining the boundary between rich peasants and landlords in terms of labor meant that some rich peasants were considerably richer than some landlords. But the landlords were regarded as being not only wealthy but undeservedly wealthy; people who really contributed to production were excluded from this category as far as possible.[13] The most important form of landlord exploitation was renting land, but many also hired laborers to work on their land, made usurious loans, etc. Those who used their power in local society most oppressively were called *local despots.* It should be noted that the despots were not necessarily the richest landlords; it might even be possible for a rich peasant to be a despot.

People who owned comparatively small amounts of land, which for one reason or another they were unable to work for themselves and therefore rented out, were called *small renters.*

The Communists obviously were not victims of the simple-minded notion that all people who rented out land formed a single class; the structure summarized above, with people who rent out land spread among five categories, appeared relatively early in the history of the land reform.[14]

People who were poor peasants at the time their villages came under Communist control could rise in class status if they worked hard and took advantage of Communist programs for the redistribution of landlord wealth. Many poor peasants and laborers became *new middle peasants;* a few poor and middle peasants became *new rich peasants.*

In this study a policy will be called *leftist* or *radical* if it attacked the interests of the wealthier classes very severely, or if it attacked people who were only moderately well off as well as the very rich. It will be called *rightist* or *moderate* if it attacked only a few of the rich, or imposed only mild penalties on them.

In many Chinese and Vietnamese sources, people advocating very moderate policies are called right deviationists while radicals are called "left" deviationists, with quotation marks. The implication is that leftist policies are those that serve the interests of the poor, and therefore it is impossible really to be too far to the left. The radicals only appear to be "leftist." I have avoided this usage as

---

13. The principle that those who did major agricultural labor would not be classified as landlords was not absolute; class-demarcation decrees generally allowed families that engaged in exploitation on a very large scale to be classified as landlords even if they did labor to some extent.

14. For the beginnings of CCP class-demarcation policy, see Huang, "Analyzing the Twentieth-Century Chinese Countryside," pp. 132–50; Huang, "Mao Tse-tung and the Middle Peasants, 1925–1928," pp. 278–88.

far as possible; I feel it reflects an oversimplification of the issues of class struggle. It seems to have become widespread only in the 1950s (some of the earlier writings of Mao Zedong have had the quotation marks added in recent editions of his works).[15]

The term *feudal* will seldom be used in this study. In many Communist documents, it had a fairly exact meaning; when a person who played no part in the productive process was able to demand a share in the goods produced, that was considered feudal exploitation. The typical feudal exploiter was a landlord who collected rent on land to the productivity of which he did not contribute and which he might never even have seen. The Communists felt, quite reasonably, that feudal exploitation in this sense usually inhibited production. They distinguished it from more capitalist forms of exploitation used by most rich peasants and some landlords, who actively managed the land that other people worked, or invested significant amounts of capital to raise its productivity. However, even when used in this fairly exact sense, the word "feudal" was seldom necessary; it was more often an expletive than a descriptive term. And often, especially in the early days of the CCP, "feudal" was used vaguely, meaning that the exploitation in question was old-fashioned, or involved a great deal of control of the exploited by the exploiters, or was just very bad. Even buying cheap and selling dear could be "semifeudal exploitation."

---

15. In an alternate formulation, the "leftists" are impetuously trying to reach at once revolutionary goals that will actually be attainable only in the future. See Hua Tse, "Left, Ultra-'Left' and Fake Left," pp. 6–10.

2

The Background to Land Reform in China

Geography

In the early years of the People's Republic, China was divided into six greater administrative regions: Northeast, North, Northwest, East, Central-South, and Southwest. These were new units; neither the Qing (Ch'ing) Dynasty nor the Guomindang would willingly have created such powerful organizational bases for regionalism. Below them were the provinces, most of which had the same or almost the same boundaries as under former governments. Each province contained several special administrative districts.

The *xian* (*hsien* or county) had long been the real base of the national administration. After the establishment of Communist power it lost that role; the CCP reached below the *xian* level in a way the Qing and Republican governments had not. The *qu* (*ch'u*)[1] was a subdivision of the *xian*, and, during the land-reform period at least, its government was largely an auxiliary of the *xian* government.

Most of the peasants lived in small villages called *cun* (*ts'un*). However, these were residential rather than administrative units. For governmental purposes these natural villages were grouped into administrative villages called *xiang* (*hsiang*), or sometimes administrative *cun*. The *xiang* was the base level of government after 1949, the place where the national administration met local society. In the late 1940s there were about 48,000 *xiang* in China. In this book the word "village" will be used both for the *cun* and the *xiang*.

The Chinese countryside was extremely poor, but it was not simple or primitive. Over the centuries, the Chinese had worked out many patterns of crop specialization, long-distance trade, and local trade by which too many people could extract some sort of living from too little land. At the same time, elite groups had devised an equal variety of systems for extracting a rather good living from the peasants. Few members of the rural population led lives of total isolation and self-sufficiency; they were affected to a

---

1. In this study the term *qu* will be used only for this subdivision of a *xian*. In Chinese documents it is also used for greater administrative regions and special administrative districts.

Figure 2-1—Land tenure and population density in southern China

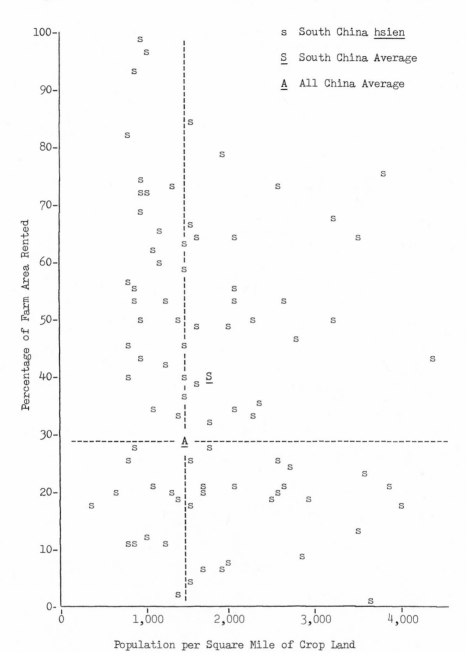

Population per Square Mile of Crop Land

Figure 2-2—Land tenure and population density in northern China

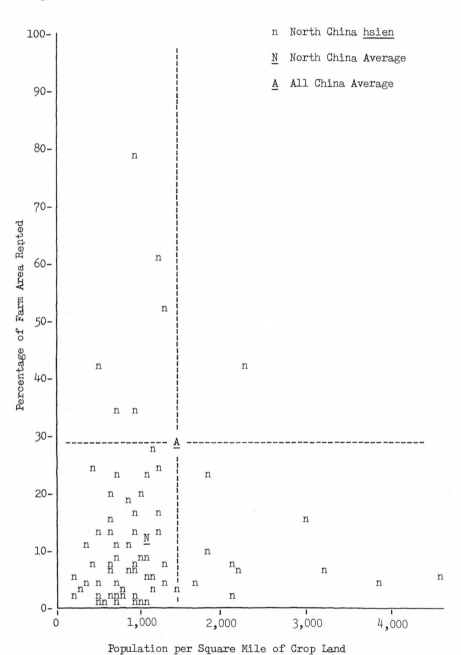

significant extent by forces outside their native villages. Peasants could supplement their incomes by household industries. Rich peasants and landlords could become brokers buying their poorer neighbors' crops for sale in the towns. Many landlords had originally bought their land with money obtained through commerce, usury, or politics. There was considerable geographic as well as occupational mobility; peasants moved into the towns looking for work, or (especially in northern China) moved from one village to another.

Conditions of land tenure, productivity, and population density varied widely not only between different regions of China but between localities within each region. Speaking in crude averages, we can say that southern China, where rice was the main crop, had a comparatively high rate of tenancy. The productivity of the land was good and yields seldom fluctuated too much from year to year. The ratio of people to cultivated land was high. The predominantly wheat-growing North had a far lower rate of tenancy. The land was less productive on the average, and there were drastic fluctuations in yield due to the uncertainty of rainfall. The ratio of people to cultivated land was therefore lower. Northern China, especially the Northwest, was far more subject to famine than the South. The landlords in the North were less often absentees than in the South. According to stereotype, the northern landlord was more savage and the southern landlord more clever.[2] The Northeast (Manchuria) must to some extent be left out of these generalizations; it had comparatively low productivity, a low population density, and large absentee landlords holding much of the land.

Figures 2-1 and 2-2 show something of the range of variation among localities. They are based on data from a considerable number of *xian* compiled by J. Lossing Buck in the 1930s. Each small letter shows the percentage of cultivated land rented, and the population density, found by a survey or surveys in a particular *xian*.[3] Capital letters show averages. Figure 2-1 is for China south of the boundary line between predominantly rice-growing and predominantly wheat-growing areas. Figure 2-2 is for China north of this line, excluding the Northeast. One can see clearly in these figures the general pattern of regional averages described above, but the variation between individual localities was so great that there hardly existed a typical village even for any particular province, much less for China as a whole. It is possible to obtain very different pictures of rural conditions by looking at different areas. Thus Ramon Myers has studied two provinces, Shandong and Hebei, which had tenancy rates that were below average even for North China. Chen Hansheng (Chen Han-seng), on the other hand, reported conditions in areas of Guangdong where the

---

2. *Xinhua yuebao*, August 1950, p. 817.

3. Buck, *Land Utilization in China*, 3:55–56. These surveys seldom if ever covered all of a *xian*.

tenancy rate was well above average even for South China. Both books are useful as studies of the particular areas with which they deal, but neither should be taken as representative of any broader area.[4]

Land Tenure and Wealth

When speaking in generalities, Communist authors often said that the landlords and rich peasants, less than 10 percent of the population, controlled 70 percent to 80 percent of the land; this included land owned by clans, schools, and other organizations, which was under the effective control of the landlords and rich peasants who managed it. This generalization is not borne out by more specific data from CCP sources. It may have originated with some surveys Mao Zedong took in the early years of the CCP, when its activities were concentrated in areas of rather high tenancy.[5] Later authors treated these figures as if they were typical long after more extensive CCP surveys had shown that they were not, presumably because the exaggerated figures made it easier to blame the landlords and rich peasants for all of China's ills. This tendency to underestimate the amount of land controlled by the peasants is shown most clearly in a study of agricultural taxation by Li Chengrui, which contains much useful information on land-tenure conditions before and during the revolution. At one point Li presents two tables showing the amounts of land owned by each class in twenty-four localities in Central-South and Southwest China. In summarizing these tables, Li says they show that the middle peasants generally owned from 15 percent to 25 percent of the land. But if we consult the tables, we will find that they actually show the middle peasants owning more than 25 percent of the land in fourteen of these twenty-four localities.[6] It is vital therefore to look at surveys from specific areas rather than at impressionistic generalizations.

For the purposes of the present study, Li Chengrui's figures from fifteen local surveys in the Central-South Region are probably the most useful. They indicate that the combined holdings of landlords, rich peasants, and "others" ranged from 46.9 percent to 76.9 percent of the land, with an average of 60.9 percent. The middle peasants, poor peasants, and laborers, on the average, formed 82.8 percent of the population and owned 38.8 percent of the land. These data probably underestimate the proportion of

---

4. Myers, *The Chinese Peasant Economy*; Chen Han-seng, *Landlord and Peasant in China*.

5. Li Chengrui, *Zhonghua renmin gongheguo nongye shui shikao*, pp. 59–60; Snow, *Red Star over China*, p. 84.

6. Li Chengrui, *Zhonghua renmin gongheguo nongye shui shikao*, pp. 118–20.

Table 2-1—Percentages of population, households, and land ownership for different classes

	Central-South Region	Southwest Region	Other Regions
Landlords			
population	4.2	7.4	7.4
land	41.4	38.4	29.3
Rich peasants			
population	5.0	7.3	3.0
land	12.1	14.3	6.4
Middle peasants			
population	26.3	44.3	38.6
land	24.8	30.8	42.3
Poor peasants			
population	55.6	38.5	
land	14.0	8.6	
Agricultural laborers			
population	0.9	0.6	
land	0.0	0.1	
Poor peasants & laborers			
population			48.8
land			17.2
Landlords			
households			2.7
land			27.7
Rich peasants			
households			5.4
land			16.0
Middle peasants			
households			30.6
land			35.0
Poor peasants & laborers			
households			58.5
land			18.8

Sources: Li Chengrui, *Zhonghua renmin gongheguo nongye shui shikao*, pp. 61, 119–20; Li Geng, *Jiefang qu di tudi zhengce yu shishi*, p. 42; Qi Wu, *Yige geming genjudi di chengzhang*, p. 127; Hinton, *Fanshen*, p. 209; Yan Zhongping et al., *Zhongguo jindai jingji shi tongji ziliao xuanji*, p. 278.

Table 2-2—Index numbers for the per capita landholdings of different classes, from Table 2-1

	Central-South Region	Southwest Region	Other Regions
Landlords	9.81	5.19	3.96
Rich peasants	2.42	1.96	2.13
Middle peasants	0.94	0.70	1.10
Poor peasants	0.25	0.22	
Poor peasants & laborers			0.35

laborers in the population; agricultural laborers seldom had to pay land taxes, and so a study primarily concerned with taxation omitted them. Li found laborers to be only 0.8 percent of the population of the Central-South Region. An earlier study not focused on taxation, which agreed very closely with Li on the overall percentage of the land owned by middle peasants, poor peasants, and laborers, had found about 8 percent of the population of the Central-South Region to have been agricultural laborers.[7] Most other areas of China, except for the Northeast, probably had less concentrated landholdings than the Central-South Region.

Table 2-1 gives the averages of Li Chengrui's data for the Central-South and Southwest regions, and averages of nine assorted surveys in other regions, four of which give the percentage of population for each class and eight of which give the percentage of households. The index numbers in Table 2-2 show the per capita holdings of each class relative to the average per capita holdings of the rural population as a whole; thus the landholding per person of landlords in the Central-South Region was 9.81 times the average for people of all classes in that region.

Division of the rural population into owners, part owners, and tenants (cultivators who owned all the land they worked, part of it, or none of it) is somewhat less useful than division into the

7. Zhang Gensheng, "Zhongnan qu gesheng nongcun shehui jieji qingkuang yu zudian guanxi di chubu diaocha," pp. 27, 34. For further discussion of the landholdings of different classes see Esherick, "Number Games."

Table 2-3—The percentages of owners, part owners, and tenants among farming households in China, 1936

Province	Number of *xian* Covered	Owners %	Part Owners %	Tenants %
Chahaer	10	43	26	31
Suiyuan	13	52	17	31
Shanxi	90	61	23	16
Hebei	126	72	18	10
North China	*239*	*66*	*20*	*14*
Ningxia	5	66	14	20
Qinghai	8	50	28	22
Gansu	29	64	18	18
Shaanxi	49	62	20	18
Northwest	*91*	*62*	*20*	*18*
Shandong	100	75	15	10
Jiangsu	56	45	25	30
Anhui	41	35	23	42
Zhejiang	62	20	33	47
Fujian	42	25	31	44
East China	*301*	*46*	*24*	*30*
Sichuan	87	29	20	51
Yunnan	39	39	25	36
Guizhou	23	27	28	45
Southwest	*149*	*31*	*23*	*46*
Henan	89	59	21	20
Hubei	48	33	26	41
Hunan	41	22	28	50
Jiangxi	57	27	33	40
Guangdong	55	21	33	46
Guangxi	50	39	23	38
Central-South	*340*	*36*	*27*	*37*
TOTAL	*1,120*	*47*	*24*	*30*

Source: Zhang Youyi, *Zhongguo jindai nongye shi ziliao*, 3:728–30.

Note: In this table provinces have been grouped into greater administrative regions, which did not exist in 1936. Averages for regions are weighted.

class categories the CCP used, because each of these three categories will include people ranging from quite rich to very poor. Also,
this division ignores the agricultural laborers. However, these
categories are clear and unambiguous, and this is the best form of
data readily available for some areas. Table 2-3 shows the situation
as of the year 1936 (with the provinces grouped into greater
administrative regions, which did not exist at that time).

It should not be supposed that the reason that some CCP
sources exaggerated the amount of land in the hands of the landlords and rich peasants was that accurate figures would have
shown land reform to be unnecessary, or necessary only in some
areas. The existence of even a limited number of rather small
landlords posed a problem, from the viewpoint of the CCP, which
needed to be solved by fairly radical measures. It does not take
much redistributed wealth to make a significant improvement in the
life of a really poor family. Land reform looked more attractive if
one had the mistaken idea that in most villages 60 percent or more
of the land would be available for distribution to the poor, but
even 10 percent would have made a very real difference. Also, the
landlords posed a threat to the revolution in their capacity as the
traditional village elite, regardless of whether their holdings were
small or large. The most important English-language study of the
land reform, William Hinton's *Fanshen*, deals with a village where
middle and poor peasants had already owned 70 percent of the land
before the revolution. This was an extraordinarily high percentage
for China, the second highest of the thirty-three surveys summarized in Table 2-1, but it was not high enough to eliminate the
need for a radical land reform. The poor of China needed every
scrap of wealth they could obtain. Death by starvation was at least
a distant possibility for a large fraction of the peasantry. In the
rural areas of northern China, famine probably claimed something
like 8 percent of every generation,[8] and an unknown additional
number starved as individuals even when there was not a large-
scale famine. Furthermore, the condition of most families was
declining from generation to generation; the average man was
significantly poorer than his father.

To say that the average man—both mean and median—was poorer
than his father is not the same as saying that the average level of
wealth per man in Chinese society was declining from one generation to the next. Intuitively these statements seem equivalent, but
intuition is misleading in this case. The average wealth of the
fathers of the men of the current generation is not the same as the
average wealth of all men of the preceding generation, because
some men of the preceding generation had no sons, and their level
of wealth would not be considered when we construct the average
for the fathers of the current generation. The difference is actually big enough to be important; if we look at all the men of a

8. Buck, *Land Utilization in China*, 3:19.

given generation in prerevolutionary China and compare each man's wealth with what his father had had, we will find a pattern of declining wealth that would be less conspicuous, or perhaps absent, if we compared the average level of wealth for this generation with the average for all the men of the preceding generation.[9]

The poorest men in China were often unable to have children. A significant fraction of them were simply unable to marry, because there were fewer women than men in the population and it was the men with the least money who usually went without wives. If they did manage to marry, their children were more likely to die young, of outright starvation or various diseases aggravated by malnutrition, than the children of families having at least average wealth. The upshot of this was that the poorest men of any given generation could not be the children of the poorest men of the preceding generation, because very few such children existed. Most of the poorest men had to have been born higher on the economic scale and to have been downwardly mobile. The bottom elements of the society were continuously disappearing and being replaced by downward mobility. As a village head told Isabel and David Crook in Hebei: "How could any man in our village claim that his family had been poor for three generations? If a man is poor, then his son can't afford to marry; and if his son can't marry, there can't be a third generation."[10]

This pattern of downward mobility ran from the top of Chinese society to the bottom, although it was most noticeable at the lower levels. Among the well-to-do, downward mobility was caused mainly by *fenjia* (the division of family wealth among several sons of a given father). Among the poor, downward mobility was more likely to be caused by a loss of wealth to the rich, as families in need had to sell land or contract loans at high interest.

This pattern was one of the driving forces behind the Chinese Revolution. The poor were desperately poor and could reasonably expect that their children would be even poorer. Many of them therefore became willing to fight very hard for a change in the system that doomed them, when the Communist Party offered them a credible hope that such a fight could succeed. The land reform was one of the major battles in this struggle. However, while the pattern of downward mobility helped create the need for land reform, it also made it more difficult. Many middle and poor peasants were the children or grandchildren of landlords and rich peasants, which created dangerous confusion in class demarcation.

---

9. What follows is a brief summary of the argument in Moise, "Downward Social Mobility in Pre-revolutionary China."

10. Crook and Crook, *Revolution in a Chinese Village*, pp. 133–34.

Early CCP Land Policies

In its first years the CCP was primarily an urban organization. A few Party members were organizing the peasants, but the Party neither drew up any detailed program for social reform in the villages, nor devoted enough resources to rural work to have been able to put such a program into effect if it had existed. This situation changed abruptly in 1927 when Chiang Kai-shek, then just consolidating his position as head of the Guomindang, turned on his erstwhile Communist allies and virtually destroyed their organization. Most Party leaders were killed, went underground, or fled abroad, but a few went into the hills and established rural bases. Mao Zedong and Zhu De (Chu Teh), operating mainly in Jiangxi province, were particularly successful. After the Jiangxi base area attained a substantial size, the top Party leadership of the early 1930s, a Russian-oriented group known as the "28 Bolsheviks," moved there and made it their headquarters. For the first time rural areas were under a Communist rule sufficiently stable for a real land reform to be practical.

The "Land Law of the Chinese Soviet Republic,"[11] applied in the Jiangxi base area from 1931 to 1934, was quite radical. The landlords were stripped of all their land and wealth; many were set to doing forced labor. The rich peasants were left with only some land of inferior quality. This severity may have been inspired, to some extent, by the harsh policy Stalin had recently adopted toward the rich peasants (kulaks) in the Soviet Union.

Article 3 of this law said that the land of the middle peasants was not to be confiscated, but Article 5 said that in some areas there would be equal distribution of the land, which meant that middle peasants who owned more than an average landholding for their village would lose part of it, without compensation and without their consent. This was an early example of a confusing terminology that has been common in both China and Vietnam. The term "confiscate" (in Chinese, *moshou*; in Vietnamese, *tich thu*) was given a restricted meaning: taking land from enemies of the people. When land was taken from those such as middle peasants who were not considered enemies of the people, some other phrase was used.

Mao Zedong, who by this time (unlike the 28 Bolsheviks) had had years of experience working in the countryside, would have preferred a less drastic policy. His need to fit his public utterances to the views of his superiors in the Party makes it difficult to trace the exact development of his thought, but in general he wanted something closer to simple equalization of wealth; he thought that the rich peasants should be allowed to retain landholdings equal to those being given to the poor and that some

---

11. Dated 1 December 1931, trans. in Hsiao Tso-liang, *The Land Revolution in China, 1931–1934*, pp. 186–91.

members of the landlord class should be left with some land.[12] His policies were not as far to the right as has sometimes been alleged. Those who criticized him for following a "rich-peasant line" wanted land reform to go beyond equalization of wealth, reducing the landlords and rich peasants to well below the level of the poor peasants.[13]

The Guomindang managed to destroy the Jiangxi Soviet in 1934, but Mao and his supporters, who gained control of the CCP soon thereafter, had learned a great deal about the techniques of revolution that they were able to apply in other regions. They had evolved a clear set of class definitions. Families that lived off land rent, etc., and did no major agricultural labor, were labeled landlords. If at least one member of a family performed major agricultural labor, but over 15 percent of the family's income came from exploitation, the family would be labeled rich peasants. Families could get up to 15 percent (or in special cases 30 percent) of their income from exploitation and still be considered middle peasants.[14]

The CCP was confronting some of the real difficulties of social revolution in the countryside, which were far more complex than had been anticipated. After the Red Army arrived in an area, it could not mobilize the peasant masses to seize effective social and economic power at once. For a while, the traditional landlord and rich-peasant elite would retain much of its control over the peasants and perhaps even infiltrate the new regime. Mao was shocked: "Petty-bourgeois elements seized control of the government committees; in the early days the small landlords, rich peasants, and intellectuals scrambled to get on to government committees, especially at the township level. Wearing red ribbons and feigning enthusiasm, they wormed their way into the govern-

---

12. "Land Law of the Chinese Revolutionary Military Council," sometimes said to have been dated 7 February 1930, trans. in Hsiao, *Land Revolution*, pp. 130–35. See also CCP Central Bureau of the Soviet Areas, "Resolution on the Land Problem," 21 August 1931, quoted in ibid., p. 49.

13. See Moise, "Land Reform in China and North Vietnam," pp. 56–58 (hereafter cited as Moise, "Land Reform"), for my disagreements on this issue with Wong, *Land Reform*, p. 8; Kim, *The Politics of Chinese Communism*, p. 121; Kuo, *Analytical History of the Chinese Communist Party*, 2:536–37; Lotveit, *Chinese Communism 1931–1934*, p. 184.

14. Mao Tse-tung, "How to Analyze the Classes" and "Decisions Concerning Some Problems Arising from the Agrarian Struggle," both issued formally by the Central Government of the Chinese Soviet Republic on 10 October 1933, trans. in Hsiao, *Land Revolution*, pp. 255–82. Do not be misled by the version of the former given in Mao Tse-tung, *Selected Works*, 1:137–39. It is actually a shortened text issued in 1948.

ment committees by trickery and seized control of everything, relegating the poor-peasant members to a minor role."[15]

This naturally affected the results of any attempted land redistribution. In June 1933, at a conference on problems of land redistribution, Mao described areas where the old village elite had been remarkably successful in adapting itself to life under a Communist regime:

> Here the landlords' and rich peasants' open counterrevolutionary struggle had already been crushed by the revolutionary masses during the first stage. After this, many of them quickly altered their appearance, taking off their counterrevolutionary masks and putting on revolutionary masks. They expressed approval of the revolution and of land redistribution. They claimed that they were poor peasants and were entitled to share in the distribution of land. They have been very active, relying on their historic advantages: "they are the ones who can speak, and they are the ones who can write." Therefore, during the first stage they were able to snatch the fruits of the land revolution. The facts from countless localities prove that they are controlling the provisional administrations, infiltrating local armed forces, manipulating revolutionary organizations, and [in land redistribution] receiving more land and better land than the poor peasants.[16]

Surface control of an area might be attained fairly easily. The establishment of a real mass base, which would make that control secure, was a longer and more difficult process. It required the development of new techniques of struggle against the landlords and rich peasants.

Mao's desire not to be too harsh on most of the victims of land reform has already been mentioned. His retrospective analysis of the Jiangxi land reform, embodied in a 1945 resolution of the CCP Central Committee, indicated the desirability of "providing certain economic opportunities for the rich peasants and also enabling the ordinary landlord to make a living."[17] He presumably wanted to set limits (albeit broad ones) on the disruption of society and to maintain agricultural production. From similar motives, he argued that in redistribution the CCP should not shift the ownership of

---

15. Mao Zedong, "Jinggangshan Qianwei dui Zhongyang di baogao" [Report of the Jinggangshan Front Committee to the Central Committee], 25 November 1928, in Takeuchi Minoru et al., *Mao Zedong ji*, 2:52. To the extent possible I have followed the translation of a substantially altered version of this report given in Mao Tse-tung, *Selected Works*, 1:92.

16. Takeuchi Minoru, *Mao Zedong ji*, 3:244–45.

17. "Resolution on Certain Questions in the History of Our Party," 20 April 1945, in Mao Tse-tung, *Selected Works*, 3:195.

land unnecessarily. Even if the Party were carrying out complete equalization of land ownership in a village, it should not simply assign each family plots arbitrarily but rather take the existing situation as a basis. It should take away from families that had too much land, or very good land, only enough to bring them down to the proper level; it would then use what had been taken to supplement the holdings of families with little land or inferior land ("drawing on the plentiful to make up for the scarce" and "drawing on the fat to make up for the lean").

These issues arose at a time when the CCP was making a fundamental shift in its whole conception of the revolutionary process. This was not merely a matter of shifting the center of the revolution from the cities to the countryside. Up until about 1930, the Communists had been trying to provoke a popular uprising. They had tried to present a program that would be attractive enough so that the masses in enemy-held areas would overthrow their rulers and place the CCP in power. This was the pattern that the European Marxists had always considered natural, the pattern that had produced the October Revolution in Russia. It had disastrous results in China from 1927 onward. The emphasis on civilian insurrection made the CCP underestimate the importance of regular military forces. The CCP repeatedly sent workers and peasants to fight against professional soldiers. This line also required the Communists to send what military forces they did have into the densely populated areas where the enemy was strongest in order to arouse the masses there. This led to many quite futile attacks on large cities. The proletariat and peasantry, which were supposed to join the revolution as soon as Red forces came to arouse them, proved reluctant to do so. As Mao noted in 1928, "Wherever the Red Army goes, the masses are cold and aloof, and only after our propaganda do they slowly move into action."[18]

The CCP had to adopt a strategy of civil war. It first acquired base areas, and then expanded them by means of the Red Army. In any given area, Communist cadres would be protected by outside military forces until they could mobilize the local peasantry. Until 1927, the Guomindang army had provided some of the necessary protection for peasant movements in parts of Guangdong and Hunan. By late 1928 Mao had raised an army, composed largely of former Guomindang soldiers and bandits, to do the same thing.[19] Only after such motley groups had established base areas were the Communists able to recruit large numbers of politically reliable peasants to defend and expand them.

Making the revolution primarily a matter of expanding the base areas, rather than of expanding the sympathy for Communism among the masses still under Guomindang rule, created the danger

---

18. Mao Tse-tung, "The Struggle in the Chingkang Mountains," in *Selected Works*, 1:97.

19. Ibid., pp. 80–81.

of a decline into opportunism. Some leaders of the Jiangxi Soviet seemed on occasion to be letting their concern for their military power distract them from the need to maintain good relations with the masses. But in the end, making the base areas the key to the revolution made the CCP far healthier than it otherwise would have been. It expanded its power not by making promises but by carrying them out; by actually providing good rule to local populations and thus winning their support for the defense and expansion of the base areas. As a result, by the time the Communists got control of really large areas they had become capable, experienced administrators, in a far better position than the Bolsheviks at the time of the October Revolution.

The need to provide effective administration and a strong economy eventually led Mao Zedong to disavow some of the extremes of the class struggle. The rich peasants in particular had been among the more productive elements in the traditional rural economy, and the Communists might do themselves more harm than good if they destroyed the rich-peasant economy completely.[20] Although a considerable amount of class struggle was clearly necessary, that struggle should not be carried to a point where it would harm the nation as a whole and thus in the long run harm the poor peasants. The question that had to be resolved was where that point lay at any given time.

The Shift to the Northwest

In 1934, most of the Communists in Central and South China were forced to flee superior Guomindang forces in the "Long March." Much of the Red Army was lost; the survivors reached the small Communist base area in Shaanxi, which later became the Shaanxi-Gansu-Ningxia Border Region, in late 1935 and 1936. The retreat marked a policy failure so disastrous that the 28 Bolsheviks were unable to retain control of the Party, and Mao Zedong emerged as its top leader.

Shaanxi, and northern China in general, were considerably poorer than the provinces of central and southern China that had previously been the centers of CCP activity; periodic droughts caused famines of a magnitude almost unknown south of the Yangze. The North and Northwest also had a considerably lower rate of tenancy; most land was owned by those who worked it (see Figure 2-2 and Table 2-3). Statistics collected by J. Lossing Buck in the 1930s indicate that only about 17 percent of the cultivated land in Shaanxi was rented; this compares with 28 percent in

---

20. There is no evidence that Mao knew of the disastrous effects of Stalin's attack on the rich peasants in the Soviet Union, but he may have observed similar problems arising in the Jiangxi base area.

China as a whole and 51 percent in Jiangxi.[21] One might conclude
that land reform was not needed in Shaanxi. However, simple
statistics on landholdings are not as important as they might seem.
Inferior but arable land was plentiful in Shaanxi and had very
little value. Edgar Snow talked with some peasants about this in
1936:

> I asked this old man how much land he had.
> "Land?" he croaked. "There is my land," and he pointed to
> a hilltop patched with corn and millet and vegetables. It lay
> just across the stream from our courtyard.
> "How much is it worth?"
> "Land here isn't worth anything unless it's valley land," he
> said. "We can buy a mountain like that for $25. What costs
> money are mules, goats, pigs, chickens, houses and tools."
> "Well, how much is your farm worth, for example?"
> He still refused to count his land worth anything at all.
> "You can have the house, my animals and tools for $100—with
> the mountain thrown in."[22]

Local Communists had carried out a land reform in considerable
portions of the Shaanxi base area in 1934 and 1935. This reform
did not just redistribute land that had been owned by landlords
and rich peasants (which would have been more important than
Buck's figure of 17 percent rented land would suggest, both
because these people's land would have been of considerably better
than average quality and because some land that they had worked
by their own labor or hired labor was redistributed, in addition to
what they had rented out). It also affected livestock, tools, seed
grain, and the other things that a peasant needed actually to raise
a crop and to avoid dependence on usurers. It had been immensely
important to the local peasants. It had been accompanied by many
of the same policy disputes as the land reform in Jiangxi. Local
leaders had wanted an essentially egalitarian reform, but the
national Party leadership had denounced this as a "rich-peasant
line" and imposed more radical policies. When Mao arrived at the
end of 1935, he intervened on the side of the more "moderate"
local leaders.[23]

The United Front

War between China and Japan broke out in 1937. The Red Army,
its main body renamed the Eighth Route Army, placed itself nominally under the command of Chiang Kai-shek for united action

---

21. Buck, *Land Utilization in China*, 3:55–56.
22. Snow, *Red Star*, pp. 262–63.
23. Selden, *The Yenan Way in Revolutionary China*, chaps. 2–3.

against the invaders. The CCP and the Guomindang achieved some genuine cooperation in the first years of the war, but their relations were never good, and after 1941 there was at best an armed truce. The United Front had more reality in the villages than at the national level.

In December 1935, the Political Bureau of the CCP Central Committee met at Wayaobao and passed a resolution calling for a broad united front against Japan. Chiang Kai-shek was not, as yet, invited to participate; he was described as a running dog of Japan and an enemy to be overthrown. Still, there was hope that some elements of the warlords and the national bourgeoisie could be persuaded to support the front. Although the CCP was not giving up its advocacy of land reform, and the best it said it expected from the landlords was that some of them would refrain from open opposition to the anti-Japanese front, the resolution contained two important modifications of the land-reform program. One was that confiscation from rich peasants would be limited to land they rented out. The other was that a thorough implementation of land reform would be gradual: "In the Japanese-occupied zone and the areas surrounding it, we should first confiscate the land and goods of the traitors, and distribute them to the peasants; later, in the course of the struggle, based on the experience of the masses themselves, we will deepen the struggle and carry out a thorough solution of the land question."[24]

The Party was realizing that mass mobilization took time; attempts to redistribute the land immediately after a given area came under CCP control simply had not worked very well. But this statement may also have hinted at the concessions the CCP was willing to make in order to broaden the United Front. In July 1936, the Central Committee ordered that there be no confiscation of land from anti-Japanese soldiers or people involved in anti-Japanese enterprises. Finally, in February 1937, the CCP announced that in the interests of the United Front it was willing to give up the confiscation of landlord land; land would not be taken except from those who collaborated with the Japanese. Instead, borrowing from Guomindang legislation that had never been enforced, the CCP ordered that land rents be reduced by 25 percent of the amount formerly paid. It also reduced the interest rate on debts, usually to 10 percent per year. The landlords were promised that rent would actually be paid at the reduced level. There were some areas where the landlords even tried to get back from the peasants land that had been redistributed before 1937, but the CCP did not condone any such reversal of old reforms.[25]

---

24. "Muqian zhengzhi xingshi yu dang di renwu" [The present political situation and the Party's tasks; commonly referred to as the Wayaobao Resolution], 25 December 1935, in Takeuchi Minoru, *Mao Zedong ji*, 5:34.

25. Selden, *Yenan Way*, p. 99; Mao Tse-tung, *Selected Works*,

In 1940, while the United Front at the national level was starting to collapse, the CCP broadened it at the local level by instituting the "three-thirds" system. The Party announced that it was voluntarily limiting itself to one-third of the positions in local governments, including elected assemblies. This quota was applied flexibly, and the Communists tried to make sure their people occupied the most critical posts, but many non-Communists, including landlords and rich peasants, were able to take positions in elected assemblies and in the bureaucracy. The Party seems to have been willing to accept a larger proportion of landlords in the middle and upper levels of the government than in the villages;[26] it wanted them where they could be watched and where they would not have too much direct control over the peasants.

There were two major reasons for the CCP's moderate policies. One was to maintain the United Front at the national level; to placate the Guomindang and perhaps also the United States. This logic applied both during the war against Japan and during the negotiations of 1945–46, which attempted to avert civil war. The other, and probably the more important reason, was to assist the expansion of CCP power at the local level. An overly radical agrarian policy could have slowed disastrously the expansion of the guerrilla bases behind Japanese lines. This is not to say that the peasants were inherently unreceptive to the idea of class struggle. CCP experience both before 1937 and after 1945 indicates that the peasants would have accepted and supported a radical land reform; the problem was that they would have done so rather slowly. The CCP would have had first to arouse the peasants to want to overthrow the traditional elite and then to organize them and give them the self-confidence actually to do so. Only after this would they have become a political force, a major asset in the expansion of CCP power. As Isabel and David Crook put it, "[The Communists] did not expect the poor and middle peasants...immediately to take their destinies entirely into their own hands. For centuries these peasants had been accustomed to regard themselves as ignorant and inferior. Now they had to learn from their own direct experience that they had the ability to govern."[27]

By arousing the peasants against the landlord power structure, the CCP could have expanded its power gradually, as it had expanded the Shaanxi base area in 1935 and 1936. But by coming to terms with as much of the old power structure as it could, the Party was able to spread over enormous areas of North China, behind Japanese lines, in a very short time. It reached accommodations with many military and paramilitary groups and with

---

1:281–82, 2:76.

26. Mao Tse-tung, "On the Question of Political Power in the Anti-Japanese Base Areas," 6 March 1940, in *Selected Works*, 2:418–19.

27. Crook and Crook, *Revolution*, pp. 37–38.

influential individuals. It absorbed areas with a population variously estimated from 50,000,000 to 100,000,000 in about three years. These areas became immediate assets, supplying the Eighth Route Army with recruits and taxes and allowing it to disperse its forces to reduce their vulnerability. Once the Communists had consolidated their position, they would begin to chip away at the power of the landlords and rich peasants regardless of the United Front.

In the early years of the war, the main programs leading to an equalization of wealth were direct outgrowths of the struggle against Japan; the Eighth Route Army confiscated land and other property of people who collaborated with the Japanese and distributed these things to the poor, and it collected steeply graduated taxes to pay for its own operations. There was little class struggle; even rent-reduction laws often went unenforced. Carl Dorris has described campaigns for the enforcement of rent reduction in the Shanxi-Chahaer-Hebei Border Region as early as 1939,[28] but in some other areas such campaigns do not seem to have started until 1942, and even then the results were uneven. Many landlords collected the legal (reduced) rent in public but later returned clandestinely to collect an additional amount from their tenants.

Serious reforms depended on the political situation in the villages—on the class composition and ideological level of local officials, cadres, and CCP members, and on the degree to which the ordinary peasants had been mobilized and politicized. The CCP began a rectification campaign, running from top to bottom and affecting both Party and non-Party cadres, in 1941. In the upper levels, this campaign emphasized reeducation of Party members, especially intellectuals, who came from the exploiting classes and had joined the Party after the formation of the United Front. Among *cun* administrations and non-Party cadres, rectification may have been less a matter of reindoctrination than of weeding out the unsatisfactory. But even after the rectification, the landlords and rich peasants were likely to form a larger percentage of the local leaders than they did of the population as a whole. After a reform of *cun* administrations and new elections for *cun* assemblies in the Taihang District of the Shanxi-Hebei-Shandong-Henan Border Region, limited but interesting surveys indicated that 21 percent of the elected *cun* representatives and 22 percent of the *cun* cadres were still landlords or rich peasants.[29]

As the balance of class forces shifted, the CCP could proceed from progressive taxation to 25 percent rent reduction and sometimes beyond. Mao had suggested as early as 1940 that once rents had been reduced by 25 percent, the peasants might demand

---

28. Dorris, "Peasant Mobilization in North China and the Origins of Yenan Communism," p. 705.

29. Qi Wu, *Yige geming genjudi*, p. 95.

further reductions.[30] The Shanxi-Hebei-Shandong-Henan Border Region government ruled at an early date that regardless of how high rents had originally been, they were not to exceed 37.5 percent of the crop after rent reduction. Near the end of the war this limit was lowered first to 30 percent and then to 22.5 percent.[31] Rent reduction was made retroactive, going back usually to the date a given area had been liberated from the Japanese, sometimes even earlier. Landlords who had to refund excess rents collected in previous years, as well as pay fines for tax evasion, out of seriously reduced incomes, often had to sell considerable amounts of land. Without any overt land reform they were being seriously weakened economically as well as politically.

The landlords defended themselves with varying degrees of success. Some maintained enough control over their tenants to keep rents "reduced by daylight but not reduced at night." Some gained influence with the new regime by taking posts in it themselves, befriending local cadres, or sending sons to join the Eighth Route Army. One very clever one joined the CCP and then formed a mutual aid team in which the members farmed their land collectively and then divided the crops, with 40 percent distributed according to the amount of land and capital each person had contributed and 60 percent distributed according to the amount of labor each person had done. Under this fine socialist rationale he was in effect getting the other members of the team, who had presumably been short of land, to cultivate his land for him and pay a 40 percent rent.[32] But the number of landlords who succeeded in resisting Communist pressures became steadily smaller.

---

30. Mao Tse-tung, *Selected Works*, 2:446.
31. Crook and Crook, *Revolution*, p. 100. For comments on other areas, in some of which rent reduction seems to have gone past 25 percent at quite early dates, see Snow, *The Battle for Asia*, p. 338; Li Geng, *Jiefang qu*, p. 44; *Renmin ribao* (*Jen Min Jih Pao*), Wuan, 1 March 1948, p. 1.
32. *Wei chunjie dang di zuzhi er douzheng*, p. 74.

3

Land Reform from 1945 to 1948

From 1945 to 1948, the CCP gradually shifted from a posture of class compromise to one of unrelenting class struggle. At first the Party seemed simply to be trying to help the poor peasants, while weakening an upper class that tended to sympathize with Chiang Kai-shek. But the policy of promoting class struggles among the rural population came increasingly to be accompanied by an attempt to purify the Party itself along class lines. Policies of class compromise were not merely abandoned, they were eventually repudiated with shock and horror. Party leaders set a very high standard of class purity, class loyalty, and service to the poor, a standard by which Party organizations in many areas were seriously inadequate. In their dismay over the situation, they exaggerated the problem, believing that the behavior of Party members had become much worse than was actually the case. By the winter of 1947–48, the Party was not only attacking the landlords and rich peasants very vigorously, but also conducting a rather paranoid purge of its own organizations.

During the war, the CCP had looked ahead to some kind of land reform after the defeat of Japan; it had never stopped advocating "land to the tiller" as a long-range goal. However, it was uncertain how radical a reform this would be. It did not wish to become too radical too fast for fear of provoking a civil war. Rent and interest reduction and progressive taxation had been able to achieve a great enough transfer of wealth during the war to form the basis for a very substantial degree of mass mobilization, without a direct assault on the landlord class. Top leaders knew that civil war, and therefore a renewed land reform, were likely. But they seem to have felt that even the moderate policies of the war years met the minimal needs of the peasants and that such policies could therefore be maintained as long as there was any hope of peace with the Guomindang. The three-thirds system was formally in effect in some areas as late as September 1946.[1] Landlords were probably being weeded out of village-level posts, where they had direct control over the peasants, and left mainly in positions where

---

1. *For Your Information: Yenan Broadcasts* (hereafter cited as *FYI*), 19 September 1946; see also 28 June 1946.

they would be visible without being able to interfere much with CCP policies.[2]

In 1945 and 1946 there were movements for "settling accounts" in many areas. These were directed partly against former collaborators, especially in the large areas that had been liberated only after the Japanese surrender of 1945. Some collaborators were killed, with or without formal trials. Many, though not all, had their land and goods confiscated. Property that had been usurped from the peasants by local despots was confiscated and, in some cases, distributed to the poor rather than simply being returned to the original owners. Finally, landlords and rich peasants had to pay compensation for collection of excess rents and underpayment of taxes during the war. To a considerable extent, the settling of accounts was a spontaneous movement arising at the village level, and the CCP leadership was later criticized for not having supported it more strongly. The CCP provided remarkably little guidance to the peasants and village cadres during late 1945 and most of 1946, so there were significant variations in the way the struggle was carried out in different areas.[3]

In the village William Hinton called Long Bow, in Lucheng *xian*, Shanxi province, Shanxi-Hebei-Shandong-Henan Border Region, the antitraitor phase of the settling accounts movement lasted until December 1945. About half the landlords and rich peasants in the village were attacked, but only in their capacity as collaborators. This was not yet a class-based movement; property was even taken from sixteen middle peasants and six poor peasants who had collaborated with the Japanese. This antitraitor movement did not really draw in the mass of the peasants; it was mainly the work of the cadres and a few activists. Three people were killed.[4]

In January 1946 the emphasis of the movement shifted. One of the people involved later told Hinton: "We were told that the Anti-Traitor Movement was over. We decided that we would now struggle against the landlords who had oppressed us for so long. Everyone who had been oppressed or exploited, who had borrowed money or rented land could now make accusations and get revenge."[5] This settling of accounts went beyond anything authorized in the formal legislation of the border region. Rent and interest reduction were applied retroactively to the period of Japanese control. In a number of cases, the amount a landlord was

---

2. Even during the war a report from the Shanxi-Chahaer-Hebei Border Region had said that 17.7 percent of the *xian* assemblymen were landlords or rich peasants, but only 7.6 percent of the *cun* chairmen were landlords or rich peasants; Li Geng, *Jiefang qu*, p. 55.

3. Ibid., pp. 15–16, 22; *Wei chunjie dang*, pp. 20–21; Belden, *China Shakes the World*, pp. 164–69.

4. Hinton, *Fanshen*, chaps. 11 and 12.

5. Ibid., p. 131.

said to owe the peasants as compensation for past exploitation was greater than the landlord's total wealth. The peasants might confiscate all his visible property—land, grain, etc.—and then beat him to make him reveal where he had buried his silver. By the summer of 1946, 97 percent of the land that had been owned by landlords in Long Bow had been taken from them, as well as 54 percent of the land that had been owned by rich peasants. The same occurred in many other areas. There was hardly a plot of rented land to be found in the whole of Wuan *xian*, Hebei. In the Jiangsu-Anhui Border Region, there were said to be no landless farming families remaining.[6]

On 4 May 1946 the CCP Central Committee issued a directive on the land question, the text of which was not released to the public.[7] The "May Fourth Directive" ordered that land reform be carried out in all areas under secure Communist control. It began by noting that the peasant movement in some areas had already led to the confiscation and distribution of land, sometimes even to the equalization of landholdings (*pingfen*). Some people had expressed doubts about the desirability of such actions. The directive argued that the Party should not fear the movement but support it, and should approve the transfers of land that the peasants had obtained or were obtaining.

The body of the document fell short, in daring and in clarity, of what one would expect from these introductory remarks. Many landlords were to lose their land; they were to be left enough to live on. But industrial and commercial properties of the landlords were not to be infringed, unless the landlords involved had committed exceptional crimes against the Communist Party or the people. The property of the rich peasants was generally to be left alone; if the masses demanded that some rich-peasant land be taken during the settling of accounts in regard to old rents, or during land reform, the rich peasants were still not to be treated as harshly as the landlords. Land that they worked themselves was to be protected. The middle peasants, including well-to-do middle peasants, were not to be touched; it was important to rally them to the side of the poor rather than driving them into the arms of the landlords.

The May Fourth Directive left extraordinary latitude to local leaders. The landlords might face outright confiscation, be forced to sell their land, have it taken away as compensation during the settling of accounts, or be persuaded to donate it to tenants

---

6. Ibid., p. 209; Crook and Crook, *Revolution*, p. 113; *FYI*, 19 September 1946.

7. "Zhonggong Zhongyang guanyu qingsuan jianzu ji tudi wenti zhishi" [CCP Central Committee directive on settling accounts, rent reduction, and the land question], 4 May 1946, in *Tudi zhengce zhongyao wenjian huiji*, pp. 1–6. The version published on Taiwan is not significantly different.

"voluntarily." There was no clear statement of how much land the landlords should be allowed to keep.[8] Furthermore, CCP cadres were not supposed to maintain an excessively tight control over the movement. The land reform was to be carried out by "the masses," and the cadres were told not to substitute themselves for the masses, or issue too many commands. The whole vaguely defined process was supposed to be completed before the end of 1946. Once it was over, there was not supposed to be any further land reform; the peasants needed to have a feeling of security so that they would work hard and try to enrich themselves.

The overall impression conveyed is one of confusion. The introductory sections had implicitly endorsed equalization of landholdings (*pingfen*) as something that the peasants were attaining in some areas and that the Party should approve. In most Communist documents, and apparently in this one, equalization of landholdings meant taking from everyone who owned more than the average amount—landlords, rich peasants, and some middle peasants. But the body of the directive did not permit cutting well-to-do middle peasants or even all rich peasants down to equality with the poor, and it seemed more worried about left than right deviations. It recommended a general policy of leniency toward former enemies. Some people would have to be executed or imprisoned after a formal trial (nature and jurisdiction of the court unspecified), but this was to be kept to a minimum and nobody was to·be lynched or beaten to death.

The CCP's public decrees and propaganda over the next few months seem to have been aimed largely at people in the cities under Guomindang control; they emphasized that the land reform was to be peaceful. Radio broadcasts from the CCP capital at Yan'an (Yenan) repeatedly discussed cases of landlords who were returning from the cities to the liberated areas in the countryside; these landlords supposedly were treated better by the CCP than by the Guomindang. There was also considerable publicity about landlords who donated land voluntarily to the peasants; those who had joined the Party, or who held high positions under the three-thirds system, took the lead in this movement.[9]

Around the end of 1946, draft laws on land reform were issued by various regional governments under Communist control; they were quite moderate. One of the stricter of them, the Shaanxi-Gansu-Ningxia Border Region law of 21 December 1946, said that the landlords' surplus land was to be purchased with ten-year bonds. The value set on the land was extremely low: the

---

8. In September 1946, landlords were still permitted in theory to retain twice the local average of middle-peasant holdings, or more. Li Geng, *Jiefang qu*, p. 17. But in practice they were treated more harshly.

9. Ibid., pp. 17, 20, 23; *FYI*, 18 May, 12 June, 15, 25, and 27 July, 1 August, and 19 September 1946.

equivalent of one to two years' harvest for small landlords, less for large landlords. The landlords were allowed to keep 50 percent more than the local average of middle-peasant landholdings, or 100 percent more if they had supported the Anti-Japanese Resistance. The land of rich peasants was not to be taken, but the law stated that the land that landlords worked themselves (*zili gengzhong zhi tudi*) should not be taken, and this implied that some people who should have been labeled as rich peasants may have been classified as landlords.[10] The laws in other border regions allowed landlords who had not participated in the Resistance to keep twice the average middle-peasant landholding.[11] The peasants were supposed to make a partial payment for the land, up to half of what the landlords were getting, if they had the financial ability.

Such moderate public statements did not have much connection with what actually happened in the countryside, but it is difficult to present a coherent picture of real CCP policies, either as they existed in the minds of Party leaders or as they worked out in the villages. There were great variations in local conditions, and problems in communications. Furthermore, the CCP had made an explicit decision not to lay out too formal a program for land reform at this time but to wait while various areas experimented freely.[12]

On its face this seems a sensible decision, given that the CCP still had a great deal to learn about land reform. But it may have been influenced by the Party leaders' desire to avoid issuing publicly a radical program that would compromise their image in the cities. To have allowed themselves to be guided by considerations of this type would have been seriously detrimental to land reform. If people cannot discuss problems in public, they will have considerable difficulty refining and improving their views and checking them against reality. The incoherence of the May Fourth Directive, an internal document of the Party, suggests that the CCP did not understand clearly what it wanted to do. In February 1947, Mao Zedong complained that the May Fourth Directive had been applied in only about two-thirds of the liberated areas and that, even there, it often had not been applied thoroughly enough.[13] But what Mao actually wanted was for land reform to go far beyond the provisions of that directive, and in many areas it was doing so.

In the villages that had been under CCP control during the war, much landlord land, rather than being distributed to the poor, had been sold off gradually as the owners became unable to withstand the pressure of rent reduction and graduated taxes. Many poor peasants had been unable to get any of it; they had not had the money to buy land even at artificially low prices. This had created

---

10. Li Geng, *Jiefang qu*, pp. 57–61.
11. Ibid., p. 25.
12. Ibid., p. 18.
13. Mao Tse-tung, *Selected Works*, 4:123–24; see also 4:116.

a rather dangerous situation. The policy that the CCP would have preferred to follow, when it resumed open land reform, was the one often described as evening out the ends without disturbing the middle. This meant that landholdings would be equalized among the landlords, rich peasants, poor peasants, and laborers, while no land would be taken from middle peasants. A survey of twenty-four *cun* of the Shanxi-Chahaer-Hebei Border Region found that before the war the middle peasants had been 36 percent of the households and had owned 41 percent of the land. If all the rest of the land had been divided equally among all the rest of the population, then each non-middle-peasant household would have ended up with 81 percent as much land as the average middle-peasant household. But between 1937 and 1943, the middle peasants had been able to buy 54 percent of all the land sold.[14] If we assume that land transfers continued in this proportion until land-lord and rich-peasant holdings had been reduced by one-fourth (by about 10 percent of the total cultivated area), then a later effort to even out the ends without disturbing the middle would have left the poor peasants with only 65 percent as much land per household as the average middle peasant. The discrepancy between the poor peasants and the richest of the middle peasants would have been considerably greater. This might have seemed quite reasonable in a country carrying out land reform as a purely economic process. To the CCP, which was trying to strengthen the poor peasants to a point where they would become the dominant social and political force in the villages, it was unacceptable.

To the extent that the poor of such villages had been able to obtain land and other wealth, they had done so unevenly; those poor peasants and laborers who had led in the struggle against the landlords had received more of the fruits of that struggle. By the time the CCP began openly shifting wealth from the rich to the poor, in 1946 and 1947, there were still poor peasants who needed much more than they had, but few landlords and rich peasants still had any surplus. There were continued efforts to search out whatever surplus individual landlords and rich peasants still had, but where this proved inadequate there were increasing pressures to strip the landlords and rich peasants not only of their surplus but of everything they owned, to take wealth from middle peasants, and to take something back from poor peasants who had gotten more than their share in the earlier struggles.

The problem might not have been so great if the CCP had been prepared to attack the fundamental legitimacy of private property in land. But the Party was not yet willing to say that a family's ownership of more than its fair share of land was in itself a justi-fication for taking some away. There had to be some excuse for saying that the people involved were enemies of the revolution, or that they had acquired their land illegitimately. The most common

14. Li Geng, *Jiefang qu*, pp. 42, 48.

excuse was that the father or even the grandfather of the current owner had been a landlord or rich peasant and had become rich by exploiting the peasants. Such accusations were very easy to make, given the high rate of downward mobility in Chinese society; many middle and poor peasants were the children of landlords and rich peasants. This damaged the revolution politically, since many peasants were being branded as enemies unnecessarily. Also, the people against whom these accusations could be made were not necessarily the richest. Lower-middle peasants and even poor peasants were sometimes attacked, while well-to-do middle peasants whose immediate ancestors had not been exploiters might escape.

This was the period when the classic pattern of mass mobilization for land reform was evolving. The landlords had to be stripped not only of their wealth but also of their prestige.

When the landlords and rich peasants ruled, theirs were the ruling ideas. Outstanding among these was the belief that the poor peasants and farm labourers were dependent on the landlords and rich peasants and should be grateful to them, for leasing land (at exorbitant rents), for lending money (at usurious rates) and for giving employment (at long hours and low wages), and that without all this the poor would starve. Thus the landlords and rich peasants were seen as benefactors, not as exploiters.[15]

As long as such attitudes persisted, the peasants would not participate actively in land reform, and their participation was vital. The goal of the campaign was for the peasants to *fanshen*. Literally this might be translated "to turn the body over"; what it meant was to change the whole basis of one's life, economically by acquiring enough wealth to become an independent farmer, socially by freeing oneself from a state of helpless subordination to the village elite, and psychologically by ceasing to think of oneself as being naturally or easily subordinated. If the peasants were not psychologically mobilized, then after the land reform they might be unable or unwilling to defend any economic gains they had made. In some areas where land reform was carried out in a hasty and slipshod fashion in 1947 and 1948, there were noticeable numbers of peasants who were so unconvinced of the legitimacy of land reform that they wanted to give the land back to the landlords and return to their old status as tenants (see below, p. 78). If land reform were to produce fundamental changes in rural society, it had to be carried out, at least partially, by the peasants themselves. Even if cadres sent into the villages from outside could carry out land reform, by doing so they would be depriving the peasants forever of the opportunity to do it. In a novel by a

---

15. Crook and Crook, *The First Years of Yangyi Commune*, pp. 208–9.

former land-reform cadre in the Northeast, there is an incident in
which the worst landlord in a village, a man responsible for
several deaths, is brought before a mass meeting to be denounced.
He tricks and overawes the peasants and walks out a free man.
The head of the land-reform work team, asked why he did not
arrest the landlord, explains: "I could easily have kept Han in
custody—or even put a bullet through him. But the point is—have
the masses risen? They must act of their own accord. If we can't
work patiently on the masses so that they take their destiny into
their own hands and level the feudalistic strongholds to the
ground, we can't overthrow feudalism. We can kill one landlord
Han, but there are other landlords."[16]

The mass struggle, once started, often went to extremes. This
extremism was encouraged by the cadres to some extent, especially
in the years 1945 to 1947. Some felt that the best way for the
peasants to show that they had really escaped the psychological
bonds of the old order was for them to beat or kill the landlords.
Late in 1945, Jack Belden heard of a prominent Japanese collabora-
tor being hauled from one village to another to be beaten, with the
cadres carefully keeping him alive so the peasants of every village
would have their chance.[17] But there was also a very real element
of spontaneity in the violence. The tensions in the countryside of
North and Northwest China were very strong. Peasants who lived
dangerously close to the starvation level had watched wealth flow
from their own families to their richer neighbors not only through
rent and interest payments, which were often seen as legitimate,
but through corrupt manipulation of the tax system and outright
extortion. Given the extremely hierarchical nature of Chinese society, it had been difficult for a peasant to express resentment
against a landlord directly, whether from a perfectly rational fear
of retaliation or from deeper emotional inhibitions against defiance
of an authority figure. When the peasants managed to break
through these barriers, they were not likely to stop with half
measures; they did not even restrict their rage always to its legitimate targets.[18] The peasants were also worried about the uncertain outcome of the civil war. If the landlords were only
dispossessed, they might be back in power after the next

---

16. Chou Li-po, *The Hurricane*, pp. 68–69.

17. Belden, *China Shakes the World*, pp. 31–32.

18. It has sometimes been suggested that the tendencies for
impulses toward violence or defiance of superiors to be repressed,
and for these impulses to lead to disorder (*luan*) if they come into
the open, form a pattern found rather broadly in Chinese culture.
There is circular causation here; the fact that these impulses lead
to disorder would be both a result and a cause of the attempt to
repress them. See Solomon, *Mao's Revolution and the Chinese Political Culture*, pp. 112–16; Byrne [Moise], "Harmony and Violence in
Classical China."

Guomindang offensive; killing them was safer.

During this period, Party doctrine stated that when the Party and the masses differed on matters of principle, the Party should submit to the wishes of the masses while trying to persuade them to change their views.[19] It was later decided that this "tailism"—trailing along behind the masses—had been a mistake and that the Party should have exercised more control over the masses. Tailism was especially unfortunate in the many areas where the bulk of the peasants had not yet become highly politicized, and where "the masses" behind whom the Party had trailed had consisted essentially of a minority of activist elements.

If the Party had ever believed that land reform should or could be completed without bloodshed, it had given up this idea by late 1947; "peaceful land reform" was attacked as a delusion. Still, there was no question of liquidating all the landlords. In contrast to what happened in the Jiangxi period, many landlords, though they lost most of their wealth and went through some very unpleasant experiences, were able to go on living in their villages.

Rectification

The Communist Party knew that its cadres in the countryside were far from perfect. This was natural; revolutionary organizations had been built up hastily, amid the tension and confusion of war. But during 1947, two factors pushed Party leaders to worry much more about the defects of their cadres than they had in the past. First, land reform, despite repeated efforts, still had not led to an adequate redistribution of wealth. Some poor peasants had obtained what they needed and had become new middle peasants, but others were still short of land, tools, housing, clothes, and food. The Party concluded that there must be something seriously wrong with the cadres who had been leading mass struggles. Second, when the Party had invited the peasants to criticize the shortcomings of local cadres in the spring of 1947, it had been shocked by the intensity of criticism that had developed. A major rectification campaign was therefore launched in the second half of 1947; it reached a peak early in 1948.

One aspect of the problem was the presence of landlords and rich peasants both within the Party itself and among the non-Party cadres. In an extreme case, a *cun* Party branch of fifty-seven members in the Shanxi-Chahaer-Hebei Border Region was reported to have contained twenty-nine landlords and rich peasants plus twenty lackeys of landlords and rich peasants. This branch had been quite corrupt and had opposed equal division of the land. It had simply to be dissolved rather than being reformed.[20] An

---

19. *Wei chunjie dang*, p. 12.
20. Ibid., p. 84.

editorial in the main newspaper of the Shanxi-Suiyuan Border Region said that in this region, most of the leadership at the *qu* level and above consisted of landlords and rich peasants.[21] Although infiltration of the Party was a genuine problem, reports such as these may have exaggerated it considerably. In an area about which very detailed information is available, Lucheng *xian* in southeast Shanxi, the Party leadership estimated in February 1948 that landlords and rich peasants formed at least 40 percent of the Party membership at the village level. By June, careful investigation revealed that there were hardly any landlords or rich peasants in the Party.[22]

Most people who were found to have come from landlord and rich-peasant backgrounds were expelled from village-level Party branches, but some who appeared to be loyal and valuable members were retained. Even those found worthy of Party membership posed a certain problem. If a Party branch contained members of the old village elite, this fact was bound to have a bad effect on peasant attitudes, no matter how good the behavior of the Party members in question. The best compromise was to require that landlord and rich-peasant elements found worthy of remaining in the Party serve away from their home villages. These people needed ideological reeducation, but so did all Party members regardless of class status.[23] People of landlord and rich-peasant origin were less likely to be expelled from the Party if they were in positions above the village level.

Renmin ribao later reported that the rectification movement had been directed mainly against landlord and rich-peasant influence in the Party,[24] and this seems to have been true at higher levels. But in the villages, misbehavior by Party members of peasant origin was in fact a more serious problem than landlord and rich-peasant infiltration and was sometimes recognized as the more serious problem. The peasant cadres occasionally sympathized with and protected members of the old village elite. Even when they did not, they were products of the same culture; it should surprise nobody that they had some of the same attitudes toward the nature and prerogatives of leadership. An open letter of 10 January 1948 from the CCP Central Bureau for the Shanxi-Hebei-Shandong-Henan Border Region to the Party members of the region criticized cadres who (1) gave themselves more than their legitimate share when the fruits of the antilandlord struggle were being distributed, or simply stole things before the formal distribution occurred; (2) behaved in an arrogant and abusive fashion toward the peasants; (3) made all important decisions themselves without

21. *Jin-Sui ribao* editorial, 27 November 1947, in ibid., p. 33.

22. Hinton, *Fanshen*, pp. 264, 491.

23. *Wei chunjie dang*, pp. 14, 18, 33–34, 40.

24. *Renmin ribao* editorial, 1 July 1950, reprinted in *Xinhua yuebao*, July 1950, p. 504.

permitting the ordinary peasants to play any role; and (4) united into a tight clique and supported one another against anyone who had the temerity to criticize one of them. In areas where the cadres had behaved in this fashion, land-reform efforts had not brought, and in the opinion of the Central Bureau could not have brought, adequate benefits to the poor. The letter stated: "Formerly the poor peasants and laborers were exploited by the landlord class; today they are oppressed by these bad Party members and bad cadres."[25] These problems were pervasive; almost every village must have had at least some of them.

The Party leaders were actually underestimating the proportion of landlord wealth that had been properly distributed to the poor. Also, they sometimes overreacted to the phenomena of arrogant and selfish behavior among the cadres. To say that such behavior was bad, and to threaten the cadres with dismissal if they did not stop it, were perfectly reasonable. To treat them as though their offenses reflected an astonishingly low level of morality was not reasonable. Such behavior had been normal in the culture in which they had grown up, and the CCP had not previously pushed them very hard to follow a higher standard.

Party leaders had formed a lower opinion of the cadres than was really justified. However, they did not generally suggest that bad cadres represented some sort of absolute evil. Documents of this period contain the following major stereotypes: (1) the cadre from a wealthy family who protected his immediate family, and perhaps some close friends, from mass struggle and the redistribution of their excess wealth; (2) the cadre from any class background who was influenced by traditional attitudes and simply could not see the need or the justification for drastic class struggle; (3) the cadre of peasant origin who exploited his position to enrich himself; (4) the cadre who did not bother to consult the masses when making major decisions; and (5) the cadre who felt entitled to curse, arrest, or beat anyone who offended him or against whom he had a grudge. All of these stereotypes were based on perfectly comprehensible human motivations, and none of them implied that the culprit was an irredeemable enemy of the revolution. During the Stalinist purges in the Soviet Union, and during the land reform in North Vietnam, there was an image of the bad cadre as a sort of monster who did evil things for which he had no clear motive, simply because he was an enemy of the revolution. The CCP, in the late 1940s, regarded very few cadres as either wholly good or wholly bad. It recognized the existence of conflicting emotions in a Party member from a landlord family who approved when the May Fourth Directive called for a harsher policy toward the landlords in general, but at the same time was pleased to see a loophole by means of which his own family could evade the struggle, or in a Party member who realized that his own family deserved to be

---

25. *Pingfen tudi shouce*, p. 22.

struggled against, but still hoped that they would not be treated too harshly.[26] Such people could be reformed. Even some people who had been dismissed from the Party for their errors were once quoted as saying that they would work hard under the Party's leadership to serve the people and reform themselves; the Party said that it welcomed this attitude.[27]

The Party members and cadres had a higher average level of altruism and public-spiritedness than the old elite they had replaced. Many of them had first joined the revolutionary forces to defend their villages against the Japanese, at a time when doing so seemed more likely to get them killed at an early age than to advance their personal fortunes. This factor of self-selection often had not been enough to make them think of themselves as servants rather than as masters of society once they were in power. Unlike their predecessors, they had little personal wealth to back up their political power; this made them more vulnerable to pressure, from the peasants and from authorities at higher levels, to improve their attitudes and behavior. The rectification involved a vigorous (indeed sometimes excessive) application of such pressure.

Peasants who were not members of the Party played a major role in the rectification. This was a break with past practice; the peasants had not even known, before this, which of their neighbors were and were not Party members. The non-Party masses could contribute much useful information at the -meetings that evaluated Party members. But beyond this, the cadres and the Party were to be removed from their pedestals and brought down to a level where the peasants could criticize or punish them if they misbehaved. The Shanxi-Hebei-Shandong-Henan Border Region Peasant Association Preparatory Committee announced to the peasants of the region on 20 January 1948: "We must...place the Communist Party under our supervision. We must take our destinies into our own hands. We loudly cry, 'All power to the peasant representative assemblies!'"[28]

Each cadre and Party member at the *cun* level had to be investigated first by a meeting of poor peasants and laborers and then by a meeting of poor peasants, laborers, and middle peasants. Some organizations at higher levels were investigated by assemblies of elected peasant representatives.[29] A meeting of peasant representatives in one *qu* of Rugao *xian*, Jiangsu, spent five days investigating 167 cadres. When the meeting began, most of the representatives were doubtful and unwilling to speak up, because of general inhibitions against attacking the mighty, or an inability to believe that the organizers of the meeting would really support peasants who criticized senior cadres. (This was not an idle fear;

---

26. *Renmin ribao*, 2 November 1947, p. 4; 7 January 1948, p. 1.
27. Ibid., 9 January 1948, p. 1.
28. *Pingfen tudi shouce*, p. 33.
29. *Wei chunjie dang*, p. 37.

peasants invited to speak out during the spring of 1947 had not been adequately protected against retaliation by the cadres.) But after the peasants had seen a member of the *qu* committee suspended from the Party, they realized that serious criticisms would be welcomed, and they became very active. Of the 167 cadres 16 were praised, 34 were both praised and criticized, 28 were criticized, 3 were suspended from their positions (presumably in local government), 7 were left in office pending further investigation, 52 were dismissed from their posts, 7 were suspended from the Party, and 20 were expelled from the Party.[30] The Party later decided that the work teams that had supervised the rectification campaign had at first been far too uncritical in believing complaints made by peasant activists against cadres and Party members, and had taken too pessimistic a view of both Party members and non-Party cadres at the village level. These errors began to be corrected, at different dates in different areas, during the first four months of 1948.[31]

The Outline Land Law

As new areas came under Communist control in this period, the Party would try to arouse some struggle against the landlords as soon as possible. The first efforts would produce limited and often superficial results; there was not time to mobilize the peasants properly, and there were seldom adequate cadres to lead the movement. In the following months, there would have to be one movement after another, stripping the targets of the initial struggles more thoroughly and also increasing the range of people struggled against. By 1947 the actual struggles had far outstripped the legislation that was supposed to be guiding them; there was no formal program to explain just what methods were supposed to be used, or how far the redistribution of wealth was supposed to go. This gap was filled by the Outline Land Law of China, which was approved by the Central Committee on 10 October 1947, circulated among the cadres, and finally presented to the public near the end of the year.[32]

It stated that the land ownership rights of all landlords and institutional owners, and all debts in the countryside dating from before land reform, would be abolished. Then not just the land confiscated from the landlords, but all land in each village, was to be equally divided among the entire population of the village. Each person, regardless of age or sex, was to get an equal share, taking into account both quality and quantity. The landlords also

---

30. Ibid., p. 80.
31. There is a good summary of the rectification in Teiwes, "The Origins of Rectification," pp. 32–49.
32. Text translated in Hinton, *Fanshen*, pp. 616–18.

would get equal shares. The only people denied land were traitors, collaborators, civil war criminals, and persons having some occupation other than agriculture which could support them adequately. Poor-peasant households of only one or two persons could in some cases be given an amount of land equal to the normal shares for two or three people.[33] Authorities at higher levels could sometimes transfer land or population between villages with much land and those with little. After redistribution, the land would become the private property of the peasants to whom it had been given; they could buy, sell, and even under some circumstances rent it. All debts dating from before land reform were canceled.

The landlords' animals, farming implements, houses, grain, and other property, and the rich peasants' "surplus" animals, farming implements, houses, grain, and other property were to be confiscated and distributed to the poor. Again, the landlords were supposed to get an equal share.[34] The property and legal operations of industrial and commercial elements were to be protected from encroachment. In places where equal division had already been carried out, it did not have to be repeated if the peasants considered the existing situation to be satisfactory.

One should not overestimate the ability of abstract provisions in such a law to reshape the intractable reality of the Chinese countryside. Although one of the purposes of the Outline Land Law was to eliminate inequalities that had arisen when past distribution of wealth had discriminated in favor of politically meritorious groups (mainly the families of cadres, activists, and soldiers), discrimination according to merit persisted to some extent.[35] Most areas took the existing landholding situation as the basis and made necessary adjustments—adding here, taking away there, and exchanging good for bad land. Redistribution *de novo*, without regard to which family had formerly operated which plots of land, would have led to greater equality but would have shifted the ownership of a very large proportion of the cultivated land, leading to an excessive disruption of production.[36] Also, the law did not even in theory

---

33. This was probably applied mostly to young adults who could work the land effectively (two adults could work at least as much land as a couple with small children), and who were likely to have children soon and thus need more land to support themselves.

34. The authorities winked at cases in which the landlords got significantly less than an equal share, but they do not seem to have wanted the landlords actually to starve. The supplementary regulations for implementing the Outline Land Law in the Shanxi-Hebei-Shandong-Henan Border Region (*Renmin ribao*, 31 December 1947, p. 1) said that landlords who had been totally impoverished in previous campaigns might have to be given some additional land; see also ibid., 21 April 1948, p. 1.

35. See for instance Chou Li-po, *The Hurricane*, pp. 375–76.

36. The Northeast Bureau of the CCP suggested on 1 December

eliminate all inequalities in the ownership of draft animals, tools, grain, and so on, which in some areas were more important than inequalities in the ownership of land.

In December 1947, the Party began limited distribution of a revised version of the 1933 document "How to Differentiate the Classes in the Rural Areas."[37] Up to then the Party had been giving its cadres little exact guidance on how to distinguish one class from another. There were occasional villages where 20 percent, 30 percent, even 60 percent of the households had been classified as landlords and rich peasants.[38]

Mao Zedong said that the Outline Land Law corrected some of the too moderate aspects of the May Fourth Directive, specifically leaving the landlords with too much land and property and not taking any from the rich peasants.[39] On the other hand, Liu Shaoqi (Liu Shao-ch'i), who had been the individual most directly responsible for the Outline Land Law, once said that it had been intended to correct radical excesses in the actual practice of 1946 and 1947:

> During the period between July 1946 and October 1947, the peasant masses and our rural work personnel in many areas of North China, Shandong and the Northeast, in carrying out land reform, were unable to follow the directive, issued by the CCP Central Committee on 4 May 1946, to leave the rich peasants' land and property basically untouched. Instead, following their own will, they confiscated the land and property of the rich peasants the same as those of the landlords. This is understandable. It is because this was the period when the struggle between the Chinese people and the Guomindang reactionaries was most intense and most bitter. This was also the period when deviations in land reform were most frequent, infringing the interests of some middle peasants and harming some sectors of rural commerce and industry. Indiscriminate beatings and indiscriminate killings occurred in some places. The main reason these things occurred lay in the tense political and military situation at that time. Another reason was that most of our rural work personnel lacked experience in land reform and did not know how to demarcate classes correctly in the countryside. They assigned some people to the wrong class status, classifying some rich

---

1947 that some areas could divide the land *de novo; Wei chunjie dang,* p. 44. It is not likely that many areas even in the Northeast chose this option.

37. The 1947 version is unavailable. For a May 1948 version see *Tudi zhengce faling huibian,* pp. 40–59.

38. *Renmin ribao,* 17 January 1948, p. 1.

39. Ibid., 1 January 1948, p. 1. The version in Mao Tse-tung, *Selected Works,* 4:164, 174, is vaguer.

peasants as landlords and some middle peasants as rich
peasants. In view of this situation, the Central Committee of
the Communist Party of China issued the Outline Land Law on
10 October 1947, under which the rich peasants were distinguished from the landlords, but the surplus land and property of the rich peasants were allowed to be requisitioned.[40]

This passage is quite misleading. In some ways the most radical
period of the land reform was that immediately after the promulgation of the Outline Land Law. The law and the brief Central
Committee statement that was published with it contain no warnings
against leftist excesses and no criteria for preventing errors in
class demarcation. The law implicitly accepted the idea of taking
land from middle peasants. It did not halt any of the excesses that
Liu listed.[41] There were only two ways in which it really was a
moderating influence: it said that the landlords should be left with
some land after land reform, and it allowed land to be taken from
people who were not guilty of any crime or sin, thus reducing the
impetus to attack people for rather far-fetched sins as an excuse
for taking their land (see above, pp. 48-49).

Liu was trying to claim, without much justification, the credit
for having seen and corrected the leftist errors that were being
committed in late 1947. After the CCP leadership was forced to
abandon Yan'an to the Guomindang in February 1947, it had split
up. One group, headed by Mao Zedong and including Zhou Enlai
(Chou En-lai) and Ren Bishi (Jen Pi-shih), had gone to northern
Shaanxi. The other, headed by Liu Shaoqi, had gone east to
Hebei. It was Liu who convened the land conference of September
1947, which wrote the Outline Land Law; Mao later complained
about not having been consulted.[42] During the Cultural Revolution
Liu had to confess that the land conference had not dealt
adequately with the problem of leftist errors.[43] However, while Liu
was not entitled to credit for stopping the errors, there is no
evidence that he should be blamed for them more than any other
Party leader. Although Mao Zedong had not been involved in writing the Outline Land Law, he seems to have accepted it after it
had been written.[44]

---

40. Liu Shaoqi, "Guanyu tudi gaige wenti di baogao" Report on
the question of agrarian reform], 14 June 1950, in *Xinhua yuebao*,
July 1950, p. 494.

41. It forbade attacks on commercialists and industrialists, but it
did not mention commercial and industrial enterprises owned by
landlords and rich peasants. Protection was extended to these
enterprises early in 1948.

42. "Talk at the Report Meeting," 24 October 1966, in Schram,
Chairman Mao Talks to the People, p. 266.

43. "The Confession of Liu Shao-ch'i," *Atlas*, April 1967, p. 15.

44. See Tanaka Kyoko, "Mao and Liu in the 1947 Land Reform,"

The poor-peasant leagues and the new peasant associations[45] were given tremendous power while the Outline Land Law was being implemented. The preexisting structure of Party and government in the villages had no control over them; indeed, it was the other way round. One directive on land reform in the Shaanxi-Gansu-Ningxia Border Region forbade not only *xiang* but also *qu* and *xian* governments to restrict the activities of the peasant associations and poor-peasant leagues, and their elected assemblies.[46] The peasant organizations were to be allowed to do almost anything they pleased; to the extent that they were guided and supervised in the land-reform and rectification movements, it was by teams of cadres sent into the villages from outside. Considered simply as an effort to go around an unsatisfactory administrative apparatus, this seems excessive. It did not eliminate completely the problem of relying on bad elements because the teams of outside cadres were themselves not perfect, and it sometimes left the land reform guided by a ·work team that did not really understand the local situation and was relying on a comparatively small group of local activists rather than on the peasant masses as a whole. (These tendencies did not reach the disastrous levels in China in 1947–48 that they did in Vietnam in 1955–56.) In addition to distrust of existing organizations, the land-reform planners were motivated by a tremendous belief in the importance of peasant spontaneity. This was the period when in the newly liberated areas the CCP was saying: "If the masses themselves act, at the beginning it will be difficult to avoid some disorder, but this should not be feared; because the masses' desires are extraordinarily urgent, we should not fear the masses' [causing] disorder; fear of disorder could lead to restriction of the masses. For the masses to take action themselves, even if they become disorderly, is better than for us to lead them. If the disorder leads to injustice, it may cause them to want to organize themselves."[47]

Such an attitude was guaranteed to produce serious problems. The poor peasants as individuals certainly wanted to escape from the poverty and abuse to which they had long been subjected, and to some extent they seem to have systematized these hopes into an ideal of egalitarianism. However, this was for the peasants a utopian dream; it had little or nothing to do with the way they thought things happened in the real world. The reform that the CCP was trying to bring to the villages during the winter of 1947–48 was so egalitarian as to appear profoundly unnatural not

---

pp. 566–93.

45. Peasant associations had existed in many villages for years, but they were dissolved and new ones were established during land reform.

46. *Wei chunjie dang*, p. 40.

47. *Renmin ribao*, 4 February 1948, p. 1.

only to village elites but to the poor. When ordinary peasants were told that they should take not only wealth but also political power into their own hands, the initial reaction of many was that this was impossible and that if they tried they would only incur the enmity of the elite by their presumptuous effort; they would do themselves more harm than good. Once persuaded to embark on such a strange adventure, they found themselves in situations so unfamiliar that they had no standards by which to judge how far they should go, or in exactly what direction. Almost certainly, a few would move into the lead and start to behave in a domineering fashion.

The two main aspects of the poor-peasant line—giving power to the broad mass of the poor peasants, and letting the peasants handle things themselves without outside interference—were totally inconsistent. The type of mass mobilization the CCP was trying to effect, in which all of the poor would become equal participants in village affairs, could only be attained by continuous interference. It required pulling into the political arena peasants who did not feel at ease there, and at the same time pushing aside peasants who really did have a natural bent for leadership in order to create an opportunity for the hesitant and shy to make themselves heard. When poor-peasant leagues were first being organized, they might be restricted to the "simple and honest," a criterion that was sometimes interpreted to exclude anyone who had a talent for public speaking. Even if the land-reform cadres were not consciously aware of it, another of the criteria for being "simple and honest" was probably a willingness to go along with the land-reform cadres' suggestions and hints, thus allowing the cadres to guide the movement without having to act domineering.

The most difficult policy problem in land reform was how to deal with the middle peasants. Bringing maximum benefits to the poor would require taking land from some middle peasants; by late 1947 there were villages where the middle peasants were the only social class whose average landholdings exceeded the average for the village as a whole. Ensuring political predominance for the poor peasants and laborers also required cutting down the power of the middle peasants, who had sometimes been able to dominate peasant associations. When the middle peasants were powerful, wealth taken from the landlords had sometimes been distributed very widely rather than going specifically to the poor; significant amounts had even gone to well-to-do middle peasants whose wealth was already well above the average for their villages.[48]

Party leaders were faced with a choice of abandoning their commitment to full equality for the poor peasants and laborers, or significantly infringing middle-peasant interests. In late 1947 and early 1948, they tended to side with the poor, but they were sometimes either reluctant to describe their decisions clearly to the

---

48. Ibid., 6 November 1947, p. 2; 30 November 1947, p. 2.

public or simply unwilling to make a genuine decision. Thus the Outline Land Law mandated that all land in each village was to be pooled and (subject to minor variations) divided equally among the entire population of the village. This obviously required that middle peasants whose landholdings were larger than the average for the village lose some of their land. But the law said nothing direct about taking land from middle peasants; indeed it avoided mentioning the middle peasants at all. The rhetoric that accompanied its publication in *Renmin ribao* similarly dodged this issue; it emphasized taking land from rich peasants and landlords, a much more pleasant topic. [49]

Supplementary measures for implementing the Outline Land Law, issued in the Shanxi-Hebei-Shandong-Henan Border Region on 28 December 1947, said explicitly that land could be taken from middle peasants, but not any other form of wealth. [50] The corresponding regulations for the Northeast, dated 1 December, said that in areas where the land redistribution was to be carried out *de novo*, the inclusion of middle peasants in the equalization of landholdings should "in general" be on a voluntary basis, [51] but this did not provide them with much protection. Their interests were seriously infringed in the following months.

The Outline Land Law had been rather ambiguous about whether the main responsibility for carrying out land reform would fall upon peasant associations (which generally included all middle peasants) or upon poor-peasant leagues (limited to poor peasants, laborers, and sometimes new middle peasants). It seemed to lean toward the former. Bo Yibo, the chief organizer of a land conference at which cadres of the Shanxi-Hebei-Shandong-Henan Border Region prepared themselves to carry out land reform, told one of the last sessions of the conference: "Only by relying on the laborers and poor peasants, mobilizing the laborers and poor peasants, organizing poor-peasant leagues, and then, using the poor-peasant leagues as a basis, uniting with all the middle peasants to establish peasant associations and peasant representative assemblies, with all power going to the peasant representative assemblies, can we carry out thoroughly the equal division of land." [52] This statement seemed to indicate that organizations including middle peasants would have the main role in land redistribution. But Bo also said (and this statement was given far more prominence): "The general spirit of the Outline Land Law is to rely on the agricultural laborers, poor peasants, rural workers, and all poor people to overthrow the landlords, equally divide the land, fully satisfy the desires of the agricultural laborers and poor

---

49. Ibid., 28 December 1947, p. 1.
50. Ibid., 31 December 1947, p. 1.
51. *Wei chunjie dang*, p. 44.
52. Report presented by Bo Yibo, 24 December 1947, summary in *Renmin ribao*, 31 December 1947, p. 1.

peasants, and fully mobilize the agricultural laborers and poor peasants."[53]

The regional newspaper soon thereafter published an approving article describing some of the decisions that had been taken by meetings of poor peasants and laborers. In one village, such a meeting had decided that all property in the hands of the peasant association should be divided among the poor peasants and laborers. In another village, the poor peasants and laborers had decided that wealth taken from the landlords in earlier struggles, which had been allocated to the village cooperative as capital and had been generating profits mostly for the middle peasants who formed a majority of the cooperative members, should be taken from the cooperative and given to the poor peasants and laborers. It later turned out that even capital that middle peasants had themselves contributed to cooperatives had sometimes been distributed to the poor.[54] Middle peasants had also been pressured into making substantial loans to their poorer neighbors.[55]

By late 1947, CCP policy had reached an extreme of egalitarianism that would not be repeated until the Cultural Revolution. It set out to help those who had never before held political or economic power: poor peasants and laborers who had not been quick enough to seize the opportunities of the revolution and had not obtained either positions of political influence in the new regime or a large share in the fruits of the antilandlord struggle.. Economically, principles of absolute egalitarianism had been modified only slightly by concessions to the middle peasants. Politically, the ordinary poor peasants were promoted relative both to members of other classes and to poor peasants who had become cadres in previous years. Political and economic decisions were to be made by the broad masses directly, not just by a minority of cadres and activists; *Renmin ribao* actually criticized one village for the fact that only slightly over one hundred people there had any genuine involvement in decision making.[56]

Implementing the Law

When this radical line was applied in the villages, it led to considerable leftist excesses; these were corrected gradually over a period of months. To some extent there was a regional pattern: the regions that got off to an early start in the campaigns for land reform and Party rectification were more radical. But what is more

---

53. Ibid. This entire passage was repeated in large print at the top of the page.

54. Ibid., 11 January 1948, p. 1; 21 April 1948, p. 1.

55. Ibid., 13 January 1948, p. 1, presented viewpoints both opposing and favoring this practice.

56. Ibid., 12 February 1948, p. 1.

conspicuous is that within each region these campaigns started out radically and then became more moderate.

In most areas implementation of the Outline Land Law did not begin immediately after the Central Committee issued it.[57] First there had to be extended conferences at which cadres discussed the law and the procedures they would use while implementing it, and carried out criticism and self-criticism of their own past attitudes and behavior. The Shanxi-Hebei-Shandong-Henan Border Region land conference, mentioned above, lasted from 3 October to 26 December. It involved over 1,700 cadres (of whom about 10 percent were subjected to various disciplinary measures following the criticism and self-criticism sessions).[58] But the Shanxi-Suiyuan Border Region had held its land conference in June, before the national land conference that produced the Outline Land Law, and it did not feel the need to hold another one.[59] In October 1947, when the Central Committee approved the Outline Land Law and land conferences began in some other regions, the Shanxi-Suiyuan Region was spreading land reform from the key points, where it had already started, to broader areas.

A "Letter to the Peasants" issued by the Provisional Committee of the Shanxi-Suiyuan Border Region Peasant Association on 15 October 1947 differed from the Outline Land Law (which it did not mention) on two points. It treated leaving the landlords with a share of land after land reform as something that would have to be approved by the peasants of every village before it would occur, rather than something that would happen automatically. Also, the Outline Land Law had divided authority in the villages between organizations limited to poor peasants and laborers and organizations that also included the middle peasants; the "Letter to the Peasants" mentioned only the peasant associations, in which "good, newly *fanshen*ed middle peasants can also participate."[60] This implied that old middle peasants might have no organizational role in the land reform. But more important than these specific ways in which the "Letter to the Peasants" was more radical than the Outline Land Law was the overall tone of the document, particularly the sections describing the peasants' right to investigate and pass judgment on cadres in all organizations at all levels:

> The landlord class must be thoroughly defeated, no matter whether they are large or small landlords, male or female, of your own village or some other village; including also those

---

57. A passage in Mao Tse-tung, *Selected Works*, 4:164, dated 25 December 1947, refers to "the Outline Land Law of China, which was promptly carried out in all areas." This is a translation error.

58. *Renmin ribao*, 31 December 1947, p. 1.

59. For the chronology see Tanaka Kyoko, "Mao and Liu," pp. 579–89.

60. *Zhongguo Gongchandang yu tudi geming*, p. 27.

who have hidden their wealth and pretended to be poor, who
have disguised themselves as merchants or peasants; you
(*dajia*, literally "everybody") can settle accounts with [all of]
them....

As for the minority of alien class elements, opportunists,
new despots, traitors, and puppet personnel, who have infiltrated the Party, government, army, people's organizations,
and all other organizations, the Communist Party has already
announced that these scoundrels certainly cannot be considered our cadres.... The Communist Party is already expelling
these people everywhere. In whatever way you want to haul
them out and struggle against them, you can struggle against
them that way; however you want to punish them, you can
punish them. These people have committed crimes against the
peasants, there is no way to reform them, and in dealing with
them we cannot regard them as cadres.[61]

The "Letter to the Peasants" did not treat all cadres who had
behaved badly as being beyond redemption. Many whose attitude
was fundamentally good, who supported the antifeudal struggle,
had done bad things—some because their superiors had imposed
wrong policies on them and some out of selfish motives. A majority
even of the latter group could be reformed. But the peasants
would have to investigate, criticize, educate, and if need be
punish all cadres from the villages up to the border-region level.

The peasants would also investigate all discharged veterans of
the Eighth Route Army, who had benefited from various special
privileges because of their status. Those who turned out not to be
legitimate veterans would have their discharge papers confiscated.
It seems likely that this was directed not so much against people
who had actually obtained their papers fraudulently (whom the
peasants would not be qualified to investigate in any case; it would
be the army that would know), as landlords and rich peasants who
really had served in the army and then had used their status to
evade the class struggle.[62] The letter said of people currently in
the army: "[The peasants] must accept responsibility for the
Eighth Route Army. The Eighth Route Army is the peasants' own
army; from now on [we] cannot permit landlords, despots, traitor
and puppet elements, feudal rich peasants, or any scoundrels to
serve in the Eighth Route Army."[63]

The peasants' investigation, interrogation, and criticism of
cadres, concentrating on question of class origin and class loyalty,
would prove demoralizing in the short run and sometimes in the
long run even to those who were found acceptable and retained in

---

61. Ibid., pp. 19, 25.
62. See *Renmin ribao*, 22 January 1948, p. 1; Crook and Crook,
Mass Movement, p. 28.
63. *Zhongguo Gongchandang yu tudi geming*, p. 27.

their positions. Authorities in other regions would later regret that this had gone as far as it did with the civilian cadres, but at least in regard to the civilians there had been important positive achievements; proper behavior and attitudes among the cadres were vital to the peasants, and the peasants really did know a lot about the people they were investigating. For the Shanxi-Suiyuan Border Region to have extended the purge to the army, where there was less reason to expect positive achievements, in the middle of a civil war that had not yet obviously been won, can reasonably be described as foolish.

Documents titled "Letter to the Peasants" were later issued in other regions: by the Shanxi-Chahaer-Hebei Border Region Peasant Association Provisional Representative Assembly on 10 November 1947, by the Northeast Bureau of the CCP on 1 December, and by the Shanxi-Hebei-Shandong-Henan Border Region Peasant Association Preparatory Committee on 20 January 1948.[64] They all said that past land-reform efforts had been inadequate and that the time had come for a thorough, equal redivision of the land. They all emphasized the predominance of the poor peasants and laborers and directed that the peasants should criticize and pass judgment upon local cadres. The attitude they represented was later considered excessively leftist. None, however, was as radical as the Shanxi-Suiyuan letter. The other letters did not imply that the old middle peasants might be excluded from the peasant associations. They did not suggest that the peasants could extend their purge of the cadres into the army. The statement that the peasants could struggle against or punish various groups in any fashion they wished, which had been endlessly repeated in the Shanxi-Suiyuan letter, appeared rarely or not at all in the others.

The extremist line of the first letter had not, then, spread to other regions. It was not even implemented in all of the relatively small Shanxi-Suiyuan Region (population about 3,000,000). As early as late November, the regional newspaper was saying that the army was basically pure in composition.[65] Mao Zedong later said that leftist deviations had been corrected quite thoroughly in this region in January 1948;[66] this was well before the land reform and rectification campaigns had been completed in all villages.[67]

Mao commented at length on land reform in "The Present Situation and Our Tasks," a report presented to a meeting of the CCP Central Committee on 25 December 1947. According to Chou Li-po,

---

64. Texts, respectively, in: *Qunzhong* (Hong Kong), 15 January 1948, p. 8; *Wei chunjie dang*, pp. 47–52; *Pingfen tudi shouce*, pp. 27–34.

65. *Jin-Sui ribao*, 27 November 1947, reprinted in *Wei chunjie dang*, p. 34.

66. Mao Tse-tung, *Selected Works*, 4:232.

67. Significant areas had not started these campaigns by mid January; *Renmin ribao*, 17 January 1948, p. 1.

this report played a major role in ending infringement of middle-peasant interests in the Northeast. Mao himself has implied that attendance at this Central Committee meeting was what prompted the Shanxi-Suiyuan Party leaders to correct leftist excesses.[68] The warnings against leftism in this report do not seem on their face strong enough to have achieved such results, although any such warnings might have appeared striking in this radical period.

> There should be no repetition of the wrong ultra-Left policy, which was carried out in 1931–34, of "allotting no land to the landlords and poor land to the rich peasants."... There must be firm unity with the middle peasants, and their interests must not be damaged.... The middle peasants show approval of equal distribution because it does no harm to their interests. Under equal distribution, the land of one section of the middle peasants remains unchanged and that of another is increased; only the section of well-to-do middle peasants has a little surplus land, and they are willing to hand it over for equal distribution because their burden of land tax will then be lightened. Nevertheless, in carrying out equal distribution of land in different places, it is necessary to listen to the opinions of the middle peasants and make concessions to them if they object.... In determining class status care must be taken to avoid the mistake of classifying middle peasants as rich peasants.[69]

Mao did not mention the problems of beatings and killings.

The first real attack on leftist errors came in a speech by Ren Bishi on 12 January 1948. Ren criticized widespread policies that dealt too violently with the rich peasants and landlords and infringed the interests of the middle peasants.

Distinguishing between rich peasants and well-to-do middle peasants was a problem. The CCP had decided in 1933 that if a man got more than 15 percent of his income from exploitation he was a rich peasant; this was still the standard in late 1947.[70] Ren said the limit should be 25 percent. Some people were being labeled as rich peasants on the basis of exploitation carried out years before, even exploitation carried out by their fathers or their grandfathers; Ren said that if a man had stopped exploiting others at least one year before the liberation of his village, his former economic status should not be considered. In one village where various incorrect criteria including life-style, personal history, and political attitude had been used in class demarcation, 22 percent of the households had been classified as landlords or rich peasants;

---

68. Chou Li-po, *The Hurricane*, p. 280; Mao Tse-tung, *Selected Works,* 4:232.

69. Mao Tse-tung, *Selected Works,* 4:164–65.

70. Hinton, *Fanshen*, p. 286.

Ren said that villages where class status had been decided in the same manner or almost the same manner had not been rare in any of the regions under Communist control.

In some areas the middle peasants were almost excluded from important affairs in the villages. Decisions were taken by poor-peasant leagues, which gave the middle peasants no share when the landlords' wealth was being divided but too large a share when taxes were being assessed. Ren said that important decisions might be discussed by poor-peasant leagues, but that they should not be implemented unless the peasant association approved them. He recommended that one-third of the membership *and leadership* of the peasant associations be drawn from the middle peasants, two-thirds in areas where they formed a very high percentage of the population.

He approved of equal division of the land as "the best and most thorough means of abolishing the feudal system."[71] This involved taking some land away from well-to-do middle peasants. Three weeks before, Mao had said that the middle peasants probably would not object to this, but that if they did, unspecified "concessions" should be made to them. Ren said explicitly that some would object and that if they did their land should not be taken. He extended the same veto power to the new rich peasants.

Policies that alienated the middle peasants could be very dangerous to the revolution. Originally, they had been only about 20 percent of the population. But in the Old Liberated Areas,[72] gradual redistribution of wealth under the CCP had made about half the population middle peasants; 30–40 percent of the soldiers in the People's Liberation Army (PLA) were middle peasants. If they came to believe that the regime was their enemy, and that if they worked hard and saved, their extra wealth would simply be confiscated, the economic and political results would be equally disastrous. (It seems likely that mistreatment of the middle peasants was most prevalent in the Old Liberated Areas, where they were most numerous and their goodwill was most necessary to the CCP.)

Ren was also alarmed that there had been "indiscriminate beatings, men beaten to death, and men driven to suicide. Men whose crimes did not deserve death have been beaten to death or executed."[73] Ren did not say that there should be no killings

---

71. Ren Bishi, "Tudi gaige zhong di jige wenti" [Some problems in land reform], 12 January 1948, in *Tudi zhengce faling huibian,* p. 18.

72. The Old Liberated Areas had been under CCP control before September 1945. The Semi-old Liberated Areas had been liberated between September 1945 and August 1947; the New Liberated Areas had been liberated after August 1947.

73. Ren Bishi, "Tudi gaige," p. 28. In the village that the Crooks called Ten Mile Inn, on the border between Henan and

during land reform, but that there should not be so many. People should be executed only after trial by a people's tribunal and approval of the verdict by the government at *xian* level or above.[74] Ren added, rather disturbingly, "When executing people, it is necessary to announce publicly the nature of their crimes and not execute them secretly."[75]

His discussion of beatings is important, since CCP documents seldom confront this issue squarely.

> We should oppose beating people. During the mass movement, when the masses out of sincere indignation go to beat up those who have oppressed them, whom they deeply hate, the Communist Party members should not obstruct or forbid this, but should express sympathy for the indignation of the masses; otherwise we will become separated from the masses. But Communist Party members and personnel of the people's governments should not organize beatings. At the proper time we should explain to the masses that they, taking a long view, should reform those landlords and old rich peasants who have already handed over their weapons and surrendered; we are eliminating the landlords as a class, not as individuals.[76]

Ren felt that even nonviolent struggle meetings directed against the landlords should be less frequent. If a comparatively small landlord were not guilty of serious crimes and bowed his head before the new order, it should not be necessary to haul him before a mass meeting to denounce and humiliate him.

Unfortunately this report did not end leftist excesses in the land reform and Party rectification. The Party's commitment to equality for the poor peasants was combined with a serious overestimation of the actual degree of economic inequality and an underestimation of the degree to which poor peasants already had political power. As long as the Party supposed that the further benefits that could

---

Hebei, four people had been stoned to death in the relevant period. Crook and Crook, *Revolution*, p. 151. In Long Bow, which had 200 to 300 households, at least a dozen people were beaten to death. Hinton, *Fanshen*, p. xi.

74. The Northeast may already have required *xian* approval, if not formal trials; see *Wei chunjie dang*, p. 46. But this requirement was implemented very perfunctorily. In Chou Li-po's fictionalized account of land reform in the Northeast, the leader of a work team simply telephones a report to the *xian* government that the peasants are struggling against a despot who deserves execution, and the *xian* government grants immediate permission for the despot to be executed; this was considered perfectly proper. *The Hurricane*, p. 148. See also *Renmin ribao*, 24 January 1948, p. 1.

75. Ren Bishi, "Tudi gaige," p. 29.

76. Ibid.

be brought to the poor by further equalization were much larger than they actually were (which implied an equal overestimation of the extent to which the cadres had harmed the peasants in the past by failing to lift them to full equality), there were likely to be excesses. A report like Ren Bishi's, criticizing particular excesses, could have only limited effect.

The actual halt to leftist errors came at different times in different regions—in January in the Shanxi-Suiyuan Border Region, around February in the Northeast, and in March and April in the Shanxi-Hebei-Shandong-Henan Border Region. This progression represents the order in which these areas had started the campaign to implement the Outline Land Law. It is hard to be sure without access to the Party's internal documentation, but the impression conveyed is that the repudiation of extremism in each region was carried out during the spread of the campaign in that region, on the basis of experience in the region; there may not have been much transmission of experience between regions. Actual difficulties of communication between areas separated by Guomindang troops could have been exacerbated by the leadership's fear that if it began spreading the idea that in some areas the problem of inequality was not bad enough to justify a really radical campaign, administrators in other areas would seize any available excuse to decide that the situation in their own bailiwicks was not so bad either, with the result that problems really demanding radical measures would not get them. If pushed too far to the left, the campaign could still produce some important and useful results, though at an unnecessarily high price. If not pushed far enough, it might produce hardly anything.

Suzanne Pepper has suggested that during this period "the land reform movement seems to have been purposely pushed to excess by the Party center in order to destroy the ruling elite and equalize land ownership. The anti-leftist campaign was not enforced until that objective had been achieved—thus representing the successful completion of a genuine mass movement."[77] This is not correct; certainly in the area about which the best information is available (the Shanxi-Hebei-Shandong-Henan Border Region), and probably in most other areas, it was only the villages that had started early that had completed or almost completed the campaign along a radical line before that line came under attack as a left deviation. It is possible the leadership was so afraid of right deviations that it deliberately sent some cadres to the countryside with what it knew to be an excessively leftist attitude, but if so the leadership did not require that the cadres persist in that leftist attitude until they had applied it in every village.

On 1 February 1948, Party leaders in the Shanxi-Hebei-Shandong-Henan Border Region approved a "Directive on Land

---

77. Pepper, *Civil War in China*, p. 400.

Reform, Party Rectification, and the Democratic Movement"[78] to guide work that would be starting in the villages near the end of the month. This directive contained several warnings against leftist errors, which look as if they might have been inspired by Ren Bishi. It also contained a relatively optimistic assessment of the accomplishments of past struggles. It divided the villages into three categories according to how many of the poor peasants and laborers had been able to rise and become new middle peasants. In villages of the first and second categories, which together were estimated to represent slightly over two-thirds of the region, 60 percent or more of all households were middle peasants.

But on 22 February the CCP Central Committee issued a directive embodying a considerably more pessimistic view. When it divided the villages into three categories, it indicated that as little as 50 percent of the population might be middle peasants in even the best of the three. In the intermediate (and by implication average) category, 50 percent to 70 percent of the population were still poor peasants and laborers. In the worst, redistribution of wealth had either been carried out very badly or not at all, and the feudal system still existed. This directive led land-reform cadres to expect that they would find the conditions ascribed to the second and third categories in more than half the villages.

In villages of the first category, the Central Committee said that minor adjustments in the ownership of wealth could be adequate, taking from "landlords, old rich peasants, and especially cadres' families that have far more land and goods than the ordinary peasants"[79] and giving to poor peasants who still did not have enough. In villages of the second category larger adjustments or a full-scale redivision of the land would be necessary; in those of the third category, a full land reform was obviously required. Land could be taken from well-to-do middle peasants and new rich peasants, if this were necessary and if they consented, in villages of all categories; in those of the second category, where this would usually be necessary, there is an ambiguity in the phrasing which suggested that it might be done even without the middle peasants' consent. In villages of the first category, where the middle peasants formed a majority, power would be in the hands of peasant associations right from the beginning of the movement. But poor-peasant leagues would be permitted to run things for a month or two in villages of the second category and for three or four months in those of the third category.

The Central Committee thought that in villages of the first and second categories, peasant dissatisfaction often focused on Party

---

78. *Pingfen tudi shouce,* pp. 76–84.

79. "Guanyu zai laoqu banlaoqu jinxing tudi gaige gongzuo yu zhengdang gongzuo di zhishi" [Directive on carrying out the work of land reform and Party rectification in the old and semi-old areas], 22 February 1948, in *Tudi zhengce faling huibian,* p. 33.

members and cadres who had acquired more than their share of the fruits of struggle during earlier campaigns.[80] Surplus property had to be taken from such people and distributed among the poor. Ordinary peasants who were not members of the Party were to play a major role in Party rectification. Some Party branches were so much under the control of bad elements that they would simply have to be dissolved and new branches organized from scratch, but most Party branches contained some good members. These good members would be identified during Party rectification, and supplemented by peasant activists newly recruited into the Party. Those Party members found to be unworthy, especially those who came from the exploiting classes, were to be expelled. Party members who came from the exploiting classes but were found to have abandoned their old class standpoint and to be worthy of Party membership could remain, provided the masses agreed.

William Hinton has described the serious misapplication of the Central Committee directive in the village of Long Bow, in Southeast Shanxi.[81] The cadres of the work team sent to Long Bow, and their superiors, were suffering from an exaggerated belief in the "distribution theory" of the causes of poverty in rural China. They felt that the concentration of land in the hands of the landlords was the essential cause of peasant poverty. Therefore, if the peasants were still poor, it must be because there had not been an effective redistribution of the land. They presumed that the land must still be in the hands of the landlords and rich peasants or of corrupt cadres. In fact, almost all the land had been properly divided; the problem was that the landlords and rich peasants of this area had never owned enough land for its redistribution to do more than partially solve the problems of the peasants. Statements both by the Central Committee and by Mao Zedong as an individual that the landlords and rich peasants owned 70–80 percent of the land in China[82] must have encouraged the cadres to take an exaggerated view of what could be expected of a proper land reform. The figure of 70–80 percent was excessive for China as a whole; it was positively ludicrous for North and Northwest China. Long Bow, which was placed in the worst of the three categories defined by the directive of 22 February, should have been placed

---

80. Some cadres had benefited from corruption in the distribution of the fruits of the struggle. Some had been given an extra share as an open and publicly accepted reward for courage and initiative in the struggle. Some had acquired conspicuous items such as draft animals and land simply by default when other peasants were afraid that accepting valuable items taken from the landlords would lead to a terrible retribution if the Guomindang ever defeated the CCP.

81. Hinton, *Fanshen*, sections III–IV.

82. Central Committee statement of 10 October 1947, trans. in Hinton, *Fanshen*, p. 615. Mao Tse-tung, *Selected Works*, 4:164.

in the best. Having underestimated the success of past redistribution efforts, the work team underestimated the worth of the village cadres and Party members who had carried them out. Many of the Party members and cadres had indeed been guilty of commandism (simply giving orders, rather than consulting the peasants), excessive brutality in the struggle, or arrogant abuse of their positions. But there had been far less corruption than the work team thought, and no landlords or rich peasants in the Party. The mistaken preconceptions of the work team caused serious problems for everyone involved—the work team itself, the village cadres, and the peasants.

Long Bow had worse problems than most other villages of the Shanxi-Hebei-Shandong-Henan Border Region, although it was not among the very worst; there were villages not far away where the hostility of the work teams actually drove local cadres to suicide.[83] Long Bow faced difficulties both because of an unusually complex situation within the village and because it had no opportunity to learn from the experience of neighboring communities; it was one of the very first villages in Lucheng *xian* to start the campaign for land reform and Party rectification, and was relatively early by the standards of the Border Region as a whole. In Wuan *xian*, about one hundred miles to the east, there is extensive documentation of the way the work teams' opinion of local cadres improved as the campaign moved from one village to the next. In Zhaozhuang, chosen as the first key point for the campaign, a work team probably arrived in late January. Its preliminary assessment was that the peasants hated the village cadres worse than they hated the landlords.[84] But within a few weeks the work team realized that the Party members in this village were relatively good and had committed only relatively small errors. Furthermore, some of the errors the Party members and other cadres in this village really had committed, notably attacks on middle peasants, were not their fault; the village leaders had simply been complying with bad policies made at higher levels.[85] Ten Mile Inn was the second key point; a work team arrived there on 26 February. The work team quickly realized that the Party members and cadres in this village were not really bad, but it remained suspicious for about ten days, thinking that things might be at least somewhat worse than they really were.[86] A work team arrived in Guzhen on 20 March. It decided that most Party members in Guzhen were not bad so quickly that this must have been the preconception with which it arrived. From the very first day, it was accepting from local Party members the names of poor peasants who could be relied upon. It was prepared to use as much pressure as necessary to cure the

---

83. *Renmin ribao*, 17 April 1948, p. 1.
84. Ibid., 12 February 1948, p. 1.
85. Ibid., 24 February 1948, p. 1; 17 April 1948, p. 1.
86. Crook and Crook, *Mass Movement*, chaps. 2, 3, and 9.

problems of greed, arrogance, and brutality that really did exist among the Party members and cadres of this and almost every other village, but it did not assume that these problems were worse than they appeared on the surface, and it was not afraid that arguing against peasants who made excessive and unjustified attacks on the Party members and cadres would intimidate the masses and prevent valid grievances from emerging.[87] The experience of Guzhen was probably the one closest to being typical of the villages in this *xian* and indeed of the whole region.

Long Bow had worse errors, especially in Party rectification, than most villages of this region. It is not so obvious how Long Bow compares with other regions, in most of which the work started earlier and under more radical policies, but it was probably worse than the average for the other regions also. The errors arose from misperception of the situation more than from policies that were unreasonable in themselves. In Chou Li-po's fictionalized account of land reform in the Northeast, where the landlords had owned enough land so that its correct redistribution really could solve most of the peasants' problems, there is no indication of such a crisis as Hinton observed in Long Bow.

As Party leaders were reassured that past redistribution efforts had not in general been terribly inadequate, they could devote more attention to cases in which redistribution had gone too far. On 21 April the Central Bureau for the Shanxi-Hebei-Shandong-Henan Border Region issued a directive criticizing attacks on middle peasants, attacks on commerce and industry, and the reduction of landlords to absolute destitution. The directive of 21 April was much more forceful than previous statements on these subjects.[88] Still, it made a careful distinction. Cadres were told very emphatically that the landlords must have a chance to make a living, and that those who did not have even minimally adequate land, tools, and so on must be given more without delay. But the cadres were not being criticized for having stripped landlords to absolute destitution in the past; that had at one time been justified. In contrast, attacks on middle peasants were treated as having been errors all along.

The Party had not only to prevent leftist errors from occurring in any more villages but also to correct them where they had already occurred. This took some time; it was still going on in November 1948. In some cases, the correction of errors included the return of expropriated property to middle peasants who had wrongly been made targets of the struggle. There were areas where the correction of errors went too far, and Party leaders felt that the work of the land reform was being undone. This might happen either if leftist errors had been extreme and local cadres overreacted to them, or if the land reform had been relatively

---

87. *Renmin ribao*, 13 April 1948, p. 1.
88. Ibid., 21 April 1948, p. 1.

superficial and portions of the prerevolutionary social order still existed under the surface, waiting for an opportunity to reassert themselves. However, such phenomena did not become widespread.[89]

---

89. *Tudi zhengce faling huibian*, pp. 66–68.

4

Moderation in the New Liberated Areas

Land policy in the spring of 1948 was considerably less radical than it had been in 1947. Much of the change, as has been explained in the preceding chapter, was simply a correction of errors and misperceptions. When the Party decided that it would not have to throw any landlords out of the Party organization in the village of Long Bow, it was not compromising its policy goals in any way; it was simply recognizing that no landlords were there to be expelled. Problems based on misunderstanding of the facts had mostly been cleared up by the middle of 1948. But beyond correcting its evaluation of the situation, the CCP was also in a genuine sense softening its policy. It no longer felt that promoting the interests of the poor peasants justified massive infringement of the rights of middle peasants, or the reduction of landlords and rich peasants to destitution. During the next two years the Party would continue much further in this direction. It was so clearly winning the civil war that it no longer had to look at everything as a struggle against its enemies. It could devote more attention to constructive goals—establishing effective administration, law, order, and a healthy climate for rebuilding a shattered economy. The new priorities often diverted Party attention away from the class struggle, and required some of the more radical aspects of the class struggle to be moderated or postponed.

Treatment of the middle peasants posed difficult problems; the idea of taking land from them only with their "consent," which became standard doctrine in the winter of 1948, was a clumsy compromise at best. There were cases in which middle-peasant families really did seem willing to give up some land, especially if they owned more than they could conveniently cultivate by their own labor.[1] Some hidden pressure had doubtless been brought to bear. The middle peasants who donated land presumably had in the backs of their minds the tremendous importance of retaining the good opinion of the poor peasants and cadres, in a fluid revolutionary situation, but few would have volunteered to give up land under such subliminal pressures unless they could really afford to lose it. However, CCP leaders cannot have been so naive as to suppose that middle-peasant consent would always be voluntary in

---

1. Hinton, *Fanshen*, p. 590.

even this superficial sense. Peasants who failed to submit to subtle pressures might be told, "You only look out for yourself and don't care about other people,"[2] or worse. Under the formula of "consent" a considerable number of middle peasants lost, or were afraid they might lose, land they really wanted to keep.

In areas where the amount of land available for distribution from landlords and rich peasants was large, the middle peasants could be given firmer guarantees. Xinmen province, in the Northeast, announced in January 1948 that no land would be taken from middle peasants.[3] The notes to Mao's *Selected Works* say it was decided that "in the land reform in the New Liberated Areas, no land was to be taken from any middle peasant,"[4] but they do not specify the date of this decision. To judge from the context it might have been in February, but the treatment accorded the Semi-old Liberated Areas in the directive of 22 February makes this seem unlikely. As late as 28 March a statement by the Northeast Bureau of the CCP, discussing policy for areas newly recaptured from the Guomindang, said only that middle-peasant land should "basically" not be touched.[5] However, no large amount of land seems to have been taken from middle peasants after the spring of 1948, and the Party eventually forbade touching their land under any circumstances.

Just as important was a decision that land reform should not proceed too hastily after any particular area came under Communist control. In texts dated 3 and 15 February, Mao said that land reform in the New Liberated Areas should go through two stages. In the first, lasting about two years after liberation, the rich peasants would be neutralized and only the landlords, especially large landlords, would lose land and goods. In the second, lasting one more year, land and goods would be taken from rich peasants as well. The question of taking things from middle peasants was not mentioned.[6]

On 25 May, the Central Committee said that land reform should be carried out only in areas that met three conditions: military control of the area had to be secure and uncontested, an absolute majority of the peasants (not just a minority of advanced elements) had to want land reform, and the cadres available to guide the movement had to be adequate in quantity and quality. These conditions excluded most of the New Liberated Areas.[7] By August the Party had called a general halt to land reform in the New Liberated

---

2. *Renmin ribao*, 1 March 1948, p. 1.

3. U.S. Consulate General, Peiping, *Translations of Radio Broadcasts of Communist Hsin Hua Station, North Shensi*, 27 January 1948.

4. Mao Tse-tung, *Selected Works*, 4:175, n. 5.

5. *Tudi zhengce faling huibian*, p. 89.

6. Mao Tse-tung, *Selected Works*, 4:194, 201–2.

7. *Tudi zhengce faling huibian*, pp. 61–62.

Areas of the Central Plains Region, [8] though it said very clearly that it was not abandoning land reform, merely waiting a bit so that adequate preparations could be made. The peasants needed more political awareness, more confidence that the revolution had really won, and better organization. If land reform were carried out too soon, then at best the struggle would be carried out by a minority of peasant activists, while the majority looked on irresolutely. Compulsion and command would be widely used. Quite possibly there would be corruption in the division of what was taken from the rich, and unnecessary violence. The benefits to the broad mass of the peasants would be relatively small. [9]

Events of the previous months provided much evidence to support this argument. Land distribution had been carried out in villages that were still vulnerable to temporary reconquest by the Guomindang or to raids by a landlord paramilitary force called the "Return-to-the-Villages Corps." An agitator sent to organize the peasants of one such village (which was indeed raided by the Return-to-the-Villages Corps a few weeks later, with considerable destruction and loss of life) told the peasants they had no right to be afraid of such weak enemies; his own village had organized a peasant association when the counterrevolutionaries were still so strong that the peasants had to sneak into the hills at night to hold meetings. [10] The peasants who responded to such appeals, who could say in another village newly taken by the revolutionary forces that "if the enemy comes, we will go into the hills with the Eighth Route Army," [11] cannot have been more than a minority of unusually brave or unusually desperate individuals. The danger was very real; Suzanne Pepper has documented the retribution suffered by peasants who had participated in land reform, in areas that were reconquered by the Guomindang. The CCP lost much of its prestige and support in some of these areas. [12] There were places where land taken from the landlords could not be distributed because the peasants were afraid to accept it. [13] Two major documents from the Central Plains Region recognized that there

---

8. The Central Plains Liberated Area was created in the second half of 1947, when the PLA reentered the area bounded by the Yellow, Yangze, and Han rivers and the Jin-Pu (Tianjin-Nanjing) Railway. It gradually extended southward until it reached Guangdong and Guangxi late in 1949; it was reorganized as the Central-South Greater Administrative Region in February 1950.

9. *Yuxi ribao* [West Henan Daily] editorial, "Tingzhi xinqu tugai shixing jianzu jianxi" [Halt land reform in the New Liberated Areas, carry out rent and interest reduction], 24 August 1948, in Jiefang she, *Lun xin jiefang qu tudi zhengce*, pp. 11–13.

10. *Renmin ribao*, 10 July 1947, p. 4.

11. Ibid., 6 November 1947, p. 1.

12. Pepper, *Civil War*, pp. 298–303.

13. *Renmin ribao*, 2 November 1947, p. 2.

were peasants who had been given land who actually wanted to give it back to the landlords and return to their former status as tenants, and the Party felt it had no choice but to let this happen.[14] Such cases, presumably caused by peasant doubts as to the morality of land redistribution as well as doubts about the longevity of the Communist regime, must have been quite widespread for the Party to have recognized them so publicly.

Whipping up as much class struggle as possible, as quickly as possible, had been a military necessity in 1947. Often the job had not been done very well. After the PLA moved south of the Yellow River in Henan, there were teams of cadres who followed behind the advance, whipping up the peasants in a process so hasty it was called "setting fires while riding on horseback." They would stay in a village for two or three days, organizing some redistribution of grain and other easily movable goods, and then move on. In one village where there were no appropriate targets, they organized a group of peasants to go and get grain from a landlord in a neighboring village, who was said to be much hated. At first a cadre passed out grain to the peasants who had come with him, but as more and more peasants who lived in the same village as the landlord saw what was happening and joined in, the crowd turned into a mob, pushed the cadre aside, and looted the house.[15] The cadres had taken no steps to prepare the peasants of the village where the landlord lived for the idea of a gang of outsiders coming in and hauling off grain, and if they had been less lucky a pitched battle could have erupted between the peasants of the two villages. Even as things worked out, the grain, furniture, clothing, and so on taken from the landlord had gone to those who learned in time what was happening and were willing to join in; those were not necessarily the people with the greatest needs. Also, peasants dubious about the moral justification for redistribution of wealth cannot have been reassured. But such class struggles, however haphazard, shifted the balance of power; they weakened the landlord class (confiscating a significant number of weapons, among other things) and aroused at least some of the peasants. The Communists could hold such an area more easily, and the Guomindang would have more trouble reoccupying and pacifying it, than if the local power structure had been left undisturbed.

Suzanne Pepper has argued that land reform in insecure areas was a fundamentally bad idea in 1947. Her well-documented account of this period contains some powerful examples, drawn from areas where land reform was carried out even though reconquest by the Guomindang was not merely a threat but a virtual certainty, and areas where the potential for basing guerrilla warfare on land

---

14. Jiefang she, *Lun xin jiefang qu*, pp. 14, 19.
15. *Renmin ribao*, 10 December 1947, p. 4.

reform was not exploited.[16] However, these were aberrations of a fundamentally sound policy, one that would later produce very impressive results in the Mekong Delta of South Vietnam. The results were not as good in China partly because social and economic conditions were less favorable (landholdings were less concentrated and the landlords were more deeply rooted in village society), but also because the CCP won the civil war before it had time to learn the best techniques for exploiting the combination of land reform with guerrilla warfare. It would have obtained better results if it had carried out land reform only where it was ready to organize paramilitary forces, thus both getting the full military benefits of the land reform and making it more difficult for the landlords to return and take revenge on peasants who had participated in land reform. It also might have done better to handle things so that not too many people were so visibly and publicly implicated in the reform that they would be in very serious danger if enemy forces retook their villages. The CCP had not been strong enough to get the maximum benefit from the combination of land reform with guerrilla warfare before 1937, was too strong to need it after 1948, and had chosen the more attractive option of a united front between 1937 and 1945. The period when political and military conditions were fully suited to such a policy was quite brief, roughly from the end of 1945 to the beginning of 1948, long enough to get significant benefit from it but not long enough to perfect it.

By the middle of 1948 the military situation had become less pressing. It was not so urgently necessary to build up peasant organizations that would resist Guomindang efforts at reconquest of the villages, or to break the power of landlords who might aid in such a reconquest; the Guomindang was no longer in a position to make many counterattacks. The Communist Party could now devote more attention to the long-run implications of its programs, and from this perspective hasty land reform had serious disadvantages. The areas that had carried it out shortly after liberation had all needed to repeat the program later, and the errors committed in the initial efforts had often complicated the later ones. The Party decided that it should wait until it had some chance of doing the job right the first time; in the interim it would limit itself to rent and interest reduction. This decision did not involve a complete halt in land reform; there were always some areas that had been under CCP control just long enough for land reform to have become practical. Indeed in the Northeast, where the highly concentrated landholding pattern made it easier than in North China to whip up peasant enthusiasm for land reform, conditions were becoming adequate even in some of the New Liberated Areas

---

16. Pepper, *Civil War*, pp. 301–9. I should make it clear that although I disagree with Prof. Pepper on occasional points such as this, I have found her book as a whole to be superbly accurate.

by November of 1948.[17] Up to October 1948, out of a Chinese rural population then estimated (underestimated) at 409,000,000, about 100,000,000 people had completed land reform. A year later, the total was 119,000,000, and by the summer of 1950, it was 145,000,000. For the most part the reform proceeded in yearly cycles, starting after the autumn harvest and lasting until spring cultivation. There was little land-reform activity in the summer, when the peasants needed to be in the fields.

Land reform had not been abandoned. However, the Party had significantly moderated its attitudes. It was quite obviously winning the civil war, which meant that it could afford to be more lenient with class enemies. Many of them could be ignored temporarily, since they no longer had the courage to oppose the new regime; some could even be persuaded to support it.[18] As the Party returned to the cities, it found it would need the cooperation of at least part of the urban bourgeoisie for several years. It did not want to alarm the bourgeoisie too much with its activities in the countryside, especially the areas immediately around the cities. Also, the fact that the CCP was tolerating exploiters in the cities made doing so in the countryside seem less unthinkable. As the Party took over southern China, it found that the landlords owned a larger proportion of the land than in the North, so less extreme measures were needed to obtain significant benefits for the poor. Finally, the Party was slightly less enchanted with the poor than it had been in late 1947. Attempting to place all power in the hands of the poor peasants had not worked out as well as had been hoped. Although the Party continued to favor them, it emphasized that they must be guided. It no longer trusted them to do the right thing spontaneously. All of these factors would contribute to a slow moderation of land policy from 1948 to 1950.

There was another, more subtle shift in attitudes at this time; the people responsible for land policy became less concerned with revolutionary virtue and more concerned with designing policies that would actually produce good results. In the environment of 1947 and early 1948, when it had been widely believed that the lack of a proper concern for the masses had caused past land-reform efforts to fail, people in authority were determined to show such a concern. But this attitude of concern did not always actually benefit the masses. In some villages the cadres became so afraid of undemocratically imposing their opinions on "the masses" that even a small minority of vocal poor peasants could exercise a

---

17. *Tudi zhengce faling huibian*, p. 93.

18. Article 4 of the constitution of the New-Democratic Youth League (the youth organ of the CCP), issued 17 April 1949, allowed former members of reactionary groups, even "persons who have held relatively responsible positions in reactionary organizations," to join the League under some circumstances. Text trans. in *Current Background* (hereafter cited as *CB*), 7:2.

veto over major decisions; the cadres did not dare tell such people that the majority was against them and that they would have to submit.[19] Leaders were reluctant to say anything openly harmful to the interests of either poor peasants or middle peasants, so when the interests of the two groups conflicted the leaders were some-times silent or ambiguous. Once fear that one would appear to have a bad attitude was reduced, conflicting interests could be handled more effectively. Eventually, some aspects of the class struggle could be openly sacrificed if they appeared likely to interfere with the functioning of the economy. This was not a matter of black and white; even the Outline Land Law had given commerce and indus-try some protection against the class struggle, and the need to show that one had the proper class standpoint did not disappear in later years. Still, there had been a change in emphasis.

The moderate line was not fully codified until the summer of 1950, but important elements of it were visible during the winter of 1949–50. In Henan, land-reform cadres were being told that altered conditions had made possible more stable and orderly techniques than had been used in the past. The PRC could avoid nonlegal struggle methods that harmed the government's prestige and did not really promote the awareness of the masses. Except in regard to a small minority of reactionaries who would have to be dealt with by the courts, the movement could use struggle methods involving persuasion and explanation. This indoctrination made many cadres rather timid. They were afraid that a vigorous development of the mass struggle would lead to infringements of policy, and some of them began to restrict the struggle. Considerable persuasion was required before they returned to a policy of mobilizing with a free hand.[20]

Land-reform regulations for Henan province were approved by the Government Administration Council (GAC, equivalent to a Cabinet) in Peking on 20 January 1950.[21] The landlords, as before, were to be left with only as much land, draft animals, grain, tools, and housing as was being given to the poor. The rich peasants, on the other hand, would only be cut down to a level equal to that of the average middle peasant in their village. There was to be no encroachment on commercial and industrial activities or on any middle peasants including well-to-do middle peasants. Confiscation of the hidden wealth of the landlords, which had been strongly encouraged at the time of the Outline Land Law and permitted in North China as late as October 1949,[22] was forbidden in these regulations. This decision was not made because the government believed in principle (as it did with industrial and

---

19. *Renmin ribao*, 3 April 1948, p. 1.
20. *Xinhua yuebao*, April 1950, pp. 1472–73; May 1950, p. 87.
21. Ibid., April 1950, pp. 1475–77.
22. *Wei chunjie dang*, p. 61; *Xinhua yuebao*, December 1949, p. 460.

commercial property) that the landlords should be allowed to keep their hidden wealth, but because the process of searching for it led too frequently to disorder and violence, which were directed not only against landlords but also against peasants suspected of having hidden things for the landlords. Many of those accused of having concealed hoards had been beaten to persuade them to surrender their wealth. Since the rich usually had more than one cache of money or gold, they were likely to put up an initial resistance, then show the peasants one cache and claim that it was all they had. They might then be beaten further to persuade them to reveal their other caches. This could become a very ugly process, especially if a landlord were less wealthy than the peasants thought he was. In Long Bow, two people who probably had not had any buried wealth to reveal were beaten to death.[23] A peasant militiaman later described the lengths to which the peasants had gone in extracting the last dregs of wealth from recalcitrant landlord households: "All you had to do to make a man talk was to heat an iron bar in the fire...but the women were tougher. They would rather die than tell us where their gold was hidden. Burning flesh held no terror for them. If they weakened at all, it was in the face of threats to their children."[24] By 1950, the CCP had decided that the landlords' gold was not worth extracting at such a cost.

Authority in the land reform rested in the peasant associations, which functioned both through mass meetings of the membership and through elected assemblies and committees. The poor peasants and laborers could convene separate meetings and elect separate assemblies. This represented a rather good compromise between the necessity of mobilizing the poor peasants and laborers and that of keeping middle-peasant support. In 1947, when poor-peasant leagues had been allowed to control land reform in some villages, they had seriously infringed middle-peasant interests and sensibilities. Under the new system the poor peasants could meet together to discuss key issues without the inhibiting presence of their richer and more confident neighbors, but all real decisions had to be taken by the full peasant associations, in which the middle peasants had a major voice. If there was a danger that middle-peasant interests would be ignored, it arose less from the separate meetings of the poor peasants and laborers than from the preponderance of poor peasants and laborers among the activists whom the land-reform cadres were training.

The suburbs of Peking led in the shift to the right. Landholding there was fairly concentrated by North Chinese standards; the landlords and rich peasants owned half the land, including most of the best land, but the way they used their land was not very "feudal." The city provided a very profitable market for vegetables

---

23. Hinton, *Fanshen*, p. 204; see also pp. 135–38, 142.
24. Ibid., p. 207.

and other special crops, and the comparative security of the area had made major investments in agriculture seem safe. Much land was cultivated by comparatively advanced methods, with electric well pumps, greenhouses, and a variety of simple machines. The rich peasants worked three-quarters of their land themselves and with hired labor, and rented out only one-quarter. In one sample of fourteen *cun* it was found that even the landlords rented out only 51 percent of their land. There was a great deal of land hunger among the peasants due to the high population density of the suburbs, but the land-reform planners were reluctant to break up productive enterprises possessing considerable capital and parcel them out to peasants who might not be able to maintain advanced techniques.[25]

Each administrative *cun* was assigned a work team, usually of five to nine land-reform cadres; this meant there was about one cadre for every 275 members of the agricultural population. They worked under tight central control. Each work team had to report to its superiors at the *qu* level once every two or three days. Inspectors checked on their work. Mass struggles were permitted only under the supervision of the land-reform cadres; the municipal government later commented:

> Spontaneous struggles by the peasants must be firmly prevented in the land reform. When the tide of land reform was unleashed, peasants in the three *cun* of Liugezhuan, Mafangsi, and Fuyousi started spontaneously to carry out land reform. Among the objects of spontaneous struggles in these three *cun*, only four families were landlords (one was the family of a despot landlord); the rest consisted of four rich-peasant families and eighteen middle-peasant families. The struggle was aimed principally at confiscating grain. At Mafangsi, the peasants bound and beat one landlord. Following these incidents, we immediately instructed each *qu* to convene a meeting of the peasant-association cadres of the villages where land reform had not yet started and explicitly order that pending the arrival of land-reform work teams, no formal action was permitted; only policy propaganda and preparatory work were permitted.[26]

In the suburbs of large cities the peasants were not given full ownership of the land distributed to them. Much of this land would

---

25. General Report of the Peking Municipal People's Government on Land Reform in Peking Suburban Areas, approved by the GAC on 21 November 1950, text in *Nanfang ribao*, 23 November 1950, p. 4, and 24 November 1950, p. 4. (The translation in *CB*, no. 72, is poor.) See also *Xinhua yuebao*, January 1950, p. 726; NCNA, Peking, 18 April 1950, in FBIS, 1950, no. 77.

26. *Nanfang ribao*, 24 November 1950, p. 4.

be needed as sites for factories, offices, and apartment blocks as
the cities expanded, and the government did not want to promise
the peasants permanent ownership of the land and then have to
break the promise. So it gave them the right to use the land, with
no rent and no more taxes than they would have paid if they had
owned it. The government promised that if the land had to be
taken for urban expansion, the peasants would be able to shift to
some other occupation producing at least as high an income, and
would get compensation for any investment they had made to
improve the land during the period they had had it.

There were 4,906 households classified as landlords, or something like 7 percent of the agricultural population, but mass
struggles were organized against only 130 despots. Most of the
despots would have been landlords, but some were probably rich
peasants and possibly even middle peasants attacked because of
their role in the *baojia* system[27] or in the Yiguandao, a secret
society. Most of the despots, after having been publicly
denounced, "bowed their heads" before the masses and were let
off. The 40 most important ones were turned over to the courts.
Of these 7 were sentenced to death, 1 to life imprisonment, 26 to
prison terms short of life, and 6 had not been sentenced by late
summer of 1950.[28]

Twenty-nine percent of the landlords were concurrently involved
in commerce or industry. The policies of not going after their
commercial and industrial property and not searching out their
buried wealth may have been enforced more strictly than in other
regions because of the close links between the suburban landlords
and the Peking bourgeoisie.

Rich peasants formed 4.3 percent of the agricultural population.
They owned 88,700 *mou*, or 8 percent of the land in the suburbs;
of this they rented out 22,050 *mou*. Only the land they had rented
out was taken from them. The municipal government explained:

> Not to touch the more than 60,000 *mou* that the rich
> peasants cultivated themselves or hired laborers to cultivate,
> or their other property, had a number of advantages:
>   a. It was beneficial to an early restoration of rural produc-
> tion. First, it helped to stabilize and stimulate the middle
> peasants' will to produce.... As middle peasant Shi Wenyuan
> said, "Even rich peasants are not touched. Then what do we
> need to worry about?" To stabilize and stimulate the middle

---

27. In Chinese tradition *baojia* was a system for arranging the
people in groups and making them mutually responsible for any
misdeeds. But at the time of liberation *baojia* seems in most areas
simply to have been a name for a system of village officials and tax
collectors.

28. *Nanfang ribao,* 24 November 1950, p. 4; *Renmin ribao,* 27
May 1950, p. 1.

peasants' will to produce is in effect to encourage the poor peasants' and agricultural laborers' will to produce, since after land reform the poor peasants and agricultural laborers will, in general, certainly rise quickly to the status of middle peasants. The poor peasants and laborers of today are the middle peasants of tomorrow. At the same time, the tools, capital, and other production conditions possessed by the rich peasants are superior to those possessed by the peasants in general. The preservation of a rich-peasant economy is bene-ficial to economic restoration and development as well as to the supply of vegetables to the cities.

b. It helped to isolate the landlords. Prior to liberation, the attitude of fear on the part of rich peasants and landlords was the same. Most rich peasants felt they would surely be among the objects of the land reform; the peasants in general also thought this would be so. But once the land reform had clearly demarcated class boundaries, and the rich peasants knew that we were not adopting the same policy toward them as toward the landlords, they began to separate themselves from the landlords and their feelings became calmer.

c. It firmly protected the middle peasants.[29]

Most of these arguments were applicable to all rural areas, and lenient treatment of the rich peasants soon became general policy. It was probably the need to maintain a supply of vegetables for city markets that make Peking take the lead in this respect, at a time when rich peasants were still being treated more harshly in Henan.

The final report on land reform in the Peking suburbs recom-mended that the category "well-to-do middle peasants" be abolished. These people were supposed to be treated exactly the same as the ordinary middle peasants, and having a separate label for them would serve only to make them nervous and to encourage local cadres to infringe their rights.[30] Unfortunately this recom-mendation was not followed.

At the end of the land reform approximately 30–35 percent of the agricultural population were in peasant associations. This is not a strikingly low figure,[31] but the overall record in the Peking suburbs reveals surprisingly little concern for real political mobili-zation of the peasants. Land reform was carried out with extreme haste; it was completed about fourteen months after the liberation of Peking. In any particular village, it usually lasted only one and a half months. There does not seem to have been much mobilization of the peasants beforehand for struggle against despots or for

---

29. *Nanfang ribao*, 23 November 1950, p. 4.

30. Ibid., 24 November 1950, p. 4.

31. The number of people ineligible through class origin and age meant that this figure could hardly ever go much over 40 percent.

reduction of rent and interest. These programs had stretched over a considerable period as necessary preliminaries to land reform in Henan. They formed part of the land reform—a short first stage—in the Peking suburbs. This did not permit the gradual evolution of village politics toward peasant dominance that was typical of other areas. Instead there was a more rapid change, supervised more closely than usual by cadres from outside the villages. The way the land reform was divided into waves, in each of which specified *cun* went through the entire process in a very short time and at about the same speed as the other *cun* of the same wave, indicates a process carried out administratively, without waiting for peasant activists to teach themselves the skills of mass organization. There was no obvious reason for such haste.

The class struggle was very mild. The policies dictating what could be taken from landlords and rich peasants, while mild by comparison with earlier periods, were approximately duplicated in most of China after the summer of 1950. But the number of land-lords classified as despots and the number said to have been executed were low by both earlier and later standards. This program was about as close as the CCP leadership ever came to what it was later to revile as "peaceful land reform."[32]

Establishing Control in the South

The Communist Party had established its rule in the North through prolonged and savage warfare, but it acquired large areas of East, Central, South, and Southwest China almost by default in the "War of the Feet," in which it had to do little more than follow the Guomindang forces as they fled southward. The beginning of 1950 found the CCP responsible for the administration of immense areas in which it had little or no organizational base.

The newspapers of the early 1950s present a vivid picture of the way the Party established itself in the villages. In recent years the Chinese press has had serious shortcomings as a source for research. Many important questions have either been ignored or been discussed in Aesopian language comprehensible only to those with a great deal of specialized knowledge. Peking transmits its views and policies to local cadres mainly through private channels. But in the first years of the PRC these private channels hardly existed; Peking had no choice but to use the public press as a major means of communication with its own local functionaries. Senior officials were warned that they should not load their subor-dinates with so much administrative detail that they would have no

---

32. There was one remarkable case in which a landlord who owed money to a laborer felt so little fear of the new regime that he simply ignored repeated orders to pay from both the administration and the courts. *Renmin ribao*, 16 May 1950, p. 4.

time to read the papers.[33] The local cadres were ideologically so unreliable that it would have made little sense to treat them as an elect group that could be entrusted with information not suitable for the broad public. In any case this was not possible; the CCP had to describe its policies and the rationale behind them in the public press if it wanted local cadres to understand those policies and carry them out effectively. Furthermore, the descriptions had to be in plain language; few of the new regime's personnel had been sufficiently educated to be able to decode ideological jargon or political doubletalk accurately. CCP leaders had a good understanding of what was going on in the countryside between 1949 and 1952—a much better understanding than they had had in 1947—and they were doing their best to describe in the press what they thought was going on. Newspapers of this period are, therefore, tremendously rich sources for a student of the land reform and the campaigns that led up to it.

The most sophisticated analyses of mass mobilization and land reform that I have seen are in *Changjiang ribao* of Wuhan, the leading newspaper of the Central-South Region. This region stretched from the Old Liberated Areas of Henan down through Hubei, Hunan, and Jiangxi to the extreme southern provinces of Guangdong and Guangxi. It was administered by the Central-South Military and Administrative Committee (MAC) in Wuhan, which was derived from the earlier Central Plains Provisional People's Government. The northern sections of the region, liberated early, were ready for most social reform campaigns before the southern provinces. The Central-South MAC was able to look at the experience acquired in the early provinces and publish very clear and informative analyses for the benefit of cadres in provinces that were carrying out these programs at a later date.

Renmin ribao of Peking, *Nanfang ribao* of Canton, and *Xinhua ribao* of Chongqing (Chungking) also provide useful information on this period. The monthly *Xinhua yuebao* provides a selection of articles from many provincial newspapers as well as from Peking.

In the newly conquered areas the Party had four immediate tasks: to establish some kind of administration, to eliminate actual and potential armed opposition, to revive production (which was far below prewar levels), and to begin the political mobilization of the masses for class struggle. In one sense, of course, these tasks were mutually supporting. In another they conflicted because they constituted enormous demands on an inadequate body of qualified personnel. Every task diverted the cadres' attention from other key tasks. It did only limited good to concentrate on the "central tasks" because, as some cadres plaintively remarked, "everything is a central task."[34]

---

33. *Changjiang ribao* editorial, 16 December 1950, reprinted in *Nanfang ribao*, 20 December 1950, p. 4.

34. *Nanfang ribao*, 2 November 1950, p. 3.

The reliable CCP personnel in the South—both those who had come down from the North and those who had been working in local underground organizations or guerrilla bands before liberation—were not nearly numerous enough to govern by themselves. The bulk of the administrative personnel were either new recruits, who in the early months were mostly intellectuals, or people inherited from the Guomindang. In northern China in the late 1940s, the CCP had expanded its control gradually enough so that it could provide some reliable personnel, able to speak a dialect the peasants could understand, to govern each area as it was liberated; the Party had not needed to use former Guomindang personnel. Also, to have done so would have been very dangerous under civil war conditions; the likelihood of betrayal would have been too great. In southern China around the beginning of 1950, the shortage of reliable people was much worse, and Chiang Kai-shek had been so thoroughly defeated that counterrevolutionaries within the new administration would not be able to do a tremendous amount of harm. Adopting a remarkably nonparanoid attitude, the CCP decided to risk clutching a few vipers to its bosom rather than reduce the New Liberated Areas to anarchy by getting rid of the Guomindang personnel before anyone was available to replace them.

The danger was that the compromises that were necessary to maintain even minimal administration in the short run might become permanent; that the new regime, having absorbed many of the base-level personnel of its predecessor, would adapt itself to fit them rather than vice versa. In its first months the new government was working through a preposterously unreliable apparatus in the villages, and furthermore the supervision it could exercise over this apparatus was so sketchy that it was sometimes called "looking at flowers while riding on horseback." The CCP had to reform the (largely non-Party) administrative apparatus while using it, as well as reforming the Party apparatus that was responsible for the first reform. The fact that these tasks were accomplished, even imperfectly, represents a monumental achievement.

At the *xian* and *qu* levels the Party increased its control gradually, as it brought in cadres from other areas and retrained or replaced personnel inherited from the Guomindang. At the village level, change came in a series of waves, as work teams arrived every few months on one mission or another. Many of the initial steps of mass mobilization were carried out by tax collection teams, which had to visit every village at least once a year anyway.

The new regime's most obvious task was to eliminate actual and potential armed opposition. There were large gangs of organized bandits, and stragglers from the Guomindang armies who had been passed by during the PLA's march to the south and who were regarded as bandits.[35] As late as September 1950 there were about

---

35. "Bandit" was a convenient label to apply to enemies of the new government. However, it would in most cases have been fairly

200,000 such people at large.[36] They had to be dealt with mainly by the PLA, with some help from local militias. Next came scattered bandits; local authorities, militias, and the police[37] could handle them with only limited help from regular troops. The policy for dealing with bandits was to punish the ringleaders, let off many of the followers, and reward those who acquired merit by changing sides and helping the government. Surrender was rewarded with leniency. There was considerable variation in the way these policies were applied in practice. In July 1950, Peking began to complain that many local authorities had become "boundlessly lenient." There were cases in which bandit leaders were arrested and released again up to eight times; there were *xian* in which a whole year went by without a single execution.[38] The Party did not stop advocating leniency, but warned that it should be restricted to those who really seemed to have repented and mended their ways.

A great many weapons were scattered about the countryside in the hands of local officials, landlords, militias and crop protection organizations usually controlled by the landlords, and even some peasants. The weapons ranged from swords and spears through pistols, rifles, hand grenades, and machine guns. The new government needed to remove some of these from the villages entirely and put the rest in the hands of reliable militias. It moved rather cautiously; in the period immediately after liberation there was not even a blanket prohibition on landlord ownership of guns.[39] The government may not have wanted to issue orders it was not yet capable of enforcing. Also, to have seemed too eager to disarm people would have implied that it was expecting to come into conflict with them.

Mass struggles against local despots required somewhat more mobilization of the masses than the simple elimination of direct opposition. Work teams tried to arouse the peasants against the strongest and most oppressive of the landlords, rich peasants, and

---

accurate. The line separating soldiers from bandits had long been a vague one in China, easily crossed in either direction. Given what is known about the armies that had been more or less under the command of Chiang Kai-shek, and especially about the less reliable units that would have been most likely to be left behind in the evacuation to Taiwan, it seems likely that many if not most of them lapsed into relatively apolitical banditry once they were cut off from their former commanders.

36. *Nanfang ribao*, 1 October 1950, p. 1.

37. *Gongan*, often translated as "public security forces."

38. *Renmin ribao* editorial, 21 July 1950, trans. in *CB*, 151:7; *Nanfang ribao*, 18 September 1951, trans. in *CB*, 124:4; *Renmin ribao*, 28 December 1950, trans. in *Survey of the China Mainland Press* (hereafter cited as *SCMP*), 39:24–25.

39. *Qunzhong ribao* (Xi'an), 30 December 1949, reprinted in *Xinhua yuebao*, February 1950, p. 957.

officials. These were not necessarily the richest landlords or even those most closely tied to the Guomindang; the truly rich were likely to have lived in the towns and therefore to have been little involved in direct abuse of the peasants. Some rich peasants were considered to be despots, but most landlords were not. The anti-despot campaign was more a political than an economic movement, and indeed not all of the people branded as despots had their wealth taken at this time. They were being attacked primarily in their capacity as a ruling class. Some areas did not need to conduct an antidespot movement, presumably because they had no despots.[40]

When mobilization of the peasants was just beginning, the CCP preferred not to try attacking the whole landlord class at once. If there were an initial stage in which only a few despots were attacked, then many ordinary landlords would remain neutral.[41] Later, when the peasants were better organized and the strongest landlords had been eliminated, the revolution could attack the landlord class as a whole. Unfortunately, this policy of attacking first the despots, then the ordinary landlords and to some extent the rich peasants, must have strengthened rumors that there would be a still later stage in which the middle peasants would be attacked.[42]

There may have been other motives for making a separate attack on the despots at first. Many peasants regarded landlord domination as natural; they respected or at least did not hate most landlords. If they could first be incited to direct action against the most vicious landlords, it might be easier later to persuade them that those who had done nothing worse than collect rents were also their enemies. The discrediting of the class as a whole started with its worst members. The peasants may also have found it easier to work up the courage to denounce a despot, who seemed clearly destined to be sent off to prison or to be shot, than to attack an ordinary landlord who was going to remain in the village and who might later have an opportunity to take revenge.

The mass-struggle meetings at which the despots were denounced had no judicial powers; they were devices for political propaganda and mass mobilization. Usually, if a despot was accused of major crimes, he would be taken off after the struggle meeting and tried at a people's court or a people's tribunal, which could impose punishments. On one occasion, a crowd was told that the despots they had just spent several hours denouncing had already been under formal sentence of death.[43] The antidespot movement was

---

40. Terminal report of Deng Zihui on the work of the Central Plains Provisional People's Government, of which he had been chairman; *Changjiang ribao*, 7 February 1950, p. 2.

41. *Xinhua yuebao*, November 1949, p. 178.

42. Ibid., July 1950, p. 562.

43. Ibid., November 1949, p. 176.

supposed to be quite severe; cases in which despots were executed were often discussed in the press. Approving accounts from East China told of one *xiang* where one despot out of six was executed, and one *cun* where two out of four were executed.[44] The exact tactics of the struggle could vary according to circumstances. Where possible, the government preferred the peasants to organize themselves and denounce the despots with only advice and guidance from outside the village. If the despots were too intimidating, it might be necessary to arrest one or two before the peasants would be willing to take any public action.

Reduction of Rent and Interest

Before the land reform proper, the program that gave the greatest economic benefits to the peasants was rent reduction. This program involved not only limitation of current payments but also a refund to the peasants of any rent beyond the reduced level that had been paid to the landlords after the area in question had been liberated. Rent reduction and refund had the virtue that if the landlords' wealth was taken gradually rather than all at once in the land reform proper, the landlords would be less likely to panic and resist confiscation.[45] At a crude estimate, the average poor-peasant household in the areas of the Central-South Region that enforced rent reduction in the spring of 1950 received a rent refund of twenty-five to thirty catties of grain per person.[46] This was enough to make a considerable difference to families that were usually hungry for several months of each year.

Rent-reduction laws dealt with a variety of matters. The Regulations for Reduction of Rent and Interest in the Central-South Region, dated 15 February 1950, included the following major points:

The rent on land rented out by landlords, old rich peasants, and institutions was to be reduced by 25 percent of the original amount, and in any case was not to exceed 37.5 percent of the main crop. There could be exceptions if the landlord contributed tools, draft animals, and so on as well as land. If a natural disaster destroyed the crop, the rent might be reduced even below the standard limit, or canceled entirely. All rent was to be paid after the harvest; there was to be no rent deposit paid in advance, and no secondary rents (unpaid labor in the landlords' fields, etc.). Old rent deposits had to be refunded by the landlords. The

---

44. Ibid.

45. Ibid., December 1949, p. 462.

46. *Nanfang ribao*, 20 September 1950, p. 1, reported that 1,020,000,000 catties of grain had been refunded in areas with a population of about 60,000,000 since February 1950. A catty is equal to 1.1023 pounds.

peasants were given security of tenure, so landlords would not be able to extract illegally high rents through threats of eviction. The rent reduction was made retroactive to the date the initial people's government had been established in each *xian*. The peasants did not have to pay any rent that had been in arrears before that date.

Small renters renting out less than 150 percent of the local average landholding could, with the permission of the local government and the peasant association, reduce the rents they collected by less than 25 percent or not reduce them at all. If land were rented out by middle peasants or new rich peasants, the level of rent they could charge would be negotiated within the village.

The interest on debts that peasants had owed to landlords and old rich peasants since before liberation was limited to 1.5 percent per month; interest payments exceeding this amount, paid after liberation, were to be refunded. The total paid on a debt—principal plus interest—could not exceed twice the original principal. Commercial loans, loans made in connection with buying and selling, and loans made after liberation were not affected by the above provisions.

Land that had been usurped from the peasants was to be returned and the culprits punished. War criminals and major counterrevolutionary criminals, designated as such by a *xian* government with the approval of the province government or an authority deputized by the province government, would have their land confiscated. Members of their families who had not participated in their crimes would be left some land.[47]

---

47. Regulations for Reduction of Rent and Interest in the Central-South Region; text in *Xinhua yuebao*, April 1950, pp. 1476–77. The Central-South MAC issued a revised version in September (text in *Nanfang ribao*, 21 September 1950, p. 1). The 37.5 percent limit on rents was not mentioned; there was simply to be a reduction by 25 percent. Rent "refunds" collected from the landlords and rich peasants could be distributed among the poor according to need rather than being returned necessarily to those peasants who had originally paid the rents in question. Debts that the peasants had owed to the landlords before liberation were canceled completely.

The East China New Liberated Areas Provisional Regulations for Rent Reduction (draft), 15 September 1949, in *Xinhua yuebao*, November 1949, pp. 170–71, were similar but not identical to the Central-South decrees. Rent was to be reduced by 25 percent to 30 percent. Small renters could apply for permission to reduce rents by less than 25 percent, or not at all, only if they rented out less than the local average of middle-peasant landholdings. Debts were freed of interest limitations if contracted after the date of the regulations, rather than after liberation, and the amount of interest to be paid on old debts was left rather vague. If old

There were some landlords, called *baodian* or *baozhong*, who made a real contribution to production and therefore collected higher rents than landlords who only rented out land. The regional rent-reduction decree discussed above had said rather vaguely that such landlords could continue to collect higher rents than those permitted to ordinary landlords; the government did not want to inhibit them from continuing to support production. This decision was strikingly reflected in some provincial decrees. In Hubei, where *baodian* had provided housing, tools, seed grain, and so on to their tenants, the regulations for rent reduction issued in January 1950 said that if the original rent collected by a *baodian* had been 80 percent of the crop, it need only be reduced to 70 percent.[48] Guangdong province issued special regulations for the *shatian* areas of the coastal river deltas, where much land was rented by its owners to *baodian*, who made substantial investments in water control and then sublet the land to the peasants who actually cultivated it. In such cases the rent collected by the *baodian* would be reduced by 15–20 percent, and in any case it could not exceed 55 percent of the main crop. Landlords in the *shatian* areas who had not made any investment in water control had to reduce their rents by 25 percent and could not charge more than 25 percent of the main crop. If the original rent had been less than 25 percent of the main crop, the reduction might be less than 25 percent, or there might be no reduction. People who rented land from its owners and then sublet it to the peasants without making any investment in its productivity simply had all their rights to the land abolished.[49]

In November the GAC issued a revised decree on the handling of debts in the New Liberated Areas,[50] which clarified the boundaries beyond which interest reduction would not apply. Loans made in connection with commerce or industry had to be repaid at the originally agreed-upon terms, even if the creditor were a landlord. Debts contracted after liberation had to be repaid at the originally agreed-upon interest, unless they were really just renewals of preliberation debts. Local governments were not to interfere in the terms of loans in the future.

All these laws were often violated. Naturally, many landlords

---

debts had been at a "high" interest rate, no further interest was to be paid on them.

48. Text in *Changjiang ribao*, 6 January 1950, p. 3.

49. Text in *Nanfang ribao*, 16 November 1950, p. 1. Some people had been obtaining large profits through subletting simply because they were powerful. Either they were in a position to make owners (usually clans or other institutions) rent them land at less than its real value, or they had a degree of control over the peasants that enabled them to extract more rent than the land's owners could have done.

50. Text in *Nanfang ribao*, 22 November 1950, p. 3.

evaded rent reduction in any way they could. They might publicly collect reduced rent and later demand additional sums from their tenants. They might increase the level of rent and then "reduce" the inflated figures. The government was quite candid about its inability to enforce rent reduction properly in the period immediately after liberation. Tax laws specified that if a landlord illegally collected full rent, he should bear the entire burden of agricultural taxation. If the tenant illegally refused to pay rent, he would have to bear the full burden. If landlord and tenant obeyed the laws on rent, they would share the tax burden.[51]

There was confusion in some places over whether to reduce rent to 37.5 percent of the main crop[52] or to reduce it by 25 percent of the original amount. The low educational level of many of the cadres who had to carry out rent reduction was the main cause of this confusion, but it may have been aggravated by a lack of concern for the basic goals of the program, particularly in some bizarre cases in which rents that had originally been below 37.5 percent were raised to 37.5 percent in the "rent reduction."[53] Part of the blame also lies in the vague nature of some policy statements on the subject. The people who wrote the laws wanted to keep them short and simple, even at the risk of making them ambiguous. The February 1950 regulations summarized above omitted two useful pieces of clarifying language that had appeared in earlier documents: an explicit statement that rents below 37.5 percent were not to be raised, and a statement that rent-deposit refunds would have to be calculated in terms of commodity purchasing power to allow for the massive inflation of recent years.[54]

There were also cases in which overly zealous cadres applied rent reduction and refund to people who were supposed to be exempt from it or made landlords refund rent they had collected several months before liberation.[55]

Not all areas gave the same emphasis to different programs; thus the Southwest Region, in general, stressed refund of rent deposits more than the Central-South Region. It was not usually practical to enforce rent reduction fully until banditry and other open opposition to the government had been reduced to a low level. If bandits and local despots were comparatively weak, the campaigns against

---

51. Ibid., 7 September 1950, p. 3.

52. 35 percent in East China, 25 percent for noninvesting landlords in the *shatian* areas of Guangdong.

53. *Nanfang ribao*, 14 September 1950, p. 2; 25 October 1950, p. 1; 26 November 1950, p. 3.

54. Detailed Regulations for Implementing Rent and Interest Reduction in Hubei Province, *Changjiang ribao*, 6 January 1950, p. 3; Outline for Rent and Interest Reduction, issued by the Central Plains Bureau of the CCP, 8 October 1948, in Jiefang she, *Lun xin jiefang qu*, p. 17.

55. *Nanfang ribao*, 11 September 1950, p. 2.

them could usefully be combined with rent reduction.

Peasants in many areas also benefited to some extent from government loans and disaster relief, but these were limited. The government told the peasants that they would have to depend mainly on the resources available in their own villages. There were cases in which hungry peasants formed mobs and looted government granaries. The problem was especially bad in Hunan, Hubei, and Jiangxi early in 1950; tens of millions of catties of grain were stolen from the granaries or burned. It is impossible to tell just how widely such things occurred or how much truth there was in government charges that despots and Guomindang agents had egged the peasants on.[56]

The need to stimulate agricultural production, which was far below normal levels, placed limits on social reforms. The preservation of the rich-peasant economy was a general slogan under which the peasants were told that making themselves rich, even by means that could be considered exploitative, would not necessarily cause the CCP to treat them as enemies. This was, in fact, a great source of worry in the New Liberated Areas. Many people were afraid that it would be dangerous to produce too much and thus become conspicuously prosperous. Landlords and rich peasants feared that if they made loans, this would be added to the list of evidence against them as exploiters; they also feared that the loans would not be repaid. They did not want to flaunt their wealth by hiring laborers. Middle peasants feared that if they hired laborers, they would be classified as rich peasants. Households farming land that might be subject to redistribution feared that if they worked hard and applied a lot of fertilizer, some other household might harvest the crop in the end. Such cautious attitudes reduced production, reduced employment opportunities in the countryside, and made the annual "spring hunger," when food stocks from the autumn harvest ran low, even worse than usual for some peasants.

Cadres in some areas made the rich peasants pay more than the going rate when they hired laborers. This practice was forbidden by the government; Zhou Enlai even said explicitly that the laborers should not demand excessive wages.[57] But it might have been hard to stop the cadres from raising wages, since in many cases they would only have had to drop a few hints. Forced loans, also formally forbidden, sometimes occurred but were probably less common. By the time the peasants were sufficiently sure of themselves to extract grain from the wealthy, they would usually have been able to take it in the form of rent refunds rather than loans.

---

56. Ibid., 25 September 1950, p. 1.
57. NCNA, 16 March 1950, trans. in FBIS, 1950, no. 53.

Organizational Development

The political structure developed gradually. From the top down came the formal government, which ran (with the Party paralleling it) from Peking to the MACs that ruled the greater administrative regions, and then to the governments of provinces, special administrative districts, *xian*, and *qu*. Below the *qu* level the government was represented by traveling work teams sent out to the countryside for various purposes. The work teams cultivated a variety of organizations actually based on the masses, the first of which was the peasant association. Work teams gathered peasants who seemed open to political education, especially poor peasants and laborers, in small discussion groups.[58] Sometimes peasants who had been especially active were sent for training outside the village first so that they could lead these small groups. Sometimes the peasants had too little confidence in the strength of the new regime to identify themselves with it publicly, and the small groups had to be clandestine for a while; as political education spread to more peasants, the small groups became the basis for a more broadly based and more public peasant association.

This process was, of course, subject to distortion. Some cadres signed up peasants for the peasant association without any discussion, or even asked the officials of the old *baojia* system to draw up lists of peasants for membership.[59] The landlords and rich peasants infiltrated peasant associations; in some cases, they took the initiative in setting them up so as to maintain their control. In September 1950, *Nanfang ribao* reported that at least 20 percent of the peasant associations in the Central-South Region were controlled by landlords and feudal forces. A few were "phony" organizations created by hostile forces, but most had gone bad simply because the cadres had set them up too hastily without educating the members or examining their qualifications, and so the landlords and rich peasants had been able to take over by virtue of their superior political skills.[60] Another problem, which was rarely mentioned openly but may have been widespread, was recruitment of peasant-association leaders from among the middle peasants rather than from the poor peasants and laborers. Middle peasants were not positively unacceptable under current policies, and some cadres responsible for supervising peasant-association development preferred to avoid the extra difficulty of promoting the poor peasants and laborers with their lower self-confidence, lower prestige, and lack of leisure time.[61]

---

58. In Gaoyao *xian*, Guangdong, the small groups had an average of thirty-three members. *Nanfang ribao*, 17 October 1950, p. 3.

59. Ibid., 11 September 1950, p. 3.

60. Ibid., 15 September 1950, p. 3.

61. *Xinhua ribao* (Chongqing), 4 January 1951, p. 3; see also 24

Some cadres, on the other hand, adopted a closed-door attitude to peasant-association recruitment, setting up elaborate procedures and criteria for membership and often excluding most middle peasants and poor rural intellectuals. They demanded that peasant-association members be unselfish, that they not own more than three *mou* of land, etc. Some were even suspicious of all laborers who worked for landlords, fearing that they might serve as agents of their employers.[62]

Other key organizations at the village level included the women's association and the militia. The government hoped eventually to have about 5 percent of the population in militias, but it warned that this was not to be treated as a recruiting quota.[63] The New-Democratic Youth League spread less rapidly, because it was to some extent an elite organization. The police were not based in the villages, but they operated in the villages to some extent.

Representative assemblies were organized at the *xiang*, *qu*, and *xian* levels. The eventual goal was to have a people's representative assembly at each level. These bodies, the formal voice of the people, would elect the chairman and other key members of governments at the corresponding levels. Their powers were circumscribed; all their decisions were subject to veto by higher levels of government. They met at intervals rather than continuously and had no standing organs to monitor the actions of local governments between their sessions. Citizens over eighteen years old of any social class were eligible for election, provided they opposed imperialism, feudalism, and bureaucratic capitalism, supported the Common Program that had been passed by the Chinese People's Political Consultative Conference, and had done nothing that caused them to be deprived of political rights.

The Communist Party did not care to entrust formal power, even nominally, to broadly elected bodies before the local political structure had been thoroughly reformed. In the interim, which in many places lasted through the end of land reform, the most important elected bodies were the peasant representative assemblies. At the *xiang* level these were closely connected with the peasant associations and had a great deal of real power. They made some important decisions themselves and elected the committees that made most of the other decisions: the peasant-association executive committee and the people's government committee of the *xiang*. But peasant representative conferences[64] at the *qu* and *xian* levels did not

November 1951, p. 2; Yang, *A Chinese Village in Early Communist Transition*, pp. 134–35.

62. *Nanfang ribao*, 6 September 1950, p. 3; 31 October 1950, p. 2.

63. Ibid., 22 November 1950, p. 4.

64. I have called bodies "assemblies" or "conferences" according to the functions they seem actually to have performed. This does not quite correspond to the distinction in documents of this period

have nearly the same decision-making power as their counterparts at the *xiang* level. There were also "all-circles" people's representative conferences, which included representatives of the bourgeoisie and other nonpeasant groups acceptable to the CCP. Some of their members were elected by the population at large, directly or indirectly, but others were chosen by mass organizations or appointed by the government. The fact that peasant and "all-circles" representative conferences at the *qu* and *xian* levels did not have formal legislative powers does not imply that they were of no importance. Some officials saw no value in them, or viewed them simply as information-gathering groups from which the leadership could learn the opinions of the masses, but they could be more. Officials were supposed to delegate to them some decisions that their members were qualified to make, and they were extremely useful as channels of communication. Most of their members were cadres or activists taking a few days from their regular work to attend the conference. They exchanged advice and comments on problems they had encountered, listened to explanations of new policies they would soon have to implement, and reported to higher authorities on the work they had been doing. When they returned to their regular jobs, they passed on to their colleagues what they had learned.

Political change in the countryside was very uneven. A single village might go through a series of upheavals as successive work teams came, talked with the peasants, trained activists, and tried to bring village politics into something approximating the desired pattern. The landlords and rich peasants were influential, clever, and tenacious. They could overawe the peasants and continue to control a village clandestinely under an apparently reformed system. Even if peasants not aligned with the landlords could be trained and helped to take over a village, there was no guarantee that they would not fall into corrupt and tyrannical habits. The work teams, which were not native to the villages in which they worked and which could not usually stay in one village long enough to make exhaustive investigations, could be deceived and manipulated. There was one *cun* in Sanshui *xian*, Guangdong, where a peasant association was created under rather good leadership at an early date. The landlords watched for opportunities to attack it. When a new work team came to the village in June 1950 and began calling peasant meetings, the landlords mobilized every peasant they could still control to charge the peasant-association

---

(see in particular four decrees on the organization of local governments and local assemblies, all passed by the GAC on 8 December 1950, all published in *Xinhua ribao*, 1 January 1951, p. 3) between the preliminary organizational form *huiyi* and the more fully developed form, with greater official powers, *dahui*. I categorize the peasant representative *huiyi* at the *xiang* level as an assembly, but those at *qu* and *xian* level as conferences.

leaders with massive corruption. The work team dissolved the existing peasant association and set up a preparatory committee for a new one; the landlords were able to gain control of the preparatory committee. This renewal of landlord power in the village lasted through the summer, with quite serious results during the collection of the summer tax; the situation was finally corrected in September.[65] By the end of 1950, the Party had decided that one should not simply dissolve a peasant association, even a fundamentally fraudulent one established at the initiative of the landlords. One should instead mobilize the masses to purify and reorganize it.[66] The only real solution to such problems was to mobilize the broad mass of the peasantry, elevating a large fraction of the population to political awareness and political participation, so that the people could keep tabs on village leaders when no work team was present. This could not be done quickly.

The cadres of the work teams were themselves far from perfect. They included a leavening of trained personnel from the Old Liberated Areas, but most were local people with little experience and a rather low political level. Many were peasants; many others were students or teachers pulled out of the schools and sent to the countryside after a brief period of training. They had to learn by doing. A great deal of their education was in matters of work style. They had a tendency, natural in China as in many other cultures, to think that governing consisted of telling people what to do. The notion of working with the masses came hard to them; more than a few were convinced that if they tried to follow the mass line, it would not be possible to get their jobs done.[67] Bureaucratic and commandist work styles were rife.

A man named Su Zheng, who was sent out to collect taxes in Gaoyao *xian*, Guangdong, was chosen as a type case to be studied in later campaigns for cadre rectification. He thought that his superiors were testing him and that their only criterion of judgment would be how much tax he could collect. He led what was in some respects a genuine mass struggle in the *cun* to which he was assigned; three or four hundred peasants participated in struggles against the landlords, despots, etc. But he ran these struggles in a bureaucratic and commandist fashion, not letting the peasants make the decisions they should have made. He was careless about whom he struggled against; he harmed commerce and industry and infringed the rights of some middle peasants. When things went wrong, he did not investigate the causes but simply arrested people or beat them. When people did not pay the taxes he thought they owed, he did not use propaganda or the massed weight of public opinion against them; he used simple fear, even to the point

65. *Nanfang ribao*, 12 November 1950, p. 3.

66. NCNA, Peking, 31 December 1950, in *Xinhua ribao*, 4 January 1951, p. 4.

67. *Nanfang ribao*, 18 November 1950, p. 4.

of organizing a fake firing squad and telling them they were about to be shot. He sometimes took the fruits of the struggle for himself.[68]

Major rectification campaigns were needed at all levels of the Party and government. In the party itself, the rectification movement that began in 1950 was primarily educational. It was not as concerned with landlord and rich-peasant influence and did not give as large a role to the ordinary peasants as had the rectification of 1948.[69] It was run from the top down. Many newly recruited cadres were doing work that could only be accomplished properly with the cooperation of the masses. At intervals they were brought together to discuss what they had been doing and how, and to exchange information on how mass mobilization could be made more effective. In the summer of 1950, these rectification meetings emphasized avoiding mistakes and leftist excesses; there seems to have been a doctrine that if the cadres mobilized just a few of the poor, the ones they would get would be the ones with a naturally radical temperament, and the result would be leftist excesses in the struggle. The radicalism of 1947–48 was still the most important example of how not to carry out mass mobilization. So the same meetings that taught the cadres that they should mobilize the broad masses of the peasantry and avoid commandism also gave some of them an overly cautious attitude regarding the policies of class struggle. This phenomenon will be discussed further in Chapter 6.

The personnel inherited from the old regime presented special problems in political reform. They were by no means restricted to people in technical jobs, such as railway employees. The CCP was determined to maintain administration in the New Liberated Areas, and it was willing to make the most extraordinary compromises to achieve that end. A significant portion of the old police forces was given some reeducation and was absorbed into the police of the new regime, apparently on a permanent basis.[70] The people's courts set up in the New Liberated Areas took over many of the

---

68. Ibid., 19 September 1950, p. 4.

69. *Renmin ribao* editorial, 1 July 1950, reprinted in *Xinhua yuebao*, July 1950, pp. 504–5. An interesting side effect to the policy of having organizations rectify themselves was that an organization in really bad shape could not carry out rectification. The New-Democratic Youth League was told not to have a formal rectification campaign in 1950, because most of its branches had been so recently organized that they would not be able to do the job properly. *Xinhua yuebao*, September 1950, p. 983. In a rectification campaign such as that of 1948, when organizations were rectified largely by nonmembers, no such logic would have applied.

70. *Renmin ribao* editorial, 8 August 1950, reprinted in *Xinhua yuebao*, September 1950, p. 985; *Nanfang ribao*, 20 October 1950, p. 1.

personnel of the old judiciary, and although these people were supposed to be given an intensive course of reeducation, the minister of justice later admitted that many of them had not in fact been put through any reform.[71] In the villages, the CCP allowed the old *baojia* system to retain some police and tax powers for several months after liberation. In parts of Hubei, it did so until the summer of 1950; in East and South Sichuan, the *baojia* system still had not been fully abolished by the beginning of 1951. Indeed, some of the *baojia* personnel not only stayed for these few months but were able to make the transition to become local cadres.[72] The CCP had to get the best use it could out of the holdover personnel, until they could be reindoctrinated or replaced. The Party also had to be rather cautious about letting itself become too closely identified with them or allowing them more power than necessary.

Within a year after liberation, the CCP could claim substantial progress on almost all of its programs for the initial transformation of the countryside: recruiting and training adequate administrative personnel, transferring wealth from the rich to the poor, destroying the political power and prestige of the traditional village elite, politicizing the peasants in general, and locating and training peasant activists who could become the new leaders of their villages. None of these tasks was even close to completion; they would be carried much further in the land reform. But substantial progress had to be made on all of them before an orderly land reform would be possible.

---

71. NCNA, Peking, 23 September 1952, in *CB*, 218:33.

72. *Nanfang ribao*, 17 October 1950, p. 4; *Xinhua ribao*, 1 January 1951, pp. 4, 5; *Changjiang ribao*, 7 February 1950, p. 2.

5

The Land-Reform Program of 1950

Early in 1950, planning began for a massive land-reform campaign during the coming winter in Jiangsu, Zhejiang, Anhui, Fujian, Henan, Hubei, Hunan, Jiangxi, Guangdong, and a few areas of northern China that had not yet been reformed. There was no desperate urgency about these plans; the government recognized that some of these areas might not be ready for reform and that it might have to be postponed until the winter of 1951–52. Reform in Guangxi, Sichuan, Yunnan, and Guizhou would also start during the winter of 1951–52. Reform in the national minority areas was postponed indefinitely.[1] The most important of the documents issued to guide this campaign were Liu Shaoqi's report on agrarian reform, delivered on 14 June 1950 to the National Committee of the Chinese People's Political Consultative Conference,[2] .the Agrarian Reform Law issued on 30 June,[3] and a revised version of the 1933 "Decisions Concerning the Differentiation of Class Status in the Countryside," issued on 4 August.[4]

The landlord class was defined by the same essentially economic criteria as in previous years; the idea that those politically hostile to the regime should be punished by being classified as landlords was explicitly denounced. People likewise were not to be classified as landlords merely because they had a high standard of living.[5] Land belonging to landlords and to institutions such as schools, temples, and clan organizations, and the "surplus" houses, draft animals, farm tools, and grain of the landlords,[6] were to be

---

1. Directive of the GAC, 28 February 1950, in *Xinhua yuebao*, April 1950, p. 1471.
2. Text in *Xinhua yuebao*, July 1950, pp. 492–96.
3. Trans. in Wong, *Land Reform*, pp. 286–96.
4. Trans. in *CB*, no. 52.
5. *Nanfang ribao*, 21 October 1950, p. 3.
6. The definition of "surplus" goods could be rather arbitrary. In September 1952, the CCP South China Sub-bureau ordered that when surplus grain was being confiscated during land reform in Guangdong, "large landlords" (about 30 percent of all landlords) should surrender an amount of grain equal to one year's rent. Medium landlords, industrialists and merchants who were concurrently landlords, and overseas Chinese landlords (about 50 percent

confiscated or requisitioned.[7] Landlords were to be given shares equal to those given to the poor peasants when these things were distributed. Collaborators, traitors, war criminals, and those who persistently sabotaged the land reform would get no land; their families, if they had not participated in such criminal acts and were willing to work the land themselves, would get equal shares of land.[8] Industrial and commercial property in theory were not to be touched. In practice the commercial wealth of the landlords was often taken, in whole or in part, when fines and penalties for their activities as landlords exceeded their total agricultural wealth. In particular, if they scattered their agricultural property in an effort to evade confiscation, capital they had invested in commerce or industry could be taken to make up for the missing items.[9] The landlords were forbidden to sell, give away, or destroy anything subject to confiscation in the period preceding land reform; they had to keep it intact to be confiscated. They were not considered really to own such property any more but merely to have custody of it.

The rich-peasant economy was in general to be preserved, especially in areas of highly commercialized agriculture. In April 1950, Liu Shaoqi had said that rich-peasant land should not be touched in the coming land reform.[10] It is unlikely that this statement could have been meant as a mere trial balloon; the speech in which it appeared was published with extraordinary prominence, occupying the whole front page of *Renmin ribao* on May Day. Yet the

---

of all landlords) were to surrender less than one year's rent. Small landlords who really could not afford to give up any grain (about 20 percent of all landlords) would not have to do so. The amount of grain taken from the landlords had formerly been larger than this. *Nanfang ribao*, 28 October 1952, trans. in *CB*, 226:6.

7. Confiscation (*moshou*) and requisitioning (*zhengshou*) were only nominally different; requisitioning was polite confiscation.

8. Regulations issued by the Central-South MAC in November 1950 specified denial of land only to criminals sentenced to over ten years in prison. *Changjiang ribao*, 17 November 1950, trans. in *SCMP*, 15:17.

9. *Nanfang ribao*, 23 October 1950, p. 1. It was suggested in 1952 that a person involved both in landlordism and in commerce or industry, who was considered to owe the peasants more than could be obtained from his agricultural assets, should be required to make payments out of his commercial or industrial assets "to the extent that such payments shall not too seriously affect the continued operation" of the commercial or industrial enterprises. *Nanfang ribao*, 15 July 1952, trans. in *CB*, 211:34.

10. *Renmin ribao*, 1 May 1950, p. 1. A posthumously published circular by Mao Zedong, dated 12 March 1950, says that he had proposed such a policy in November 1949 and again in March 1950. *Selected Works*, 5:24–25.

Agrarian Reform Law issued in June said that land rented out by rich peasants of a semilandlord character (those who rented out more than half their land) could be requisitioned in all areas, and that in certain areas designated by province governments, where there would not otherwise have been enough land to satisfy the needs of the poor, land rented out by any rich peasant could be requisitioned. Province governments seem to have approved the requisitioning of land rented out by ordinary rich peasants rather freely; near the end of the land reform *Renmin ribao* said that there had been areas where small amounts of land rented out by rich peasants had not been taken, as if these areas had been exceptions to the general rule.[11] An examination of statements by regional CCP leaders on what types of areas should be designated for requisitioning of land from ordinary rich peasants shows no consistent pattern; apparently, in 1950 at least, the Party imposed no overall policy. One common view was that land rented out by rich peasants not of a semilandlord character should be requisitioned in areas where it would otherwise be impossible to raise the average landholdings of the poor peasants to 80 percent of the average level for the rural population as a whole; this principle appeared in reports by the secretary of the Jiangxi Province Party Committee on 31 August 1950, by the chairman of the Hubei Province Land-Reform Committee on 6 October, and by Fang Fang (the de facto head of the Party apparatus in Guangdong) on 8 October.[12] However, Zhang Gensheng (the head of the Central-South MAC Land Committee's Research Department) said that if the poor peasants could be brought up to about 70 percent or 80 percent of the average landholding without requisitioning land from ordinary rich peasants, this would be adequate; in areas where the land ownership pattern was such that the poor peasants might otherwise be left with only 50 percent of the average landholding, the ordinary rich peasants' land would have to be requisitioned. Exactly where he was intending to draw the line, between 50 percent and 70 percent, was not clear.[13]

Rao Shushi, chairman of the East China MAC, said that land rented out by ordinary rich peasants should not be requisitioned in the areas around Shanghai, Nanjing, Hangzhou, and Ningpo, where the population was dense, productivity high, and the economy closely linked to that of the cities.[14] Authorities in Shaanxi province decided not to requisition rented land from ordinary rich

11. *Renmin ribao*, 28 September 1952, p. 2.

12. Texts in *Zhengfu gongzuo baogao huibian*, *1950*, pp. 856, 883; *Nanfang ribao*, 6 November 1950, p. 5.

13. *Renmin ribao*, 6 September 1950, p. 2.

14. Report of 14 July 1950, in *Zhengfu gongzuo*, p. 571. There were considerable variations in the way this directive was interpreted by Rao's subordinates. See reports from North Jiangsu and South Jiangsu in ibid., pp. 652–53, 677.

peasants in any of the areas scheduled to carry out land reform during the winter of 1950, although this meant that only 5–6 percent of the cultivated land would be available for distribution; there hardly existed a landlord class in these areas.[15] The rich peasants owned enough land not rented out, and other wealth, so that they would have remained an extremely important part of the rural economy even if their rented land had been taken. It was not worth antagonizing them to obtain for the poor the very small amount of land they rented out (5–10 percent of the land they owned, or about 1 percent of the total cultivated area).

Nothing other than land could be taken from either ordinary or semilandlord rich peasants in any area. The property and interests of the middle peasants were not to be infringed in any way; in fact, one reason the rich peasants were treated as leniently as they were was to reassure the middle peasants. The criterion for distinguishing middle peasants from rich peasants continued to be whether a family got more than 25 percent of its income from exploitation.

The poor peasants and laborers were to be the social base and the main beneficiaries of land reform, but they were not permitted to form separate poor-peasant leagues. Middle peasants were supposed to form one-third of the membership and leadership of the peasant associations at all levels. (The rule about one-third of the membership may not have been meant to be taken literally, since they formed less than one-third of those eligible for membership in many areas, and the CCP cannot have contemplated excluding poor peasants in order to maintain the ratio.) This was important because peasant associations at the *xiang* level would be responsible for distributing confiscated property, and some middle peasants would be entitled to share in the distribution.

Confiscated land was to be distributed to the laborers, poor peasants, and those middle peasants who did not already own enough land in such a fashion that every beneficiary family in a given *xiang* would end up with about the same level of landholdings per person. Where possible, ownership of a given piece of formerly rented land was to go to the peasant already farming it rather than to some new cultivator. Peasants who had operated rather large farms as tenants could even be given slightly more land than would normally have been allotted to them, so that not too much land would be transferred from one operator to another. Cadres could also arrange for them to continue renting some land after land reform;[16] the land they had worked might be distributed to someone who was too old or sick to work it and would need to rent it out.

---

15. Report of Ma Mingfang, Chairman of the Shaanxi Province Government, on land reform and other tasks, 14 August 1950, in *Zhengfu gongzuo*, pp. 469–72.

16. *Zhengfu gongzuo*, p. 655.

The new program was more moderate and was kept under tighter control than had been the reform of the 1940s. The economy of China was in a shambles. In most areas it took several years after liberation just to get production up to prewar levels. The CCP was determined to carry out its social reforms in such a way as to help rather than hinder economic reconstruction. Top leaders explained:

> The Communist Party has always struggled for the interests
> of the laboring poor, but the viewpoint of the Communist
> Party has always differed from that of the philanthropists.
> The results of agrarian reform are beneficial to the poor
> laboring peasants and can help the peasants partially to solve
> the problems of poverty. But the basic aim of agrarian reform
> is not simply to relieve the poor peasants, it is to free the
> rural productive forces from the shackles of the landlords'
> feudal land-ownership system, so as to develop agricultural
> production and open the way for New China's industrializa-
> tion....
> This basic reason for and basic aim of agrarian reform are
> intended for production. Hence, every step in agrarian reform
> should involve practical consideration of, and close coordina-
> tion with, the development of rural production. Precisely
> because of this basic reason and aim, the Central Committee of
> the Communist Party of China has proposed that in agrarian
> reform from now on the rich-peasant economy shall be
> preserved, not destroyed. This is because the existence of
> the rich-peasant economy, and within certain limits its devel-
> opment, are advantageous to the development of the people's
> economy in our country and are therefore also beneficial to
> the broad mass of the peasants.[17]

> Agrarian reform shall be subservient to agricultural produc-
> tion.[18]

There was a widespread feeling in the CCP that the landlords had been cowed by the total victory of the Communist armies and would submit to the land reform without serious resistance. They could therefore be stripped of their land without the necessity of socially disruptive struggles. The Party wanted not only to preserve the rich-peasant economy but also to avoid alarming the urban bourgeoisie too much. Many capitalists also owned some land in the countryside; many landlords had long had ties in the cities, and others fled to the cities when land reform became imminent. The rural struggle would be badly harmed if there were a way for

---

17. Liu Shaoqi, "Report on the Question of Agrarian Reform," 14 June 1950, in *Xinhua yuebao*, July 1950, p. 493.

18. Ye Jianying, in *Nanfang ribao*, 22 September 1951, trans. in *CB*, 125:15.

such landlords to escape land reform completely. Yet good relations between the Party and the bourgeoisie, necessary for the revival of the urban economy, would be harmed if land-reform cadres and peasant activists were able to come into the cities and make impromptu arrests of people who owned or had owned land in the countryside, especially if exaggerated rumors about the fate of the victims arose in the cities. Formal channels were set up through which the peasants could obtain the arrest of landlords who had fled to the cities,[19] but problems continued; the authorities in some cities were not very responsive to the demands of peasants who did not live in their jurisdictions. Landlords living in the cities generally owed rent refunds and rent-deposit refunds to their rural tenants, but from some cities the peasants had only been able to obtain about 30 percent of what was owed up to the spring of 1951.[20]

It was very important that the land reform take the form of a class struggle in the villages, rather than something that government officials did for the peasants. For one thing, it was unlikely that land-reform cadres sent out by the government would be capable, during the few weeks they spent in a village, of learning enough about the village to carry out land reform correctly if they tried to do all the work themselves instead of leading the peasants to do it. Also, if the peasants simply watched while the land-reform cadres took land away from a landlord and distributed it, there was a considerable chance that after the land-reform cadres were gone, the landlord would be able to overawe the peasants and get his land back.[21] Finally, one of the main purposes of the land reform was to locate and train peasants who had the capacity to become the new political leaders of the villages. Late in the land-reform campaign, Du Runsheng of the Central-South MAC suggested that an average *xiang* should end up with a guiding core of five or six peasant leaders, with a broader group of peasant activists around them, and with the mass of the peasants, who would have participated in land reform to a lesser extent, around them.[22] The new village cadres would not learn what they needed to know by watching other people make decisions; they had to exercise real political leadership and perform real administrative functions while the land-reform cadres were available to guide them and make suggestions, if they were to be effective after the land-reform cadres had departed. Du treated commandism and substituting oneself for the masses as cardinal sins for land-reform cadres: "It is true that the masses, at first, are inexperienced in handling

---

19. Central-South MAC directive of 1 December 1950, in *Nanfang ribao*, 15 December 1950, p. 3.

20. *Changjiang ribao*, 18 April 1951, p. 2.

21. *Nanfang ribao*, 19 September 1951, trans. in *CB*, 125:9; *Changjiang ribao*, 9 December 1951, p. 1.

22. *Changjiang ribao*, 9 December 1951, p. 1.

affairs, but it would be wrong to substitute ourselves for the masses in handling things, out of fear that the masses cannot handle them. There is no task relating to the masses' own interests that the masses are not capable of learning to do. If they temporarily can't do something, and make some minor errors, this can only awaken us to our responsibility for educating and leading them; it should not lead us to ignore their legitimate political powers."[23]

The class awareness of the peasants had first to be aroused in private conversations with land-reform cadres and activists, or in the small-group meetings of the peasant associations. The peasants had to be taught to look at the oppressive and exploitative activities of the old elite as a pattern rather than as a series of isolated incidents. There were long discussions about whether the landlords had supported their tenants by renting them land without which they could not have survived, or whether it was the tenants who had supported the landlords by working on their land and paying rent. The peasants were invited to denounce, in private, the injustices to which the landlords had subjected them. This was valuable not only as a means of raising their consciousness but also as a source of information for the cadres and activists.

After the peasants had come to believe that the landlords deserved to be overthrown, they still had to be convinced that the landlords could be overthrown. Here the best technique was the public struggle meeting, a morality play in which the landlord had to stand before a great crowd while one person after another denounced him for various past crimes and sins. These meetings had to be carefully prepared, with peasants who could be depended upon to get things off to a proper start by repeating denunciations they had made previously in peasant-association small-group meetings. If these rehearsed speeches established a proper atmosphere, other peasants would take courage from seeing the landlord actually being humiliated in public and unable to retaliate, and they would join in with more spontaneous denunciations. Ideally, the peasants would go home hating the landlords somewhat more than before the meeting and fearing them much less. If possible, the landlords were broken down to the point that they would bow their heads and admit their crimes before the meeting.

Controls over the class struggle were considerably tighter from 1950 onward than they had been in the 1940s. There had been a time when the CCP had allowed the struggle at the village level to proceed almost without restriction; the same thing could not be permitted to happen again. In the late 1940s one cadre had said: "It has been our experience that whenever the peasants are mobilized to struggle, they push on toward extreme egalitarianism and the cadres are apt to be swept along with them. In this case, we senior cadres must take the blame for not having given the junior

---

23. Ibid., p. 2.

cadres full explanation and education on this point beforehand."[24]
A *Renmin ribao* editorial of July 1950 took a similar attitude:
"Peasants, long oppressed and exploited by landlords, and having
been subjected to endless miseries and humiliation, will naturally
want to take reprisals against the landlords once they are freed
from feudal bondage. Such feeling on the part of the peasants
must be kept under control and properly led. It must not be
allowed to go its natural course, or it will lead to indiscriminate
beatings and killings and so upset the social order."[25]

As the Party shifted its activities southward, it found increasing
numbers of peasants who did not in fact feel such an intense
hatred for the landlords. Some later policy statements placed most
of the blame for leftist excesses on a minority of "brave elements"
among the peasantry, or on *liumang* or *erliuzi*.[26] The policy implications, however, were the same; land reform could be carried out
only under careful supervision. Liu Shaoqi told the cadres, "In the
areas where it has been decided not to carry out land reform this
year, do not carry out land reform. If there are peasants who
spontaneously rise up to carry out land reform, persuade them to
stop."[27] The municipal government of Peking used even blunter
language: "Spontaneous struggles by peasants must be firmly
prevented in land reform."[28]

The land-reform work teams were supposed to maintain close
contact with their superiors and ask for advice on difficult problems. An extensive network of telephone lines was established in
the countryside in preparation for land reform.

Peasant meetings in the villages could not function as courts.
They made decisions on class demarcation and the confiscation of
property, subject to approval by higher authorities, but they
could not try purported criminals. Ordinary legal and criminal
cases went to the people's courts. But if the personnel of the
people's courts were familiar with legal procedures, they were not
always reliable from an ideological standpoint, so cases involving
land reform and the class struggle were handled by special
people's tribunals. There was one tribunal in every *xian* during
land reform, and branch tribunals were eventually set up in most
qu. The tribunals could travel around, trying cases in the villages
where the people involved lived. Each tribunal had a panel of
judges. The presiding judge, his deputy, and half the ordinary
judges were appointed by the *xian* government. The remainder of
the judges were elected by popular organizations, usually peasant

---

24. Quoted in Crook and Crook, *Revolution*, p. 135.
25. *Renmin ribao* editorial, 21 July 1950, trans. in *CB*, 151:8.
26. Vagabonds; the rural lumpenproletariat; people accustomed to
living by their wits rather than by consistent physical labor.
27. Liu Shaoqi, "Report on the Question of Agrarian Reform,"
Xinhua yuebao, July 1950, p. 492.
28. *Nanfang ribao*, 24 November 1950, p. 4.

associations or peasant representative assemblies. The judges appointed by the government were often quite important people; at one of the first trials held before a people's tribunal in the suburbs of Canton, the five-judge panel included one judge from the Canton People's Court, the head of the *qu* administration, a member of the *qu* Party committee, and two peasants' representatives.[29]

Sentences of less than five years' imprisonment had to be approved by the *xian* government. Sentences of more than five years' imprisonment, or death, had to be approved by the province government or by officials at the level of the special administrative district, deputized by the province government. Major trials often drew several thousand spectators, from a fairly wide area. Members of the public could speak out at trials, but authoritative documents stressed that "the order of the tribunal [had to] be maintained,"[30] and that "care [had to] be taken to prevent the people's tribunal from becoming a mass meeting for struggle."[31] In general, the regulations for people's tribunals issued in 1950 reflect a tighter control over land reform than those issued in 1948.[32] The 1950 regulations gave the tribunals jurisdiction in disputes over the demarcation of land lots, and so on, which would have been left to peasant associations or poor-peasant leagues within the villages in 1948. The 1950 regulations placed much less stress on the role of the masses. Indeed, in 1950· *Renmin ribao* said: "The existence of the People's Tribunal, which is an organ for systematic and orderly suppression of law-defying landlords, will prevent peasants from taking justice into their own hands and so maintain normal order throughout the agrarian reform."[33]

The CCP said, clearly and often, that government officials and Party cadres were not to carry out beatings or torture. There was to be no violence at the people's tribunals, and the police were forbidden to use force to extract information or confessions from suspects.[34] But on the question of peasants beating up landlords, the Party was rather vague. It generally advocated "legal" (in other words verbal) means of mass struggle. It repeatedly denounced "indiscriminate beatings" (*luan da*) and hardly ever said

---

29. Ibid., 29 September 1950, p. 2.

30. Regulations Governing the Organization of People's Tribunals, 19 July 1950, trans. in *CB*, 44:2.

31. *Renmin ribao* editorial, 21 July 1950, trans. in *CB*, 151:8.

32. See the regulations issued by the Shanxi-Hebei-Shandong-Henan Border Region Government, 6 January 1948, published in *Renmin ribao*, 24 January 1948, p. 1.

33. *Renmin ribao* editorial, 21 July 1950, trans. in *CB*, 151:8.

34. The police did in fact use torture to extract information, if they considered a case sufficiently important; Yang, *Chinese Village*, pp. 139–40.

anything good about beatings.[35] However, during periods when the Party was imposing firm and explicit controls over most other aspects of land reform, it would not say clearly either that all beatings were forbidden or that beatings were permitted under some circumstances. A few statements are available indicating that all beatings were considered undesirable,[36] but even these are absent in many documents where one might expect to find some comment on this issue. One might suppose that the Party was being vague in an effort to conceal the more brutal aspects of its policy, from the Chinese people or from the world. That is implausible, however, since the CCP was quite open on the subject of killings. It was perfectly willing to say, with large headlines in *Nanfang ribao*, that people were being shot. It even published statistics, and the totals were quite large. It therefore seems more likely that the Party was vague on beatings because it was worried about the reactions of its own subordinate apparatus. Many cadres tended to implement directives from above in a wildly exaggerated manner: "You point out to them that it is wrong to stage colorful demonstrations, and they stop the struggle completely and the rest is silence. You point out to them that 'peaceful agrarian reform' is out of the question, and they stage colorful demonstrations, indulging in riotous struggles and riotous redistributions."[37]

The Party may simply have decided that any explicit statement of policy on beatings would generate more errors than it prevented. Du Runsheng, secretary-general of the CCP Central-South Bureau, told the cadres they should correct deviations involving excesses against landlords in such a way as to promote the class struggle rather than bring it to a halt. The cadres were to persuade the peasants that beating the landlords was not in their interests, but the cadres were not to use compulsion or commandist methods.[38] If there had been a clear statement that beatings were forbidden, many cadres would simply have told the peasants, "You can't beat the landlords because that is against policy." On the other hand, a statement that beatings were permitted would have been widely abused. Even the line the Party actually took, warning against indiscriminate beatings at one extreme and against binding the

---

35. There was one guarded endorsement of beatings published early in 1950, when the antidespot movement was in a radical phase; *Changjiang ribao*, 16 February 1950, reprinted in *Xinhua yuebao*, April 1950, p. 1348.

36. A rather confusing discussion by Liu Ruilong of the East China MAC, in *Xinwen ribao* (Shanghai), 19 March 1951, trans. in *CB*, 92:7–8, ends with the conclusion that even when farmers have good cause to beat a landlord, "these could not be good methods," but the Party "should not unkindly criticize or reprimand the farmers."

37. *Nanfang ribao*, 18 April 1952, trans. in *CB*, 184:27.

38. *Changjiang ribao*, 18 April 1951, p. 2.

hands of the masses at the other, led to problems in deciding when "the masses" really wanted to beat a landlord. Cadres who took a radical view of class struggle sometimes felt that if nobody was hung up and beaten, it was not a real "free hands" struggle. In a given village there were likely to be some peasants who approved of beatings and others who did not. The radical cadres regarded the former as representing the views of "the masses" and the latter as being mindless, backward, or even "running dogs of the enemy."[39]

Land-reform work teams played a greater role than in the land reform of 1947, but they did not generally push aside local cadres to as great extent as had happened in some areas in the first half of 1948. They came to any village as the latest in a series of teams, which had been coming ever since liberation to mobilize the peasants for tax collection, rent reduction, bandit eradication, and so on. The land-reform work teams generally stayed longer and made their work more thorough than previous teams. The cadres were supposed to eat, sleep, and work together with the people—the "three togethers." They located new peasant activists and gave further training and indoctrination to peasants who had already been activists.

Land reform was the responsibility of the regular government hierarchy; China did not establish a separate land-reform administration of the type that would later be created in North Vietnam. The land-reform cadres might be trained by the government of a greater administrative region, a province, a special administrative district, or a *xian*. Many were peasant activists who had arisen during the campaigns preceding land reform and who were given extra training for land reform mainly by *xian* governments. Others came from the People's Liberation Army, the Youth League, various levels of the administration, and from schools and colleges. Their training could not be purely theoretical; much of it had to be handled on the job. It had to help the cadres not only to understand their work but to approach it with the correct attitude. Some of those from urban backgrounds had trouble adjusting to the villages. Some of the peasant activists, especially the illiterate ones, lacked self-confidence. Almost all land-reform cadres needed prolonged indoctrination to persuade them to be less bureaucratic and commandist.

The land-reform work teams, like most other governmental organizations of this period, accepted members from all class backgrounds. Many intellectuals who came from the exploiting classes were assigned to work on land reform as part of their reeducation. At one conference of land-reform cadres held in Guangxi early in 1952, it was found that almost 18 percent of those present came from landlord or rich-peasant backgrounds (Table 5-1). One land-lord from Xingning *xian*, Guangdong, observing how many

---

39. Ibid., 9 December 1951, p. 2.

Table 5-1—The class origins of a group of 565 land-reform cadres, Guangxi province, early 1952

Class	Percentage
Landlords	12.7
Rich peasants	5.1
Middle peasants	20.0
Poor peasants and laborers	24.5
Capitalists (bourgeoisie)	9.2
Urban poor residents	1.6
Workers	1.9
Petit bourgeoisie	24.4

Source: *Nanfang ribao*, 13 April 1952, trans. in *CB*, 184:57.

---

intellectuals there were among the land-reform cadres assigned to his village, hoped to discourage local peasants from cooperating with the land reform by warning them that "all the people in the land-reform work team are the children of landlords and rich peasants, and in the end they will surely side with the landlords; you poor peasants and laborers will get the worst of it."[40]

The land reform and related campaigns can be divided into three broad stages. The preliminary campaigns discussed in Chapter 4—bandit eradication, struggle against despots, reduction of rent and interest, refund of rents and rent deposits, and preliminary reform of village political structures—together constituted the first stage. These campaigns were supposed to break the landlords' political control and shift the balance of forces within the villages in favor of the peasants. They brought significant but not over-whelming economic benefits to the peasants.

The second stage was the land reform proper. It began with extensive propaganda work that informed the people about land-reform policy, and that tried to persuade the landlords that

---

40. *Nanfang ribao*, 15 December 1950, p. 3.

resistance was hopeless and that they should submit to the inevitable. Large numbers of secondary teachers and students were sent out to the countryside to help with this propaganda work. In some villages where the preliminary campaigns had been incomplete, the land-reform work teams had to make up deficiencies, particularly in regard to rent reduction and refund, while they were carrying out this first step of the land reform proper. The next step was class demarcation. Each household was first carefully investigated by the cadres and activists. Then the head of the household had to declare what class he felt he belonged to, and why, at a public meeting. The peasants would comment and usually reach a consensus fairly soon. It was a good idea to handle the simpler cases first, so that the peasants would have some families falling clearly in one class or another to use as standards of comparison when they were trying to classify those on the borderline. In really difficult cases a decision could be postponed for a considerable period to permit more extensive investigation. Decisions on class demarcation reached in the villages were supposed to be checked and approved by authorities at the *qu* level. It is hard to see how this could have been more than a formality, but one report presented to the Central-South MAC late in 1951 suggested that it was taken very seriously.[41] People who felt they had been misclassified could carry appeals up to the *xian* level. After the classes had been demarcated, land and other goods would be confiscated or requisitioned from the appropriate people and distributed to the poor. The final step in this stage was to sum up the work and push for an increase in agricultural production. The peasants who had benefited in the land reform were encouraged to invest in fertilizer, new tools, and so on rather than hold expensive celebrations.

The third stage was reinvestigation. It was inevitable that in some villages land reform would not be thorough or would lead to incorrect results. Some of the mistakes could only be seen clearly after it was over. So in the months immediately after land reform, the peasants would farm their new land on provisional titles only. Then a new work team would come to investigate, settle any remaining problems, and issue deeds to the redistributed land. In some areas, even the reinvestigation did not settle all problems, and it had to be repeated. This could lead to a very unfortunate sense of uncertainty in the minds of the peasants, which undermined their enthusiasm for production. In extreme cases villages might be investigated as many as seven times.[42]

Land reform in the Central-South Region was seasonal, lasting from late autumn to early spring. Work usually started in a limited number of *xiang* and spread; this was known as proceeding from

---

41. *Changjiang ribao*, 9 December 1951, p. 2.

42. Grigorii Sukharchuk, personal communication, Ann Arbor, Mich., 15 May 1974.

points to areas. The 1950–51 campaign, for instance, started in a few experimental *xiang* in the autumn of 1950. Then during the winter, land reform spread in three waves—first to the key point *xiang*, then to the *xiang* around the key points, then to the broad areas between. The areas covered by the three waves were in a ratio of approximately one to three to nine. There was relatively little land-reform activity in the summer, when the peasants needed to be in the fields. In the Southwest Region, on the other hand, there were no long seasonal gaps in land reform.

When the Agrarian-Reform Law was issued in 1950, the CCP predicted that it would finish land reform in all the ethnically Chinese areas of China by 1953, and it met that goal. Most of the country underwent land reform during the winters of 1950–51 and 1951–52. By the summer of 1952, all but 12 percent of the rural population (including national minorities) had completed the land reform proper,[43] and the central leadership was turning to other matters. The land reform almost disappeared from the index to *Renmin ribao* after this time, although it remained a major preoccupation of local authorities in the areas that had still to complete it.

---

43. Aggregate figures from Wong, *Land Reform*, p. 129.

6

Guangdong and the Central-South Region

The Central-South Region

The authorities in the Central-South Region seemed, in 1950, to be in about as good a position to administer a land reform as anyone could have asked.[1] They had a good understanding of the actual situation in the countryside, and they had a program for land reform that seems, even with hindsight, to have been close to the optimum policy for achieving Communist goals. Even so, they had a great deal of difficulty getting the job done. They were trying to change the whole nature of village society so drastically that even with the best of cadres and propagandists, many peasants would have been reluctant to go along. In fact, the cadres and propagandists were far from being the best; most lacked adequate training and experience, and many did not themselves believe the things they were supposed to be telling the peasants. In Guangdong it proved exceptionally difficult to whip up enthusiasm for the campaign; those reluctant to cooperate ranged from peasants who placed clan loyalty above class loyalty all the way to CCP leaders at the province level who wanted to keep land reform relatively slow and moderate. No matter how good the leadership and policies might be at the regional level, the land-reform program was going to have problems down in the villages.

Large portions of Henan had already completed land reform before the Agrarian Reform Law of 1950 appeared; the other five provinces were New Liberated Areas and had at best completed rent reduction. The Central Plains Provisional People's Government issued regulations for rent reduction in September 1949, but these were widely ignored. At its first session, in February 1950, the Central-South MAC passed new regulations (see Chapter 4). Between February and September campaigns for rent reduction, for

---

1. The Central-South Military ana Administrative Committee in Wuhan was derived from the earlier Central Plains Provisional People's Government. Its nominal chairman was Lin Biao (Lin Piao), but he was unable to devote much time to it. In practice it was headed by one of its vice-chairmen, Deng Zihui (Teng Tzu-hui). The vice-chairman who most specialized in land reform was Li Xuefeng (Li Hsueh-feng).

the refund of excess rent collected from the peasants since liberation, and in some cases for the refund of rent deposits were
carried out in areas with a population of 60,000,000 (about half of
the region). The total refund was over 1,000,000,000 catties of
grain. This was of great importance in helping the peasants stave
off the annual spring hunger, which was especially bad that year,
since the civil war and some fairly serious floods had disrupted
production. The CCP later decided that too much of the "refunded"
rent had been distributed on the basis of need, and that too little
had gone to the tenants who had originally paid it to the landlords.[2]

The movement for rent-deposit refunds had to be halted after a
few months; it was leading to too much disorder. The problem was
presumably similar to that with the landlords' buried wealth. The
amounts involved were too large for most landlords to be able to
pay in grain. Many would have tried to claim that they did not
have enough money either, and a significant number would have
been telling the truth; the CCP victory had rendered many of
their investments worthless, especially usurious loans. The CCP
decided that it would wait until conditions were more settled before
extracting large amounts of money from landlords whose wealth was
uncertain. Deng Zihui later said that the Party should have
stressed, more clearly than it did, that the cessation of rent-
deposit refunds was only temporary.[3]

In many areas rent refunds went together with the abolition of
the *baojia* system, the establishment of new *xiang* and *cun* administrations, and the establishment or expansion of peasant associations. The results were of course far from perfect. By September
1950 the peasant associations were still seriously impure in every
province except Henan. Twenty percent or more of them were said
to be controlled by the landlords and feudal forces.[4] During the
summer of 1950 there was much rectification work in the peasant
associations and reinvestigation of rent reduction.

In September 1950, the Central-South MAC decided that during
the next three months rent reduction should be enforced in all
areas where it had not yet occurred (total population about
40,000,000) and in areas where past efforts had not been thorough. It also scheduled 161 *xian*, with a population of about
50,000,000, to carry out land reform during the coming winter.
Experimental *xiang* and then key point *xiang* would start land
reform late in 1950, but the greater portion of these 161 *xian*
would not get started until January 1951.[5] In November, the MAC
decided to accelerate these plans and reform a population

---

2. *Nanfang ribao*, 25 September 1950, p. 3.
3. Ibid.
4. Ibid., and also 15 September 1950, p. 3.
5. *Nanfang ribao*, 20 September 1950, p. 1; 16 October 1950, p.
1.

approaching 65,000,000 during the coming winter. The acceleration turned out to be impractical; by the time spring cultivation halted land reform everywhere except in some parts of Henan, the actual results were almost exactly the original goal of 50,000,000. Some provinces had covered more than their original targets, and others had covered less. In October and early November of 1950, in the experimental *xiang*, some cadres were carrying out what was branded as "peaceful division of the land." Then, when land reform was going on in the key point *xiang*, there were problems with cadres trying to go too fast.[6] But overall, this winter's land reform seems to have been fairly satisfactory.

Land reform did not come to a complete halt in the spring of 1951; areas with a population of about 12,000,000 were covered in the summer. After the autumn harvest, work resumed on a really large scale, and approximately another 50,000,000 people were covered by the spring of 1952. The areas remaining, largely in Guangdong, completed land reform in the summer of 1952 and the winter of 1952–53.

The Preliminaries to Land Reform in Guangdong

The People's Liberation Army reached the city of Canton on 14 October 1949. There was little Guomindang resistance in this area, and all the mainland of Guangdong[7] can be considered to have been liberated at approximately this time. Even militarily, CCP control of the countryside was rather superficial at first; there were an estimated 100,000 "bandits" (probably Guomindang straggglers for the most part) in Guangdong. Bandit activities declined at first, but then increased again for a few months starting in December 1949.

There had been some CCP guerrilla activity in Guangdong before the PLA arrived, but it had been on a rather small scale. *Nanfang ribao* mentions "Old Liberated Areas" in Longchuan *xian*,[8] but this was an exaggeration probably motivated by local pride; these areas would not have been entitled to such a description by the standards used in North China. The Guangdong guerrillas were to be important not so much for the limited mass mobilization, rent reduction, and so on, which they had carried out in the areas where they were strong enough, as for the role that their leaders played in the postliberation politics of Guangdong. There was considerable conflict between the veteran cadres of Guangdong and the personnel sent down from the north after 1949.

The first thing the new government did in most areas was to

---

6. *Changjiang ribao*, 18 April 1951, p. 2.

7. This chapter will not discuss the island of Hainan, which was liberated later.

8. *Nanfang ribao*, 25 October 1950, p. 3.

collect the 1949 autumn tax. The tax collectors really needed to rely on the old *baojia* heads to some extent in this tax collection, although some tried to abolish the *baojia* system. There was much inequity, and the amount collected fell far below what it should have been. Rent reduction was widely ignored.

Conditions were very bad from February to April of 1950. The annual spring hunger, which occurred every year while the peasants were waiting for the first spring crops, was aggravated by banditry and by the way political turmoil and floods had disrupted production. The government tried to alleviate the hardship partly by direct disaster relief, but mostly by mobilizing the peasants to demand the refund of part of the rent that had been collected from them in the autumn of 1949. The rent-refund movement, which reached its peak in April and was associated with antibandit and antidespot campaigns, represented the first real attack on the old rural elite.

The work of reforming local political structures—abolishing the *baojia* system, establishing peasant associations and new village administrations, and then rectifying and purifying these new organizations if they proved unsatisfactory—occurred continuously. At first there was so much to do that progress was very haphazard. There was a *cun* in Xinxing *xian* where the head of the peasant association was a reactionary and a long-time Guomindang official. When the province government found out about this and started an inquiry, the *xian* government admitted that it had known about this situation for some time but claimed that it had been too occupied with other work to correct it.[9] Unless there were some particularly bad problem that demanded the dispatch of a special team, the reform of village political structures was usually carried out by work teams that were also busy with other tasks like taxation and rent reduction. It was not until late 1950 that some areas got far enough ahead in their work to be able to send out teams without specific tasks to look around the villages and see what needed to be done;[10] for the most part there had been more known jobs than work teams to do them.

The CCP leadership had to deal with the Guangdong peasants through several layers of often unreliable intermediaries. First were the Guangdong CCP members, who while clearly committed to the revolution, had little administrative experience and had not benefited from the campaigns of Party education and rectification that had occurred in northern China. Next were the work-team cadres, most of whom were not Party members. Below these came village political organizations, made up at best of peasants without much administrative experience. Finally, especially in the early days, there might be the landlords.

The traditional elite did all it could to maintain its position as a

---

9. Ibid., 10 September 1950, p. 4.

10. See ibid., 26 November 1950, p. 3, for work in Panyu *xian*.

mediator between the peasants and the government. The old *baojia* heads had a recognized role in the 1949 autumn tax collection. Even in the summer of 1950, after the *baojia* system had been abolished, there were *cun* in Zhongshan *xian* where the landlords told the peasants not to talk to the cadres of the tax-collection work teams; the landlords went to the work teams themselves with complete registers indicating who should pay how much tax. The work teams, eager to finish their task as quickly as possible, were inclined at first to accept the "assistance" of the landlords.[11]

Some landlords either took the lead in setting up peasant associations or infiltrated existing associations thoroughly enough to acquire partial or total control. Others, who could influence large numbers of peasants, used them to attack the leaders of peasant associations not under landlord control. One landlord in the Dongjiang Special Administrative District was able to mobilize 200 peasants to protest to the *xiang* authorities when *cun* cadres did things he did not like.[12]

Many landlords were able to exploit conflicts between villages, or between clans within a village. Peasants belonging to the same clan as the landlord might support him in his refusal to pay rent refunds to peasants who were not members of the clan.[13] The situation could become very difficult if the government allowed itself to become identified with one side or another in local disputes. There was a *cun* in Chaoan *xian* that was divided into five *she*. Before liberation there had been two really powerful landlords in the *cun*. One, Li Mingquan, controlled the administration as *bao* head. The peasants of the *she* in which he lived tended to be identified with him. After liberation the other major landlord, Li Caixiong, mobilized peasants of the other *she* and overthrew his rival; he then ruled the *cun* through the peasant association. His control was harsh. When a work team came to the *cun* in September 1950 to rectify the peasant association, it looked for peasants who could be mobilized quickly to act against Li Caixiong. The peasants it found all turned out to be from the *she* where Li Mingquan lived; they were the ones who had no connection with Li Caixiong. Many people in the other four *she*, seeing this, rallied around Caixiong. After one cadre of the work team was beaten up by supporters of Caixiong, the *qu* authorities stepped in and arrested Caixiong and some of his henchmen, but it is to be doubted whether that action completely solved the problem.[14]

In the first months after liberation some landlords, if peasants asked them for rent reduction, threatened to report the peasants

---

11. Ibid., 11 September 1950, p. 2.
12. Ibid., 2 October 1950, p. 3.
13. Ibid., 19 November 1950, p. 3.
14. Ibid., 16 November 1950, p. 3.

to the government as bandits.[15] As time went by their activities had to become less blatant, but for a considerable period they retained enough control over some peasants to make rent reduction a sham, with rent paid formally at reduced levels but covertly at higher levels. By the time of the land reform itself some landlords were developing more subtle schemes. One in Xingning *xian* put up money for extensive repairs on the local water-control system, so the peasants would be busy with this project when the land-reform cadres were trying to mobilize them for class struggle.[16]

Once the old elite had been overthrown, it was necessary to make sure that the new village leaders would behave properly. Sometimes there were problems of simple personal corruption—for example, stealing from public funds. Other cases were less clear-cut. Local militias might expect to be paid by the people and to be given tips on holidays. Some activists demanded the return of any land they had mortgaged or sold for decades before the revolution, claiming that it had been "usurped" from them.[17] Very often there were problems of work style. Government by command rather than by discussion with the masses was a deeply rooted pattern in Chinese political culture, and it did not disappear merely because the new officials were recruited from among the peasantry. Investigations in the summer of 1951, of 1,100 villages in the Central-South Region that had undergone land reform, found that about 80 percent of the *xiang* cadres had abused their positions at least in minor ways.[18] Tax collection in particular tempted new cadres to use threats and make arbitrary decisions rather than discuss matters with the masses. It must be borne in mind that the cadres in question thought of this as perfectly normal behavior and often were not even secretive about it. In one *cun* where the peasant-association leaders had been keeping for their own use the taxes they collected, and capriciously branding as reactionaries people they disliked (usually because of clan rivalries), it was pointed out in their defense that they had been reporting all their actions to their superiors.[19]

Bureaucratism and commandism were, inevitably, major problems among the work-team cadres. They were supposed to work with the masses, but most of their work involved spending a short time in a village where they did not know the people, trying to get some job done, and then moving on to the next village. Making real contact with the masses would have been hard for them even if they had been experienced in peasant organization, which most of them were not. They had to learn by doing, with help from frequent study sessions at which they discussed their work and the ways it could

15. Ibid., 1 October 1950, p. 5.
16. Ibid., 15 December 1950, p. 3.
17. Ibid., 26 October 1950, p. 3.
18. *Changjiang ribao*, 9 December 1951, p. 1.
19. *Nanfang ribao*, 26 October 1950, p. 3.

be done better. As they grew more accustomed to mass organization, and as peasant activists got more experience working with
them, the situation improved.

The Communist Party apparatus in Guangdong began a formal
rectification in June and July of 1950. It did not give great emphasis to identifying and expelling people not qualified to be Party
members, like the campaign of 1947–48 in China and that of 1955–56
in Vietnam. It was aimed rather at helping people do their jobs
better, like the rectification of the early 1940s. The main targets
were bureaucratism and commandism, not only in relations with the
masses but also within the Party; during the years when the Party
in Guangdong had been a clandestine organization the leaders had
not been able to consult the lower ranks of the Party much, and
bad habits had arisen. Ordinary Party members had to be taught
to speak up more than they had formerly done, and Party leaders
had to learn the habit of listening.[20]

In the middle of 1950, rectification sometimes caused both Party
and non-Party cadres to become rather conservative in leading the
class struggle. They were supposed to provide active leadership in
rent reduction and other campaigns, but they were also warned
against repeating the excesses of 1947 and against indiscriminate
beatings and arrests. They were told of the dangers of substituting themselves for the masses and taking action against landlords
and despots themselves when the peasants were unready, or even
leading a small minority of the peasants against the landlords when
the broad mass was not yet ready for drastic action. Many of them
ended up with an excessive fear of making mistakes, an attitude
sometimes described as "bound hands and bound feet." Their position was really very difficult. They were eager to please their
superiors, but these superiors, with whom they were not closely
acquainted, were assigning them difficult tasks with instructions
that often seemed ambiguous or contradictory.

The Progress of Land Reform in Guangdong

Land reform in Guangdong lasted from late 1950 to early 1953. It
was marked by almost continual conflict; authorities at the regional
and national level did not feel that the Party apparatus in Guangdong was moving fast enough or radically enough with the
program.

In February 1950, the Central-South MAC decided that Guangdong would start land reform in the winter of 1950–51 and complete
it in the winter of 1951–52.[21] But when detailed plans for the
winter of 1950–51 came out in October, Guangdong was planning

---

20. Ibid., 17 September 1950, p. 1; 15 October 1950, p. 1; 23
November 1950, p. 1.

21. *Xinhua yuebao*, April 1950, p. 1348.

little more than an experimental program; only three *xian* plus the suburbs of Canton, or a population slightly over 2,000,000, were scheduled for reform.[22] By contrast, the adjacent province of Guangxi scheduled reform in seventeen *xian* with a population over 4,000,000, despite the fact that Guangxi had been liberated after Guangdong, had experienced more difficulty eradicating bandits, and therefore had been expected to put off land reform until the winter of 1951–52.

The three initial *xian* in Guangdong were Xingning, Longchuan, and Jieyang, all in the eastern part of the province. These were areas where CCP guerrillas had been active before the PLA had come down from the North and where banditry had been eradicated by the summer of 1950. Because of this strong base, the CCP used these *xian* as testing grounds for a variety of programs in Guangdong.[23] Fifteen hundred land-reform cadres trained at the province or special administrative district level reached these three *xian* around 10 October. They were supplemented by peasant activists (over seven hundred in Xingning *xian*) who had been trained at the *qu* or *xiang* level. In addition there were a considerable number of teachers and students from the local primary and secondary schools, who were not really part of the land-reform work teams but could help spread information and propaganda about the land-reform campaign in the villages.[24] Late in November, probably as a result of pressure from above the province level, an additional eight *xian* were designated for land reform, making a total of eleven. The expansion of the program was announced to the public early in December, and another two *xian* were added soon after.

Performance lagged far behind these plans. Of the first eleven *xian*, which should have completed land reform by April 1951, six had not finished even by April 1952. The thirteen *xian* in which land reform occurred in the winter of 1950–51 had a total population of about 6,300,000; of these about 4,000,000 had been covered by April 1951 and 4,600,000 by August.[25] As late as the spring of 1952, less than one-third of Guangdong had completed land reform. At that point Fang Fang, who had controlled both the Party apparatus in Guangdong and the provincial land-reform committee, was demoted. Tao Zhu (T'ao Chu), a native of Hunan, replaced him. The pressure for speed in land reform increased greatly; the normal practice of halting or almost halting land-reform activity during the summer was abandoned, and work proceeded with only

---

22. *Nanfang ribao*, 16 October 1950, p. 1; 10 November 1950, p. 2.

23. Vogel, *Canton under Communism*, p. 96.

24. *Nanfang ribao*, 5 October 1950, p. 1; 24 October 1950, p. 3; 27 November 1950, p. 3.

25. Ibid., 2 December 1950, p. 1, and 19 September 1951, p. 1; ibid., 5 May 1952 (trans. in *CB*, 184:33), and 11 August 1952 (trans. in *CB*, 211:53).

brief halts at times of peak labor demand.[26] In a startling decision, the Party ordered areas in which the initial stage of land
reform had not achieved adequate results to move on to the second
stage anyway to avoid losing momentum.[27] Land reform was finally
completed early in 1953.

Guangdong, in a remarkably poor performance, had fallen behind
a number of regions, notably Sichuan, which had been liberated
later and which had originally been scheduled not to start land
reform until one year after Guangdong. Although the problems that
plagued Guangdong probably affected most other provinces to some
extent, Guangdong was an unusually bad case.

The Leftward Shift of Late 1950

Around September and October of 1950, CCP leaders in Guangdong
formulated plans for the implementation of land reform. These plans
were not very radical, either in the social content of the program
envisaged or the speed with which it was to be pushed. Late in
November, orders came down from Peking and Wuhan for a faster
and more radical application of the reform. Many people in Guangdong, including large sections of the Communist Party, were
antagonized by this often violent new policy. Friction between the
moderates in Guangdong and the radicals in Peking and Wuhan
lasted until the end of land reform. Some of the moderates felt that
they had been betrayed; that the plans laid out in Guangdong had
been fully in accord with central policy at the time they had been
written, but that Peking had changed its mind, had become more
radical, and had defined the Guangdong Party leaders retroactively
as right deviationists.[28] In fact, Peking's policies had never been
as far to the right as the Guangdong moderates had supposed.
Although there had been a slight leftward shift in central policies
late in 1950, the main problem was that the Guangdong policies had
been right deviations by the standards of the time at which they
had been formulated.

Peking and the Central-South MAC might have liked the cadres
in Guangdong to finish land reform ahead of the original schedule,
but the end result of their demands for more speed, which became
most pressing during 1952, was simply to get the land reform in
Guangdong completed during the winter of 1952–53, which was the
latest date that had ever been suggested by anyone and was one
year after the target date set in February 1950. It seems likely,

---

26. This may have been planned as early as autumn 1951; see
Nanfang ribao, 19 September 1951, trans. in *CB*, 125:12.

27. *Changjiang ribao*, 29 June 1952, trans. in *CB*, 211:12.

28. Ezra Vogel, who accepts the Guangdong cadres' view of
events, gives a good summary of it in *Canton under Communism*,
pp. 97–105.

then, that conflict arose more because Guangdong cadres were trying to slow down the original schedule than because higher authorities were trying to speed it up. Roughly the same applies to conflicts over the content of land reform. Ezra Vogel has summarized the "new" policy imposed at the end of 1950, and the Guangdong cadres' reaction to it, as follows:

> The new policy was profoundly disturbing because it struck at the very heart of social organization [in Guangdong]. The essence of the new hard line lay in drawing sharp lines between social classes and dealing severely with rich peasants and landlords, the leaders of the traditional rural order....
> Before 1949 it was to be expected that one would help look after and protect his family, his friends, his previous associates. The hard line on land reform meant that local cadres had to cut their personal ties to those classified as rich peasants and landlords. If class lines were to be drawn, many cadres hoped that they might be able to make exceptions for their friends. With new pressure from above, this could be done only at great risk.[29]

Clearly this was not a new policy but an old one. The increased pressure applied to cadres in Guangdong and elsewhere starting in November 1950, to follow the hard line described above, had nothing to do with any leftward shift that may have been occurring in Peking at this time; it was simply an effort to achieve compliance with the longstanding principles of land reform.

The thinking of the leadership had probably been most moderate in April of 1950, when Liu Shaoqi said that no land should be taken from the rich peasants. When the Agrarian Reform Law came out in June, it allowed significant amounts of rich-peasant land to be taken. There is no direct evidence as to the reasons for this change; conjectures must depend on one's impression of the general nature of policy changes in the PRC. The scholars I have consulted feel that there must have been an experimental application of land reform by Liu's formula, somewhere, which had unsatisfactory results and led to the abandonment of the formula. I believe that although this may have happened, it is also possible that a debate along ideological lines had one outcome in April and another in June, without new information from any specific locality having played a key role.

The formal outline of the land reform reached its final shape in June 1950. From then on the changes that occurred were subtle ones—shifts in the way the program was applied. In the treatment of bandits and counterrevolutionaries, for instance, there was a policy of "combining suppression with leniency" throughout the period under consideration. It is very difficult to measure

---

29. Ibid., pp. 102, 104–5.

accurately the shifts of emphasis between suppression and leniency. The central government began complaining as early as July
1950 that local authorities in some areas were far too lenient.

> The key to [victory] lies in Chairman Mao's policy "combin-
> ing suppression with leniency," i.e., "relentless punishment
> for principal criminals, condonation of accessories under coer-
> cion, and reward for those who have rendered meritorious
> service." It should be pointed out with emphasis here that the
> suppression part of the policy is absolutely essential. If prin-
> cipal criminals are not suppressed, law and order will be a
> mockery, the people's wrath will not be mollified, other crimi-
> nals will not be discouraged, and accessories under coercion
> will not repent. Unqualified leniency will actually be an
> encouragement to counter-revolutionaries. For instance, in
> certain areas where the work of suppression was inadequate,
> unnecessary damage has been done which caused dissatisfac-
> tion among the masses. In some of these areas, the people
> have described the policy of the People's Government as
> "boundlessly lenient," which reflects their dissatisfaction.[30]

It will be worthwhile to trace the attitudes to class struggle
expressed in several reports starting in June of 1950. The first is
Liu Shaoqi's authoritative commentary on the Agrarian Reform Law,
delivered to the National People's Political Consultative Conference
on 14 June. Although Liu did not advise that the policies applied
during the preceding winter be continued without change, he
considered them basically quite good; land reform had been carried
out without major deviations. His comments on future policies
included a lengthy discussion of the need to preserve the rich-
peasant economy; he gave briefer warnings against infringing the
interests of the middle peasants or of commerce and industry. He
explained that some types of wealth owned even by the landlords
would have to remain untouched simply because trying to confiscate
them would lead to excessive disorder and waste. However, he also
stressed that land reform was a fierce class struggle. Many landlords might stubbornly attempt to sabotage it, and they would have
to be firmly suppressed. A small number would be imprisoned or
executed for sabotage activities or for past crimes against the
peasants.[31]

On 15 September Li Xuefeng, head of the Land Reform Committee

---

30. *Renmin ribao* editorial, 21 July 1950, trans. in *CB*, 151:7.
See also Zhou Enlai's National Day speech in *Xinhua yuebao*,
October 1950, pp. 1218–20. By the beginning of October, Dong
Biwu (Tung Pi-wu) was saying that the error of "boundless
magnanimity" was being corrected; NCNA, Peking, 7 October 1950,
in *CB*, no. 16.

31. Text in *Xinhua yuebao*, July 1950, pp. 492–96.

for the Central-South Region, reported to the Central-South MAC on land-reform plans.[32] During the coming winter and spring a rural population of about 50,000,000 would be affected, out of a total rural population of about 120,000,000 in the region. Areas not yet ready for reform would continue with rent reduction, struggles against bandits and despots, and efforts to increase production. Li criticized comrades who either overestimated or underestimated the readiness of the region for land reform. Some people did not realize the difficulty of mobilizing the broad masses of the peasantry. They mistook the eager attitude of the peasant activists for the attitude of the peasantry as a whole. Some even mistook the attitude of some enlightened landlords, who approved of land reform, for the attitude of the landlord class as a whole. Some reactionary landlords were hoping for land reform to occur very quickly so it would not be thorough. Landlords had been cutting down trees and scattering land subject to confiscation. They had been spreading antigovernment rumors dealing with the Korean War, crop failures, etc. Comrades who underestimated landlord resistance wanted to broaden land-reform plans prematurely.

Some other cadres exaggerated the difficulty of land reform; they wanted mass education to be perfect and all cadres to be perfectly trained before the campaign could begin. They wanted to restrict the area to be covered by land reform in the immediate future or even avoid carrying it out at all for a while. They did not understand that both cadres and masses had to be tempered in struggle and could not be properly educated except during struggle.

The main difference between Li Xuefeng's report and that of Liu Shaoqi was Li's greater preoccupation with the role of the masses. Li was worried that "free hands" mobilization might be wrongly implemented, freeing the hands of the land-reform cadres and a few peasant activists, but not involving the peasant majority. Many cadres in the Central-South Region, during their studies of land-reform policy, had been quite uncertain about the proper forms for mass struggle. They were being told both to organize peasant confrontations with the landlords and to use "legal struggle," and they doubted that the two ideas were compatible. Li opposed excesses in the antilandlord struggle—cursing people, beating people, and so on. He believed that activists and land-reform cadres who did such things would simply become isolated from the masses; he even thought the enemy might deliberately incite the cadres to excessive radicalism to create such a situation. But he did not want to abandon public struggle meetings, leading to "peaceful land reform"; he only wanted to restrain them. The peasants still had to speak their bitterness against the landlords, denounce their past crimes, and threaten them with dire retribution for any sabotage of the land reform. The masses could show

32. Text in *Nanfang ribao*, 11 and 12 December 1950.

their stature by expressing their emotions; this did not have to lead either to formal rhetoric without content or to excesses and disorder.

Li implied[33] that if only a few peasant activists were mobilized they would be likely to commit excesses, but that the mass of the peasantry would not commit such excesses. He did not harp on the possibility of *liumang* or *erliuzi* becoming activists;[34] he seems to have been talking about a minority of genuine peasants. It is hard to tell how much truth there was in the doctrine that the broad masses would behave in a more stable fashion than a small group of activists; it is an idea that the CCP wanted very much to believe. It may well have been valid. A few activists trying to substitute for the masses as a whole could have wanted to make up by fierceness what they lacked in numbers. (Du Runsheng applied the same logic in a slightly different context. He said that denying the land-reform cadres the right to use physical violence against the landlords was a means of pressuring the cadres into going really deep among the masses; if they could not be fierce they would have to make up for it by mobilizing great numbers of peasants.)[35] False or exaggerated accusations against supposed reactionaries would have been better able to pass the scrutiny of a small group than that of a large one, including all the neighbors of the accused. The Vietnamese land reform was later to illustrate the disastrous results of relying just on the land-reform cadres and a few activists.

Fang Fang, head of the Guangdong Land Reform Committee and de facto head of the CCP in Guangdong, reported on land reform to the First All-Circles People's Representative Conference of Guangdong province on 8 October.[36] He was very moderate. He said next to nothing about the involvement of the masses; land reform as he described it could have been an administrative program rather than a class struggle. His comments on the anti-despot struggle were all in the past tense; there was nothing to indicate that during the coming land reform any landlords would be punished for their past treatment of the peasants. He said a little about preventing landlord resistance to the reform, but he did not mention the possibility that any landlords would be imprisoned or executed for either past or future crimes. He was in fact talking about a "peaceful land reform," although he did not use that phrase. The lack of radicalism in Fang Fang's report is quite

---

33. This implication was made more explicit in a *Changjiang ribao* editorial, 14 December 1950, reprinted in *Nanfang ribao*, 19 December 1950, p. 1.

34. See Du Runsheng, in *Changjiang ribao*, 18 April 1951, p. 2.

35. *Changjiang ribao*, 9 December 1951, p. 2.

36. *Nanfang ribao*, 6 November 1950, p. 1. *Warning*: the translation in *CB*, no. 51, is badly abridged, more so than the translator's introduction admits.

striking when it is compared with the earlier ones by Liu Shaoqi and Li Xuefeng; this was probably among the charges against him when he was demoted in 1952.[37]

In October, land reform started on an experimental basis in a number of areas. On 18 November, Du Runsheng reported to the Central-South Land Reform Committee on the results of land reform in about one hundred experimental *xiang*. He was not very satisfied; land reform had been good in about 20 percent of these *xiang*, not so good in 50 percent, and very unsatisfactory in 30 percent. He said that the most dangerous deviation in land reform at that time was "peaceful division of the land." According to Du, some cadres believed:

> Land reform is just dividing the land; after you have divided the land everything is decided.... The purpose of dividing the land is production; dividing the land peacefully will benefit production....
> Chiang's bandits have been overthrown, local bandits have been eradicated, the landlords have been divided, and universal peace has been established; the only task today is to overthrow bureaucratism....
> After the accomplishment of bandit eradication, the anti-despot movement, and rent reduction, it will not be necessary once again to mobilize struggles during the land reform.

Those who held such attitudes regarded the landlords as "dead tigers." Du did not agree. The landlords could not be expected graciously to hand over their land; they would offer substantial resistance to land reform. The peasants would have to seize the land by revolutionary methods. This did not mean chaotic methods; there was to be no infringement of middle peasants or of commerce and industry. Du warned: "Do not carry out disorderly beatings or disorderly killings (*luan da luan sha*); free the hands of the poor peasants and laborers, but don't free the hands of the *liumang*; free antifeudal hands but don't free anticapitalist hands;

---

37. Vogel, *Canton under Communism*, p. 97, defends Fang Fang on the grounds that none of the statements in his report contradict what Liu Shaoqi and Li Xuefeng had said. However, it was Fang Fang's omissions that were crucial.
Aside from these reports by Fang Fang's superiors, I checked reports analogous to Fang Fang's, made at about this time, in seven other provinces or province-level units: Shaanxi, North Jiangsu, South Jiangsu, North Anhui, Zhejiang, Jiangxi, and Hubei (texts in *Zhengfu gongzuo*, pp. 469–79, 650–59, 674–83, 688–91, 704–8, 853–59, 879–85). Only two were as moderate as Fang Fang's: Wan Zhongyi's report for North Jiangsu and Li Shinong's for North Anhui. These two men were noticeably less successful in their later careers than their five more radical colleagues.

free the hands of legal struggle but don't free hands for disorderly beatings and disorderly killings." However, Du's report stressed more than other recent ones that there should not be a one-sided emphasis on order. What he wanted was a revolutionary order, an order in which the peasants imposed their will on the landlords. Even when the masses committed excesses, which would surely happen in some places, the Party needed to guide and correct them, rather than pouring cold water on them.

> We should talk about the law, but first talk about opposing feudalism, because this is the basic spirit of the law....
> To talk about order without struggle is equivalent to not wanting a revolution....
> To press the landlords down into the ground, that is order.[38]

Du did not want the peasants to feel that the government was giving the land to them. They had to take the land, themselves, from the landlords. It would be dangerous if the land-reform cadres and a minority of activists became separated from the masses and tried to substitute themselves for the masses. Du advised that the peasant representative assemblies include representatives of the backward elements as well as the activists to make sure that radical actions would only be taken after the peasantry as a whole understood and approved of them. Some cadres, however, either did not believe in mobilization of the masses or did not know how to go about it. They adopted an attitude of "I talk and you listen." Some made the peasants go through the motions of class struggle like actors in a play, making them "speak bitterness" as an obligation. Where such problems occurred the land reform might not be thorough, and the peasants might regard what they had gotten as a gift rather than as something they had won for themselves.

The rather radical view of land reform that Du espoused finally appeared in *Nanfang ribao* on 2 December, at the same time that the expansion of land-reform plans from three to eleven *xian* was announced. By this time the CCP leadership was probably advocating a slightly more radical land reform than it had planned in June, but that would be hard to prove. There was no inconsistency between policy statements of the two periods, only a sharp difference in emphasis. Thus an article in *Nanfang ribao* on 19 December pointed out that shedding a little blood could serve a useful educational function. Party leaders had certainly believed this six months earlier, but they would have been unlikely to say it so bluntly. The outbreak of the Korean War may have made their policy slightly more radical than it had been, but this should not

---

38. Du Runsheng, in *Nanfang ribao*, 10 December 1950, p. 3.

be overemphasized.[39] What had happened was less a shift in their ideas on correct land-reform policy than a shift in their perception of the land-reform cadres. When they discovered the rightist tendencies of many cadres in the New Liberated Areas, they began to emphasize the dangers of right deviations. In the Central-South Region as a whole the problem of "peaceful land reform" was considered to have been a relatively brief aberration, widespread only in November and December of 1950.[40] It may have been unusually persistent in Guangdong.

At the end of 1951 Du Runsheng offered some minor refinements in land-reform policy, designed to reduce the danger that the land-reform cadres would substitute themselves for the masses. The number of land-reform cadres per village was to be reduced. Du said the land-reform cadres should join the peasant association in the villages where they worked, and thenceforth all decisions in land reform should be taken by the peasant association, in which the land-reform cadres would have only one vote apiece like the ordinary peasants. They should have no right to overrule the association if they were outvoted on some issue. This report by Du also emphasized, more than earlier ones, that the recruitment of peasant activists was not to be done only by land-reform cadres; the early activists should themselves go out to recruit other activists.[41]

In March 1952, the CCP South China Sub-bureau still considered inadequate struggle against the landlords and inadequate mobilization of the peasants to be the main problems among land-reform cadres. There were cadres who felt that the landlord class had been overthrown to a sufficient extent so that they could relax a bit, moderate the class struggle or even suspend it altogether, and give up the arduous chore of practicing the "three togethers" among the peasants.[42] Later in 1952, the Party finally stopped pushing so hard for more radicalism. The land-reform cadres were becoming more radical, and the Party leaders may also have felt that by this time the enemies of the revolution really had been defeated, so they could be treated a bit more leniently. A decree of July 1952 gave measures for surveillance of people who had been counterrevolutionary criminals before 1949, who showed no evidence of repentance, but who had committed no flagrant counterrevolutionary acts since liberation and therefore were not worth

---

39. "To expand the area of land reform, and carry out land reform more quickly, are concrete measures for resisting America and aiding Korea, protecting our homes and defending the fatherland, since to eliminate the landlord class as a class is to eliminate the social base on which imperialism and the reactionary forces rely." *Nanfang ribao*, 2 December 1950, p. 1.

40. *Changjiang ribao*, 13 December 1951, p. 1.

41. Ibid., 9 December 1951, pp. 1–2.

42. *Nanfang ribao*, 15 March 1952, trans. in *CB*, 184:13–14.

arresting.[43] The idea that such people should only be watched, not imprisoned, represented a significant softening of CCP policy. By October, the movement of the land-reform cadres to the left and of the leadership to the right had reached a point where Tao Zhu (Fang Fang's replacement as head of the CCP in Guangdong) was complaining of radical excesses in the land reform: taking too much "surplus" grain from the landlords (especially overseas Chinese landlords and those involved in commerce or industry), mistakes in class demarcation, and excessively broad attacks on counterrevolutionaries.[44]

Obstacles to Land Reform in Guangdong

The record of land reform in Guangdong was rather poor. Guangdong had been one of the last provinces liberated by the PLA in 1949 and had to carry out land reform quite soon after liberation, but several other provinces with the same problems were able to deal with them better.

The pattern of land tenure in Guangdong was very unequal, even by the standards of southern China. Highly concentrated land ownership should have made land reform easier; the CCP could give very large amounts of land to the poor while expropriating only a limited number of landlords and rich peasants. However, there was a comparatively high level of commercial development and considerable capitalist agriculture. Care had to be taken to avoid disrupting these patterns too much. There were also problems with the overseas Chinese, who owned a great deal of land in Guangdong but who could not be alienated too much. Special measures were developed to deal with land held by the overseas Chinese.[45] Such problems led some people to say, "In the North emphasize struggle; in the South it is necessary to emphasize peace."[46]

The clan (zu) system was far stronger in Guangdong than in most of China. Since most clans embraced all social classes from landlords to laborers, this system was a serious obstacle to class struggle. The CCP had to create cleavages within clans and try to avoid getting involved in feuds between clans.[47]

The CCP blamed many of its problems in Guangdong on the cadres, of all levels. Tao Zhu, his nerves perhaps frayed by

---

43. NCNA, Peking, 17 July 1952, in *CB*, 193:1–3.
44. *Nanfang ribao*, 28 October 1952, trans in *CB*, 226:6.
45. Ibid., 6 November 1950, p. 6.
46. *Changjiang ribao*, 18 April 1951, p. 2.
47. Secret societies like the Yiguandao may have performed some of the same functions for their members, and caused some of the same problems for the CCP in other provinces, that the clans did in Guangdong.

almost two years of not very satisfactory results in land reform, told a conference of land-reform cadres in April 1952:

> Are the ranks very pure? We should say that the agrarian reform ranks in various [xian] in the Central [Guangdong] Special District, having gone through several reforms, are no longer as gravely impure as in certain other areas, but the phenomenon of impurity still exists, the principal expression of which is the extremely vague line of demarcation between the enemy and ourself....
> We have gone astray so much and there is still not a path that is relatively straight. This is what defies explanation. Why has it often been difficult to fulfill the policies? Why have we always gone astray...? Especially to be mentioned is the tendency of violating law and discipline, indulging in willful practices, protecting landlords either openly or illicitly, employing depraved persons, abetting the landlords' animus, suppressing the voice of the peasants—these things have occurred incessantly. Can one say that these are signs of lack of experience? If we want to make a success of agrarian reform in [Guangdong] Province today, we have to start by "reforming" standpoint, ideology, and style of work.[48]

Problems occurred both among holdovers from the old regime and among poor peasants who had been promoted and saw a chance at an easy life. *Nanfang ribao* reported inflated salaries paid to village heads and militia officers, feasts held for cadres at public expense, and inflated bureaucracies (a number of *xian* had from 100 to 200 more salaried land-reform cadres than they were supposed to have). The tax system was in serious disarray. The CCP had nominally suppressed all but a few fairly simple taxes, principally on grain production. But local administrations continued to collect a wide variety of illegal taxes, often through tax farmers. The Agrarian Reform Law had said that all land rented out to support schools should be confiscated and distributed to the peasants, leaving the schools to be supported by public funds. Local governments quickly invented special taxes to pay for the schools, and these became a source of corruption.[49]

Many cadres and officials did not attack the landlords vigorously; some even sheltered them. This could be due to an affirmative belief that coexistence with the landlords was good, to personal ties with the individuals in question, to simple apathy, or to bribes in the form of money, fine meals, and women. In Xingning *xian*, one of the first three to undergo land reform, it was later estimated that only 20 percent of the landlords had been

---

48. *Nanfang ribao*, 18 April 1952, trans. in *CB*, 184:25–27.
49. Ibid., 27 August, 17 and 22 September, 4, 6, and 8 October 1951, trans. in *CB*, no. 129.

hit.[50] In Huiyang, one of the slowest *xian*, it was reported that the head of the *xian* government had appointed landlords, despots, and counterrevolutionaries to administrative posts at the *qu* and *xiang* levels and that the local cadres often did not seem even to be trying to mobilize the peasants.[51] Enping, in Central Guangdong, was perhaps the worst case. The *xian* administration and police remained riddled with landlords and former Guomindang functionaries until 1952. An incident in which three poor-peasant activists were executed on a framed murder charge finally led to an investigation and a thorough purge. The head of the *xian* government was imprisoned; the director of the Public Security Bureau and the vice-president of the People's Court were executed. None of these three men seems to have had a Guomindang background himself, but they had gotten along entirely too well with those who had.[52]

At the village level many cadres were lenient to the landlords. Some cases of accommodation with the landlords arose from social and kinship ties dating from before liberation. Others had originated immediately after liberation, when the CCP had needed the cooperation of the old village power holders to maintain administration for the short run. It is hard to say how the attitudes of the majority of land-reform work-team personnel, who were not Communist Party members, differed from those of Party members native to Guangdong. Party members brought in from other provinces were far more antilandlord than either.

The number of cadres from other provinces increased steadily. By August 1952, the PLA alone had assigned almost 10,000 men to work on land reform in Guangdong.[53] If left to itself, the Party in Guangdong would eventually have carried out at least part of what Peking and Wuhan were demanding, but the higher leadership wanted fast and massive results. The outcome was that issues of social policy, on which there must have been dispute both in Peking and in Guangdong, were turned into questions of regional autonomy. In the end, Guangdong leaders had to submit to higher authority.

Imposition from Above

Land reform between 1950 and 1953 was much more a centrally directed campaign and less a matter of spontaneous action at the village level than it had been in 1947. This was especially true in Guangdong, since the central government was so dissatisfied with

---

50. Ibid., 5 May 1952, trans. in *CB*, 184:36.

51. Ibid., 23 May 1952, and *Changjiang ribao*, 7 April 1952, trans. in *CB*, 184:10, 39.

52. *CB*, no. 204 passim.

53. *Nanfang ribao*, 2 August 1952, trans. in *CB*, 211:51.

the initial performance of the local cadres that it sent in large numbers of northerners to supervise the campaign. The imposition of land reform from above meant that social mobilization often was not as thorough as it should have been. In North China in 1947, serious land redistribution had usually taken place in a village only after the local Communist Party organization, peasant association, and/or poor-peasant league had become strong enough to impose their will on the landlords. After the land reform these forces had continued to dominate the village. In the New Liberated Areas, however, land-reform work teams played a much larger role. Once such a team had supervised the land reform in one village it would move on to another, not necessarily leaving behind it a really strong peasant association or Communist Party branch. A newspaper in East China described some of the resulting problems as follows: "In *xiang* where the masses were not mobilized, after land was distributed, the landlords would dare to launch a counterattack, tearing up notices and posters and forcibly taking back land, farm implements, draft animals, foodstuffs, and houses which had already been distributed to peasants. Some even dared to obstruct the peasants in undertaking winter farming, to intimidate peasants into concluding lease contracts with them, and to continue openly the collection of rent from the peasants."[54] The same thing happened in parts of Guangdong.

The peasants themselves seem to have been less radical in Guangdong and the rest of the South than they had been in North China. This may have been due partly to differences in social structure and partly to the fact that mass mobilization and propaganda efforts were neither as prolonged nor as radical as in the North. Du Runsheng told the Central-South MAC that the peasants were easily fooled by landlord arguments that "people of the same *cun*, of the same clan, can reach a peaceful understanding." This was especially true if the landlords were really sophisticated in their efforts to save themselves; in some *xiang* the illegal scattering of landlord property before land reform was so wide that 80 percent of the peasants got some.[55]

The work teams were told very frequently that they were supposed to organize local peasants to carry out land reform for themselves; the cadres were not supposed to do the work for the peasants. But they were also under pressure to finish the reform quickly and to make sure that proper procedures were obeyed. The temptation to settle for mobilizing a few peasants, to tell the peasants exactly what to do at every stage, or simply to do it for them was great. In extreme cases "the cadres monopolized the work and acted for the peasants in all activities from the most important

---

54. *Xinwen ribao* (Shanghai), 19 March 1951, trans. in *CB*, 92:4. See also *Nanfang ribao*, 19 September 1951, trans. in *CB*, 125:9.

55. *Changjiang ribao*, 9 December 1951, p. 1.

to the most trivial."[56] Mass meetings for the peasants to "speak bitterness" could become a farce; there were cases in which the cadres scheduled a certain period for the peasants to express their indignation and then started looking at their watches and tugging at the peasants' sleeves to tell them their time was up.[57] "The cadres clapped hands till they were swollen, the activists shouted till their throats were hoarse, the backward elements slept through the whole thing peacefully, and the despots and landlords still did not bow their heads."[58]

There would have been advantages to the heavy emphasis on land-reform work teams sent into the villages from outside, compared with a dominant role for local cadres, even if the local organizations had not been so new and untested. Cadres from other areas were insulated from clan ties and clan feuds. They were more likely to uphold central government policy against local pressures. Their main defect was that they were not planning to remain in the villages where they worked, so if they were slipshod they would not have to live with the results. They tended to concentrate on the specific tasks to which they were assigned, neglecting problems such as the annual spring food shortage, which obviously needed attention but which were not obviously part of the land reform. Some PLA cadres were in a hurry to get back to their units. All were eager to report quick success to their superiors. They were tempted simply to go through the motions of mass mobilization: "In the field of *visiting the poor and inquiring into their sufferings,* some cadres proceeded with their tasks like making new year calls, or taking a census. Some were known to have visited 50 families in a single day."[59] Just during the demarcation of classes, the first half of the second stage of land reform, there was supposed to be half a day of group discussion and public mass struggle devoted to each landlord, preceded by careful investigation and preparation behind the scenes.[60] It is not surprising that many cadres cut corners.

Land reform was a major task and potentially a major source of discomfort for all officials in the countryside, not just those formally designated as land-reform cadres. The Communist Party had little respect for bureaucratic regularity. When it said that land reform was the most important task in the countryside, it meant that officials and cadres assigned to other tasks were supposed to place a higher priority on helping the land reform than on getting their own jobs done. They were supposed

56. *Nanfang ribao,* 15 March 1952, trans. in *CB,* 184:14.

57. *Changjiang ribao,* 7 April 1952, trans. in *CB,* 184:11.

58. Ibid., p. 9; see also *Changjiang ribao,* 15 December 1951, p. 2.

59. *Nanfang ribao,* 13 April 1952, trans. in *CB,* 184:54 (emphasis in the original).

60. *Nanfang ribao,* 9 March 1952, p. 2.

continually to be taking time away from the work they had been assigned in order to do things they had not specifically been told to do but which would help the land reform, either at their own initiative or at the request of the land-reform cadres. Their imme- diate superiors were supposed to hold the number of their assigned tasks down in order to permit this,[61] but they did not always do so. To inexperienced and confused personnel, eager to win a place for themselves by getting the approval of their superiors, this must have seemed a nightmare.

Land reform was not so completely a program imposed from above that we can regard it as a mechanical process, carried out "by the numbers." Land-reform plans laid down by the Party and govern- ment were continually being helped, hindered, or altered by the actions of land-reform cadres, local officials, landlords, and peasants. When peasants in some villages of Enping *xian* confis- cated certain landlord property, the former owners proceeded by sedan chair to the *xian* administrative offices and obtained orders that their property be restored to them.[62] Almost certainly these incidents involved two consecutive violations of policy—the peasants should not have carried out the confiscation without waiting for proper authorization, and the *xian* authorities should not so blatantly have supported landlords against peasants even if the peasants had not followed proper procedures. But in a political struggle at the local level—which land reform most definitely was—policies made in Peking could not always prevail.

---

61. *Changjiang ribao* editorial, 16 December 1950, reprinted in *Nanfang ribao*, 20 December 1950, p. 4.

62. *Guangming ribao* (Peking), 1 September 1952, trans. in *CB*, 211:13–14.

7

The Results of Land Reform in China

Economic Results

There is no good statistical summary of the results of land reform for China as a whole. The State Statistical Bureau tried to write one shortly after the end of the reform, but it found that adequate data were not available. Various data exist on particular questions, usually covering only a limited part of China.

John Wong has estimated that about 43 percent of the cultivated land in China was transferred during the land reform.[1] This seems roughly compatible with what is known about the prereform tenure situation and the policies applied to it, but regional surveys show variations from 20 percent to 60 percent,[2] and there were even wider variations among individual villages. Only in a few areas, most of which underwent land reform before 1949, was there something approaching full equalization of landholdings. For the most part, the CCP roughly equalized the holdings of the people at the top and the bottom of the economic scale, while leaving untouched people ranging from slightly below average to considerably above average.

Table 7-1 shows the situation after land reform in a few sample areas, unfortunately not including the Northeast. The top portion of the table gives the percentage of population and land held for each social class. The index numbers give the per capita landholding of each class relative to the per capita landholding of the rural population as a whole; thus the landlords in the *xiang* studied in East China had 0.82 times as much land per person, after land reform, as the average person in these *xiang*. North China is represented by a single village, which underwent land reform in the 1940s; the other regions are represented by varying numbers of villages where land reform was carried out after 1950. The land reform had not followed policies of complete egalitarianism, especially if we consider that in the areas that underwent land reform after 1950, the redistribution of draft animals, tools, and so on was less complete than the redistribution of land. In these areas the middle peasants retained their former level of landholdings or

---

1. Wong, *Land Reform*, p. 161.
2. Ibid.

Table 7-1—Percentage of population, percentage of land owned, and index numbers for per capita land ownership, for different classes after land reform, in sample areas

Region	Central-South[a]	SW[b]	East[c]	NW[d]	North[e]
Landlords					
population	4.3	4.6	4.2	7.4	0.2
land	4.3	4.4	3.4	5.6	0.2
Rich peasants					
population	4.8	6.9	4.8	6.6	1.3
land	7.0	8.1	8.0	10.1	1.0
Middle peasants					
population	22.9	30.9	40.5	50.7	90.0
land	26.1	31.8	44.3	59.0	90.8
Poor peasants					
population	55.0	50.6	44.6	32.8	8.5
land	52.4	48.1	37.7	24.7	7.4
Laborers					
population	5.2	5.8	3.7	4.2	none
land	4.8	5.8	3.3	3.1	none
Index Numbers					
Landlords	0.99[f]	0.97	0.82	0.75	1.15
Rich peasants	1.47[f]	1.17	1.67	1.53	0.79
Middle peasants	1.04[f]	1.03	1.09	1.16	1.01
Poor peasants	0.95[f]	0.95	0.84	0.75	0.87
Laborers	0.92[f]	0.98	0.90	0.74	none

    a.   Data from 89 *xiang*, in Li Chengrui, *Nongye shui*, p. 123.
    b.   Data from 2 *cun*, in ibid.
    c.   Data from 20 *xiang*, in ibid.
    d.   Data from 5 *xiang*, in ibid.
    e.   Data from one village, in Hinton, *Fanshen*, p. 592. Figures for middle peasants, poor peasants, and laborers reflect upward changes in class status brought about by land redistribution. Figures for landlords and rich peasants include only those who were still in the village in 1948. Most landlords and rich peasants had lost all their land and had been killed or had fled. If the land owned in 1948 were compared with the original (1944) numbers of landlords and rich peasants in the village, the index numbers would be 0.06 for the landlords and 0.36 for the rich peasants.
    f.   *Changjiang ribao*, 9 December 1951, trans. in *CB*, 157:35, gives significantly different figures: landlords 0.80, rich peasants 1.30, middle peasants 1.10, poor peasants and laborers 0.90.

even gained a little; most owned slightly more than the average for their areas, but some would have owned a bit less. The rich peasants lost a significant part of their land, but they still had considerably more than the average. The landlords, poor peasants, and laborers ended up owning what might be considered their minimal needs—somewhat less than the average landholding, or about what the lower ranks of the middle peasants had held before land reform. When many poor peasants were reclassified as middle peasants after land reform, this was a reasonable reflection of the changes in their economic status,[3] though we should not make too much of the exact figures; the criteria of class demarcation may have changed a bit.

It is hard to judge from a distance how far actual distribution deviated, in individual cases, from the ideal patterns described in land-reform legislation. In theory, almost all families receiving land in a given village should have ended up with essentially equal landholdings, taking into account quality as well as quantity. In practice, those considered especially meritorious could be favored.[4]

The new social order, much more egalitarian than the old, was not completely stable. There was no longer a class of very poor people whose average yearly expenses exceeded their average yearly incomes, but most families were still potentially at the mercy of unusual events—crop failures, the expense of weddings and funerals, and so on. Such things could lead them to sell land or borrow at very high rates of interest, just as in the old days. In the area the Crooks studied in Hebei, about 2 percent of all households sold land in the year 1951. In parts of Shaanxi interest rates as high as 60 percent to 180 percent were being charged for loans five years after land reform.[5] Some of the poorer peasants were still supplementing their incomes by wage labor.

There probably was no longer an average trend to downward mobility, either in absolute or relative terms. The overall level of wealth in the society was rising. Famine had essentially been eliminated. In general, the obtrusively horrible aspects of the old

---

3. See Moise, "Land Reform," pp. 217–20, for my disagreements on this point with Wong, *Land Reform*, p. 177.

4. See Chou Li-po, *The Hurricane*, pp. 375–76. After 1948 CCP leaders generally discouraged such things, although they remained fairly common at the village level. The only late document I have seen that suggested that participation in the struggle could be a legitimate factor in distribution of the fruits of the struggle was a statement by the mayor of Wuhan, who said that nonagricultural laboring people (who would not otherwise have been eligible) might be given a share in the fruits of the struggle against the landlords if they had helped the struggle. *Changjiang ribao*, 28 November 1951, p. 2.

5. Crook and Crook, *First Years*, pp. 6, 33. *Renmin ribao*, 11 November 1951, trans. in *CB*, 143:5.

society had been ameliorated. But the land reform by itself had provided only minimally adequate conditions for the peasants.

Political Results

The overthrow of the old rural elite, while not total, had been adequate in almost all areas. The landlords had been stripped of most of their wealth and had been publicly humiliated. Most peasants had shared in their wealth when it had been distributed, and many had attacked them at public meetings; the peasants had learned that it was both possible and profitable to fight those they had once thought to be the ordained masters of their world. In the early stages of the mass mobilization there had been areas where the landlords retained enough moral authority to keep effective control of their property after work teams from outside the villages had nominally redistributed it. Even after land reform, reinvestigation in the Central-South Region, during the summer of 1951, found landlords still exerting significant control over the peasants in almost 30 percent of the villages checked.[6] But by the time the whole process of land reform and reinvestigation had been completed, landlord power cannot have been great in very many villages. The best most landlords could even try to do was to carve out a niche in the new system rather than defy it. Their assets were their land, which was usually less than the local per capita average; their other wealth, which must have varied widely from individual to individual but would seldom have been great; their remaining prestige, also variable but usually low to negative; and their literacy and business skills. These were not enough to make them a genuine threat to peasant domination of rural society.

Some landlords suffered more than the loss of their wealth and power. Large-scale forced labor was most typical of the Jiangxi period; it was reminiscent of, and probably copied from, contemporary Soviet practice. In the 1940s and 1950s the proportion of landlords set to forced labor was smaller, and its conditions were probably less severe. Beatings of the landlords by the peasants occurred in all periods of the land reform but were most typical of the years 1945–47. Imprisonment probably did not become really common until the early 1950s, after the regime had become well-enough established to operate large prisons.

Finally, more than a few landlords were killed, with or without formal trials. Mao Zedong said in 1957 that the total number of people liquidated by the government's security forces up to 1954 had been 800,000.[7] This figure probably represented the number

---

6. *Changjiang ribao*, 9 December 1951, p. 1.

7. "On the Correct Handling of Contradictions among the People," 27 February 1957, excerpt quoted in the *New York Times*, 13 June 1957, p. 8. The statement cited here is not in the official

of executions from the founding of the PRC in 1949 up to 1954; before 1949 executions had often taken the form of lynchings, in which the security forces had not been involved and for which there would not have been any statistical record. It seems a good assumption that the figure of 800,000 would not be far from the total number of people executed, before and after the founding of the PRC, in the areas that underwent land reform between 1950 and 1953.[8] These areas had a total population estimated at the time of land reform at 310,000,000, of which 264,000,000 was rural population. If the rate of executions in rural and urban populations had been the same, there would have been about 680,000 executions among the rural population. If the rate of executions had been twice as high for the rural as for the urban population, there would have been about 735,000 executions among the rural population. Among the rural population of about 145,000,000 that underwent land reform before 1949, the rate of executions was considerably higher. Allowing for this uncertainty and for the fact that some executions in the countryside would have had no connection with land reform, the best that can be said is that the number of executions in the land reform and the campaigns that led up to it (including bandit eradication) was probably between 1,000,000 and 1,500,000. This comes to about 0.3 percent of the population involved if we use the population estimates of the land-reform period, somewhat less if we use the larger figures that came out of the 1953 census.

The figures for Guangdong province are lower but not suspiciously so. From 10 October 1950 to 10 August 1951 there were 28,332 executions reported in Guangdong.[9] This period includes the time of maximum violence in Guangdong, but there would have been significant numbers of executions both before and after this. Overall, slightly over 0.1 percent of the province population were probably executed. Given the fact that cadres in Guangdong took an unusually moderate approach to land reform, this seems consistent with the deductions that can be made from Mao's figures.

During the campaign for the suppression of counterrevolutionaries in the Central-South Region, between November 1950 and December 1951, it was reported that, of all criminals arrested, about 28 percent were executed, 2 percent were sentenced to death but had their sentences stayed for two years to give them a last chance to reform, 50 percent had to undergo reform through labor as prisoners, and the remaining 20 percent were handed over to

---

version of this report, but I believe in its authenticity. See also Loh and Evans, *Escape from Red China*, p. 291, which quotes Mao as saying slightly over 700,000 were executed.

8. Both the number of executions in these areas before 1949 and the number in other areas after 1949 would have been relatively small.

9. *Nanfang ribao*, 18 September 1951, trans. in *CB*, 124:4.

the masses for surveillance and reform.[10] If we assume that the proportions were about the same for the larger area and longer time span covered by Mao's figure of 800,000 executions and that this area had a real population (crudely estimated from the 1953 census) of 385,000,000, we will have about 0.75 percent of the population arrested. If the rural population were considered separately, the percentage probably would not be very different. This is a rather high percentage, given that it includes only the people arrested and not their families. It may include a large number of people, especially bandits and prominent members of the Guomindang, whose arrests had little or no connection with land reform. It may also be seriously inaccurate; the chain of reasoning that produced it contains several unprovable assumptions.

There were also many people, about half (?) as many as were formally arrested, who were put in the custody of the masses for surveillance and reform through labor without being formally arrested.[11] Most of these were probably ordinary landlords, who were required by law to labor on the land that was left to them after land reform.

The new order that replaced landlord rule was firmly established in almost all areas. At its base were the peasant associations, whose membership usually included from 30 percent to 40 percent of the total population of each village, or well over half of the adult peasants. All had been exposed to some political education, and most had listened at least to some extent. Many, perhaps a majority, had actually been politicized to some serious degree. The peasants had tried intervening in politics, which had seemed a strange and dangerous experiment, and they had found it profitable. The number of activists—people who could be counted upon to participate voluntarily in government programs—was huge by comparison with previous eras. Many peasants also belonged to women's associations or local militias.

Some peasant activists were recruited into the Communist Party, but this usually happened after land reform. The Party preferred to let an activist get a considerable amount of training and experience, and preferred to have time to consider the activist's talents and accomplishments, before it invited him or her to join. This is an important point to note; excessive haste in Party recruitment was to be an important error in the land reform in North Vietnam.

Village administrations were recruited from among the peasant activists. There had been repeated upheavals in most villages, as the search went on for people who not only would be competent to run an administration and would resist the temptation to enrich themselves by means of their new power, but would maintain a healthy relationship with the peasants, thinking of themselves as first among equals rather than as a superior class entitled to give

---

10. *Changjiang ribao*, 13 December 1951, trans. in *CB*, 157:12.
11. Ibid.

orders without consulting those below them. This was not easy; it contradicted attitudes to authority that were deeply ingrained in Chinese culture as in many others. The rectification campaigns of the 1940s and the early 1950s were the first stages of the struggle that eventually led to the Cultural Revolution. [12]

At the *qu* level and above, it took a considerable period for peasant activists to acquire important positions. By 1953 there had been time for this in some of the Old Liberated Areas, but in most of the New Liberated Areas higher administrations were staffed by intellectuals, retrained Guomindang personnel, and experienced cadres from the Old Liberated Areas. Still, the land reform had given the peasants most of the positions of power at the village level and had made higher administrations at least attentive to peasant interests. This was a very impressive accomplishment.

Sending cadres into the villages from outside to supervise political reforms was a process with a tremendous potential for error. The cadres might bring mistaken preconceptions to the village, or make bad judgments about which peasants were worthy of promotion. Leaders at higher levels could do their best to supply the cadres with reasonably accurate preconceptions, and to make them respect the opinions of a broad range of peasants in the villages, but serious problems were certain to remain. The land reform needed, therefore, some mechanism to protect it from the imperfections of the land-reform cadres. By 1951 the CCP had worked out such a mechanism. A team of cadres came into each village and carried out, or helped the peasants to carry out, a reform of the local power structure. Then the team would leave, and the peasants had a few months to think and talk about what had happened, without the inhibiting influence of outside cadres. They also had a chance to see how competent and reliable the new village leaders were when not supervised by outsiders. Then another team came. Its misconceptions and prejudices would probably not duplicate those of the previous team, and if it were willing to listen it could hear the peasants' conclusions about the work of the previous team. It would carry out another effort at reform, and the cycle would repeat. Most villages of the Central-South Region were visited by at least four teams, over a period of at least one and a half years. Furthermore, massive redistribution of wealth was usually held off until at least the third visit, by which time village activists would be able to provide serious assistance to the outside cadres. The end result was generally satisfactory even if there had been some carelessness or ineptitude along the way, or if some of the peasants who had seemed qualified for leadership had turned out not to be. The remaining problem cases would have been villages that had suffered from an extraordinary succession of

---

12. There is a report on Party rectification by Chen Boda, published in *Renmin ribao*, 7 July 1947, p. 2, which seems remarkably similar to documents of the Cultural Revolution.

incompetent work teams, or where traditional loyalties or traditional hatreds had been so strong that large numbers of peasants could not be persuaded to cooperate in the reorientation of politics along class lines.

The Chinese Communist Party used the system of successive teams, but I have seen no document that explained the full logic behind it. It was not passed on to the Vietnamese, who carried out land reform in many villages with only two visits by outside work teams and sometimes tried to get by with only one.

8

The Background to Land Reform in Vietnam

The Democratic Republic of Vietnam (DRV) carried out land reform between 1953 and 1956. The war to establish Vietnam's independence from the French, who had ruled Vietnam since the late nineteenth century, was just ending. It was logical that the DRV should choose land reform policies resembling those that had worked in China; the social and political situations in the two countries seemed quite similar. In Vietnam, however, the results were less satisfactory. In October 1956, the DRV announced that serious excesses had occurred. Truong Chinh had to resign his position as general secretary of the Lao Dong Party, and the ensuing correction of errors lasted well into 1958. The extent of the disaster was not as great as has been suggested by some anti-Communist authors, but it did occur. The usual explanation in the West has been that Vietnam blindly applied Chinese policy to a situation it did not fit. There has been too little research on how closely the Vietnamese really did copy the Chinese model.

Geographical Units

From the early nineteenth century up to 1954, Vietnam was divided administratively into three parts,[1] which for the sake of consistency will be described here by the names used in recent Communist sources. In the North was Bac bo (also known as Tonkin, Bac ky, Bac viet, and Bac phan). In the Center was Trung bo (Annam, Trung ky, Trung viet, Trung phan). In the South was

---

1. There has been repeated debate for over a century between those who say that Vietnam is basically one nation and those (usually representatives of a foreign power wanting to "protect" one region against another) who say that it consists of two or three natural units that should be mutually independent. It is therefore worth noting that the tripartite division of Vietnam was carried out in the nineteenth century by the Gia-long Emperor, who controlled all three regions. This division had no roots in previous Vietnamese history; suggestions that the country had been divided along approximately the same lines between the Tay-son brothers in the late eighteenth century are unfounded.

Nam bo (Cochinchina, Nam ky, etc.). The main levels of administration below the three *bo* were the province, the *huyen* (district,
equivalent to the Chinese *xian*), the *xa* (administrative village,
equivalent to the Chinese *xiang*), and the *thon* (the natural village
or hamlet, equivalent to the Chinese *cun*). There were also administrative units called *xom* within the *xa*. The boundaries of many of
these units have been shifted since 1945.

In addition to these traditional units the DRV created groupings
of provinces, equivalent to the greater administrative regions of
China. The most important of these were the interzones (*lien khu*);
when these were first created during the war against France there
were six, numbered from North to South. Interzone I, the Viet
Bac, was the northeast section of Bac bo, and contained substantial ethnic minority groups. The Viet Minh had its headquarters
there. Interzone II, western Bac bo, had very large minority
populations, especially Thai and Meo. Interzone III, the valley of
the Red River, contained most of the ethnic Vietnamese in Bac bo.
Interzone IV was the northern half of Trung bo, stretching down
to just south of Hue. Interzone V was the southern half of Trung
bo. Interzone VI was Nam bo.

The interzones were originally made up of zones (*khu*),[2] but the
use of this term has not been consistent. The interzones have
often been referred to simply as zones. After 1954 there were
zones that did not seem to be part of any interzone, as well as
provinces that were not part of any larger unit. The term *zone*
will occur in this study in reference to the Hong Quang Zone on
the coast northeast of Haiphong, which was for practical purposes
simply a province, and the Left Bank Zone, made up of several
provinces on the north bank of the Red River, which had formerly
been part of Interzone III.

Social Structure and Land Tenure

Vietnam had a society quite similar to that of China, more so than
any other nation of Southeast Asia. Some of the common characteristics—a severe crowding of population on the land and a long
tradition of active administration by the central government—have
been noted in Chapter 1. In some other respects Vietnam was not
quite so close to China. The status of women was somewhat higher
in Vietnam. The family unit was very strong, but broad kinship
groups stretching beyond the family were less powerful in Vietnam
than in China. The material and psychological gap separating the
elite from the peasants was substantial, but perhaps not as wide as
in China. In the absence of a fixed hereditary class system, both
upward and downward mobility were possible, but probably not to
the extent that was true in China. In Bac bo and Trung bo

---

2. See Palmerlee, "Viet Cong Political Geography," p. 3.

especially, the communal landholding system tended to minimize both upward and downward mobility. With the limited data available, it is not possible to say whether downward mobility predominated over upward to the extent that was true in China.

The Vietnamese economy was not as commercialized as the Chinese; it had more of a subsistence character. One aspect of this was that a considerable portion of the land had not yet become private property. Most land in China was owned by some individual, who could dispose of it freely. The main exceptions were land belonging to clans and other organizations, which could buy and sell it like individuals, and land subject to the rules of customary tenure. Even in the last case the land could be considered to be owned by several persons, each of whom owned certain rights. But in Vietnam much of the land was "communal." This meant that it was owned by the village; it was usually supposed to be shared among the population of the village. The system of communal land had been encouraged by indigenous Vietnamese governments to increase tax revenues, to promote the welfare of the people, and to keep the peasants tied to their villages by making it impossible for individuals to sell the land they farmed. During the French period a considerable amount of communal land passed into private hands. Figures from the 1930s indicate that the proportion of land that was communally owned was about 21 percent in Bac bo, 25 percent in Trung bo where French influence had been weakest, and only 3 percent in Nam bo, where there had been little communal land even before the French conquest. Figures collected by the Viet Minh in 1952 indicate that 17 percent of the land was communal in Bac bo, 21 percent in Trung bo, and 2 percent in Nam bo.[3] Most land-reform statistics treat the communal land as if it had been a disguised form of landlord land, but this is a serious exaggeration. It was not always the case even that wealthy and powerful individuals got more than their share when the communal land was being parceled out, and when they did get an unreasonably large amount they do not usually seem to have gotten all of it.[4]

Private landholdings were very concentrated in the Mekong Delta and moderately so in Trung bo and Bac bo. In the early 1930s, Yves Henry collected comprehensive statistics on landholdings in the three regions, which have formed the basis for most later writing on the distribution of land ownership in this period. However, aside from the fact that they underestimate the concentration of landholdings to an unknown but possibly significant extent, Henry's statistics are in a form that limits their utility. They simply group the owners of land into categories according to size of landholding. They do not indicate what percentage of the

3. Tran Phuong, *Cach mang ruong dat o Viet-nam*, pp. 29–30.

4. For comments on this issue see Truong Chinh and Vo Nguyen Giap, *The Peasant Question (1937–1938)*, pp. 78–83.

total land area was owned by people in each of the size categories or how many peasants there were who owned no land. They use different size categories for the three regions, which inhibits effective comparison. Other authors have tried to flesh these figures out by the addition of data from other sources, by extrapolation, and by sheer guesswork, but the results must be considered unreliable.[5]

We will do better to use the figures collected in the 1950s in connection with land reform, although these likewise present problems both of accuracy and of interpretation. It is impossible to give a single set of figures for the landholdings of different social classes before the revolution, because of shifts in class demarcation. During the land reform, very harsh standards were applied and probably over 5 percent of the rural population of North Vietnam were classified as landlords. In late 1956 and 1957 the DRV decided that this had been a mistake, and many of these people were reclassified as rich or middle peasants. We will therefore get two different pictures of the tenure situation before land reform, depending on whether we use the class-demarcation standards used before the correction of errors (during the land reform) or the standards used during the correction of errors. Table 8-1 shows the variations in figures for the prereform holdings of different classes between data collected before and after the correction of errors. Data collected during land reform indicate a great many people in the landlord class, with an average of about 0.6 hectares per person. Data collected after the correction of errors show fewer people in the landlord class, but with an average of about 1.0 hectares per person. Data reflecting the class-demarcation standards used during the land reform would be the most useful type for our purposes, but unfortunately it is neither as comprehensive nor as reliable as that collected after the correction of errors.

Table 8-2 gives the results of sample surveys from selected villages in sixteen provinces of North Vietnam; the data were collected after the correction of errors. It is probably quite accurate for the areas covered, although these areas might not be perfectly representative. Table 8-3 gives data for all the areas of North Vietnam covered by the land reform (essentially all the

---

5. Henry, *Economie agricole de l'Indochine*, pp. 23–25, 108–9, 144, 182–83, gives actual survey data. Gourou, *L'Utilization du sol en Indochine Française*, pp. 229, 274, supplements the survey data with estimates. There is a more complete set of figures, likewise estimates rather than survey data, found in Le Thanh Khoi, *Le Viet-Nam, histoire et civilization*, p. 422, and a variety of Communist sources. They indicate a considerably higher concentration of landholdings than does Gourou. I have no confidence in these estimates; they may have arisen partly from misinterpretation of Henry and Gourou.

Table 8-1—The landholdings of different classes *before* land reform, in hectares per person; *data collected* before and after the correction of errors

	Landlords	Rich Peasants	Middle Peasants	Poor Peasants	Laborers
Before					
From Table 11-1	.650	.214	.115	.046	.020
From Table 11-1	.512	.228	.115	.147	.019
After					
From Table 8-2[a]	.980	.427	.155	.059	.014
From Table 8-3	1.009	.398	.137	.043	.012

a. Data showing land per household has been converted to show land per person, on the basis of information on household size in Tran Phuong, *Cach mang ruong dat*, pp. 156, 160, 162, and Mazaev, *Agrarnaia reforma v Demokraticheskoi Respublike V'etnam*, p 87. Inaccuracies may have crept in during this conversion.

Table 8-2—The percentage of households and of land owned by different classes before August 1945; data collected after the correction of errors

	Landlords	Rich Peasants	Middle Peasants	Poor Peasants	Laborers
Households	3.3	2.2	32.9	35.4	20.6
Land	22.5	7.1	30.4	10.8	1.2

Source: Tran Phuong, *Cach mang ruong dat*, following p. 82. Data from 93 *xa* and 31 *thon* of North Vietnam.

Table 8-3—The land-tenure situation in 1945 in the 3,653 *xa* (after division of *xa*) of North Vietnam that underwent land re*form between 1953 and 1956; data collected after the correction of errors

	(1) Population	(2) Land Owned	(3) Land Owned	(4) Land Owned per Person	(5) Land Owned or Used per Person
	(%)	(hectares)	(%)	(hectares)	(hectares)
Colonialists		15,952	1		
Churches		23,928	1.5		
Landlords	3.2	390,825	24.5	1.009	1.136
Rich peasants		113,259	7.1	0.398	0.468
Middle peasants	31	462,609	29	0.137	0.169
Poor peasants	\ / 58.9	159,520	10	0.043	0.068
Laborers	/ \	17,547	1.1	0.012	0.025
Others		12,761	0.8	0.024	0.028
Communal and semipublic		398,801	25		

Source: Tran Phuong, *Cach mang ruong dat*, p. 14

ethnically Vietnamese areas and some of the national minority areas). Unfortunately it cannot be considered fully reliable. Column 1 is seriously inconsistent with columns 2 and 4. Also, a close examination will show that the figures for the percentage of land owned by each class, in column 3, were not derived from the amounts of land owned by each class in column 2. Rather, someone took a figure for the total amount of land in the country and multiplied it by the percentages in column 3 to get the absolute figures in column 2. If the real figures for column 2 were not available, one must wonder where the percentages came from.

The available data are not very satisfactory, but they can probably be taken as a crude approximation of reality. They indicate that some kind of land reform was definitely needed. The poor peasants and laborers, even if we allow for their share of the communal land, had only about half as much land as the average for the rural population as a whole. [6]

The Vietnamese Revolution

The Indochinese Communist Party (ICP) was founded in 1930, growing out of movements dating from 1925. It was involved in several peasant revolts in different parts of Vietnam between 1930 and 1940. However, these revolts were brief, and the top ICP leaders did not always have close control over them, so there was never an occasion for the Party to draw up and implement a serious program of land reform.

The Japanese moved into Vietnam in 1940, but they allowed the French colonial administration to continue operating under Japanese control. In May 1941, the ICP leaders in exile in South China formed a national front for resistance against the French and Japanese, the Viet Nam Doc Lap Dong Minh Hoi (League for the Independence of Vietnam), or Viet Minh. The Viet Minh soon began spreading an underground network of political and eventually military organizations within Vietnam. Vo Nguyen Giap later described its strategy thus:

> The most appropriate guiding principle for activities was *armed propaganda; political activities were more important than military activities, and fighting less important than propaganda;* armed activity was used to safeguard, consolidate and develop the political bases. Once the political bases were consolidated and developed, we proceeded one step further to the consolidation and development of the semi-armed and

---

6. Beware the statement that 98.7 percent of the land in Bac bo was owned by those who cultivated it, found in Fall, *The Viet-Minh Regime,* p. 118, and later works. Fall had misinterpreted figures coming originally from Henry, *Economie agricole,* p. 108.

armed forces. These had to be in strict secrecy.... A position of legal struggle was maintained for the broad masses. The setting up of revolutionary power was not then opportune. There were regions in which the whole masses took part in organizations of national salvation, and the village Viet Minh Committees had, as a matter of course, full prestige among the masses as an underground organization of the revolutionary power. But even in these localities, we had not to attempt to overthrow the enemy, but try to win over and make use of him. [7]

The Vietnamese have often tried to use political more than military tactics even against armed opponents. In the early 1960s, "the NLF initially approached the entire Revolution not as a small-scale war but as a political struggle with guns, a difference real and not semantic. It maintained that its contest with the GVN and the United States should be fought out at the political level and that the use of massed military might was in itself illegitimate." [8] This follows the European Marxist tradition of building one's base of mass support in an area before one takes open control of it, and it even contains traces of the European pattern of essentially unarmed political organization. It stands in sharp contrast to the strategy Mao had followed in China, especially in the Jiangxi period, under which the CCP seldom had much power in areas where it was not supported by substantial armed forces. The idiosyncracies of individual leaders may have had something to do with this; from 1927 to 1936 Mao was more concerned with the use of regular armed forces than were most other CCP leaders, and his attitude left a lasting imprint on Chinese Communism. But the nature of the opposition the Communists faced was probably more important. When the enemy had powerful armed forces and was willing to use them ruthlessly to uproot the Communist political structure, the only answer was an equally powerful Communist army. Thus the Vietnamese had to abandon their preference for primarily nonmilitary activity when faced with massive invasions by the French after 1946 and by the Americans after 1964. Small-scale political activity is practical under almost any circumstances, but a primarily political struggle can reach a massive scale and create an organized structure of political power only if the enemy is numerically weak or very indecisive.

In March 1945, the Japanese dismantled the French administration that had been running Vietnam for them. However, Japan did not have the manpower to replace the French soldiers and officials who were interned or killed or who fled to China. The Viet Minh was able to expand into the resulting power vacuum. In August

7. Vo Nguyen Giap, *People's War, People's Army*, pp. 78–79 (emphasis in the original).

8. Pike, *Viet Cong*, pp. 91–92.

1945, after Japan surrendered, the Viet Minh seized most of Vietnam and proclaimed the Democratic Republic of Vietnam. The new government had to deal immediately not only with political and military problems, but with the most terrible famine Vietnam had experienced for generations. Malnutrition had long been a way of life for the peasants of Bac bo and Trung bo. In normal years, with their own rice plus imports from Nam bo, they could stay alive even if hungry. But in 1944 very heavy Japanese demands for rice and industrial crops (passed on to the peasants by French administrators), a poor harvest, and disruption of the transportation routes that might have brought food from Nam bo, caused a disaster in Bac bo and to some extent in Trung bo. The head of the French colonial administration estimated that 1,000,000 people died; DRV historians say that 2,000,000 died.[9] In the short run, the DRV dealt fairly well with the problems of allocating food supplies and reviving production. In the long run, it benefited from the intensification of an already revolutionary situation. Foreign rule had become so horrible that the Vietnamese people became willing to endure almost unlimited hardships to eliminate it.

The DRV administration at each major level (interzone, province, *huyen*, and *xa*) was controlled by a resistance administrative committee (*uy ban khang chien hanh chinh*), later renamed administrative committee (*uy ban hanh chinh*). The Indochinese Communist Party was the guiding core of the government. It nominally dissolved itself in November 1945 to reduce the appearance of Communist domination of the nationalist movement, but this meant only that its leaders had to use euphemisms like "the Organization" when discussing it in print. It continued not only to exist but to grow. It came into the open again as the Vietnam Lao Dong (Workers') Party in February 1951. It was not a tiny elite; there were sometimes over 100 Party members in a single *xa*.[10] The most important organizations in each *xa* were: the *chi bo* (*xa* level Party branch), headed by a secretary; the (resistance) administrative committee, headed by a chairman; and the peasant association, headed by a secretary.

The French began to return soon after the Japanese surrender. The conflict between Vietnam's desire for independence and France's determination to restore colonial rule proved too strong for a negotiated settlement, and full-scale warfare broke out in December 1946. The French quickly captured all the major cities

---

9. Buttinger, *Vietnam*, 1:581; *An Outline History of the Vietnam Workers' Party*, p. 38. See also Tran Van Mai, "Who Committed This Crime?", excerpts trans. in Ngo Vinh Long, *Before the Revolution*, pp. 221–76. Mai, like many Vietnamese, believed that the French had caused this famine deliberately.

10. One very large *xa* in Nghe an province had 1,500 Party members. It was too unwieldy and was split into seven smaller *xa*. *Nhan Dan*, 8 October 1955, p. 3.

and much of the densely populated lowlands, especially in the Mekong and Red River deltas. The Viet Minh retained large base areas in Trung bo and northern Bac bo, and smaller ones elsewhere. The French were fatally handicapped by the fact that they did not dare group those Vietnamese who opposed the Viet Minh into a powerful and unified organization; they feared that any such organization would turn on them and seek independence for Vietnam. They waited until 1949 to organize a puppet government covering all of Vietnam—the State of Vietnam under Bao Dai—and even then they gave it no real power. They formed a Vietnamese National Army (VNA), but were slow to recruit troops for it and were careful not to give the State of Vietnam real control over it. Most Vietnamese who supported the French were in regional groups: the Binh Xuyen, Cao Dai, and Hoa Hao organizations in Nam bo, and the Catholic communities of Phat diem and Bui chu (in Ninh binh and Nam dinh provinces respectively) on the southern edge of the Red River Delta in Bac bo. The war was stalemated until 1950, when the Chinese People's Liberation Army reached the Sino-Vietnamese frontier. With a moderate amount of aid from China the Viet Minh was able to break the deadlock. By the middle of 1954, the French, despite considerable assistance from the United States, were losing ground rapidly in both the Red River Delta and the Central Highlands. There was no realistic prospect that reinforcements could be found to stem the tide on either front. On the contrary, it was the Viet Minh that could expect very heavy reinforcements within a few months, when the elite units resting and refitting after their victory at Dien Bien Phu were ready to move into combat once more. France had lost the war.

Early DRV Agrarian Policies

Shortly after its creation, the DRV issued an order for a 25 percent reduction in land rents, cancellation of all secondary rents, and cancellation of all arrears in rent owed by tenants since before the revolution.[11] This order had little practical effect, because the government did not mobilize the peasants to force the landlords to obey. Many cadres felt comparatively little concern for the class interests of the peasants.

The DRV confiscated land from Frenchmen and from Vietnamese who served the French. Some was distributed to the peasants as early as the summer of 1945,[12] but a considerable portion was rented out by local authorities. Aside from placing the revolutionary movement in an invidious position, this led to a certain amount of economic irrationality. Such land was rented very cheaply. Some

---

11. Russian translation in Arturov, *Demokraticheskaia Respublika V'etnam*, p. 154.

12. Truong Chinh, *Tien len duoi la co cua dang*, p. 70.

peasants rented more than they were able to cultivate and either left some fallow or sublet it at a profit.[13]

In January 1948, the Second Plenum of the Party Central Committee defined the main lines of the Party's agrarian policy:

1. Thoroughly implement the 25 percent rent reduction (not yet done in many areas).

2. Abolish secondary rents....

3. Abolish the system of subletting land.

4. Temporarily allocate the land and property of traitors to the poor cultivators, or give it to military units to cultivate so they can be to some extent self-supporting....

5. Redistribute communal land more rationally and justly.

6. Allocate the land of the enemy to the poor cultivators....

11. Fix the wages of [agricultural] laborers (by the day and by the season); protect the landowners against losses.

12. The rent of estates whose owners have long been absent, or who live in enemy-occupied territory, shall temporarily be given to the provincial resistance administrative committee.... (The government promises to return these rents to the landowner whenever he returns and is judged entitled to receive these rents.)[14]

The Fifth Cadres' Conference, convened by the Party Central Committee in August 1948, decided that a land reform (judging by the phraseology, a rather drastic one) was needed to win full mass support for the nationalist struggle. But because the landlords were divided and because most of them (especially the medium and small landlords) had supported or at least submitted to the independence movement, it was not advisable simply to strip them of their land at that time. The Party had to "use reformist methods gradually to restrict the scope of the native feudal landlords' exploitation (for example: rent reduction), and at the same time modify the land system (within limits which do not harm the united front against the French colonialist aggressors)."[15]

Statistics collected in 3,035 *xa* that underwent land reform between 1953 and 1956 (in other words, most of the ethnically Vietnamese areas of North Vietnam) show that in 1945 the French had owned 19,033 hectares of land in these *xa*. Between 1945 and 1949 the DRV confiscated 11,656 hectares of this land, presumably all that lay within its control, and also 8,280 hectares of land

---

13. *Sinh Hoat Noi Bo* [Internal activities], no. 7 (April 1948), reprinted in *Cuoc khang chien than thanh cua nhan dan Viet-nam*, 2:33–34.

14. Quoted in Tran Phuong, *Cach mang ruong dat*, p. 59. As regards item 12, I know of no cases of back rent actually being given to a returning landlord.

15. Quoted in ibid., pp. 63–64.

belonging to Vietnamese in these *xa* who were considered traitors.[16] The rent-reduction program was less successful; relatively
few landlords reduced rents in accord with the law.

Directives in the second half of 1949 established a new system
for dealing with land confiscated from Frenchmen and traitors.[17]
Land growing rice and similar crops was to be divided among the
peasants. They did not become the owners of this land; it was
only being allocated to them for terms of five years, renewable by
the government. They had to work the land themselves rather than
rent it out, cultivate it carefully, and pay taxes, including a
special levy of 10 percent of their production to support the
army.[18] If they failed to cultivate the land or otherwise violated
these conditions, or if they committed some act causing them to be
deprived of the rights of citizens, they would lose the land.
Peasants already working the land in question as tenants, and the
families of revolutionary soldiers and cadres, had priority in the
allocation.

Decree 78 SL[19] of 14 July 1949 repeated the old demand that
rents be reduced 25 percent below the level of 1945. In special
cases where this would have left the rent unreasonably high or
unreasonably low, provincial rent-reduction committees could set
some other level. A supplementary order of 23 July exempted DRV
government personnel from the rent reduction, provided they
rented out less than three *mau* of land. A decree of May 1950
ordered interest reduction and the cancellation of some debts. It
did not try to regulate future loans, but it also did not stress that
future loans were to be free from interference; we should not be
surprised that such interference did occur.[20]

In this period the Lao Dong Party was beginning to talk about
mobilizing the peasants to demand rent reduction and similar
reforms. In June 1950 the Party journal *Su That* pointed out that,
for three years, the idea of rent reduction had been brought up
every year at the time of the autumn harvest but not actually
carried out, and that many people expected the same thing to

---

16. Ibid., p. 65.

17. Texts in Arturov, *Demokraticheskaia Respublika V'etnam*,
pp. 156–57, 160–70.

18. It is not clear whether this represented more than peasants
had to pay when they farmed land that they owned.

19. The DRV numbered its decrees in two series. The more
important ones were in the SL (*sac lenh*) series; the less important
were in the TTg series. *Warning*: these series sometimes (perhaps
at the beginning of each year) went back and started over with
no. 1.

20. Arturov, *Demokraticheskaia Respublika V'etnam*, p. 158;
Fall, *The Viet-Minh Regime*, p. 119; *Nhung cai cach moi cua chinh
phu*, pp. 7–11; *Nhan Dan*, 29 November 1951, in *Cuoc khang
chien*, 3:149.

occur during the coming autumn. *Su That* urged that the peasant associations be strengthened and the peasants aroused to struggle for rent reduction.[21]

These policies resemble those followed by the CCP during the Resistance against Japan. The basic situations were similar; Communist parties were trying to win peasant support, but they could not carry out a radical attack on the landlord class both because this would disrupt a united front against foreign invasion and because their own organizations were not ready for such a program. The most important innovation the Vietnamese introduced was temporary allocation of land to the peasants. This effort to keep ultimate control of the land in the hands of the government, rather than giving it to the peasants, may have been an early symptom of the serious commandist tendencies in the central leadership that plagued the land reform from 1953 to 1956. However, there were rational arguments for it. The DRV was probably trying to avoid the problems that had occurred in some parts of China, where land had been taken from the landlords in a haphazard fashion between 1942 and 1946. By the time the CCP decided to distribute land systematically to the poorest peasants, most of the land was already in the hands of the middle peasants and a minority of the most enterprising poor peasants. The DRV, fearing a similar situation, kept open the option of shifting some of the temporarily allocated land to different recipients during a future land-reform campaign. This was actually done between 1954 and 1956; it is hard to tell on how large a scale.[22]

The DRV also had to deal with abandoned land. Fields were being left fallow because the peasants were off fighting in the war, had fled to safer areas, or had given up their old plots when local authorities gave them better ones. It was vital to bring as much of this land as possible back into production. However, the DRV could not be too hasty about giving the new cultivators title to the land, because the original owners might return. Temporary allocation was a good way of dealing with land that had been left uncultivated, and this could have helped inspire a similar procedure for land confiscated from Frenchmen and traitors.

The decrees discussed above were somewhat more flexible than their Chinese equivalents. The provision in the decree on debts that allowed the cancellation of pre-1945 debts if the debtors were too poor to pay could have been used to cancel virtually all of these debts and probably was so used; the best DRV history of the land reform simply states that this decree abolished all pre-1945 debts of the peasants.[23] The decree on rent reduction allowed provincial authorities to modify the 25 percent reduction of

---

21. *Su That*, 15 June 1950, in *Cuoc khang chien*, 2:391–92.

22. *Nhan Dan*, 17 November 1956, p. 2; 22 March 1957, p. 2; 24 September 1957, p. 3.

23. Tran Phuong, *Cach mang ruong dat*, p. 67.

rents in either direction. At this early stage, when the DRV had little experience with social reform, an argument could be made for flexibility, but in the long run it clearly became a vice. Although the DRV generally planned major programs ahead of time, in considerable detail, it did not always define these programs clearly in formal legislation; the legislation might be ambiguous or the policies actually followed might be at variance with the legislation. Such practices were conducive to misunderstanding among the base-level cadres and sometimes to unclear thinking among the leadership. Flexibility in regard to debts was a mistake even for the early period. The main reason the DRV had not legislated abolition of all pre-1945 debts was that it had wanted to minimize disruption of rural credit. It hoped to reassure lenders that if they made loans in the future, those loans would be repaid. But to see pre-1945 debts being canceled in practice, even though the law had not required that they be canceled, would have seemed even more ominous to lenders than having the law cancel them.

Results of DRV Agrarian Policies up to 1953

Early in 1958, the Central Land Reform Committee collected a considerable amount of data on the pattern of land transfers between 1945 and 1956. The committee found that the landlord class had lost 40–50 percent of its land during the piecemeal reforms up to 1953 (see Tables 8-4 and 8-5). This figure would presumably have been higher if only villages controlled by the Viet Minh during this period had been considered. Outright confiscation and requisitioning accounted for less than half of the transfer.

The rent-reduction decree of 1949, although essentially a reiteration of old policies, spurred a significant improvement in the enforcement of rent reduction. In Interzones III and IV, after this decree was promulgated, about 30 percent of the landlords reduced rents properly, 40 percent reduced rents but not to the extent required by the law, and only 30 percent of the landlords in areas under Viet Minh control still did not reduce rents at all. In sixteen provinces of North Vietnam, rents had been reduced properly on 147,690 *mau* (one *mau* varies from 0.36 to 0.497 hectares) of land by May 1952.[24]

Reduction of rent and interest had a significant effect on land-lord incomes. Even more important was the steep graduated tax imposed on agricultural production. The theoretical tax rate was from 6 percent to 10 percent of total agricultural income for poor peasants, from 15 percent to 20 percent for middle peasants, and from 30 percent to 50 percent for landlords. In practice, with various surcharges added, the tax rate on the rental income of the

---

24. Ibid., pp. 66–68.

landlords could approach 100 percent.[25]

The landlords had several ways of preserving their incomes. Some had enough influence in local administrations to be able to evade the rent-reduction and tax laws. Some gave nominal ownership of part of their land to their former tenants or let them cultivate it with little or no overt rent, but collected clandestine payments in various forms. The peasants were willing to give the landlords what were in effect clandestine rents—unpaid labor, "gifts," unrepaid "loans"—out of respect or fear of the landlords and because the amounts in question were often much less than the original rent. Tran Phuong cites the case of a peasant in Bac giang province who originally rented a plot of land for 470 kilos of rice per year. In 1951 the landlord reduced the rent by about 25 percent, to 350 kilos. In 1952 the landlord did not ask for any overt rent, but the peasant had to give him unpaid labor and various other things with a total value of 281 kilos. The arrangement was in the interest of the landlord because it placed him in a substantially lower tax bracket; if he had still been collecting 470 kilos per year in direct rent, he would have had to pay a real tax rate, including the surcharge for rental income, of 79 percent.[26]

During this period most landlords started farming part of their land themselves, usually the best quality land. This lowered their tax rate and made it easier to claim that they were really rich peasants. Some of them divided their land among their children. As the pressures on them grew stronger in 1951 and 1952, they became increasingly willing actually to give up part or all of their land. Many sold land. As this drove prices down to a fraction of their former level, others gave land away or allowed tenants to cultivate it rent free. This caused trouble for the land-reform cadres in later years, because even if these land transfers were in fact motivated by pressure from the DRV, they looked to the peasants like acts of landlord generosity.[27] Communist publications of 1954 to 1956 complained repeatedly about the landlords worming their way into the good graces of the peasants and thus hampering the class struggle.

As in China between 1942 and 1946, the actual degree to which wealth was redistributed depended on the political situation in a given *xa*. If the landlords were strong, they could resist rent reduction and similar programs. If the peasants were strong and ideologically conscious, they might go beyond the provisions of the rent reduction laws.[28]

Some landlords also donated land to the government, as part of the Patriotic Emulation Movement launched on a nationwide basis in

---

25. Ibid., pp. 70, 73.

26. Ibid., pp. 74–75.

27. *Nhan Dan*, 28 January 1955, p. 2.

28. Ibid., 29 November 1951, reprinted in *Cuoc khang chien*, 3:149.

June 1948. On 1 August 1948 Ho Chi Minh (perhaps anticipating the facts) said: "Landlords have emulated one another in reducing rents 50 percent, and donating land to the nation to be divided among the poor; many have donated from 500 to 2,000 acres."[29] In 1952 it was reported that "a big number of landlords have...donated hundreds of thousands of hectares of land to the government."[30] But figures collected after land reform indicate that in the area that was to become North Vietnam, very little land was donated to the government between 1945 and 1953—less than 2,000 hectares in a sample of 3,053 *xa,* which probably included most of the landlord land in North Vietnam (see Table 8-4). We could reconcile these conflicting reports by supposing that most of the donations of land took place south of the seventeenth parallel, but this does not seem very plausible. Indeed, given the regional variations in the nature of landlordism, the southern landlords (most of whom were in Nam bo) would appear less likely to have donated land to the DRV.

In 1958, the Central Land Reform Committee released statistics on the changes in landholdings and class status that had occurred between 1945 and 1953. Table 8-4 shows the amounts of land from various sources transferred to the peasants during different periods. It is derived from a table covering the whole period from 1945 to the end of land reform, which distorted data from the period 1953–56 by dividing landlord land into subcategories not appropriate for that period. The distortion is reflected in the large amount of land categorized as "remainder" in column 1 of Table 8-4, and therefore in the percentage but not the absolute figures in columns 2 and 3. Table 8-5 gives some figures for land ownership and use in a much smaller sample of 93 *xa* and 31 *thon.* The lack of data on land use before 1945 makes it impossible to judge how much communal land had already been in the hands of the peasants before 1945. The villages chosen for this sample appear to have been mainly in areas under Viet Minh control before 1953. However, it is possible that Tables 8-4 and 8-5 exaggerate the real influence of the Viet Minh in the villages in question. The Vietnamese Communists have been known to go through the procedures of confiscating land and distributing it to the peasants in areas where they did not have enough military control to back up their actions.

The DRV was fairly slow in changing people's class status to match changes in their actual economic positions. By 1953, something like 45 percent of the rural households probably had the real economic status of middle peasants. However, Table 8-5 gives a figure of only 33.6 percent because poor peasants who had risen to

---

29. Ban van dong thi dua ai quoc trung uong, *Thi dua yeu nuoc,* p. 5. This passage was omitted from Ho Chi Minh, *Selected Works,* 3:167.

30. Quoted in Fall, *The Viet-Minh Regime,* p. 119.

Table 8-4—Transfers of land from French, landlord, communal, and institutional ownership in 3,035 *xa* of North Vietnam, which underwent land reform between 1953 and 1956

Original Ownership	(1) Total, 1945 to End of Land Reform	
	Hectares	%
French	19,034	100
Landlords: total	244,451	100
—traitors (confiscated)	24,194	100
—left fallow (requisitioned)	29,753	100
—donated to the government	2,291	100
—remainder (sold, given away, scattered, purchased by the government)	188,213	100
Catholic church	15,411	100
Communal and semipublic	239,815	100
Total	518,710	100

Source: Tran Phuong, *Cach mang ruong dat*, table following p. 70.

(2) August 1945 to July 1949		(3) August 1949 to April 1953		(4) April 1953 to Beginning of Land Reform	
Hectares	%	Hectares	%	Hectares	%
11,656	61	5,323	28	1,770	9
25,522	10	75,366	31	37,074	15
8,281	34	12,228	51	2,803	12
6,812	23	14,837	50	6,317	21
a	b	a	b	a	b
10,430	6	48,301	26	26,001	14
c	d	c	d	c	d
76,127	32	108,744	45	27,372	11
113,306	22	189,434	37	73,647	14

a. Combined total for columns 2, 3, and 4 is 1,914 hectares.
b. Combined total for columns 2, 3, and 4 is 84 percent.
c. Combined total for columns 2, 3, and 4 is 7,472 hectares.
d. Combined total for columns 2, 3, and 4 is 48 percent.

Table 8-5—Changes in the number of households and amount of land owned by various classes between 1945 and 1953: 93 *xa* and 31 *thon* of North Vietnam

	Before August 1945			
	Households		Land Owned	
	Number	%	*Mau*	%
French			960	0.8
Catholic church	3	0.0	1,921	1.6
Landlords	1,985	3.3	27,338	22.5
Rich peasants	1,278	2.2	8,651	7.1
Middle peasants	18,422	32.9	36,849	30.4
Poor peasants	20,246	35.4	13,151	10.8
Laborers	11,785	20.6	1,513	1.2
Other laboring classes	3,480	6.1	911	0.7
Communal and semipublic land			29,844	24.6
Total	57,199	100%	121,138	100%

Source: Tran Phuong, *Cach mang ruong dat*, table following p. 82.
Note: Data collected after the correction of errors. All figures in *mau* equal to 0.36 hectares.

1953 (Before Land Reform)

Households		Land Owned[a]		Land Owned[b]		Land Used[c]	
Number	%	Mau	%	Mau	%	Mau	%
		1,169	1.0	1,169	1.0	398	0.3
3	0.0	1,908	1.6	1,908	1.6	772	0.6
1,311	1.8	27,071	17.3	11,593	9.5	12,201	10.0
854	1.2	5,359	4.4	5,003	4.1	5,429	4.5
23,774	33.6	42,095	34.6	45,490	37.4	55,760	45.8
30,706	43.5	19,065	15.7	23,751	19.5	36,173	29.7
10,216	14.5	2,600	2.1	4,266	3.5	7,711	6.3
3,736	5.3	973	0.8	1,061	0.9	1,466	1.2
		27,420	22.5	27,420	22.5	1,749	1.4
70,600	100%	121,660	100%	121,660	100%	121,660	100%

a. Counting land that landlords and rich peasants had scattered (illegally, according to retroactive decisions of the DRV) as still belonging to the landlords and rich peasants.

b. Counting land that landlords and rich peasants had scattered as belonging to the persons to whom it had been scattered.

c. Land that was rented out, and on which the tenants were still paying rent, is counted here as being "used" by the owner, not the tenant.

middle-peasant levels of wealth after 1949 were still officially labeled as poor peasants in 1953.[31]

Although many laborers became poor peasants and some poor peasants became middle peasants, DRV sources that might be expected to mention new rich peasants conspicuously fail to do so, and it seems unlikely that many existed. The Communists were intervening on the side of the poorest peasants more openly than during the corresponding period (1942–46) in China, and less land was going on the market to be sold to those with adequate money.

The pattern in Vietnam was similar to that in North China in two important ways. One was that large amounts of land were being transferred to the peasants before the formal land reform; in the areas covered by Table 8-4, 41 percent of the land transferred from the landlords to the peasants had been transferred by April 1953, and 56 percent was transferred before the land reform proper.[32] The other is that large amounts of land were passing into the hands of middle peasants, though probably not as much as in North China. In the areas covered by Table 8-5, 34 percent of the land scattered by landlords up to 1953, and 33 percent of the communal land, went to middle peasants.[33] Many middle peasants rose to a level where radicals in the Party would be seriously tempted to infringe upon their interests.

31. Tran Phuong, *Cach mang ruong dat*, p. 82.
32. Ibid., table following p. 70.
33. Ibid., table following p. 82.

9

The Beginning of Mass Mobilization

The DRV carried out mass mobilization for rent reduction, in most villages, between 1953 and 1955. Its economic goals were similar to those of the rent-reduction campaigns that had paved the way for land reform in southern China between 1949 and 1951. Politically it aimed not only at mobilization of the poor peasants, but also at purification of existing revolutionary organizations; it thus resembles the rectification efforts of 1947–48 in northern China.

Mass mobilization in Vietnam was more tightly and more uniformly organized than in China. Each village underwent the campaign at some particular time, supervised by a work team that reported to the central authorities of the DRV without necessarily going through the local government. The typical village in China had undergone the equivalent processes in several stages, a few months or years apart, at least some of which had been supervised by *xian* governments without the direct intervention of higher authorities.

Rectification

A major rectification campaign affecting the Lao Dong Party, the government, and other organizations began in 1952. It eventually developed into a tremendously destructive witch-hunt, but in the beginning it was fairly moderate and seemed to be primarily educational. The Party had expanded rapidly and rather carelessly between 1948 and 1950. Since 1950 there had been a period of consolidation, but the conditions of revolutionary warfare had made it very hard to give Party members coherent education and help in reforming their work styles. The same applied even more to cadres and local officials who had not yet joined the Party. In 1952, Le Van Luong[1] described Party rectification as being directed against bureaucratism, commandism, subjectivism, individualism, separation

---

1. Le Van Luong was the Party's specialist on rectification between 1952 and 1956. Because of his leftist errors he was dismissed in 1956 from the Politburo and from the chairmanship of the Party's Central Organization Committee. He finally regained membership in the Politburo in 1976.

from the masses and from reality, corruption, and waste. He blamed these problems on the fact that over 90 percent of the Party members came from peasant or petty bourgeois origins, and, despite some Party education, had not yet rid themselves of petty bourgeois thought processes. He said rectification would start at the top and proceed downward.[2]

During 1953 the rectification movement became more preoccupied with class struggle. On 1 December 1953, Ho Chi Minh told the National Assembly that in the past the leaders of the DRV had overemphasized unity with the landlords in the Anti-French Resistance and had not paid enough attention to the peasant question and the land question.[3] In February 1953, Pham Van Dong had used considerably stronger language:

> Here, I want to speak especially about the condition of our government in the rural areas. There are places where this government has nothing which entitles it...to be called a government of the people, for the people, and by the people, because it does not truly defend the interests of the peasants and does not truly serve the peasants, but on the contrary defends the interests of the landlords and serves the land-lords while it is carrying out the government's policies, such as the land policy, the agricultural taxation policy, and the corvee labor policy; because it not only does not, in the interests of the peasants, oppose the oppression and exploita-tion of the landlords, but on the contrary uses all methods to support the oppression and exploitation of the landlords; because it has become separated from the masses in the rural areas and even stands in opposition to the masses.
>
> For a long time, we have been criticizing the administrative cadres in the rural areas whose thought and work style do not have the mass standpoint and do not correctly follow the mass line. Recently, we have seen the impure organizational condition of the administrative organs in the rural areas (resistance administrative committees and people's assemblies). In many places, these organizations include a large proportion of landlords, rich peasants, and despots, or have been influ-enced by landlords, rich peasants, and despots.
>
> This is a serious situation which we must rectify.
>
> How can we rectify it? There is no method other than mobilizing the masses with a free hand and relying on the strength, awareness, and ability of the masses to rectify it.[4]

---

2. *Nhan Dan*, 3 July and 17 July 1952, reprinted in *Cuoc khang chien*, 3:294–302.

3. Text (Chinese translation) in *Yuenan minzhu gongheguo tudi fa ji qi youguan wenjian*, p. 21. This passage appears to have been mistranslated in Fall, *Ho Chi Minh on Revolution*, p. 239.

4. Pham Van Dong, *Nha nuoc dan chu nhan dan Viet-nam*, pp.

Le Van Luong said that in 1953 the rectification movement, in addition to the goals toward which it had worked in 1952, should *"especially emphasize correcting the rightist thoughts which have been expressed in the execution of the* [united] *front policy and the land policy of the Party"*[5] (emphasis in the original).

This new preoccupation with class struggle as the basis of rectification did not have to lead to the expulsion of everyone with the wrong class background. One article on rectification work in the army described how such individuals could be reeducated through group study and discussion:

> Those who came from the exploiting classes saw, comparatively deeply, their mistakes expressed in ideology and feelings, such as: despising labor, despising the peasants, protecting and feeling sympathy for the landlords, and doing things which benefited the landlords and harmed the peasants; there were people who had directly participated in exploiting and suppressing the peasants. The ideology of the exploiting classes expresses itself in work in ways such as: not working and struggling enthusiastically, having thoughts and actions harmful to the army and harmful to the revolution, etc. After undergoing a fierce ideological struggle, many of them came clearly to distinguish the progressive from the anti-progressive path, and saw clearly how evil the landlord ideology is. Therefore, they took a standpoint of being completely on the side of the peasants, and struggling to serve the interests of the peasants. There were comrades who came from the landlord class who sincerely said: "I am grateful to Chairman Ho and the Party for opening my eyes and saving me; I promise to stand fully on the side of the peasants to struggle."...
>
> Only after you have seen clearly the degree of seriousness of your own mistakes can you correct them decisively, and progress. As regards other people, you should be tolerant; decisively struggle to help them correct their mistakes, but do not be impatient or prejudiced against them.[6]

But even in the army there were people who were more concerned with attacking and humiliating people from dubious backgrounds than with reeducating them during rectification meetings. In the Party and government, the emphasis on educating and saving people was probably weaker than in the army even in 1953, and it declined over time.

66–67.

5. *Nhan Dan*, 1 March 1953, in *Cuoc khang chien*, 4:38.

6. Ibid., 6 October and 11 October 1953, reprinted in ibid., 4:128–29, 131.

Mass Mobilization Is Announced

The Fourth Plenum of the Lao Dong Party Central Committee, held from 25 to 30 January 1953, decided that the time had come for a real class struggle to weaken feudalism economically and smash it politically. A month later Pham Van Dong told a joint meeting of the Standing Committee of the DRV National Assembly and the National Committee of the Lien Viet Front:

> Only the masses can defend the interests of the masses in a thorough fashion....
> Our goal is not only to carry out the land policy in order to satisfy the economic demands of the peasants; it is [most?] important to mobilize the masses to gain political preponderance for the masses and overthrow the political preponderance of the landlords and despots....
> The work of mass mobilization will be managed by the masses and organizations of the masses, which they have established and which they trust. The people's democratic administration will not play the leading role. [7]

Provisional regulations on class demarcation were drawn up in March 1953 and published later in the year. In broad outline they resembled the decrees that had been used in China, but there were differences in details. The life-style—level of living—of a family could be taken into account in class demarcation. It was the main criterion for deciding whether people who owned land that for various reasons (such as service in the Viet Minh) they were unable to cultivate, and therefore rented out, could be classified as middle or poor peasants despite living primarily on land rent. If they did not live better than the middle peasants, they could be classified as middle peasants. In other contexts, such as distinguishing landlords from rich peasants, criteria such as level of living could be taken into account in borderline cases.

The size of the family holding relative to the average holding of small-landlord families in the area could be relevant in deciding whether to designate a family as a landlord family. Ordinarily, families that did major agricultural labor could be classified as landlords only if they rented out three times as much land as the combined total of the land they worked by their own labor and hired labor. However, if they owned twice the average small-landlord holding, or more, they could be classified as landlords if they rented out twice what they cultivated by their own labor and hired labor. Families that did not do major agricultural labor, and rented out land, but wanted to be classified as small renters rather than landlords, could be classified as small renters only if they owned less than the local average of the holdings of

---

7. Pham Van Dong, *Nha nuoc*, pp. 68, 70.

small-landlord households. This was not a very equitable way of handling these problems; using landholding per person rather than per family, and comparing the holding of a particular family to the average for the whole population of the area rather than to a category as arbitrary (and, as far as I have seen, undefined) as "small landlords," would have been better. [8]

The regulations said a considerable amount about people who did not fit into any of the main class categories, such as peddlers and salt producers. They even listed the vagabonds (*luu manh,* equivalent to the Chinese *liu mang*) as a separate class. There was also the separate category of revolutionary soldier, for which people from landlord families could qualify by having served in the Viet Minh armed forces for at least one year. The regulations also explained how to classify people whose economic status had been radically altered by the war, young people who had left home and adopted an occupation different from that of their parents, and people who had married across class lines. [9]

A revised version of these regulations, dated March 1955, seems to have adhered more closely to the principles that had been used in China. [10]

The special targets of the mass mobilization were the traitors, reactionaries, and despots. Traitors were people who served the French. Reactionaries were those who did not directly serve the French but who opposed the Resistance and the DRV. Despots were those who had power and influence that they used to oppress, rob, and beat the people. The Party announced that "people who use their positions in the [DRV] government and organizations now to do such things shall also be considered despots." [11] The Lao Dong Party linked class status closely to social and political behavior. Some DRV sources have acknowledged that a rich peasant could be a despot. [12] But during 1953 the Party at one point said that only landlords should be considered despots,

8. It also must have been confusing to have two completely different principles (total land owned and level of living) for deciding whether people who rented out land and did not labor could avoid classification as landlords, depending on whether they were seeking to be classified as small renters or middle peasants.

9. Provisional regulations on class demarcation in the rural areas, dated 5 March 1953, published in *Nhan Dan,* 1 August to 8 August 1953, made available to me through a tape recording of the text made by Dr. Ngo Vinh Long. (There is a very bad translation of these regulations in Fall, *The Viet-Minh Regime,* pp. 172–78.)

10. The text is not available, but there are excerpts and comments in Tran Phuong, *Cach mang ruong dat,* pp. 147–61. See also *Nhan Dan,* 22 March 1955, p. 3; 24 March 1955, p. 2; 11 February 1957, p. 2; 29 March 1957, p. 2; 11 April 1957, p. 2.

11. *Nhan Dan,* 16 June 1953, in *Cuoc khang chien,* 4:71.

12. Ibid., 4:70; Tran Phuong, *Cach mang ruong dat,* p. 125.

and later said that rich peasants who acted like traitors, reactionaries, or despots and who were really hated by the people should
be classified as landlords.[13]

Decree 149 SL of 12 April 1953 defined the formal goals for
which the masses were being mobilized.[14] All landlords, rich
peasants, and organizations would be made to reduce rents on land
they rented out, if they had not already done so. In general,
rents were to be 25 percent below the level that had prevailed
before 1945, not counting any special rent increases that might
have been imposed because of high tax levels during the Japanese
occupation. If the original rent had been very high, it would be
reduced to one-third of the crop. If the land were of low quality
or hard to work, the local peasant association could decide to
impose a reduction of more than 25 percent, perhaps more than 50
percent. The landlords could also be made to reduce rents by more
than the above amounts, or cancel them entirely, if crops were
damaged by natural disaster or military action. Landlords had to
refund excess rent, collected in violation of rent-reduction laws
since July 1949. They also had to pay all wages that had been
arbitrarily withheld from the peasants in the past (in practice, this
was probably directed mainly at unpaid labor the peasants had
done for landlords as a form of rent). There was to be no deposit
required when land was rented, and tenants were to be given
considerable security of tenure. If persons who rented out land
had in the past habitually rented out draft animals, houses,
gardens, and so on to their tenants, they could be compelled to go
on doing so.

All debts dating from before the August Revolution, debts owed
by peasants to traitors, and debts of soldiers and cadres who had
been killed or wounded in the service of the revolution would be
canceled. Debts could be postponed, with no interest accruing
during the postponement, if the creditor were living in the
French-occupied areas, if the debtor were a soldier or cadre of the
revolution, or if the debtor were a peasant unable to pay because
of natural disaster or enemy action. On other debts peasants owed
to the landlords before the promulgation of this decree, interest
was to be reduced to 18 percent if the debt were in money, 20
percent if in grain, and in any case the total amount repaid was
not to exceed twice the original principal. Interest reduction would
apply to debts owed to rich peasants only if these debts dated
from before 1950. Interest reduction would not apply to any debt
owed to middle or poor peasants, or to debts in connection with
commerce and industry. On any debt subject to cancellation,

---

13. Tran Phuong, *Cach mang ruong dat*, p. 125; report by
Truong Chinh to a national Party conference, November 1953,
trans. in *Yuenan minzhu*, p. 50.

14. Russian translation in Arturov, *Demokraticheskaia Respublika
V'etnam*, pp. 178–88.

postponement, or interest reduction, the creditor would have to return to the debtor any property that had been pledged as security or taken in lieu of payment. The government would not attempt to regulate interest rates on any debts contracted in the future, but would forbid fraud leading to excessive exploitation.

All land and other property belonging to Frenchmen, traitors, and reactionaries would be confiscated. The land would be distributed to landless and land-poor peasants with full ownership. The same would be done with communal land and land donated to the government. Soldiers, cadres, and the families of people who had died in the service of the revolution would have priority in the distribution of land. The amount of land given to each family would be proportional to the number of persons in the family, regardless of age.[15]

The most important change that took place in 1953 was not in the content of DRV agrarian policy but in the mass mobilization used to implement it. As in China in 1947, top leaders had ceased to trust the existing local administrations, Party branches, and peasant associations to carry out social reforms. From this point on they began sending *doi* (teams) of specially trained cadres into every *xa*. The mass-mobilization cadres made direct contact with the poor peasants by practicing the "three togethers." After they had mobilized the poorest strata in the *xa*, they could purify and reorganize all the key village organizations and then carry out the reduction and refund of rents. This campaign was only to be carried out where the proper conditions existed:

1. The military and political situation must be comparatively calm.
2. The majority of the masses must want it.
3. There must be cadres to lead it directly.

If we mobilize the masses without these three conditions having been fulfilled, the mobilization will be premature and will certainly create complications; the imperialists and feudalists will work together to counter-attack against the masses and suppress the struggle, some activist elements will become separated from the broad masses and will advance in an isolated fashion, and policy will not be followed correctly; reactionary and despotic landlords may take the opportunity to set up, or have their lackeys set up, peasant mobilization organizations to sabotage policy.[16]

---

15. The DRV returned to a policy of temporary allocation soon after, on the ground that the land reform proper was about to start, so it would be better to postpone any final division of land until then. In April, the DRV may still have been planning to put off land reform until after the end of the war. Tran Phuong, *Cach mang ruong dat*, pp. 98, 137.

16. *Nhan Dan*, 6 June 1953, reprinted in *Cuoc khang chien*,

The mass mobilization was usually split into four steps in each *xa*.[17] During the first, the cadres publicized government policy at various meetings for the population as a whole and for particular social groups. Then they went down among the masses to mobilize them and find out the real situation in the *xa*. A cadre would go into a poor peasant's or laborer's home to live together, eat together, and work together with the peasant. By sharing the peasants' poverty and asking about their sufferings (*tham ngheo hoi kho*), the cadres would try to win their trust and to convince them that the landlords, not fate, had caused their sufferings and that it was both necessary and possible to attack the landlords in order to win a decent life. A peasant who was ideologically mobilized in this manner was called a root (*re*). Once the root had been mobilized he or she would go to mobilize other peasants, who were called beads (*chuoi*). The whole process was called "getting roots and stringing beads" (*bat re xau chuoi*). Actual accounts of mass mobilization mention roots much more often then beads; the work of "stringing beads" may not have been emphasized in practice as much as it should have been.

The second step was to open a *xa* peasants' assembly and mobilize the masses to struggle against and overthrow the traitors, reactionaries, and despots. The third step was to carry out rent and interest reduction, rent refund, and the collection of payment for unpaid labor the peasants had done for the landlords. The fourth step involved strengthening the various key organizations in each *xa*, reviewing accomplishments, and pushing production. The rectification of organizations began during the first step and continued through all four steps.

The roots, who were among the most important elements in the whole program, had to be poor peasants or agricultural laborers with reasonably good personal histories. The first beads chosen in a given *xa* also had to be poor peasants and laborers. It was only after the mobilization of the poor was well advanced that middle peasants began to be chosen as beads, and a peasant association could be organized, or reorganized if it had already existed.

After the roots and some of the beads had been trained to some extent they were called *cot can*, or "backbone elements."[18] The *cot can* were not quite equivalent to the activists (*jiji fenzi*) of the Chinese land reform; their role seems to have been more formal, intermediate between the role of activists and that of local cadres in China.

In old liberated areas rent refunds were calculated from July 1949. In areas liberated between 1949 and 1953, rent refunds were

---

4:61–62.

17. There could be variations in the arrangement of steps summarized below; see *Nhan Dan*, 10 August 1954, p. 2.

18. The Chinese equivalent of this term, *gugan*, was hardly ever used in this sense during land reform in China.

calculated from the date of liberation. In areas liberated after 1953, rent refunds, when they eventually occurred, were calculated from April 1953.[19] In practice the size of the rent refund could be modified according to the type of person who owed it; rich peasants and small landlords were treated more leniently than large landlords and despots. The peasant association first calculated how much each landlord or rich peasant owed and then decided on the basis of his means how much he would actually have to pay.[20]

In the first wave of the mass mobilization for rent reduction, most of the rent refund actually went to the peasants who had originally paid the rent in question. Only as much of the rent refund as these people could be "persuaded" to forego, plus any property confiscated from traitors, reactionaries, and despots, was available for distribution on the basis of need. In later waves most of the rent refund was distributed according to need, and only 10–20 percent was earmarked specifically for the peasants who had originally paid the excessively high rents.[21]

The nominal figure of 25 percent for the reduction in rent was widely ignored; rents were either reduced much more or eliminated altogether. The strongest evidence here is negative; in articles about villages that had completed the rent reduction, the question of rent payments was seldom mentioned. In particular, *Nhan Dan* conspicuously failed to complain about villages where the landlords still had not reduced rents by 25 percent after the mass mobilization for rent reduction. The results of a campaign of this sort vary a great deal from village to village. The only way the DRV could have obtained a reduction of at least 25 percent in every village would have been to reduce rents by much more than 25 percent in most villages. An article on one *xa* in Thai nguyen province indicated clearly that the reduction was by more than 25 percent, and said that after rent reduction rents amounted to only 10 percent of the crop.[22] Tran Phuong states that the determination of the legal reduced rates for the payment of rent and interest was not a problem, because after the mass mobilization the landlords did not actually collect rent or interest.[23]

---

19. Tran Phuong, *Cach mang ruong dat*, p. 132. In the Hanoi suburbs, rent refunds were calculated from July 1954; *Nhan Dan*, 17 January 1956, p. 2.

20. Tran Phuong, *Cach mang ruong dat*, pp. 133–35.

21. Ibid., pp. 136–37.

22. *Nhan Dan*, 8 February 1955, p. 3.

23. Tran Phuong, *Cach mang ruong dat*, pp. 135–36. A peasant in Bac giang told a Russian visitor in 1955 that he had originally paid a rent of two-thirds of his crop. In 1951 he had reduced this to one-third, and the landlord had not dared to protest. After this, the peasant had paid no rent. Sergeyeva, "Liberated Vietnam," p. 23. This passage was omitted when portions of the

Each mass-mobilization *doi* was part of a larger group called a *doan* (brigade), which was assigned a fairly large number of *xa* in a given wave of mass mobilization. One *doan* seldom if ever was responsible for as much as one whole province, but one might cover portions of two provinces. This may have been a device to keep the *doan* from falling too much under the control of provincial administrations.

Implementation

In all, there were eight consecutive waves of mass mobilization for rent reduction, covering 1,875 *xa*[24] with 1,106,955 hectares of cultivated land and a population of about 7,800,000. The campaign obtained 31,110 tons of rice as rent refunds, and confiscated 15,875 hectares of land from traitors, reactionaries, and despots, as well as 8,246 cattle (mostly buffalo and oxen) and various other property.

Wave One (the experimental wave) of mass mobilization took place in twenty-two *xa* (later split into fifty-six) of Thai nguyen, Phu tho, and Thanh hoa provinces. It started in April 1953 and lasted until August. The movement was credited with having uncovered a very serious situation in the Lao Dong Party. The class composition of the Party organization in these *xa* is reported to have been: landlords, 13.5 percent; rich peasants, 15 percent; middle peasants, 61.4 percent; poor peasants, 3.7 percent; and petit bourgeois, 3.5 percent. After the mass mobilization the proportions were: poor peasants and laborers, 53 percent; middle peasants, 44 percent; and petit bourgeois, 3 percent.[25]

Wave One followed what was later considered to have been an excessively radical policy. From ten to fifteen people per *xa* were branded as despots and subjected to mass-struggle meetings. The settling of accounts in regard to economic exploitation had been too broad and had attacked a good many rich peasants. The Party found the slogan, "Rely fully on the poor peasants and laborers, unite with the middle peasants, and neutralize the rich peasants," to have been unsatisfactory; it had made the rich peasants nervous and had not effectively weaned them away from the landlords. In

---

article were translated into Vietnamese and published in *Thoi Moi*, 9 August 1955, p. 3.

24. *Warning*: Many of these *xa* were divided into smaller ones after mass mobilization. When comparing the area covered by mass mobilization for rent reduction with the area covered by the land reform proper, use figures for the population covered rather than the number of *xa*.

25. *Nhan Dan*, 6 October 1953, in *Cuoc khang chien*, 4:124–25. I have little confidence in these figures on the class composition of the Party; see Chapters 11–13.

practice, some mass-mobilization cadres must have acted fairly threatening toward the well-to-do middle peasants; this is the most plausible reason why seventy middle peasants of Dong bam *xa*, in Thai nguyen, would have "donated" about 29 hectares of land to the poor peasants and laborers. When higher authorities found out about this, they ordered that the land be returned.[26]

In August, the Politburo moderated the mass-mobilization program in a number of ways. Fewer people were to be branded as despots. The despots were to be separated into first-, second-, and third-class despots, and only the first-class despots were to be subjected to full-scale struggle meetings. The slogan, "Neutralize the rich peasants," was changed to "Ally with the rich peasants." Resistance landlords, ordinary landlords (nondespots), and rich peasants would no longer be asked to pay compensation for unpaid labor the peasants had done for them in the past. These changes had a real effect; the fruits of the struggle available for distribution to the peasants in later waves declined enough to require changes in the system of distribution (see p. 175).[27]

As has been noted, the slogan, "Ally with the rich peasants," was probably just a very emphatic way of saying that they were not to be treated as outright enemies. For the comparative study of Communism it is interesting, because it represents the end point of a long series of improvements in the treatment of the rich peasants in various countries. Stalin had dealt with the rich peasants (kulaks) by mass deportations to Siberia. Successive land-reform laws in China had first ordered that the rich peasants be reduced to below the level of the poor peasants (1931), then that they be reduced to equality (1947), and then that they be allowed to remain above the level of the poor peasants while being politically neutralized (1950). The Japanese Communist Party adopted something very close to the Vietnamese formula in 1956, saying that the peasant movement in Japan should base itself on the poor peasants, unite with the middle peasants, and draw in the rich peasants.[28]

Wave Two of the mass mobilization started soon after the end of Wave One and covered 163 *xa* with a population of over 770,000. Thanks to the new and less radical program, it was completed quite rapidly. Waves Three and Four lasted through July of 1954 and covered 443 *xa*.[29]

---

26. Tran Phuong, *Cach mang ruong dat*, pp. 98-99, 123–25.

27. Ibid., pp. 98–99, 123–25, 136–37.

28. Dore, *Land Reform in Japan*, p. 463.

29. *Nhan Dan*, 16 February 1954, p. 2, 1 April 1954, p. 2, 26 April 1954, p. 1, 1 August 1954, p. 2, 13 August 1954, p. 2, and 4 September 1954, p. 2. *Renmin ribao*, 30 June 1954, p. 4, and 2 September 1954, p. 3.

10

The Land Reform Proper, 1953–1956

In North Vietnam the land reform proper lasted slightly less than three years. It started out on a very small scale but spread over steadily wider areas. Successive waves of land reform from December 1953 to December 1955 covered about half the country; the remaining half was covered in a final massive wave in 1956. As the program accelerated, it also became more radical; by late 1955 and early 1956 leftist excesses and leftist paranoia, especially in the form of purges within the revolutionary movement, had reached astonishing levels.

The Land Reform Law

The DRV National Assembly approved a Land Reform Law for Vietnam on 4 December 1953.[1] It set out three methods for taking land from the landlords. Confiscation (*tich thu*) was reserved for the worst enemies of the regime and of the masses. Requisitioning (*trung thu*) was substantively the same, but it constituted a public acknowledgment that the person so treated was not among the worst enemies. Government purchase (*trung mua*) was the most desirable from the landlord's point of view, less for the actual compensation than for the symbolic statement that the man whose land was purchased was not accused of major crimes. The value of the land was fixed at one year's crop,[2] and payment was by ten-year, 1.5 percent bonds of dubious value. The true value of the compensation is shown by the fact that the DRV felt it was doing a landlord a favor if it permitted him to donate his land to the peasants and thus win moral credit, rather than have it

---

1. "Loi sur la reforme agraire," in Le Chau, *Le Viet Nam social-iste*, pp. 393–402. For details on the debates over preliminary drafts of this law, see White, "Agrarian Reform and National Liberation in the Vietnamese Revolution, 1920–1957," pp. 204–16.

2. Actual market values of land before the revolution had been from three to ten times the value of a year's crop. In the early 1950s DRV social reforms drove market prices down to between two and five years' crop and occasionally as low as one year's. Tran Phuong, *Cach mang ruong dat*, p. 77.

"purchased." When people who had been wrongly classified as landlords were reclassified, and the question of compensating them for the land they had lost arose, the government did not suggest that they had already been compensated through government purchase.

Traitorous, reactionary, and despotic landlords were to have their land, livestock, agricultural tools, surplus food stocks, and surplus housing confiscated or requisitioned. Progressive personalities, landlords who had participated in the Anti-French Resistance, and ordinary landlords were to have the land actually in their possession purchased;[3] their livestock and tools were also to be purchased, at local market values, with bonds. These landlords' other goods were not to be touched. The land of absentee landlords was usually to be treated the same as if they were living in the villages. If a landlord had gone to live in the French zone, this was not to be treated as automatic proof that he was a traitor. All communal land, semipublic land, and land owned by religious institutions was to be requisitioned or purchased. All land left uncultivated for over two years without a valid reason was to be requisitioned. Land owned by the landlords was to be requisitioned if left uncultivated for any length of time for any reason. All debts that working peasants had owed to the landlords were canceled.

The Land Reform Law said clearly that rich peasants as well as middle peasants should be left untouched, but the Provisional Decisions for the Execution of the Land Reform Law said: "In general, do not touch the land rented out by rich peasants. But in areas where the landlords are few and small, and the rich peasants are many and large, the land rented out by those rich peasants who rent out a lot of land shall be purchased."[4] The official history of the land reform says simply that the Party decided not to touch the land of the rich peasants "except for the portion which they exploited by feudal means"[5] (i.e., rented out).

Small amounts of land rented out by people unable to farm it because of physical disability, or because they were busy with some other occupation or working with the Resistance, were not to be taken.

Some of the land affected by the land reform, notably coffee and rubber plantations, railroad rights of way, temples, forests, canals, and dikes, would remain in the hands of the state. Some land was to be kept by *xa* authorities to be given later to local

---

3. Sergeyeva, "Liberated Vietnam," p. 21 (based on a visit to Vietnam around May 1955) says that the land of ordinary landlords was requisitioned, not purchased.

4. The exact date is unavailable, but it was probably June 1954; quoted in *Nhan Dan*, 23 May 1956, p. 2.

5. Tran Phuong, *Cach mang ruong dat*, p. 144; see also *Nhan Dan*, 23 December 1955, p. 2.

citizens who had not been in their home villages at the time of the reform (especially Viet Minh soldiers) and to provide for government offices, schools, etc. The rest was to be distributed without payment to local peasants and sometimes to other categories of needy people, with special priority for the families of those who had died for the fatherland, revolutionary fighters, and war wounded.

Peasants serving in the French puppet army were to be assigned land in their home villages, which would be managed by the *xa* resistance administrative committee or peasant association until they returned home to claim it. "Progressive personalities," resistance landlords, and ordinary landlords were supposed to be given shares of land approximately equal to those being given to the peasants (in reality they were given much less). Progressive personalities and resistance landlords were supposed to get special consideration. Traitors, reactionaries, and despots, sentenced to less than five years' imprisonment, would get land; those sentenced to more than five years would get nothing, but their families would still get land.

Land-reform committees were to be set up at the national, regional, and provincial levels. In each *xa*, the council of peasant delegates and the executive committee of the peasant association would manage the land reform.[6]

The local average landholding per capita was to be used as a norm in land distribution. This was supposed to mean that in dealing with land that under the law might or might not be taken from the current owner, such as land that had been scattered by landlords to middle peasants in the years before land reform, the policy to be followed was to take enough land so that, after redistribution, the poor peasants would end up with landholdings that did not fall far short of the average for the whole rural population of the area.[7]

This was a very dangerous policy and must have been among the major causes of errors and illegalities in the later stages of the land reform. Chinese land policies of 1947 had attempted to bring the landholdings of the poor up to the average for the whole rural population and had accepted (in however hesitant a fashion) that

---

6. Provincial land-reform committees, councils of peasant delegates, and peasant-association executive committees were not mentioned as often as one would expect in actual accounts of land reform; much of the power that should have been exercised by these groups was taken over by representatives of the central authorities. In some provinces, provincial land-reform committees do not seem to have been established at all. *Thoi Moi*, 19 December 1956, p. 1.

7. Tran Phuong, *Cach mang ruong dat*, p. 177. I am indebted to Christine White, who noticed that this passage was more important than I had at first realized.

this would require major inroads into the holdings not only of the rich peasants but even of the middle peasants. The Chinese policy of 1950 had given absolute protection to the middle peasants and partial protection to the rich peasants, and had accepted that this would mean leaving many of the poor well below the average level. The Vietnamese were trying to have it all ways. The poor were supposed be raised almost to the average for all classes. The landlords were supposed to be left with about as much as the poor were getting. At the same time, even if all borderline cases were decided in favor of the poor, the law required that many middle and rich peasants be left with significantly more than the average landholding. Unfortunately, it is inherent in the nature of an average that if some people have more than the average amount of land, some others must have less. Some class had to end up with less land than land-reform policy specified. Given the leftist atmosphere in which most of the campaign was conducted, the poor were not likely to be the ones whose rights were slighted. Under the resulting pressures, people who should have been classified as middle peasants or small renters were classified as landlords and rich peasants so their land could be taken, and the amount of land the landlords were allowed to retain was much less than it should have been under the law.

Truong Chinh, general secretary of the Lao Dong Party, delivered a report amplifying and explaining the Land Reform Law to a national Party conference held from 14 to 23 November 1953.[8] He was quite critical of the past actions of the Party; it had delayed too long in starting a serious rent reduction. When it had begun policies like rent reduction, it had not recognized that they had to involve a bitter class struggle; it had tried to work in a bureaucratic and commandist fashion and had not therefore been very successful.

He was very hostile toward the bulk of the landlords, but he emphasized that the rich-peasant economy was to be left alone; rich peasants should still be allowed to hire laborers. This would isolate the landlords and ease the minds of the middle peasants. A few rich peasants, who had been extremely traitorous or had viciously oppressed the laboring peasants, should be considered as landlords.

He said that people should no longer be demarcated according to the class status they had held before the August Revolution; changes in each person's economic circumstances and way of life up to December 1953 should be taken into account.

Firm central control was vital. No area was to carry out land reform without orders from above; a strict schedule should be maintained. When enough trained cadres were available, some areas would be able to proceed directly to land reform without going

---

8. Referred to hereafter as the Truong Chinh Report; Chinese translation in *Yuenan minzhu*, pp. 32–88.

through a separate mass mobilization for rent reduction. (These statements do not recognize that development in the villages might have to be gradual and uneven; such impatience would later cause much trouble in the land reform.) Truong Chinh mentioned that Interzone V and Nam bo were not ready to begin land reform and that the program might have to be modified somewhat to suit the special conditions of Nam bo.

The Hanoi newspapers *Nhan Dan* and *Thoi Moi* are the most important sources for a study of the DRV land reform. They were not as good as the Chinese newspapers had been between 1950 and 1953. Vietnam was a smaller country and had a better developed system for nonpublic communications; leaders were not forced to describe their policies accurately in the press in order to convey them to the people who would implement them. Furthermore, during the land reform, neither the Party leaders nor the people who wrote for the newspapers had a very good understanding of what was really going on in the countryside. The best information we have is in their retrospective analyses, written several months after the land reform ended.

Nhan Dan was the Party organ; it had begun publication in the mountains of the Viet Bac in 1951. It devoted considerable attention to land reform both during and after the campaign. *Thoi Moi* was addressed primarily to the bourgeoisie and petite bourgeoisie of Hanoi and Haiphong. It had hardly any coverage of land reform up to about the middle of 1955 and relatively little from then until the end of the campaign. However, its taste for sensationalism did lead it to say more than *Nhan Dan* about executions of landlords, and about espionage and sabotage carried out by agents of Saigon, France, and the United States. In 1957, after the land reform was over, *Thoi Moi* published some extremely valuable accounts of the errors that had been committed during land reform and the efforts that were being made to correct them.

The land reform was carried out in waves, like the rent reduction. The organizational pattern of *doi* and *doan* was the same.[9] However, there was a greater impression of haste in the implementation of land reform. Rent reduction in 1,875 *xa* was spread over eight waves; land reform in 3,314 *xa* was completed in six waves. Each wave of land reform, in turn, affected more *xa* and a larger population than all previous waves put together.

In each *xa*, the land reform was divided into steps; the standard grouping listed four. The first was publicizing land-reform policy, finding roots, and investigating the situation. The second was demarcating classes. The third was confiscating, requisitioning, and purchasing the landlords' land and goods and distributing them to the peasants. The fourth was reviewing and summing

---

9. Late in the land reform there were occasional references to a subdivision of the *doan*, containing several *doi*, called a *cum*.

Figure 10-1—Rent reduction and land reform, 1953–1956

 Land Reform

 Rent reduction but not land reform

Source: *Nhan Dan*, 20 July 1956, p. 2

Figure 10-2—Administrative boundaries at the time of land reform

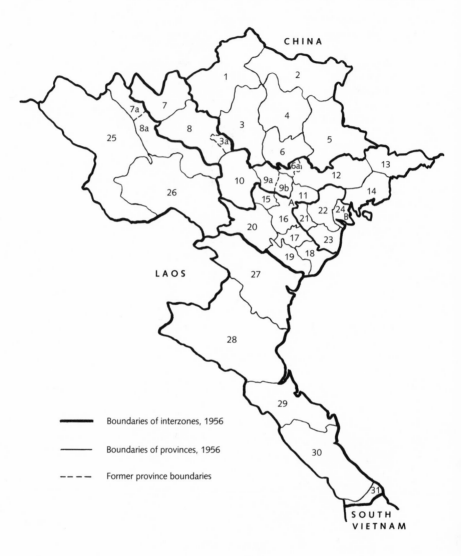

Viet Bac Autonomous Region, 1956
1 *Ha giang*   4 *Bac kan*
2 *Cao bang*   5 *Lang son*
3 *Tuyen quang*   6 Thai nguyen

Areas that do not seem to have been in any interzone in 1956
A   Hanoi (exact boundaries not shown)
B   Haiphong (exact boundaries not shown)
3a *(transferred from Tuyen quang to Yen bay)*[1]
6a *(transferred from Thai nguyen to Bac giang)*[1]
7   *Lao kay*[2]
8   *Yen bay*[2]
9a (the former Vinh yen)   \
                               Vinh phuc[1]
9b (the former Phuc yen)   /
10 Phu tho[1] [2]
11 Bac ninh[1]
12 Bac giang[1]
13 *Hai ninh*[1]
14 Hong Quang Zone[2]

Interzone III, 1956
15 Son tay   18 Nam dinh
16 Ha dong   19 Ninh binh
17 Ha nam   20 *Hoa binh*

Left Bank (Inter-)Zone, formerly part of Interzone III
21 Hung yen   23 Thai binh
22 Hai duong   24 Kien an

Thai-Meo Autonomous Region
7a *(formerly part of Lao kay)*
8a *(formerly part of Yen bay)*
25 *Lai Chau*
26 *Son la*

Interzone IV
27 Thanh hoa
28 Nghe an
29 Ha tinh
30 Quang binh
31 Vinh linh Zone (formerly part of Quang tri)

Note: Areas listed in italics were not involved in land reform.

[1] Formerly part of the Viet Bac Interzone.
[2] Formerly part of Interzone III?

Table 10-1—The number of *xa* undergoing land reform in each province, by waves

	Experimental	Wave 1	Wave 2
Viet Bac Interzone			
Thai nguyen	6	47	22
Phu tho[a]			100
Bac giang[a]			22
Vinh phuc[a]			
Bac ninh[a]			
Left Bank Interzone			
Hai duong			
Hung yen			
Thai binh			
Kien an			
Interzone III			
Son tay			
Ha nam			
Ninh binh			
Ha dong			
Nam dinh			
Interzone IV			
Thanh hoa		6	66
Nghe an			
Ha tinh			
Quang binh			
Vinh linh Zone			
Other units			
Hanoi			
Haiphong			
Hong Quang Zone			

Source: Tran Phuong, *Cach mang ruong dat*, pp. 107–8.
a. These four provinces had been part of the Viet Bac, but by the end of the land reform all of them (except for Huu lung *huyen*

Wave 3	Wave 4	Wave 5	Total
			75
106	17		223
84	16		122
65	111		176
	60	86	146
		217	217
		149	149
		294	294
		85	85
22	71		93
	98		98
	47	45	92
		163	163
		171	171
115	207	19	413
74	5	250	329
	227	6	233
		118	118
		21	21
		47	47
		9	9
		40	40

of Bac giang) had been removed. They were not thereafter part of any interzone; they were controlled directly by Hanoi. See *Thoi Moi*, 26 October 1955, p. 1, and 15 June 1956, p. 4.

Table 10-2—Results of land reform in North Vietnam, by waves

	Experimental	Wave 1	Wave 2
Total number of *xa*	6	53	210
Population (thousands)	11[a]	110[a]	481[a]
Hectares expropriated[c]	939[a]	10,664[a]	32,939[a]
Land expropriated per person[e]	87	97	69

a. *Nhan Dan*, 20 July 1956, p. 2.
b. *Nhan Dan*, 10 October 1956, p. 2.
c. These figures are carelessly discussed in some DRV sources as if they included only land taken from the landlords, but in fact they must also include communal land, etc. See Table 8-4.
d. There were 1,571,873 hectares of cultivated land in these *xa* (*Nhan Dan*, 10 October 1956, p. 2), so the figure given here for

Wave 3	Wave 4	Wave 5	Total
466	859	1,720	3,314
1,207[a]	2,564[a]	6,142[ab]	10,514[b]
86,738[a]	183,858[a]	387,406[ab]	702,544[bd]
72	72	63	67

the amount expropriated is 44.7 percent of the total.

e. Square meters expropriated, divided by total population. The official figures for the size of the plots of land expropriated in the last waves of land reform tended to be inflated, so the decline in the ratio of land expropriated to total population, as we look from the earlier to the later waves, was probably greater in reality than it appears in this table.

up.[10] The work of purifying and strengthening the major organizations in the *xa*—the *chi bo* of the Lao Dong Party itself, the
peasant association, the militia, and the (resistance) administrative
committee—was spread over all four steps, especially the last. In
the later waves, when land reform was carried out in some *xa* that
had not previously undergone mass mobilization for rent reduction,
some of the tasks of rent reduction were included in the early
steps of land reform.

The Experimental Wave of Land Reform

The DRV carried out land reform between December 1953 and
March 1954 in six *xa* of Dai tu *huyen*, Thai nguyen province,
which had undergone rent reduction earlier in 1953.[11] This was a
comparatively remote region of small villages. Much of the Vietnamese population there had only moved up from the lowlands in
recent decades; Tan thai *xa,* for instance, had been settled in the
1890s by peasants fleeing from the chaos surrounding the French
conquest. Dai tu had a relatively large number of big landlords,
but otherwise the area did not provide easy conditions for land
reform. The Tho minority group was not on good terms with the
Vietnamese, and there may also have been difficulties involving the
Catholic minority among the Vietnamese.[12]

One hundred forty-five cadres were sent into these six *xa* to
mobilize the masses. Where the rent reduction had classified an
average of six households as landlords in each of these *xa*, the
land reform found an average of sixteen per *xa*; this would have
been 3.5–4 percent of the households, and 4.5–5 percent of the
population. This was not uniform, however; there was considerable
variation between *xa*. The land-reform cadres reported that landlord infiltration of key village organizations had been a serious
problem.[13] Several years afterward, the government decided that
too many people had been classified as landlords in the Experimental Wave and that the land-reform cadres had been prejudiced
against the village organizations. Articles in *Nhan Dan* early in
1954 emphasized the danger of rightist more than leftist errors and
criticized mass-mobilization cadres who seemed too friendly toward

---

10. Tran Phuong, *Cach mang ruong dat*, p. 145. This numbering
scheme could be varied. Confiscation and distribution could be
treated as two steps, leading to a total of five; *Nhan Dan,* 7
August 1954, p. 2; 2 August 1955, p. 3.

11. These *xa* had not necessarily been involved in Wave One of
the rent reduction; see *Renmin ribao*, 13 July 1954, p. 3.

12. Ibid; Henry, *Economie agricole*, p. 100; Burchett, *North of
the Seventeenth Parallel*, p. 112.

13. See below, p. 220; Burchett, *Seventeenth Parallel*, pp. 103,
105–6.

the landlords and rich peasants, but this was not because the cadres were in fact committing mainly rightist errors; it was because leftist errors were going unrecognized.[14]

Land-Reform Wave One

The first full wave of land reform was carried out from May to September 1954, in 53 *xa* of Thai nguyen and Thanh hoa.[15] Rent-reduction Wave Five, at about the same time, covered between 195 and 200 *xa* of Ha tinh, Phu tho, Thanh hoa, Tuyen quang, Yen bay, Vinh phuc, Cao bang, Bac kan, and Lang son provinces, with a population of 637,359. In this period, *Nhan Dan* criticized leftist slightly more than rightist errors. Two articles criticized cadres who were prejudiced against all old organizations at the village level. However, "relying on old organizations" was also held to be a mistake. The Central Committee attacked the attitude of "better left than right," but this attack did not have an adequate impact at the local level. Tran Phuong gives the impression that leftist errors actually became slightly worse in this period than at the beginning of 1954.[16]

The Land Reform Law had called for creation of a Central Land Reform Committee, but it did not hold its first formal meeting until June 1954. Pham Van Dong, vice-president of the DRV, became chairman; the three vice chairmen were Lao Dong Party General Secretary Truong Chinh, Minister of Agriculture Nghiem Xuan Yem, and Vice-Minister of Agriculture Ho Viet Thang. The committee passed provisional regulations on the demarcation of classes and on the implementation of the Land Reform Law.

At about this time the DRV issued several decisions affecting areas that had not yet undergone land reform. The government guaranteed that whoever planted a crop would get to harvest it; this was to encourage an adequate application of labor, fertilizer, etc., by people who feared that the land they farmed (their own or rented) was about to be expropriated. Secondary crops were freed from agricultural taxes to encourage diversification of production. Finally, the government ordered that hired laborers be paid an adequate wage and not be fired arbitrarily.[17] This last

---

14. *Nhan Dan*, 26 February 1954, p. 2, and 1 April 1954, p. 2; Tran Phuong, *Cach mang ruong dat*, p. 103.

15. Some of these *xa* were probably transferred from Thai nguyen to Bac giang soon after.

16. *Nhan Dan*, 10 August 1954, p. 2; 13 August 1954, p. 2. The latter article was written by C. B., reputedly a pseudonym of Ho Chi Minh; see Murti, *Vietnam Divided*, pp. 187–88; Tran Phuong, *Cach mang ruong dat*, p. 104.

17. *Renmin ribao*, 6 July 1954, p. 4, citing *Nhan Dan*, 30 June 1954.

item, though it was natural considering the spirit of the time, was probably a mistake. The labor shortage created by wartime conditions and the Viet Minh distribution of land to some former agricultural laborers, plus the growing fear of being considered an exploiter, would have been adequate to make employers pay reasonable wages. Overt political interference in the labor market would have made people reluctant to hire laborers at all, thus lowering an already disastrously low level of production, and it must have worsened the regime's relations with the rich peasants. As a means of class struggle against the landlords, this measure was in a sense gratuitous, since the landlords were about to be ruined by the land reform. In mid 1956 the DRV recognized these problems and ordered local cadres not to interfere in the hiring of labor.[18]

The Geneva Accords

Peace agreements of 20 and 21 July 1954[19] declared a cease-fire for all of Vietnam and temporarily partitioned the country. Within 300 days, all Viet Minh armed forces were to move north of the 17th parallel and all forces of the French Union were to go to the South. From then until July 1956 the DRV was to administer North Vietnam, and the French Union (not, as is commonly supposed, the Saigon government) was to administer the South. Then general elections were to be held to choose a single government to rule all of Vietnam. An International Control Commission composed of equal numbers of representatives from Canada, India, and Poland was set up to supervise the implementation of the accords. Division at the 17th parallel gave the DRV less territory than the military situation would have entitled it to expect, but the USSR and China pushed for acceptance of the accords, and the DRV could hope to win the South soon anyway, either through the promised election or by a simple collapse of the anti-Communist forces in Saigon.

The portions of the Geneva Accords that had the greatest impact on land reform were in Article 14 of the cease-fire agreement. Section 14(c) guaranteed democratic liberties and forbade reprisals or discrimination against persons or organizations because of their activities during the war. In compliance with this clause, the Central Land Reform Committee withdrew the slogan "Overthrow the traitors and reactionaries" in September 1954. However, this formal change had only a limited effect in practice. The DRV really was prepared to forgive ordinary peasants who had fought for the French, but support for France continued to be cited in *Nhan Dan* among the major crimes of the landlord class. It is surprising that

---

18. *Nhan Dan*, 11 June 1956, p. 2.

19. Texts in *Foreign Relations of the United States, 1952–1954*, vol. 16: *The Geneva Conference*, pp. 1505–20, 1540–42.

the reports of the International Control Commission contain so little evidence of persecution directed against important French collabo- rators. The ICC teams could move with a fair degree of freedom in North Vietnam—more so than in the South—and they should have been aware of any widespread violations of the accords.[20] It is possible that the ICC teams in the North were spending much of their time investigating complaints made by the Saigon government and that landlords who had collaborated with the French were not a group with which Saigon wished to identify itself publicly by protesting when they were mistreated.

Section 14(d) of the agreement said: "From the date of entry into force of the present Agreement until the movement of troops is completed [18 May 1955], any civilians residing in a district con- trolled by one party who wish to go and live in the zone assigned to the other party shall be permitted and helped to do so by the authorities in that district."[21] Between 800,000 and 900,000 people moved from the North to the South under this clause.[22] Most of them were Catholic peasants, who went south because of social and religious ties and propaganda pressure. Whole Catholic villages moved south en masse. There was more involved than just the atheistic tendencies of Communism; the hostility between Catholic and non-Catholic Vietnamese went back more than a century. The Catholics might have been nervous about living under any govern- ment dominated by the non-Catholic majority.

The DRV had an official policy of freedom of worship. However, even when local officials obeyed this policy (which they often did not),[23] there was conflict. Catholicism was not simply a religious institution; it was a system of political, economic, and paramilitary power. The Communists were not willing to let the Catholic church retain large amounts of land or any strong influence over local administrations, much less local militias. Though they may sincerely have felt that they were demanding only that which was Caesar's, they were attacking the social institution that represented Catholi- cism in the eyes of the people. The ordinary peasants did not always understand just what was happening, but when community leaders told them that the Virgin Mary had gone to the South, they listened.

Both the United States and the Saigon government were eager to get the largest possible number of people to flee to the South. They helped spread a massive wave of rumors across North

---

20. See in particular *Sixth Interim Report of the International Commission for Supervision and Control in Vietnam*, p. 30.

21. *Foreign Relations of the United States, 1952-1954*, 16:1509.

22. Most sources say that 800,000 to 900,000 civilians moved south. However, the U.S. Operations Mission to Vietnam, *Activity Report*, p. 14, says that only about 660,000 were Vietnamese civil- ians; the rest were Frenchmen, VNA troops, etc.

23. See *Thoi Moi*, 13 December 1956, p. 1.

Vietnam. The Viet Minh was going to destroy the Catholic religion; the Viet Minh would not maintain the value of the currency; the Viet Minh had brought into Vietnam large numbers of Chinese soldiers, who were abusing the population; the United States was going to help the French and/or the Saigon government to invade the North; the United States was going to wipe out North Vietnam with atomic bombs once the anti-Communist elements had all gone south.[24]

Finally, it has been suggested that "the first and foremost reason why so many Catholics wanted to leave the North was hunger. The regions in which the Catholic population lived were extremely poor. In 1954–55 there was a famine in which thousands of people perished; there was no hope for rapid relief."[25]

Hundreds of thousands of ordinary peasants migrated southward, and the Communists were furious. It seemed to them that potentially loyal citizens were being corrupted and enticed away. The Party was not comforted by the fact that the DRV would be better off with fewer mouths to feed. Indeed, one pamphlet claimed that the United States was trying to impede national construction in North Vietnam by draining off human beings, a valuable economic resource. Those who "forced and enticed" (*cuong ep du do*)[26] people to go south were endlessly denounced. The DRV even argued that propaganda to persuade people to move south was a violation of the Geneva Accords; this was one of the very few occasions on which the DRV misrepresented the accords.[27]

The top Party leaders decided, rather reluctantly, to comply with the accords and allow the peasants to leave. They were under pressure from the International Control Commission, and for as long as they retained any hope that Vietnam might be peacefully reunified, they could not afford to defy this pressure. But even

---

24. *The Pentagon Papers*, 1:575, 579; Murti, *Vietnam Divided*, p. 83; Fall, *The Two Viet-Nams*, pp. 153–54; *Chong am-mu bat ep du do di dan cua de quoc My va be lu Ngo-dinh-Diem*, pp. 5–8, 12.

25. Maneli, *War of the Vanquished*, pp. 38–39. Maneli, who was a senior Polish member of the International Control Commission in Vietnam early in 1955, complains that other authors have not given the food shortage the emphasis it deserves. It is possible that the Vietnamese exaggerated their plight to him, hoping that he could influence potential donors of foreign aid.

26. The way this phrase was used leads one to suspect that much more enticement than force was involved. However, there do exist some DRV accounts which if true would indicate the use of genuine force; *Thoi Moi*, 6 April 1955, p. 1, and 25 June 1955, p. 1. Some of the people who had gone south later demonstrated and asked to return to the North; *New York Times*, 23 January 1955, p. 8.

27. *Chong am-mu bat ep*, pp. 17–20.

after Hanoi had reached this decision, many local officials refused to implement it. They continued to obstruct the migration, whether from a reasoned belief that people wanting to leave for the South should be delayed long enough to let them reconsider, or from a reflexive unwillingness to cooperate in any way with people who were flaunting counterrevolutionary sentiments by asking to leave the DRV.[28] To say that the people whose departures were being obstructed were distressed would be an understatement. A considerable number of them had let their land go fallow and sold their tools. Some local officials were discriminating against them in the distribution of famine relief and could be expected to treat them badly in the future.[29] They felt that they no longer had any choice but to leave.

After a few months the situation eased, and by the deadline of 18 May 1955, most of those who wanted to go south had done so. The DRV allowed an additional 4,797 people, who had been unable to get past the obstructionism of local officials before the deadline, to go south between 18 May and 20 July. The only large concentrations of people who wanted to go south but still had not been able to do so were in the provinces of Nghe an and Thanh hoa, in Interzone IV. Conflict between Catholic peasants and local officials led to bloody riots in both provinces early in 1955. It must also have been among the main reasons why tax collectors in these provinces fell well below their quotas—more so than in most other areas—when collecting land taxes during the winter of 1954–55.[30] The tension became less visible after the middle of 1955, but it would reappear in the famous riots of November 1956 in Nghe an (see Chapter 12).

Land-Reform Waves Two and Three

Land-reform Wave Two, in Thai nguyen, Phu tho, Bac giang, and Thanh hoa, lasted from October 1954 to January 1955. At about the

---

28. Maneli, *War of the Vanquished*, pp. 41–42, describes conferences in which he participated, at which top leaders of the DRV tried to persuade local officials to stop obstructing the migration. It is not likely that Maneli is portraying the DRV leaders as more reasonable than they actually were. Having defected from Poland to the West about three years before writing this, Maneli would if anything have been biased against Communist officials trying to hold in unwilling populations.

29. *Nhan Dan*, 25 July 1955, p. 2; 30 July 1955, p. 2; 1 August 1955, p. 2; *Thoi Moi*, 13 February 1955, pp. 1, 4.

30. *Fourth Interim Report of the International Commission for Supervision and Control in Vietnam*, pp. 12–14; *Thoi Moi*, 3 June 1955, pp. 1, 4; 6 June 1955, pp. 1, 4. See Moise, "Land Reform," pp. 313–15, for details on the riots of early 1955.

same time, rent-reduction Wave Six was occurring in 179 *xa*, with a population of about 710,000, in Vinh phuc, Son tay, Ha tinh, Phu tho, and perhaps Thanh hoa and Bac giang provinces. Many of these *xa* were in newly liberated areas where the organizational base of the DRV was still weak. There were more peasants who had collaborated with the French, and therefore were fearful of the DRV, than in the areas that had been long under Viet Minh control.

Land-reform Wave Three, in Thanh hoa, Phu tho, Bac giang, Vinh phuc, Son tay, and Nghe an provinces, lasted from February to June 1955. This was the first time the land reform had extended into the newly liberated areas. Rent-reduction Wave Seven started in January in 344 *xa* of Thai binh, Son tay, Ha nam, and other provinces, with a population of about 1,400,000.

There were several important changes in the land-reform program in early and mid 1955. First came a decree modifying the Land Reform Law, dated 1 March and released to the public on 20 March.[31] It incorporated decisions passed by the Politburo and the Central Land Reform Committee in September 1954. The 1954 version had restricted peasant struggle meetings; the 1955 version abolished them. The peasants would still be allowed to denounce the landlords, but only in the somewhat more formal atmosphere of a people's tribunal.

People involved both in the renting of land and in commerce or industry would have to reduce rent and refund rent, and in the land reform their land would be taken in the same way as from other landlords. But in general they would not be brought out to the villages for class demarcation, much less subjected to mass struggle. They would just have to write a declaration of what they owned and send it to the peasant association of the *xa* where they rented out land. Priests and monks who managed land rented out by religious institutions, or who rented out a little land of their own, would have to comply with DRV land policies but would not be labeled as landlords.

More land was to be taken by government purchase and less by confiscation and requisitioning. Resistance landlords, landlords whose children had become Viet Minh soldiers or cadres, and some people involved both in landlordism and in commerce or industry would be permitted to donate land to the government more easily than before, rather than having it taken from them in the normal course of the land reform.

Some further decisions concerned primarily with land reform in the newly liberated areas were passed by the Cabinet in mid May 1955 and published in late June.[32] In densely populated areas

---

31. Text published in *Nhan Dan*, 20 March 1955 (not available). See *Nhan Dan*, 22 March 1955, p. 3; 24 March 1955, p. 2.

32. Ibid., 28 June 1955, pp. 1, 4; see also Tran Phuong, *Cach mang ruong dat*, pp. 155–56.

where the average landholding was small, the land-reform cadres were advised to investigate the land situation very carefully and ask for advice from their superiors. They were not simply to say that whoever had more than three times the local average landholding was a landlord, as had been suggested by the provisional regulations for class demarcation.[33] Also, the government ordered that churches and temples be left with some land, rather than being stripped completely. The cadres were particularly warned to avoid commandism when discussing with the peasants the disposal of land owned by religious institutions. A decree on religious freedom was published in July.[34]

Such changes in legislation suggested that DRV policies were growing more moderate during 1955. However, one should not overestimate the importance of formal regulations, which were widely abused. Key provisions were sometimes misinterpreted or simply ignored. A person who did major labor 120 days per year was supposed to qualify as a laboring person, but unreasonable standards could be set as to how much work represented a full day's labor and some people could then be accused of not having done 120 full days of labor in a year. Facts could be falsified; thus land registers were altered, and some families were accused of owning more land than they actually did own. The result was that the number of households classified as landlords was at least twice what it should have been.[35]

As laws and decrees became more moderate during 1955, the actual conduct of the land-reform campaign was becoming more radical. The Seventh Plenum of the Lao Dong Party Central Committee decided in March 1955 that the implementation of the land reform had been too moderate, too rightist, although it admitted that there had also been some leftist errors. The Seventh Plenum resolved: "Struggle on two fronts, to oppose rightism and 'leftism,' but opposing rightism is basic." This attitude spurred a campaign against real and supposed rightist errors that eventually led to an immensely harmful wave of leftist excesses.

The Seventh Plenum ordered: "When opposing rightism prevent the cadres from going over to 'leftism.'"[36] This was probably quite sincere. But discussion of leftist errors in this period focused too much on such secondary issues as raising too high the official figures (used for tax assessment as well as land distribution) on the productivity of land, taking too much land by government purchase, and not making an adequate distinction between the worst landlords and those who were not so bad. The most important of the leftist errors actually being committed in this period

---

33. Probably a version issued in June 1954.

34. Text in *Nhan Dan*, 4 July 1955, p. 1.

35. Tran Phuong, *Cach mang ruong dat*, pp. 156–57; *Nhan Dan*, 13 August 1957, p. 2; 18 April 1958, p. 2.

36. *Nhan Dan* editorial, 21 June 1955, p. 1.

involved the fundamentals of the class struggle: class demarcation, the peasants' public denunciations of the landlords' exploitation and other crimes, and the expulsion of "reactionaries" from the Lao Dong Party. People who complained that these policies were becoming too radical were exposing themselves to serious criticism. A *Nhan Dan* editorial said that reports coming up from the local level told of more leftist than rightist errors, but it simply took this as evidence that the people who had written the reports were rightists. "Why do some cadres only talk of 'leftism' and not mention rightism? Because these cadres do not see or do not want to see rightism and the damage it does."[37]

The DRV was building up a dangerously oversimplified view of rural society. The poor peasants and laborers were idealized, while the landlord class was depicted as the repository of all evil. The landlords had been the main basis for French rule, and after the reestablishment of peace they had plotted frantically to obstruct DRV policies. *Nhan Dan* declared: "The more we study, the more clearly we see that all the disagreements and divisions in the rural areas are caused by the landlords."[38] Many land-reform cadres did not know what to do if they encountered a really vicious criminal who did not happen to be a landlord.[39] The overthrow of the landlords and the establishment of poor-peasant supremacy were made the most important bases (sometimes the only important bases) of politics in the villages, and people who had other concerns than these were often treated with suspicion.

This was an exaggerated form of an attitude that had been fundamental to land reform in both China and Vietnam, and the degree to which it was becoming exaggerated was not readily visible in the public policy statements of the period. Ho Viet Thang and Truong Chinh explained that land-reform cadres should not show compassion for the landlords but should mobilize the poor peasants and laborers with a free hand to launch an all-out attack on the landlords. Cadres should not worry about the peasants committing radical excesses if given a free hand; the peasants could be trusted to follow policy.[40] However, there was little startling in these statements; they could have appeared in a Chinese newspaper of 1950. Only with hindsight can we tell that the class struggle was being whipped up to a point where the cadres were classifying considerably more people as landlords, and were treating them more harshly, than had been envisaged in the laws and decrees that supposedly governed the land reform.

A more startling effect of the exclusive focus on class struggle was the forgiveness offered to peasants who had served the French. The fact that a man was a poor peasant, and thus could

---

37. Ibid.
38. *Nhan Dan*, 30 June 1955.
39. Ibid., 9 March 1956, p. 2.
40. Ibid., 6 April 1955, p. 2; 15 June 1955, p. 1.

be presumed to be inherently good, outweighed the fact that he had fought against the fatherland. High-ranking collaborators (mostly from the upper classes) were still attacked, but the peasants who had made up the bulk of what the DRV called the "puppet" army were offered not merely amnesty but complete forgiveness. *Nhan Dan* hinted at this in May 1955, saying that the DRV was working to reduce the misunderstandings between veterans of the Resistance and former soldiers of the French forces. Six thousand former puppet personnel joined peasant associations in Son Tay province. By July *Nhan Dan* was saying that some former puppet troops had been given posts in *xa* administrations; by October they were becoming chairmen of *xa* administrations. Some were probably being allowed to join the Lao Dong Party at this time; they definitely did so the following year.[41]

At the same time, service in the Resistance was being devalued. The land-reform cadres charged that the "old organizations"—peasant associations, militias, Lao Dong Party branches, and village administrations that the DRV had established during its war against the French—were unreliable and contained large numbers of reactionaries. *Nhan Dan* described not merely infiltration but outright reactionary domination of Party organizations in many areas:

> During Waves Six and Seven of the mass mobilization for rent reduction in the provinces of Bac giang, Vinh phuc, Son tay, Ha nam, Thai binh, etc., the work of rectifying the Party branches in various areas has shown that the situation in the rural Party branches is very complex. Many branches have been controlled by the landlords ever since they were established. When an area was temporarily occupied by the enemy, the imperialists and reactionaries sought every means to sabotage the Party's base. On the one hand, they tried to arrest or kill the good Party members; on the other, they had their lackeys slip into the Party and take over leadership in the branches to oppress and exploit the people and sabotage the Resistance. While these areas were still occupied, they [the lackeys] cooperated with the enemy to sabotage the revolution and massacre the people. Since peace was reestablished, they have continued to work with the imperialists to sabotage the people's peace and order and to oppose mass mobilization. In some *xa* of Bac giang, the reactionaries who had slipped into the Party branches plotted together with those outside to hoard arms and cause disturbances and acts of sabotage such as destroying railroad tracks, burning granaries, enticing or forcing people to go south, etc. During

---

41. Ibid., 25 May 1955, p. 4; 4 June 1955, p. 2; 26 July 1955, p. 2; 20 October 1955, p. 2; see also *Thoi Moi*, 29 September 1955, p. 3; 3 June 1956, p. 4; 28 July 1956, p. 3.

the mass mobilization, they sent lackeys among the ranks of the poor peasants and laborers, hoping the cadres would mistakenly choose them as roots. They misrepresent the principles of Party and government policy. They slander, attack, and murder peasants and activists. Aside from the reactionary elements and enemy lackeys who had slipped into the Party, there were some Party members who, when their areas were occupied and they were faced with the terrorism, threats, deception, and enticements of the imperialists, kept silent, ran away, or went over to the enemy. The rural Party branches described above also had many good Party members who courageously and persistently struggled against the enemy and who led the people to maintain the struggle within the enemy areas. But most of these comrades either were killed or were mobilized to work in other areas. The very small number who remained were no match for the reactionaries and could not act.[42]

This was, as the Party recognized before the end of 1956, a paranoid fantasy. Most of the people active in these Party branches at the time of the mass mobilization for rent reduction were loyal Communists. The available sources say little about the reasons for the Party's extraordinary misjudgment of its own rural membership, but we can deduce some of the causes, with a fair degree of assurance, from the situations and behavior of the people involved. The first was the united-front character of the Viet Minh. Members of all classes had been invited to join in the struggle against France, and some landlords and rich peasants had risen to leading positions. The land-reform cadres, with their overriding concern for matters of class struggle, regarded such people as enemy infiltrators within the ranks of the revolution. The belief that one's own forces contain concealed enemy agents usually arouses a violent emotional reaction and often causes an exaggeration of the actual threat; consider the events of the early 1950s in the United States. The land-reform cadres exaggerated the number of landlords and rich peasants within revolutionary organizations, and distrusted other members of these organizations because of their association with real or supposed landlords and rich peasants.

A second factor accentuating the first was that the "old organizations" of the Viet Minh in the villages posed by their very existence a problem for the class struggle. The land-reform cadres were trying to polarize the villages along class lines—to make poor-peasant status and vigorous support for the primacy of the poor peasants the key criteria for participation in politics. If a man had joined the Lao Dong Party and risen to a high position in the Resistance, then even if he were a poor peasant, he might be

---

42. *Nhan Dan,* 12 July 1955, p. 3.

reluctant to accept the notion that class status and class loyalty were the sole criteria for political legitimacy. Either pride or self-interest would lead him to continue emphasizing the importance of achievements in the nationalist struggle, a criterion under which he would outrank not only the landlords but also most of his fellow poor peasants.[43] If in addition he lacked respect for the land-reform cadres, many of whom had far less political and administrative experience than himself, and if he decided that some of the people being classified as landlords in his *xa* were not really landlords, then he might begin to appear as a serious obstacle to the conduct of the land reform. Land-reform cadres might welcome any excuse to undermine his power and prestige. They did not openly deny that accomplishments in the Resistance were praiseworthy, but they often denied that a particular Resistance organization had accomplished much, or denied credit to individuals for the accomplishments of their organizations. Many people were expelled from the "old organizations" on unfounded charges that they were reactionaries; sometimes a whole organization was simply dissolved.

It is difficult to give an exact chronology for the development of these tendencies, because almost all the information available is in retrospective analyses written after the end of the land reform. Also, the development of the errors was very uneven; it depended on local circumstances and on the attitudes of land-reform cadres in each area. Still, it is clear that suspicion of village Party branches and other "old organizations" had become fairly widespread by the middle of 1955. This problem will be discussed at greater length in Chapters 12 and 13.

The Climax: Land-Reform Waves Four and Five

The eighth and final wave of rent reduction started in June 1955 in 529 *xa*, with a total population of over 2,000,000, in Lang son, Bac giang, Bac ninh, Hung yen, Hai duong, Thai binh, and Quang binh provinces, and the Vinh linh Special Zone. Most of these *xa* were in newly liberated areas.[44]

Wave Four of the land reform was carried out from June to December 1955 in 859 *xa* of ten provinces, with a population of about 2,564,000. Wave Five covered 1,720 *xa* with a population of about 6,140,000 (see Tables 10-1 and 10-2), more than 58 percent of the total population affected by all waves of the land reform. The rigid pattern of waves, in which many areas were supposed to

---

43. Conversely, it was those poor peasants who had served the French who had the best reasons to put class over other matters, and thus they would have made a good impression on the land-reform cadres.

44. *Nhan Dan*, 18 June 1955, p. 1; 6 September 1955, p. 2; 20 September 1955, p. 2.

do land reform on the same schedule, broke down in this final wave. Tran Phuong says that Wave Four ended on 31 December 1955 and Wave Five began on 25 December, an overlap of only one week. But in fact Gia lam *huyen* of Bac ninh province, which started land reform in the first half of October, and the Hanoi suburbs, which started in November, were included in Wave Five. Hong Quang, on the other hand, did not begin land reform until late April of 1956, when the Hanoi suburbs had already finished.[45]

Leftist excesses, already serious, reached their peak during Waves Four and Five of the land reform. This was particularly true of the purge conducted within the Lao Dong Party. During Wave Five, the land-reform authorities in Bac ninh said that the landlords and bad elements had been the predominant influence in the Party at the village level before mass mobilization. A member of the executive committee of a land-reform *doan* in the Left Bank Zone is reported to have said: "100 percent of the Party members here are bad."[46]

The special regulations drawn up for land reform in the suburbs of Hanoi and Haiphong were quite moderate. In particular, they enabled some people who had some occupation outside agriculture but who also rented out some land and would have been classified as landlords under previous decrees to avoid such a classification.[47] This theoretical moderation of policy seems to have been carried out to a significant extent in practice. The same factors that acted to moderate land policy in the Peking suburbs would have applied, especially the need to reassure the urban population. Also, the immediate proximity of the national leadership may have persuaded the land-reform cadres to adhere more closely to the laws and decrees supposedly guiding the land reform than they did in other areas.

Not many landlords seem to have been executed in the suburbs. Only one such case was reported in available issues of Hanoi newspapers,[48] and it is not likely that this could have represented concealment of a large number of executions. Several executions in more distant areas were reported. The government was trying to persuade city residents that the nasty rumors they had been hearing about the excesses of land reform were false, but the suburbs formed a small enough area with good enough communications so that an attempt to understate the number of executions

---

45. Tran Phuong, *Cach mang ruong dat*, pp. 107–8; *Nhan Dan*, 16 November 1955, p. 2; 6 January 1956, p. 2; 12 May 1956, p. 1.

46. *Nhan Dan*, 4 May 1956, p. 2; 29 May 1956, p. 1.

47. Moise, "Land Reform," pp. 328–29, contains a summary drawn from *Nhan Dan*, 19 November 1955, p. 2; 24 November 1955, p. 2; 17 January 1956, p. 2; Tran Phuong, *Cach mang ruong dat*, p. 154. See also *Thoi Moi*, 25 March 1956, p. 1; 22 July 1956, p. 4.

48. *Thoi Moi*, 15 December 1955, p. 1.

there would have been ridiculous and would have served only to fan the rumors about excesses in more distant areas. Indeed the government was organizing groups of city residents, eventually totaling over 100,000 people, to go out to suburban villages and observe trials of real or supposed landlord despots.

Errors of other sorts also seem to have been less common in the suburbs than in most of North Vietnam. The strongest evidence here is negative; after the land reform was over, when the Hanoi press was filled with accounts of land-reform errors, it said rather little about the suburbs, the area in which its readers would have been most interested. But occasional accounts show that the suburbs had not been immune. Long bien *xa* was mentioned repeatedly; it was an unusually bad case and may have been the worst. This *xa* had established a good record in the Resistance, but during land reform most of the families that had participated in the Resistance came under suspicion, and several Lao Dong Party members including the *xa* Party secretary were arrested on unfounded charges. At least ten families were wrongly classified as landlords.[49] There was also a rather bizarre case in Haiphong, where some employees of the municipal electric plant were hauled out to the suburbs and wrongly classified not only as landlords but as despots and saboteurs of the revolution.[50] Possibly these people had made the mistake of trying to assert their legal rights or had allowed their behavior to show that they thought the land-reform cadres were crazy.

The Reexamination Campaign

During the Resistance, the DRV had stressed the importance of investigating major programs after they had been completed to find out how well they had been handled. After the end of the war, in its haste to complete the social and economic reconstruction of North Vietnam, the DRV had allowed investigative organs to atrophy and had transferred many of their personnel to other work. In the first half of 1956, as the leadership began to fear it did not have proper control over the way its directives were implemented, it revived the investigative organs.

The Seventh Session of the Central Land Reform Committee, in January 1956, discussed plans to reexamine the results of land reform before the end of the year in all areas where it had been carried out. Teams of cadres had already begun work in five key point *xa* of Phu tho province, and the campaign soon spread to Vinh phuc and Thanh hoa. Aside from collecting information, the reexamination cadres helped local cadres deal with any problems

---

49. Ibid., 28 October 1956, p. 2; 9 November 1956, p. 2; 2 December 1956, p. 4.

50. Ibid., 27 November 1956, p. 3.

they might be facing. They corrected some leftist errors, but they may have committed more than they corrected. They also worked on some problems that had no particular rightist or leftist character, like promoting agricultural production.[51]

In April 1956, the Lao Dong Party began a slow retreat from the radical excesses of land reform that led before the end of the year to a massive campaign for the correction of errors (see Chapter 12). It seems plausible that the reports of the cadres involved in the reexamination may have helped inform the leadership about the serious errors that were being committed, but there is no indication of this in the published record.

---

51. Ibid., 20 January 1956, p. 4; *Nhan Dan,* 30 January 1956, p. 2; 23 April 1956, p. 1; 12 May 1956, p. 1.

11

Immediate Effects of the Land Reform

There was a certain basic sense in which the land reform was a success. Vietnam had possessed a landlord class—the upper stratum of traditional village society—consisting of people who did little or no labor themselves but who lived better than the peasants by means of rents, usury, and so on. In many cases they had been extremely unpopular, abusing the peasants without mercy and relying on their economic power and the support of the colonial government to maintain control of their tenants, rather than behaving well enough to appear "legitimate" in the eyes of those below them. Vietnam had also possessed a very numerous class of poor peasants and laborers, many of whom had lived on the edge of starvation. Almost everyone who should have been classified as a landlord had been so classified and had been subjected to expropriation. Most of those who should have been classified as poor peasants had been so classified and had received much-needed assistance in the form of redistributed wealth. The influence of the landlords and rich peasants had been almost totally eliminated within the Lao Dong Party, and much reduced in the informal relations of village society. Poor peasants who had not previously participated in politics had begun to do so; at least a few were active in almost every village and a great many in some villages.

The price of these accomplishments, however, had been far higher than it needed to be. In addition to the actual landlords, many people who should not have been classified as landlords had had their property expropriated. Many of those classified as landlords had been treated with excessive severity. The number of peasants who had really become involved in political decision-making was smaller than it should have been, and it was partly counterbalanced by the number of veteran peasant cadres who had been thrown out of their positions for no valid cause.

It is difficult to measure the exact extent to which wealth had been redistributed. Table 11-1, based on data published during and immediately after land reform, has two main shortcomings. First, it does not distinguish what should have been three categories of land: land taken from the landlords during land reform, land that had actually passed out of landlord hands a few years earlier but to which the peasants did not get legal title until the land reform, and communal land, much of which had been in the hands of the peasants for generations. Thus the before and after

figures in Table 11-1 exaggerate the real change in the landholdings of the laborers, poor peasants, and middle peasants.

Second, the figures are simply inaccurate. During the land
reform, each *xa* measured the area and productivity of each plot of
land in the *xa*. These new figures served as a basis both for
redistribution of land and for the calculation of agricultural taxes.
They were distorted in many *xa* by a wildly exaggerated belief that
all social classes, and especially the landlords, had been cheating
on their taxes in past years by underreporting both the area and
the productivity of their land. If a land-reform cadre could
persuade a landlord to admit that the plots he owned were larger
than the existing land registers showed, the cadre would have
made the "accomplishments" both of having increased (on paper)
the amount of land available for distribution to the peasants and of
having uncovered another crime of the landlord class. The cadres
may also have been under pressure to exaggerate the figures so as
to get more grain taxes from the peasants in order to feed the
urban population (see below). The landlords went along because it
was safer; they could usually win more lenient treatment by
confessing and acting repentant than by arguing when accusations
were made against them. At a time when they had very few pleas-
ures, some landlords must have felt vindictive satisfaction at the
thought of the poor peasants, who were taking their land, trying
to pay four hectares' worth of taxes on three hectares of land.

The overestimation of area and productivity seems to have been
worst in the newly liberated areas of the Left Bank Zone and
Interzone III, which underwent land reform in Wave Five. In Ha
dong province the 1955 land registers had probably been reasonably accurate. The figures in these registers were raised an
average of 6 percent for land owned by poor peasants and laborers, 7–15 percent for land owned by middle peasants, 16–20
percent for land owned by rich peasants, and 30 percent or more
for land owned by landlords. In Interzone III, the figures for the
total land area were raised 5–10 percent in most *xa*. Some peasants
to whom plots were distributed with particularly inflated figures
refused to accept the land; the taxes would have been too high.[1]

The available data therefore can be taken as at best a rough
indication of the real changes in landholdings up to the end of the
land reform. Table 11-1 gives both the averages of figures for
particular areas published in *Nhan Dan* at various times during
land reform, and comprehensive figures released shortly after the
end of the campaign. It indicates the development of a fair degree
of equality in landholdings, except that the landlords ended up
with much less land than the other classes, less than they should
have retained according to the Land Reform Law. The index
numbers show more directly the degree of equality attained by the
reform; they give the holdings of each class relative to the

---

1. *Nhan Dan*, 28 November 1956, p. 2; 3 December 1956, p. 1.

holdings of the poor peasants after land reform. They show slightly more equal landholdings than those achieved after 1949 in China, except for the extraordinarily small amount of land left to the landlords. If one were to adjust the figures to compensate for the inaccuracy of the land registers at the time they were compiled, the result would probably be to reduce the index numbers for the landlords and laborers and to increase those for the middle peasants. The most surprising thing about these figures is that they show the landlords and rich peasants to have retained more land near the end of the land reform than they did in the earlier waves. Since in most respects the last waves were more radical, one would have expected that the index numbers for the landlords and rich peasants would have been lower in the late waves. If this is not a statistical fluke resulting from the small number of surveys available, it probably means that the radical excesses of Waves Four and Five were tempered with some degree of mercy. Many of the people classified as landlords in these last waves should not have been so classified, and the plots of land allowed to them had a lower productivity and a higher tax rate in actuality than they did in theory. Cadres distributing land may consciously or subconsciously have taken these things into account when deciding how many plots to give to a family labeled as land-lords.

The class categories used in these figures conceal·a wide range in actual levels of wealth; class demarcation was not carried out in a very consistent manner. When the Party spoke in generalities, the estimate that 5 percent of the rural population were landlords had an appeal based on simplicity; it still appeared occasionally even after the correction of errors had reduced very drastically the proportion of the population actually classified as landlords. During the land reform, between 4 percent and 5 percent of the rural households, or over 5 percent of the population, were proba-bly placed in that category. This proportion was considerably higher than it should have been. The land-reform cadres, and the *cot can* whom the land-reform cadres had recruited from among the local peasants, classified as landlords many people who actually belonged to other classes. The cadres and *cot can* paid excessive attention to exploitation committed in the distant past, refused to consider secondary wives and adopted children who did agricultural labor as real members of the "landlord" family and thus denied the family credit for the labor they had done,[2] or told and incited others to tell simple falsehoods about this or that person's past behavior. Substantial numbers not only of rich peasants but even

---

2. Land-reform cadres classified one secondary wife as a de facto agricultural laborer rather than as a genuine family member, and denied the family credit for her labor, even though she steadfastly refused to denounce her husband and regarded herself as his wife. *Thoi Moi*, 7 May 1957, p. 4.

Table 11-1—Some figures collected before the correction of errors on the average landholdings of different classes before and after land reform, in hectares per person

	Laborers	Poor Peasants
Before		
Nhan Dan figures, early waves[a]	.030	.065
Nhan Dan figures, late waves[b]	.008	.024
Nhan Dan figures, all waves[c]	.019	.042
Average for North Vietnam[d]	.020	.046
After		
Nhan Dan figures, early waves[a]	.152	.161
Nhan Dan figures, late waves[b]	.132	.129
Nhan Dan figures, all waves[c]	.142	.144
Average for North Vietnam[d]	.153	.143
After (index numbers)[e]		
Nhan Dan figures, early waves	94	100
Nhan Dan figures, late waves	102	100
Nhan Dan figures, all waves	99	100
Average for North Vietnam	107	100
China[f]	101	100

a. Average of figures from various areas published in *Nhan Dan* at various dates between September 1954 and July 1955; see Moise, "Land Reform," pp. 335–37.

b. Average of figures published in *Nhan Dan* between November 1955 and August 1956; see ibid.

c. Average of all figures published in *Nhan Dan*; see ibid.

d. V. Zelentsov, "Uspekhi demokraticheskoi respublike V'etnam v vosstanovlenii i razvitii narodnogo khozyaistva," p. 62, citing a

Middle Peasants	Rich Peasants	Landlords
.136	.206	.547
.103	.242	.498
.115	.228	.512
.115	.214	.650
.178	.193	.076
.163	.198	.087
.170	.196	.083
.166	.214	.101
111	120	47
126	153	67
118	136	58
116	150	71
123	163	99

report of Nguyen Duy Trinh to the DRV National Assembly, [4?] January 1957.

e. The average landholding of the poor peasants has been set at 100.

f. This is an unweighted average of those figures from Table 7-1 that represent areas that underwent land reform after 1949 in China. The index numbers in Table 7-1 were not computed on the same basis as those in this table; they have been recomputed here to make comparison possible.

of middle peasants were mistakenly classified as landlords.

A considerable number of people were categorized as "other exploiting classes." This was an illustration of the fundamental lack of respect for socialist legality that characterized the land reform in Vietnam. There is no evidence that any such category existed in any class-demarcation decree; the land-reform personnel seem to have invented it on their own. The "other exploiting classes" were mostly people who rented out small amounts of land. Such people were also classified as small renters in some cases in which they should have been designated under their other occupations: fisherman, petty trader, and so on.

Poor Peasants and Laborers

The poor peasants and laborers, 50–60 percent of the rural population, were the main beneficiaries of the land reform. Almost all the land really redistributed went to them. They also got houses, draft animals, tools, and grain.

Cot can of poor peasant and laborer origin were given political control of their villages. They were fairly numerous, although this varied from area to area; in Wave Four there were an average of forty-six *cot can* per *xa* in Bac ninh and Bac giang provinces, over seventy per *xa* in Ha nam and Son tay.[3] Ten to twenty new Party members (all or almost all *cot can*) were supposed to be recruited in an average *xa* during land reform.[4] Their position was not very secure. For one thing, the land reform had been carried out so hastily that in many *xa* the great mass of the peasants had not really been politicized. Individual poor peasants had been promoted to key positions, but they could not depend on effective, organized support from their neighbors. In addition, most of the new village leaders lacked education, organizational experience, and self-confidence. One agricultural laborer in Vinh phuc, twenty years old and apparently without political or administrative experience, was recruited as a root by the land-reform cadres and within five months was both chairman of the *xa* administration and Party secretary for the *xa*.[5] Although he may have tried hard, it seems unlikely that he performed the functions of these offices very competently. At the same time, those poor peasants who had become important in their villages during the Resistance and had been leaders for long enough to have learned how to lead had often lost influence during the land reform. The official history of the land reform commented:

We underestimated our organizations in the villages and

---

3. *Thoi Moi*, 9 November 1955, p. 4; 17 December 1955, p. 2.
4. Le Van Luong, in *Hoc Tap* 1, no. 3 (February 1956): 22.
5. *Thoi Moi*, 21 November 1955, p. 4.

overestimated the control of the landlord class; we did not clearly recognize that during the Resistance War a rather large proportion of the poor peasants and agricultural laborers had had their ideological and political consciousness raised, and that some of the [more] advanced poor peasants and laborers had participated in village organizations. As a result, during the land reform we did not emphasize strengthening and relying upon these poor peasants and laborers; we even grew suspicious of them and attacked them.[6]

Middle Peasants

The basic slogan of the land reform enjoined the poor peasants to unite with the middle peasants. Those middle peasants who did not own much land were given shares in what had been taken from the landlords. But land that they had used without having legal title, including communal land, land illegally scattered by the landlords, and perhaps some land temporarily allocated to them during the Resistance, could be taken from them. The net effect was a slight decline in the amount of land actually controlled by the middle peasants, as compared with the period immediately before land reform. They were probably still better off than they had been before the August Revolution.

Politically, the middle peasants were not in the mainstream of the land reform. No middle peasant was supposed to be chosen as a root. Some could be chosen as beads, but they were not likely to become *cot can*. The large number of new members brought into the Lao Dong Party during land reform did not include many middle peasants; they were permitted to join only under the most exacting conditions. In other village organizations, of which the most important were the *xa* administrative committee and the peasant-association executive committee, the middle peasants were supposed to be guaranteed one-third of the positions. This quota often went unfilled; there were also cases in which the same middle peasant was made a member of several organizations and then counted in the quota of each.

A significant number of middle peasants were harmed by the land reform. Some were wrongly branded as rich peasants or landlords. Others (like some poor peasants and laborers) were accused of being "connected with" landlords or reactionaries.

Rich Peasants

The official slogan of the mass mobilization was changed late in 1953 from neutralizing the rich peasants to allying with them. The

---

6. Tran Phuong, *Cach mang ruong dat*, p. 189.

Party probably did not mean this change to be taken literally; it was just a very emphatic way of saying that the rich peasants were not to be treated as enemies. Rich peasants would be permitted to continue some activities that the Communists considered exploitative, such as making loans at interest and hiring laborers to work on their land.[7] They were allowed to keep most of the land they had owned, although communal land, land that had been scattered to them by the landlords, and land that they had rented out could be taken from them.

Their political activities were restricted. They could not become members of the peasant associations, the *xa* administrative committees, the militia, or the police. They could not join labor-exchange groups. They could, however, vote and theoretically even run for office in the *xa* people's assemblies.[8] There were some sections of the Lao Dong Party apparatus in which some rich peasants who were already members were allowed to remain, but virtually all rich peasants were expelled from village-level Party branches.

Cadres in many areas infringed upon the rights of the rich peasants in various ways. They were probably encouraged to do so by Party terminology that grouped the landlords and rich peasants together as "the exploiting classes." Some cadres regarded the rich peasants in almost the same way as they did the landlords; indeed, there were cases of poor and middle peasants who got in trouble for being "connected with rich peasants."[9] The rich peasants might be forbidden to attend *xom* mass meetings or be forced to sit in a section by themselves. They might be prevented from hiring laborers or be made to pay more than the prevailing wage. Their movements might be restricted. And like members of other classes, many of them were wrongly classified as landlords.

The Landlords

Class-demarcation regulations had in general defined the landlords as people who lived by renting out land and did not do major agricultural labor. However, the regulations in fact had classified as landlords not only capitalist farmers whose land was worked by hired laborers, but even some people who worked part of their land themselves but had a very large income from exploitation. Statistics collected in some sample areas after the correction of errors indicate that the landlords had only rented out about half of their land and that 9.8 percent of the landlord households

---

7. It was not until the Sixteenth Central Committee Plenum, in April 1959, that the Party decided to restrict and progressively eliminate rich peasant exploitation.

8. Tran Phuong, *Cach mang ruong dat*, p. 144.

9. *Nhan Dan*, 23 May 1956, p. 2.

contained someone who had done major agricultural labor.[10] If one were to include the people who had been wrongly classified as landlords during land reform but were reclassified during the correction of errors, the former figure would have been still lower and the latter figure much higher. The landlords were not, then, as parasitic a class as the DRV liked to say they were.

The landlords were the main targets of the land reform. However, there was supposed to be a considerable differentiation in the treatment given to different types of landlords. Despots (at first, traitors, reactionaries, and despots) fared the worst; they will be discussed below. Ordinary landlords were supposed to be given shares of land approximately as large as those given to the peasants, so that they could reform themselves by labor. After five years, they would be eligible for a change in class status. Resistance landlords (a very small category during land reform)[11] were given better land and generally lenient treatment.

All categories of landlords were treated worse in practice than they should have been under the law. This was often done with the knowledge and consent of the leadership but without formal modification of the law. Thus *Nhan Dan* never commented on the discrepancy between decrees saying that the landlords were supposed to get about as much land as the peasants and statistics saying that they were actually getting much less. There were even cases of landlords who were reduced to working as hired laborers.[12] Under the Land Reform Law ordinary landlords should not have lost any housing; even despots should only have lost their "surplus" houses. In practice many landlords, probably a majority, were stripped of their homes. This happened particularly in the later waves of land reform. A reporter from the Soviet Union who visited Vietnam in 1955 wrote that the ordinary landlords "are allowed to retain possession of part of their homes or are moved to other quarters."[13]

During the reform, the landlords became the pariahs of village society. Many peasants did not want to associate with them, after having been deluged with accounts of real and imaginary landlord crimes. The rest knew that it was unwise to risk acquiring the label "connected with landlords." The result was an informal isolation of the landlord class. The stringency of this isolation and the

---

10. Tran Phuong, *Cach mang ruong dat*, pp. 150–51.

11. There was about one resistance landlord for every forty *xa* during Wave Three of the land reform, and about one for every six *xa* in the Left Bank Zone during Wave Five. *Thoi Moi*, 4 August 1955, p. 1; *Nhan Dan*, 23 July 1956, p. 2.

12. *Nhan Dan*, 30 September 1955, p. 2.

13. Sergeyeva, "Liberated Vietnam," p. 21; this passage was not included when portions of the article appeared in *Thoi Moi*, 9 August 1955, p. 3. See also Tran Phuong, *Cach mang ruong dat*, p. 166.

degree of open pressure the land-reform cadres applied to enforce it varied considerably. A system of formal surveillance called *quan che* was applied to some landlords. Decree 175 of 18 August 1953 had stated: "*Quan che* is the use of the government's and the people's power to punish (*xu tri*) elements who have committed crimes against the revolution and against the people [but] whose crimes do not merit imprisonment, or who have completed their terms of imprisonment but have not really mended their ways."[14]

In some areas the whole landlord class was *quan che*.[15] The peasants regulated all the activities of a person who was *quan che*. This does not seem to have gone to the point of complete house arrest, but it may have come close; even under more relaxed conditions after the end of land reform, landlords who were not *quan che* still needed a permit to leave their home *xa*.[16]

Bao vay was a severe form of house arrest involving complete isolation; the term connotes besiegement. Cadres in Thanh hoa province told David Marr that *bao vay* had been a comparatively rare punishment applied to a few families in each *huyen* who were so hated by the peasants that they would have been in danger of lynching if they had not been guarded and isolated.[17] At best, this description dodges the issues. If it had simply been a matter of protecting a despot from mob attack, he could have been put in prison. The purpose of *bao vay* was to inflict the maximum possible shame and humiliation on the victim right in his home village. Some of the people who were *bao vay* died, whether as a result of shock and shame, outright suicide, or (as has been suggested by otherwise unreliable anti-Communist propagandists) simple starvation.

The families of the landlords were not supposed to be treated as harshly as the landlords themselves. The degree of differentiation must have varied a great deal according to the feelings of local cadres. In the spring of 1956, when land-reform policy was just beginning to moderate, statements appeared in *Nhan Dan* that indicated that the children of the landlords were hardly to be treated as members of the landlord class at all. In the public schools they were to be treated the same as the other children; that they should be permitted to attend school was either stated explicitly or simply taken for granted.[18] Potentially they were a valuable human resource; a large proportion of the educated young people in the countryside came from landlord families.

---

14. Quoted in *Nhan Dan*, 30 November 1956, p. 2; see also 10 December 1956, p. 2.

15. Ibid., 30 November 1956, p. 2.

16. Cabinet decision on treatment of the landlords after land reform, *Thoi Moi*, 9 November 1956, p. 1.

17. Notes, given to me by David Marr, of his conversations with cadres in Thanh hoa province, 6 January 1975.

18. *Nhan Dan*, 11 December 1955, p. 2; 30 May 1956, p. 2; see also 18 May 1956, p. 2.

The differentiation between the landlords and their children tended to break up families. A letter to the editor of *Nhan Dan* published shortly after the end of land reform complained that cadres in many areas had not permitted the children of landlords to visit them and help them out, even if they were old or weak and were having trouble supporting themselves.[19] One son of a landlord family said that for three years he had been afraid to visit his parents for fear of being called "connected with land-lords."[20] This would have been less likely to happen in China, where the idea that staying away might enable the son to avoid being connected with landlords would have seemed rather implausible. Near the end of the reform *Nhan Dan* published advice on how people related to the landlords should treat them; it is hard to tell whether this advice was directed specifically toward Party and government personnel or toward anyone related to a landlord. *Nhan Dan* said that if people came and went visiting their landlord relatives during land reform, they could be harming both the mass struggle and themselves. After the reform was over, it would be acceptable for people whose families were resistance or ordinary landlords to visit them. The relatives of families that had been *quan che* were advised to limit themselves to writing letters rather than visiting, even after land reform.[21]

Late in 1956 the magazine *Giai Pham Mua Thu*, published by a group of Hanoi intellectuals with anti-Communist leanings, printed a poem about a land-reform cadre who was severely reprimanded for having fed and sheltered a starving orphan from a landlord family.[22] This story may have recorded a real event; there were radical excesses of various types happening in so many villages during Waves Four and Five of the land reform that almost every imaginable excess must have occurred in at least one place. It probably did not represent standard policy, even for the most radical period; the principle of lenient treatment for landlords' children does not seem to have been ignored in practice to the extent that the theoretical property rights of the landlords were. The rumors about wild leftist excesses that circulated in the cities during land reform were probably correct in broad outline, and the Lao Dong Party's denials of these rumors were definitely false. But the urban intellectuals, who had no sympathy for the fundamental principles behind land reform, were in a poor position to distinguish which of the stories to which they listened with such horror represented fundamental aspects of the campaign and which represented isolated aberrations.

---

19. Ibid., 22 September 1956, p. 3; see also 10 December 1956, p. 2.

20. Ibid., 10 December 1956, p. 2.

21. Ibid., 6 August 1956, p. 2.

22. Hoang Cam, "The Enemy's Child," trans. in Hoang Van Chi, *New Class*, pp. 120–22.

Despots and Executions

The special targets of the mass struggle were those landlords considered to be traitors, reactionaries, and despots. In the first wave of mass mobilization for rent reduction, ten to fifteen landlords per *xa* were branded as despots. The Party decided that this had been too high a number and that the struggle should concentrate on a few of the very worst individuals. In September 1953 the Politburo ordered that the total number of despots be reduced, and that only one to three individuals per *xa* (four or five in *xa* with populations over 10,000) should be branded as first-class despots and subjected to the most intense forms of mass struggle. These included prolonged public denunciation, with the despot often standing in a shallow pit to make sure he would have to look up at his accusers. The second- and third-class despots had to appear at somewhat more restrained mass meetings and attend group-indoctrination sessions, run by provincial cadres, for intensive analysis of their crimes.[23] The Central Land Reform Committee later decided that the number of despots of all types should not exceed 25 percent of the total number of landlords in a given area. However, some cadres treated the figure of 25 percent as a minimum rather than a maximum. During the whole of the mass mobilization for rent reduction, an average of 25.0 percent of the landlords are reported to have been branded as despots. There were 2.1 first-class despots per *xa*, or 8.8 percent of the landlords, and 3.8 second- and third-class despots per *xa*, or 16.2 percent of the landlords.[24] Working from these figures, and assuming that there were 5.1 persons per landlord household, we get 2.9 percent of the population classified as landlords during the mass mobilization for rent reduction. During the land reform proper, the percentage of despots in the total population would have been considerably higher, but the ratio of people classified as despots to people classified as landlords would not necessarily have increased.

The Vietnamese seem to have been more sure than the Chinese had been that there should be some people classified as despots in every area. In theory the despots were supposed to be a subcategory of the landlords, but some land-reform cadres applied the label "despot" promiscuously to anyone they considered an enemy, including (perhaps even especially) those who were well thought of by the peasants. In an extreme case we read of two sisters aged seventeen and twenty, both with good reputations in their village as strong and enthusiastic workers in the rice fields, who were assigned to do corvee labor wearing hats labeled "despot." Their father had been arrested, and the land-reform cadres were

---

23. Tran Phuong, *Cach mang ruong dat*, pp. 125–26; Burchett, *Seventeenth Parallel*, p. 116.
24. Tran Phuong, *Cach mang ruong dat*, pp. 126, 131.

presumably trying to undermine the prestige of the whole family.[25]

Probably most of the despots were only imprisoned or *quan che* as a result of the rent-reduction and land-reform campaigns, but a considerable number of them lost their lives. Most accounts published in the West have described the land reform as a blood-bath; there have been widely varying estimates of the number of people killed. The highest estimate, made by Richard Nixon, is that 500,000 were executed and another 500,000 died in slave labor camps.[26] What might be called the standard estimate, by Bernard Fall, is that about 50,000 were executed.[27] D. Gareth Porter demonstrated a few years ago that these figures were completely unfounded.[28] He discovered that various people in Saigon had been manufacturing counterfeit North Vietnamese documents and falsify-ing translations of genuine documents in order to support the idea that large numbers of people had been killed in the land reform. The documentary evidence for the bloodbath theory seems to have been spurious almost in its entirety. Thus Hoang Van Chi's book *From Colonialism to Communism*, the most influential source of the bloodbath theory, attributes the statement, "Nghe-An is the prov-ince in which...the most serious mistakes have been made, and the greatest number of Party members have been executed during Land Reform," to an issue of *Nhan Dan* that contains no passage remotely resembling this.[29] A speech by General Giap, which said that the leaders responsible for land reform "did not attach impor-tance to taking precautions against deviations [and] did not emphasize the necessity for caution and for avoiding unjust punishment (*xu tri*) of innocent people,"[30] was translated, "We made too many deviations and executed too many honest people."[31]

---

25. *Thoi Moi*, 15 February 1957, pp. 1, 3.

26. *New York Times*, 28 July 1972, p. 10.

27. Fall, *The Two Viet-Nams*, p. 156.

28. Porter, *The Myth of the Bloodbath*. Porter overreacted to some extent against the falsehoods he was refuting. His estimate of the actual land-reform death toll, lower than my own, is based partially on misunderstanding of the available data. See Moise, "Land Reform," pp. 361–62.

29. Hoang Van Chi, *From Colonialism to Communism*, p. 225, citing *Nhan Dan*, 21 November 1956. This is in fact a mistransla-tion of a passage from *Nhan Dan*, 27 March 1957, p. 2, which had not mentioned executions.

30. *Nhan Dan*, 31 October 1956, p. 2.

31. Hoang Van Chi, *From Colonialism to Communism*, p. 210. *Xu tri* might be translated "punish," "convict," or "discipline." In practice it usually meant either expulsion from an organization such as the Lao Dong Party, or imprisonment, but it could be used for anything from demotion within an organization to execution.

Hoang Van Chi, attempting to justify his mistranslation of *xu tri* as "executed," has argued that during the land reform *xu tri* was

Porter's argument was an essentially negative one: the evidence for the bloodbath theory is demonstrably false, so there is no reason to believe in the theory. That is an adequate argument. However, it can be supplemented by some positive evidence. The land reform lasted roughly from December 1953 to July 1956. Throughout that period, the Saigon government was pouring out propaganda about how terrible the Communists were. Yet that propaganda contained very little about the land reform and related matters. In October 1956, Saigon learned from international press agency dispatches that the DRV was admitting that serious land-reform excesses had occurred. Only after this did Saigon's anti-Communist tracts become filled with supposed eyewitness accounts of mass slaughter in the land reform.

For an example of this kind of belated revelation, let us look again at Hoang Van Chi. His book *From Colonialism to Communism* comes largely from his personal observations; he was in North Vietnam for the first one and a half years of the land reform. In this book, Chi estimates (supposedly extrapolating from what happened in his home village) that 5 percent of the North Vietnamese population were massacred in the land reform. Yet texts are available of two interviews he gave in Saigon in mid 1955, shortly after he came from the North. In one of these interviews, he did not mention land reform at all while he was describing the supposedly horrible situation in North Vietnam; in the other he mentioned it but did not make it sound terribly bad. Only in later years did his memories alter.[32]

A superficial survey of the Saigon press suggests that even as late as October 1956, well after the end of the land reform, nobody

---

a euphemism for "execute" and could properly be so translated. He says the meaning shifted to include nonlethal punishments only after the land reform had ended; see U.S. Senate Judiciary Committee, *The Human Cost of Communism in Vietnam*, 2:44–45. This argument is false in its entirety. There were a variety of euphemisms for "execute" used in DRV sources, mostly based on the verb *trung tri* (to punish), but I have seen no document of any date in which *xu tri* was so used. Most passages using *xu tri*, including several in the very speech in which Chi made this mistranslation, make it clear that after people have been *xu tri* they are still alive; see for instance *Thoi Moi*, 25 July 1956, p. 1, which describes how some people who had been *xu tri* in the rent reduction were afraid that something worse would happen to them during the land reform proper. In the rare passages that discuss people who died as a result of *xu tri*, one is always told that they were *xu tri* and also that they died; *xu tri* alone would not have conveyed the meaning.

32. Hoang Van Chi, *From Colonialism to Communism*, p. 212; *Washington Post*, 13 September 1972, p. A2; Hoang Van Chi, *The Fate of the Last Viets*, pp. 30–35.

in Saigon had heard of massive land-reform atrocities. When Truong Chinh announced his resignation as general secretary of the Lao Dong Party at the end of October, Saigon's official press agency had difficulty understanding the fact that this had been caused by the crisis over land reform.[33] If there had in fact been a bloodbath, Saigon would have known about it. During the first half of the land reform, the DRV had been allowing large numbers of refugees to go to the South.[34] During the second half, the International Control Commission had been circulating quite widely about the North Vietnamese countryside. It is conceivable that a wave of executions such as the bloodbath theorists describe could have occurred without the ICC having been able to prove it, but such things could not have occurred without the anti-Communist elements on the ICC knowing about them and passing the word informally to their friends in Saigon.

How many people actually were killed in the land reform, if the usual estimates are wrong? It is impossible to judge from the Hanoi press, which never published overall statistics on this subject and did not mention very many specific cases. Even when *Nhan Dan* did publish articles about people who had been convicted of crimes such as multiple murders of peasants or government cadres for which anything less than the death penalty would have been most unlikely, these articles often did not mention any result of the trial, or they reported only that the criminals had been made to bow their heads and admit their crimes, or that they had been "appropriately" or "severely" punished (*trung tri*), or that they had "paid for their sins."[35]

One possible reason for this reticence is that the Party may have wanted to avoid provoking too many executions. Most of the land-reform cadres did not have adequate training or experience. They tended to follow blindly patterns they thought they were expected to follow, and to see in the villages what they expected to see. Some of them thought they were supposed to fill quotas of

---

33. The *Times of Vietnam*, 3 November 1956, p. 4, carried an article from the Vietnam Press Agency, 30 October, based in turn on a dispatch of Agence France-Presse (AFP), Hanoi, 29 October. The portion of this story written by AFP mentioned land reform repeatedly in connection with Truong Chinh's resignation; the commentary by the Vietnam Press Agency, amounting to six column-inches, did not mention land reform once.

34. Hoang Van Chi, *From Colonialism to Communism*, p. 163, in an apparent effort to obscure this point, makes the rather ludicrous claim that the land reform was halted in late 1954 and early 1955 during the period of maximum refugee outflow.

35. *Nhan Dan*, 29 June 1955, p. 2; 2 July 1955, p. 2; 4 November 1955, p. 2; 18 November 1955, p. 2; 24 January 1956, p. 2. In the last case it is known that the two despots in question were sentenced to death; see 13 January 1956, p. 2.

landlords and despots in each village.[36] The Party leadership did not understand the full extent of this problem, but it may have understood enough not to want the land-reform cadres to be going into the villages expecting to find a certain number of landlords who deserved to be executed.

Nhan Dan was the newspaper of the Lao Dong Party. Materials addressed to other audiences were more frank on the subject of executions. *Thoi Moi*, the paper read by the Hanoi bourgeoisie and petite bourgeoisie, mentioned deaths of landlords about as often as *Nhan Dan* did, but while *Nhan Dan* alternated between reporting that people had been sentenced to death and using euphemisms, *Thoi Moi* alternated between reporting that people had been sentenced to death and reporting that they had been executed on the spot.[37]

When speaking to a foreign audience, the Party even gave some statistics. In a report published in *Renmin ribao* on 2 September 1954, Hoang Quoc Viet said that in 600 *xa* that had undergone rent reduction, the peasants had exposed the crimes of 10,147 landlords, of whom 12 percent were despots brought before peasant struggle meetings. This is 16.9 landlords, including 2.0 despots (presumably first-class) brought before struggle meetings, for an average *xa*. 1.3 percent of the landlords, or about 132 men, were executed in these 600 *xa*. If this number of executions per *xa* had been typical of the whole rent reduction, about 415 people would have been executed in the 1,875 *xa*, with a population of 7,800,000, covered by the campaign. On the other hand, if we compute the number of landlords affected by rent reduction from data in Tran Phuong (see above, p. 216) and assume that 1.3 percent of them were executed, we get 575 deaths during rent reduction.

In the land reform proper the number of people classified as landlords was larger than in the rent reduction, and those people were treated more harshly. The Experimental Wave of land reform took place in six *xa* of Thai nguyen province, in which thirty-eight households had been classified as landlords during rent reduction. In the land reform this was increased to ninety-eight households. According to Hoang Quoc Viet all the landlords had to admit their crimes before the people, and 8 percent of them were executed.[38] This means that there were eight executions, or 1.3

---

36. Tran Phuong, *Cach mang ruong dat*, pp. 131, 195; see also *Nhan Dan*, 6 September 1956, p. 2.

37. *Thoi Moi*, 23 August 1955, p. 4; 30 September 1955, p. 3; 15 December 1955, p. 1. The only article I have seen in *Thoi Moi* that restricted itself to euphemisms in discussing an apparent case of execution was published on 8 July 1955, p. 1.

38. *Renmin ribao*, 2 September 1954, p. 3. Voice of Vietnam, 4 May 1954, trans. in FBIS, 12 May 1954, CCC 13–14. The translation mistakenly places these *xa* in Interzone V; they were actually

per *xa*, or 0.07 percent of the population. If we assume that the same percentage of the population was executed throughout the land reform, we get a total of about 7,800 executions. On the other hand, if we assume that the number of executions per *xa* was the same throughout the reform, we get about 4,400 executions. This is a more reasonable form of extrapolation than it might seem. The main point of the executions lay in their psychological effect. Although there is no direct evidence, it seems likely that to have the proper effect on the whole population the Party wanted to have a few executions, but not too many, in each area. The Party definitely made the number of despots denounced for their crimes at mass struggle meetings in each *xa* much more uniform than the actual distribution of brutal and oppressive landlords would have justified. It would not have been necessary to have an execution in every *xa*, since it was common for peasants from several *xa* to gather for important trials.

When David Marr visited Thanh hoa province early in 1975, cadres who had been involved with land reform told him that on the average one to two landlords had been executed in each *xa* in the province.[39]

Can we properly extrapolate from these figures for Thai nguyen and Thanh hoa to the land reform as a whole? It is not likely that we are being misled by purely random fluctuations. Thanh hoa is extremely large; it contained over one-tenth of all the *xa* involved in the land reform. Hoang Quoc Viet would not have released the figures from the Experimental Wave in Thai nguyen as he did, months after that wave was over, if he had not considered them relevant to other areas. Still, there are several possible sources of systematic error.

First, Thai nguyen and Thanh hoa had been under firm Viet Minh control for years before land reform. In the Red River Delta, much of which had been ruled by the French up to 1954, far more landlords might have been accused of collaborating with the enemy. On the other hand, landlords in such areas often fled along with the French when the Viet Minh came, and the net result might have been fewer executions than in the areas that the Viet Minh had held since the beginning of the war.

Second, there is the issue of timing. The Experimental Wave was in early 1954, and most of Thanh hoa underwent land reform during Waves Three and Four in 1955. Most of North Vietnam did not undergo the reform until Wave Five in 1956, and by that time it is known to have become more radical in such respects as the number of families classified as landlords and the number of people

---

in Interzone I.

39. Notes, given to me by David Marr, of conversations on 6 January 1975. D. Gareth Porter, who participated in the same discussion, remembers it differently; he thinks the figure of one to two executions per *xa* was a maximum rather than an average.

accused of being reactionaries. It is therefore plausible that there might have been considerably more executions than we would expect on the basis of data from 1954 and 1955. On the other hand, Hoang Van Chi states that Khrushchev's revelation of Stalin's crimes, at the Twentieth Congress of the Soviet Communist Party in February 1956, led the DRV to reconsider its policies and halt all land-reform executions as of March 1956.[40] Chi's work is in general so unreliable that it cannot be trusted even when what he says is favorable to the Communists, but his statement is plausible. Mao Zedong responded to Khrushchev's revelation by proposing a halt to the execution of some categories of counterrevolutionaries in China.[41] Such a decision would have been logical in Vietnam if the DRV leadership had been starting to worry about leftist excesses and wanted time to investigate matters. The fact that no particular cases of landlords being executed were mentioned in available issues of *Nhan Dan* or *Thoi Moi* after January 1956 supports this hypothesis.[42] An alternate explanation is possible, however. The Party may have been failing in its efforts to persuade the urban population that the land reform was not leading to radical excesses and might therefore have decided to stop publicizing even occasional executions.

Third, there is the question of whether the data for 1954 and 1955, from Communist sources, were accurate in the first place. I tend to think they were. The number of people executed cannot have been much higher than the Communist sources indicate, or there would have been more genuine evidence of it in the anti-Communist sources. Allowing for these uncertainties, the most that can be said is that the total number of people executed during the land reform was probably on the rough order of 5,000 and almost certainly between 3,000 and 15,000.

It is hard to tell what the exact grounds for execution were, because details are available for so few cases. Almost all the people executed would have been accused of having been both landlords and active counterrevolutionaries, but so were many people who were not executed. It is not even possible to be sure whether it was better for a person accused of serious crimes to deny them or confess and throw himself on the mercy of the court; there is evidence in each direction.[43]

---

40. Hoang Van Chi, *From Colonialism to Communism*, pp. 213–14.

41. Mao Tse-tung, "On the Ten Major Relationships," in *Selected Works*, 5:298–300.

42. The last case of a land-reform execution I have seen in *Thoi Moi* was 15 December 1955; the last in *Nhan Dan* was 24 January 1956. Hardly any issues of either paper are available for February 1956, but one would expect to find executions mentioned between March and June. I have seen none.

43. *Nhan Dan*, 30 October 1956, p. 3; 12 November 1956, p. 2.

The Role of Women

The position of women in traditional Vietnam, as in most Southeast Asian cultures, had been considerably higher than in China; this fact affected the role of the women's movement in the revolution. In China women were organized to free themselves from their particular disabilities as women. Female cadres were likely to be leaders of women's organizations, working for specifically female goals, with women under their leadership. In Vietnam there had been less discrimination, so it was said that "the interests of women are, for the most part, the general interests of peasant households."[44] Female cadres worked on the problems of the peasantry as a whole, and came into positions of command over men, more than in China. The greatest example was a woman named Do Thi Than (a.k.a. Nguyen Thi Than), who was chosen as the land-reform cadre whom all others in the country, of both sexes, were to emulate. She was in fact worthy of emulation; she had not become the most admired member of a paranoid organization by being the most paranoid. She was conspicuous for thinking of things she could do, beyond the normal duties of a land-reform cadre, which would improve the economic situation of the peasants with whom she was working.[45]

The land-reform cadres who carried out rectification of village-level organizations were suspicious of the old cadres in those organizations. The land-reform cadres therefore needed to find peasants who had the talents and personality for political leadership but had not held important positions in the Resistance. Many of those they found were women, and the proportion of women in key positions increased remarkably. In one extreme case, two young women acquired between them the posts of Party secretary, assistant Party secretary, and chairman of the *xa* administration in a *xa* of about 3,700 people. In Trung hoa *xa*, just outside Hanoi, women held six out of seven places on the executive committee of the peasant association and headed both the *xa* administration and the Lao Dong Party.[46] This advantageous situation lasted only a short time, however. The women had become identified with the disastrous policy of pushing aside the old cadres of the Resistance, and when this policy was discredited and reversed, the policy of promoting women cadres suffered by association.

---

44. Ibid., 20 January 1956, p. 3.

45. Ibid., 20 November 1955, p. 2; 27 January 1956, p. 2; *Thoi Moi*, 17 May 1956, pp. 1, 4.

46. *Nhan Dan*, 27 September 1955, p. 2; *Thoi Moi*, 30 January 1956, p. 3.

Production

While the land reform was going on, the ravages of war were being repaired, and agricultural production was increasing very rapidly. The land reform may well have contributed to this rise; if it did not contribute, at least it did not prevent a rise. For all its errors, it was not comparable to the collectivization of the 1930s in the Soviet Union, which led to a substantial fall in agricultural production.

DRV statistics are difficult to use, for a variety of reasons. Figures for the area of cultivated land and yields per hectare usually refer to crop area; land that is double cropped is counted twice. Thus one hectare of double-cropped land producing three tons of rice per year will appear in the statistics as two hectares producing 1.5 tons per hectare. Another problem is that percentage changes may be calculated as a percentage of the final rather than the initial figure; thus an increase from 40 to 50 may be called a 20 percent rise rather than a 25 percent rise. But the worst problem is that many of the figures are simply inaccurate. Vietnamese society had not reached a high enough economic and educational level to make the collection of really accurate statistics possible, and the government was not sufficiently concerned with this matter even to work very hard at turning out the best figures possible.

Table 11-2 shows some of the figures that were published in *Nhan Dan* on rice production in North Vietnam. The significance of the postwar figures clearly depends on which estimate we accept for production in the peak prewar year, 1939. Official French figures indicate it was about 2,400,000 tons, but DRV historians feel that many landowners had been underestimating their production very substantially in order to evade taxes and that the amount actually grown had been approximately 3,500,000 tons.[47] This higher figure should probably be accepted; the DRV would hardly have wanted to exaggerate the productivity and thus the prosperity of the colonial regime. The figures given for 1954 in the table may well be underestimates; those for 1956 are probably fairly accurate. It should be repeated that double-cropped land is counted twice in this table; if we treated one hectare of double-cropped land simply as one hectare, then for 1956 we would have about 1,600,000 hectares producing about 2.6 tons per hectare per year. Between 1954 and 1956 the production of other crops grew faster than rice production.[48]

In 1954 and most of 1955, there was a severe food shortage in North Vietnam. The Soviet Union began sending some rice around

---

47. Ibid., 29 November 1957, pp. 2–3.
48. Corn increased from 165,900 to 258,500 tons, potatoes from 461,600 to 1,062,000 tons, and cassava from 133,000 to 366,600 tons. Ibid., 21 August 1957, p. 2.

Table 11-2—Available figures on rice production in North Vietnam (post–1954 boundaries) between 1939 and 1956

	1939 Official	1939 Modified	1954	1956
Production (tons)	2,453,200	3,500,000	2,600,000	4,210,000
Crop area (ha.)	1,836,000	?	1,898,000	2,308,000
Tons per hectare	1.34	?	1.37	1.82
Tons per person	0.21	0.30	0.18	0.31

Source: Derived from a wide variety of figures, often mutually contradictory, published in *Nhan Dan*, 1 January 1957, p. 6; 5 January 1957, p. 1; 8 January 1957, p. 2; 14 January 1957, p. 2; 21 April 1957, p. 1; 23 June 1957, p. 2; 21 August 1957, p. 2; 29 November 1957, pp. 2–3; 7 February 1958, p. 2.

Note: The figure for tons per person is rice production divided by the total population of North Vietnam, not just the agricultural population.

May 1955 and the Chinese began sending some around August, but neither sent very much; the Vietnamese had to depend essentially on their own production. A good autumn rice crop in October and November 1955 eased the food crisis in the countryside but not in the cities. The DRV food-distribution system was based on the assumption that the peasants would pay their grain taxes, set aside enough for their own consumption, and sell the remainder of their crops. But in the autumn of 1955 the peasants held on to their surplus rice; they wanted to rebuild their personal reserves as insurance against future crop failures.[49] Their grain taxes alone were not adequate to feed the cities. The continued urban food shortage must have been among the factors that made land-reform cadres raise the official figures on the area and productivity of land, thus raising the peasants' tax obligations, during land-reform Wave Five in the first half of 1956.

The autumn of 1956 brought a second good crop, and the peasants then became willing to sell large quantities of rice. The

---

49. *Thoi Moi*, 8 March 1957, pp. 1, 4.

crisis concerning the revelation of land-reform errors, then at its peak, would have been far worse if there had not been enough food to go around. There were serious inequities in the land-tax registers for many areas, especially those that had undergone land reform in Waves Four and Five. The moral authority of the government was at a low ebb. With the peasants selling adequate rice to feed the cities, the government was able to accept a substantial reduction in tax quotas and a delay of several months in tax collection while it was setting its house in order.

Most of the production increases represented the repair of wartime damage. Many people had been unable to cultivate their land properly during the war; about 135,000 hectares had fallen out of use altogether. Of this about 70,000 hectares had been restored by the end of 1955, and about 105,000 hectares by March of 1956. This marked the end of what could be restored quickly and easily; the total only reached 115,000 hectares by the end of 1956.[50] Further production increases would require genuinely new construction, which was much slower. Rice production was actually less in 1957 than in 1956 because of bad weather, but this was not a disaster; food supplies were adequate if very austere.

Fundamental Errors

The land reform was afflicted by "commandism" at all levels; leaders and cadres decided what should be done and then issued the appropriate orders without really consulting the peasants very much. This defect was conspicuous right from the beginning, when the Land Reform Law was drawn up and officially promulgated without prior experiments in so much as a single *xa*.

The campaign was carried out with desperate haste. It was completed in the middle of 1956, little more than a year after the last French troops withdrew from North Vietnam. In Guangdong, at an equivalent date, land reform was still in its early stages. At the local level, the haste of the campaign in Vietnam was even more conspicuous. In each *xa*, land reform was part of a specific wave, covering a much wider area. When the wave was finished, all the land-reform cadres would assemble in large conferences, usually at the province level, to discuss their experiences and plan for the next wave. There probably were villages where the cadres could not finish on time and were unable to attend the summing-up meetings, but such cases never seem to have been mentioned in the press, and they must have carried a severe stigma. The impression conveyed is that in a given wave and a given province, most of the *xa* proceeded at about the same speed. Mass mobilization for land reform was so subtle and difficult a process that it

---

50. Ibid., 2 January 1956, p. 2; 21 May 1956, p. 4; 4 January 1957, p. 1.

could not possibly have been fully effective if jammed into so rigid a schedule. Even when the CCP was pushing for speed and working in a framework of waves, it allowed flexibility in special cases. There were *xian* in Guangdong that were over a year late in completing land reform. Except for Hong Quang, where work was broken off in mid 1956 so that leftist errors could be corrected, no specific area in North Vietnam is known to have been late at all. Haste led to such ridiculous occurrences as befell one woman cadre of middle-peasant origin who lived in Hong Quang. *Three days after the land-reform cadres arrived in her village she was branded as a landlord*, for no very clear reason, and was thrown out of the Lao Dong Party.[51]

The Party does not seem to have recognized the wave pattern as a problem, even after the errors of land reform had become apparent. The most extensive history of the land reform accepts this pattern and in fact makes it seem more rigid than it really was, mentioning an overlap of only six days between the end of Wave Four and the beginning of Wave Five.[52] In fact, the overlap was more like two months.

The land-reform apparatus ran all the way from the Central Land Reform Committee in Hanoi down to the village level. It was a chain of command separate from both the Party and the government, although many of the people who worked on land reform had been recruited from the Party or government, and some of them continued to hold their old positions while also working on land reform. In China things had been quite different; land reform in each province or *xian* had been the responsibility of the regular Party and government authorities of that province or *xian*. The creation of a separate land-reform system in Vietnam was partly a result of distrust of the old organizations of the Resistance in the countryside. It eventually became a factor increasing that distrust, because it placed the land-reform apparatus in the position of competing for power against the previously existing organizations. Another unfortunate effect was that it reduced the coordination between land reform and other tasks in the countryside.

During land reform, the Party looked at society in black and white terms and wanted the peasants to do the same. Land-reform leaders needed to polarize sentiments in the countryside, to focus the attention of the peasants on the ways in which peasant interests conflicted with landlord interests. They needed to persuade the peasants to forget the conflicts that pitted one peasant against another, or one group including both landlords and peasants against another such group. They firmly denied that there could be any common interests between landlords and peasants. Their attitude was symbolized by the terminology used for right and "left" deviations, with quotation marks used to indicate that it was

51. *Nhan Dan*, 18 November 1956, p. 2.
52. Tran Phuong, *Cach mang ruong dat*, pp. 107–8.

impossible actually to be too far to the left. The implication is that rightist policies serve the interests of the rich while leftist policies serve the interests of the poor, and that a given policy can usually be fitted into one and only one of these two categories. It followed that policies that harmed the interests of the masses should be considered basically rightist even if they took the form of excessive radicalism.

The Party assumed that the landlords would do anything to harm the revolution and the peasants, whether or not such actions were of any visible benefit to themselves. Thus Truong Chinh claimed that before the land reform the landlords had had no desire to see agricultural techniques improved but on the contrary had opposed any such improvement;[53] he ignored the fact that the bulk of the profits from any such improvement would have gone to the landlords. In order to believe some of *Nhan Dan*'s descriptions of the role of the landlords as American lackeys in 1955 and 1956, one would have to believe that the landlords were so selflessly loyal to an American government with which they had at the moment no contact at all, and with which they had never been close, that they were willing to risk letting themselves and their families go hungry if by doing so they could cause the enemies of the Americans also to go hungry.

Almost any action of the landlords could be interpreted as having been in some way directed against the revolution. To give a few extreme examples: *Nhan Dan* considered suicide by the landlords as a form of sabotage activity; among other things it deprived the mass struggle of the targets it needed. When some landlords, totally impoverished by the land reform, hired themselves out as manual laborers at low wages, this was considered to be a reactionary plot because peasants who could hire them cheaply would not want to join labor-exchange groups.[54]

The landlords were also charged with a great many things they had not actually done. While there surely must have been genuine cases in which landlords murdered peasant activists, the landlords were likely to be suspected of having murdered almost any person of any social class who had died during or immediately before land reform. These suspicions arose even if a landlord had died; the land-reform cadres could suggest that the deceased had been a member of a reactionary organization and had been killed by his co-conspirators to keep him from talking. In a village where the land-reform cadres had aroused a great deal of baseless excitement over one supposed case of murder and one of attempted murder, and where at least sixty people had come under unjust suspicion as reactionaries, later investigators commented: "The *doi* had not been clear-sighted...and had regarded every unusual event occurring in

---

53. *Yuenan minzhu*, p. 35.
54. *Nhan Dan*, 25 June 1955, p. 2; 30 September 1955, p. 2.

the village during the land reform as having been caused by enemy sabotage."[55]

A *cot can* who had conducted investigations under the supervision of a *doi* of exceptionally bad land-reform cadres later described the lengths to which the cadres had gone in search of counterrevolutionary crimes and criminals. An old man in the village had fallen ill and died a few months before land reform. The land-reform cadres decided that he must have known something about the reactionaries in the village and been killed to keep his mouth shut. When the *cot can* tried to explain that the man had been over eighty years old and seemed to have died of natural causes, the *doi* criticized them for lack of vigilance. The *cot can* finally extracted a confession from somebody after prolonged interrogations including the use of physical torture, but the land-reform cadres were not satisfied. If the old man had been killed by enemies of the revolution, it would have been done not by a single individual but by a conspiracy. There had to have been a ringleader, someone to pin the old man's feet, someone to pin his hands, someone to pin his head, someone actually to strangle him, someone to hold a light over the proceedings, and someone to stand guard outside. Only after these people had been found could the case be closed.[56]

There were four main groups victimized by the land reform. The first group consisted of the landlords themselves. The second included the people wrongly classified as landlords. The third was made up of those considered to be "connected with landlords." Some of those people had supported or defended real or supposed landlords in the land reform, but others were given this label simply because they had been friends of some landlord, or relatives, or even because they had worked as wage laborers in some landlord's fields.[57] Members of this category perhaps bear a closer resemblance to the *podkulachnik* (sub-kulak) of the Soviet Union than to the nearest Chinese equivalent, "dog's leg." The injustices committed against people "connected with landlords" were among the first land-reform excesses to arouse the uneasiness of the Lao Dong Party leadership; *Nhan Dan* complained as early as 1954 that this label was being too broadly applied, and ordered in May 1956 that it no longer be used.[58]

The fourth group of victims in the land reform was a large fraction of the veteran cadres of the Lao Dong Party and the DRV administration. In a process similar to what William Hinton witnessed in North China in 1948, but one that was carried to greater extremes, the land-reform cadres decided that the reason the poor peasants and laborers had not received the benefits of a

---

55. Ibid., 8 September 1956, p. 2.
56. Xuan Chi, in *Thoi Moi*, 13 April 1957, pp. 1, 4.
57. *Nhan Dan*, 20 January 1956, p. 2.
58. Ibid., 4 September 1954, p. 2; 21 May 1956, p. 2.

radical land policy much sooner was that the Party and government had been heavily infiltrated by the landlords and agents of the landlords. They launched a veritable witch-hunt among the cadres who had served in the Resistance against France. Old Party members, and administrative cadres not in the Party, were accused of being landlords and even despots, of personal corruption, or of having secretly served the French. When the land-reform cadres and *cot can* became suspicious, "every word these comrades had spoken and everything they had done was regarded in a biased fashion and turned around so as to harm them."[59] There was one *xa* chairman in Ha dong province who had done very good work for the Resistance while his area had been occupied by the French. In order to reduce the amount of taxes that the *xa* paid to the French, he had juggled the land registers to make the 900 *mau* of land in the *xa* appear as 500 *mau* or less. During land reform this underregistration of the land owned by the peasants was inter- preted as an effort to shift the land into his own hands. Once when he was very busy with administrative duties and could spare little time for his own farm, a group of peasants had volunteered to come work his land. This was later described as exploitation of the peasants and cited as evidence that he should be considered a landlord. During the land reform he was branded a landlord despot and sentenced to death, though he was not actually executed.[60] A woman Party member who had worked as a courier, carrying messages between Resistance units on opposite sides of a French- controlled highway, was accused of having been a liaison between the French forces and French agents in the Viet Minh areas.[61] An agricultural laborer named Co had served with great heroism in the Resistance and had risen to become Party secretary for Van duong *xa* of Bac ninh province. During mass mobilization for rent reduc- tion he was dismissed from his position and thrown out of the Party. During land reform he was classified as a rich peasant and treated as belonging to a reactionary organization. At first he thought he had been the victim of an isolated mistake. "But gradu- ally, as he looked at [what was happening in] neighboring *xa*, he saw comrades whom he knew to be devoted and [self-] sacrificing also being pursued and attacked. He began to see that the errors were widespread. Co became confused and uncertain; he shriveled up inside like a man standing helplessly before a burning house."[62]

By early 1956, when the purge reached its peak, the land- reform cadres were treating the existing organizations in the villages—the Lao Dong Party, the local administrations, the militia, etc.—as hostile forces. "Relying on old organizations" was a

---

59. Ibid., 8 February 1957.
60. Ibid., 12 November 1956, p. 2.
61. Xuan Chi, in *Thoi Moi*, 13 April 1957, p. 4.
62. *Thoi Moi*, 21 August 1957, p. 1.

cardinal sin; in some areas the land-reform cadres had been taught that "our organizations are basically organizations of the enemy."[63] The result in seventy-six *xa* of Bac ninh province was that in only twenty-six *xa* were any veteran members at all allowed to remain on the executive committee of the *chi bo* (*xa* level Party branch).[64] The purge started in the villages and proceeded upward to the *huyen* and then the province level. In some provinces it had not yet reached the higher levels when the radical policy was discredited and brought to a halt.

There exists a detailed account of what happened in one of the very worst *xa*. It was written by Xuan Chi, a cadre who worked on the correction of errors early in 1957 in the *xa* he calls "T.N.," in Hung yen province a little east of Hanoi.[65] The Communist organization in this *xa* dated back to before 1945. It had established an exceptionally good record in the Resistance; the *xa* had been hotly contested because of its strategic position astride Highway 5 between Hanoi and Haiphong. The land-reform cadres sent to T.N., during Wave Five, won commendation from higher authorities for having uncovered an unusually large number of landlords and enemies of the revolution. The way they had done this had been to brand the entire Viet Minh leadership of T.N. a gang of reactionaries; all were dismissed from their positions, most were imprisoned for at least a brief period, and some were tortured. A *cot can* later described the way the land-reform cadres had attacked comrade Kiet, who had done very well as a platoon commander in the Resistance: "The *doi* came and said: 'Kiet is a [member of] reactionary organizations, a lackey of the enemy.' We said that he had been [politically] aware since the dark days and that all the people loved and respected him. The *doi* explained to us: 'The more dangerous the enemy, the more methods he will have for fooling the people.'"[66]

There was a considerable variation among land-reform cadres. Many *doi* avoided falling into the extremes of paranoia described above. Even the *doi* assigned to T.N. contained at least one cadre who wanted to reconsider the evidence against those who had been arrested as enemies of the revolution, but his comrades said he was lacking in vigilance and overruled him.[67] Each *doi* was a separate unit; its authority did not stretch very far outside the *xa* to which it had been assigned. Comrade An, who had been the first Communist in T.N. and was one of the most prestigious,

---

63. *Nhan Dan*, 5 November 1956, p. 3.

64. Ibid., 6 July 1956, p. 2.

65. Xuan Chi, "Sau nhung ngay song gio" [After the days of adversity], serialized in *Thoi Moi* from 5 to 20 April 1957, and "Trong khong khi diu mat cua dem xuan" [In the cool air of spring nights], serialized in *Thoi Moi* from 7 to 23 May 1957.

66. Xuan Chi, in *Thoi Moi*, 13 April 1957, p. 1.

67. Ibid., 12 April 1957, p. 3.

escaped harm despite being branded "leader of the reactionaries," because he was away at the time, working as a land-reform cadre in another province.[68]

The new power structure established in the villages during land reform was composed of those old cadres who had not been purged, plus the *cot can* recruited and trained by the land-reform cadres. The relative proportion of the two groups varied from *xa* to *xa*. The main criterion, within both groups, was purity of class origin and class loyalty. The poor peasants and laborers were promoted. The exploiting classes and all those connected with the exploiting classes were cast down. "Classism"—the belief that social class determines or should determine everything—was one of the fundamental causes of the land-reform errors.

The promotion of poor peasants and laborers was intended to be, and sometimes was, a method of spreading political power more broadly in the countryside, enabling the mass of the peasants to play a dominant role. But too often the *cot can*, lacking adequate political experience, prestige, education, and training, simply served as mouthpieces for the land-reform cadres. After the campaign was over, when *cot can* who had publicly accused many people of crimes they had not committed were attacked by their former victims, *Nhan Dan* repeated many times that they should not be blamed too much, because they had only been doing what the land-reform cadres told them to do. This was to a large extent true.

The land-reform cadres were trained to see enemies everywhere, and they passed the same attitude on to the *cot can*. It was considered a great "achievement" to expose as a reactionary plotter or a landlord someone who had not previously seemed to be one. After the land reform there were bitter comments on "achievements in wrecking the rural areas and wrecking the Party."[69] In retrospect it appears that a majority of the people denounced during the land reform were innocent.[70] Some of the pressures pushing land-reform cadres and *cot can* to do these things are apparent—demands coming from above for more radical results, and the

---

68. Ibid., 5 April 1957, p. 4.

69. *Nhan Dan*, 23 April 1957, p. 2.

70. Tran Phuong, *Cach mang ruong dat*, p. 180, says that 4.6 percent of the Party members had been landlords, rich peasants, or "bad elements"; p. 214 says that 8.8 percent had been expelled as landlords, rich peasants, or "bad Party members" (both figures from after the correction of errors). The proportion of Party members assigned to these categories during land reform had been much higher. In Thanh binh *xa*, Hai doung province, there were sixteen Party members; during land reform fourteen were expelled. Later investigation showed that only one had done anything for which he should have been expelled. *Nhan Dan*, 10 December 1956, p. 2.

difficulty of raising the class struggle to a paramount role in village affairs while Resistance organizations not based on class were powerful—but there still remains the question of how those of the cadres and *cot can* who succumbed to these pressures justified their actions to themselves; no single explanation seems adequate. The land-reform cadres, who had been sent out to work in villages where they were strangers and had been required to form political judgments after a brief stay, were in many cases genuinely ignorant of the characters of their victims. Even some of the *cot can* may not have known much. The worst land-reform errors were in the areas covered by Wave Five, and many of these areas had been occupied by the French up until late in the war. In such areas the Viet Minh had of necessity been clandestine, and *cot can* who had not belonged to the underground might have been relatively ignorant of the real accomplishments of local leaders.

In the cases where *cot can* fabricated accusations against individuals whom they did know or should have known to be upright people, we cannot rule out a crudely cynical desire for political and economic advancement, but other factors certainly contributed and may have been more important. Psychological research in the United States has begun to explore the extent to which people will do things that violate their normal moral codes, simply because some person in a position of authority tells them to do so. The same thing can also apply to beliefs; most human beings will believe, or act as if they believe, quite absurd things if everyone around them also seems to believe. Most of the *cot can* were relatively young people from poor families; they had never enjoyed much status or respect before they became involved in land reform. For them to have asserted a personal sense of truth or of justice against the consensus of those around them, accepting the opprobrium of their colleagues, would have required extremely strong characters. One of the leading *cot can* in T.N. *xa* later explained: "At that time we used physical torture and made incorrect denunciations; a few times I felt our consciences were bothering us. But we would have been unable to bear being accused of 'sabotaging the revolution,' and we would do anything to avoid this."[71]

There may also have been resentment over the power and prerogatives that had been enjoyed by the leaders of the Resistance, although there is no evidence that this was as big a factor in the attacks on veteran cadres in Vietnam as it had been in North China in 1948.[72] Many cadres of the Resistance must have abused their positions to some extent; they were only human. Even their legitimate prerogatives were great enough to create the possibility of bad feeling. They could demand labor and grain that the peasants could not easily spare, and they could ask people to

---

71. Xuan Chi, in *Thoi Moi*, 13 April 1957, p. 4.
72. See Hinton, *Fanshen*, especially pp. 222–31, 326–49.

risk their lives. When two guerrillas in Thai binh province were fleeing from a French patrol one night and came for shelter to an old woman who could hide only one man properly, she unhesitatingly put the guerrilla who was a Party member into her safe spot; he was more important and would be in more danger if caught. The man who was not a Party member was left to conceal himself as best he could, hiding under the water in a pond. That solution was legitimate and proper, but it also may have had some connection with the fact that the non-Party member later made false accusations against the Party member during land reform.[73]

The land reform grew more radical as it went on. Excesses in class demarcation, in setting the official figures for the area and productivity of land, and in the search for reactionaries both among the population at large and among the old cadres were worst in Waves Four and Five. If we are evaluating the mentalities of the DRV leaders, we can treat these two waves as a comparatively brief aberration, lasting only about one year. But from the viewpoint of the people, these two waves constituted almost the whole of the land reform; 78 percent of the *xa* and 83 percent of the population covered by land reform were covered in Waves Four and Five.

It is very hard to tell how far the formal decisions of the land reform penetrated into informal social relations. Some people classified as landlords but not imprisoned were shunned by their neighbors and even their families. Others had friends willing to stay in contact and help them, openly or covertly. This was especially true in Catholic communities, where the land reform involved an attack on the leaders of the faith, in which many Catholic peasants refused to join. Even some people who were imprisoned had friends willing to work for their release. For them to do so was dangerous, but not as dangerous as it would have been, for instance, in the Soviet Union of 1937.

The Question of Foreign Influence

It has sometimes been suggested that North Vietnam went disastrously wrong through slavish imitation of the Chinese land reform. In its extreme form[74] this argument is simple nonsense; the patterns of action that Vietnam allegedly copied from China had not actually occurred in either Vietnam or China. But the question of Chinese influence is a real one. Vietnamese policies both for mass mobilization and for land reform were clearly based on Chinese models, although they did not copy these models precisely.

---

73. *Thoi Moi*, 11 February 1957, p. 3.
74. See Hoang Van Chi, *From Colonialism to Communism*, pp. 12, 72, 190, and passim. Chi is very ignorant of the history of Chinese Communism; see ibid., pp. 48, 72, 110, 148, 154n.

Mieczyslaw Maneli, who was in Hanoi for part of the period of the land reform, states that the Soviet Union was the main adviser to the DRV on foreign policy and China the main adviser on domestic policy, but that the DRV did not always follow the advice given.[75] In regard to land reform, the Soviet Union and Poland advised a moderate program; the Chinese, whether by their advice or simply by their example, helped inspire the more radical line that Vietnam actually followed.[76]

However, if we look at the errors of the Vietnamese land reform there is little appearance of Chinese inspiration. The principal errors were two: (1) classifying many people as landlords whose actual economic status was not that of landlord and (2) carrying out wild purges within the Party and other organizations at the *xa* level, promoting new members too rapidly while throwing out old ones. In the Chinese land reform of 1950–53, there was much closer adherence to class-demarcation decrees, and the decrees themselves relied more firmly on economic criteria in defining the landlord class. When old Party members in Guangdong genuinely obstructed the class struggle, Peking concluded not that the Party had been taken over by counterrevolutionaries but simply that a lot of Party members had bad attitudes and had to be pressured into reforming themselves. The Chinese had decided not to bring poor-peasant activists into the Communist Party during land reform, because they believed that to do so would not allow enough time for training and testing.

The closest Chinese parallel to the leftist excesses of Vietnam came early in 1948 in northern China. A summary of land-reform errors made by the Northeast Bureau of the CCP in March 1948 has sections dealing with large-scale misclassification of middle peasants as rich peasants,[77] with gross underevaluation of the members of existing village organizations, and so on, which are remarkably similar to the reports made by the Lao Dong Party in late 1956.[78] But the necessity of avoiding such errors became a permanent part of CCP land-reform doctrine after 1948 and would have been thoroughly dinned into the Vietnamese land-reform cadres if they had in fact been operating under Chinese supervision.

Imitation of Chinese patterns may have distorted Vietnamese policies in one way. There is a definite possibility that the Vietnamese were copying provisions from Chinese laws into their own

---

75. Maneli, *War of the Vanquished*, pp. 26–27.

76. Maneli, personal interview, New York, 30 December 1975.

77. Given the harsh policy being followed toward the rich peasants in 1948, this would have been almost as great a misfortune for the people concerned as misclassification as a landlord was in Vietnam.

78. "Basic summary of the movement for equal division [of land]," 28 March 1948, in *Tudi zhengce faling huibian*, pp. 72–82.

legislation as a diplomatic gesture, and then doing what they pleased in practice. Vietnamese rent-reduction laws issued between 1949 and 1953 appeared on the surface to order a 25 percent rent reduction, but loopholes and simple lack of respect for the law allowed very different levels to be applied in practice. Contempt for formal law was one of the factors that contributed to errors in Vietnam, and copying of foreign laws may have contributed to that contempt.

There may have been specific aspects of Chinese land-reform policy that did not fit Vietnam, but in general the situations were similar, and Chinese policies seem equally suited to both countries. Criticism of policy copying, by Western scholars, has generally been based either on a misunderstanding of the nature and accomplishments of land reform or on an aversion to violent social reform that would lead to disapproval of radical land reform in any country.

On the opposite side, Truong Chinh, who believes that Vietnam should have begun mass mobilization for rent reduction in 1949 and land reform in 1952,[79] has argued that imitation of China led to unnecessary delays in the Vietnamese land reform:

> We mechanically applied the experience of the Chinese revo-
> lution in the period of the Anti-Japanese Resistance. We did
> not see that the reason why China carried out only rent
> reduction during the eight years of the Anti-Japanese Resis-
> tance was because the Chinese people were collaborating in
> the Resistance with the Chiang Kai-shek regime, which repre-
> sented the landlord class and the bureaucratic capitalist class.
> As for us, we are not in the same position; we have no such
> partner in our Resistance, so we do not need to restrict
> ourselves to rent reduction.[80]

The argument again is weak. The political situation in the villages was at least as big a factor in the CCP's moderate policies as was the alliance with Chiang Kai-shek. In this respect China and Vietnam were similar, so Vietnamese imitation of Chinese moderation does not seem unreasonable.

---

79. Truong Chinh, *Tien len duoi la co*, pp. 73–74.
80. Report of November 1953, text in *Yuenan minzhu*, p. 43.

12

The Correction of Errors

The Party realized the seriousness of the land-reform excesses very gradually. Its awakening began by April 1956 but was not complete until August or September. There are a variety of possible explanations why the errors became visible to the top leaders at this particular time.

The simplest explanation is based on the slow circulation of information. Top leaders became aware that something was seriously wrong about a year after the situation became bad. This may simply have been the amount of time it took, with the land-reform apparatus and its allies dominating the official channels of communication from the villages, for enough disturbing rumors and reports to reach Hanoi from the countryside. A considerable amount of information would have been needed; the Party was denouncing as counterrevolutionary propaganda the rumors that the land reform was running out of control,[1] so an individual would have wanted to be very sure of his ground before he said that he took these rumors seriously and asked for an investigation.

The top leaders of the Party may have begun to doubt the charges being made against old cadres when these charges began to affect men with whom they were personally acquainted. The purges of the Party and other organizations had been mostly at the *xa* level, but in 1956 they had moved up to the *huyen* and province levels. The teams sent out to recheck the land reform, although they had been intended to push local cadres to the left and probably had done so in most areas, may have sent back some disquieting reports to their superiors. Finally, it is possible that the Twentieth Congress of the Soviet Communist Party in February 1956, at which Khrushchev made his famous denunciation of Stalinism, may have made the DRV reexamine some of its practices. It definitely helped inspire reforms increasing collective decision making and inner-Party democracy.[2]

The first step in the retreat from extremism was a Central Committee directive titled "Correct Errors Committed in *Chi Bo*

---

1. *Thoi Moi*, 6 April 1955, pp. 1, 4.
2. Report of Truong Chinh to the Ninth Plenum (April 1956) and a resolution of that plenum, both trans. in FBIS, 30 April 1956, CCC 4, 7; see also *Thoi Moi* editorial, 31 October 1956, p. 1.

Rectification during Wave Five," which was probably passed at the Ninth Plenum in April.[3] Starting roughly with step three of Wave Five, some of the left deviations began to be corrected. *Nhan Dan* had been warning for some time that people were being wrongly branded "connected with landlords," sometimes as a result of deliberate slander by hostile elements. In late May, an article appeared that said that no one should be called "connected with landlords."[4] There was increasing emphasis on reeducation for old Party members, rather than on wholesale expulsion of "bad elements." *Nhan Dan* complained: "Some cadres do not clearly distinguish comrades who have shortcomings from bad elements and saboteurs."[5] Some who had been wrongly expelled had their Party membership restored.[6] In late June *Nhan Dan* editorialized:

> At the beginning of Wave Five of the land reform, we overestimated the enemy. Naturally, we could not underestimate the enemy's plots. Events in various regions had shown that since the reestablishment of peace, the landlord class had been sabotaging [us] in a serious fashion. During Wave Five of the land reform they opposed the peasants even more drastically and cunningly than during the previous waves. But we treated the situation of enemy sabotage breaking out in some areas as if it were the general situation, to the point of making incorrect judgments, such as believing that there were enemy organizations within our organizations or controlling our organizations in the villages everywhere, believing that the enemy was deployed and ready for the work teams to arrive everywhere, etc.

Many land-reform cadres had said that the *chi bo* in general were seriously "complex,"

> but they did not see that the level of complexity in every area was different, that not every *chi bo* of ours in the rural areas was bad, and that not every old Party member in the rural areas was bad.[7]

Party leaders, however, were thinking in terms of scattered excesses; they had no idea how widespread and fundamental the errors had become. Efforts at correction up to July 1956 were hopelessly inadequate; indeed leftist errors continued to occur on a large scale.

---

3. *Nhan Dan*, 22 June 1956, p. 2.
4. Ibid., 21 May 1956, p. 2.
5. *Nhan Dan* editorial, 29 May 1956, p. 1.
6. *Nhan Dan*, 13 June 1956, p. 2; 15 June 1956, p. 2; 16 June 1956, p. 2; 23 June 1956, p. 2.
7. *Nhan Dan* editorial, 27 June 1956, p. 1.

After the land-reform cadres had finished Wave Five, they went to the usual summing-up meetings, at the *doan* or province level, which probably lasted over a month. However, at the end of these meetings they had to attend a further course of reeducation, instead of returning as they had expected to whatever jobs they had held before they became land-reform cadres. After this, some of them were sent back to the villages to work on correction of errors.

Hong Quang had started land reform several months later than the other areas covered by Wave Five. Therefore, when the other areas finished, Hong Quang was still working on step three. The land reform there was broken off in the middle and the cadres were pulled out for reeducation. Some of them were sent back to the villages in September.

On 18 August Ho Chi Minh published a major statement on the land reform. In many areas, it was this statement that marked the real beginning of the correction of errors. Considering that it was used as a guide to action at the village level, it was remarkably vague. The Lao Dong Party normally worked out detailed plans for all major programs and discussed them at length before presenting them to the public and implementing them. However, in August 1956 there was not time for such orderly procedures. Ho's statement, which seems to have been released directly to the public without having first been studied within the Party, gave only a brief summary of errors committed in the land reform. However, it directed cadres at the village level to go ahead and start to correct these errors without waiting for their leaders to finish working out plans for a formal campaign.[8]

At about this time the Central Land Reform Committee sent small groups of cadres out to Bac ninh, Hung yen, Thai binh, and Nghe an provinces to investigate the situation and help with the correction of errors.[9] An article published at the end of August suggests that the Party even then may not have realized the full extent of the problem it faced. For one thing, it complained that the cadres supervising the correction of errors were disrupting the villages too much; it was almost as though the cadres were trying to repeat the whole mass mobilization for land reform instead of building on the successes already attained. For another, it expressed outrage that peasants who had been wrongly classified as landlords, and thus had had property taken from them, were being given back only part of their lost land and goods when their class standing was corrected. They had really suffered; the Party felt that the least it could do was to give them back what they

8. Ho Chi Minh, "Letter to the Peasants and Cadres on the Successful Completion of Land Reform in the North," *Nhan Dan*, 18 August 1956, translated in Fall, *Ho Chi Minh on Revolution*, pp. 275–77.

9. *Nhan Dan*, 25 August 1956, p. 1.

should never have lost in the first place.[10] As late as September the Party was saying that not many people had been misclassified.[11] When it found out how many had in fact been wrongly classified as landlords, it would realize that there was no way to give full compensation to all of them.

Phu chan *xa* of Bac ninh province provides a good example of some of the early efforts at correction of errors. This *xa* had established an extraordinarily good record in the Resistance, but during land reform, a great many "reactionaries" had been found. In one *xom* of eighty-two families, fifty-two had been branded as "enemies." The land-reform cadres probably pulled out of the *xa* by the beginning of June 1956. For most of June and July and part of August, land-reform cadres of the whole province met together to sum up the results of land reform and undergo reeducation. In July, before these meetings had ended, the chairman and two other members of the land reform *doi* for Phu chan went back to the *xa* to correct errors. They did not expect to find much that needed correcting. They hoped to lower the official figures on land area and productivity, let back into the Party three people who had been expelled, investigate the cases of five people who had been arrested, and be finished within ten days. At this point the land-reform apparatus was still functioning as an independent system, separate from the normal chains of command of both the government and the Party. The Bac ninh land-reform *doan*, plus a team of cadres sent in by the Central Land Reform Committee, were handling the correction of errors. Both seem to have accepted past land-reform policies as having been fundamentally correct.[12]

The proportion of households classified as landlords had been slightly higher in Phu chan than in the surrounding area. The cadre assigned to deal with this issue apparently decided, without even investigating particular families within the *xa*, that what should be done was to bring the proportion of households classified as landlords closer to the average for the area. This required that of the 705 households in Phu chan, the number classified as landlords be reduced from 37 to 34 (from 5.2 percent to 4.8 percent). The man who made this decision did not have to carry it out. Lower-ranking cadres actually working in Phu chan were afraid of the difficulty of paying compensation to those reclassified, so they dragged their feet. Up to the end of August only two landlord households were reclassified.[13]

In the early stages, the cadres sent into Phu chan from outside took most of the initiative in correction. Only after Ho's statement

---

10. Ibid., 31 August 1956, p. 2.

11. Ibid., 24 September 1956.

12. *Hoc Tap* 1, no. 10 (October 1956): 57; *Nhan Dan*, 4 June 1956, p. 1; 21 August 1956, p. 2; 6 September 1956, p. 2.

13. *Nhan Dan*, 6 September 1956, p. 2.

of 18 August reached the *xa* did the peasants begin speaking out to the cadres. One important beneficiary of the peasants' new willingness to express their real opinions was an old Party member who had been wrongly accused of being the ringleader of reactionary activities in Phu chan and had been imprisoned during the land reform. The people of Phu chan had known that the charges against him were false but had not dared to defend him openly. He was released in mid September. Before he went home, he had to attend a study session at which he was persuaded that he should not take revenge against those who had wronged him.[14]

By early September the people of Phu chan knew that this would not be the final correction campaign; a special *doi* of correction cadres would be coming later in the year. In this later correction, after the land-reform apparatus had lost its power, considerably more people must have been reclassified from landlord status. By November the chairman of the province government was saying that every *xa* that had undergone land reform during Wave Five had had "many" people corrected in class status.[15] Figures were published in 1957 for two of the three *xa* that were used as key points in the correction of errors for Bac ninh. The number of households classified as landlords had been reduced from 30 to 14 in one of these *xa* and from 15 to 5 in the other.[16]

The initial efforts at correction had been carried out by the land-reform apparatus, though Party and government leaders who were not part of this apparatus were presumably applying pressure to it. In August 1956 these other leaders began getting into the work directly; Ho issued his statement on correction, and the government of at least one province (Ha dong) began sending its own correction cadres to the villages.[17] In September the land-reform apparatus was stripped of its power. One of the first public signs, around the beginning of September, was that *Nhan Dan* stopped printing articles on the correction of errors embodying the viewpoint of the land-reform apparatus.[18] The Central Land Reform Committee had been planning to present an exposition on land reform in Hanoi from 3 to 30 September; its indefinite "postponement" was announced on 31 August.

In much of the countryside, meanwhile, an open power struggle was developing. The victims of land reform and the old cadres (people who had been village cadres before the mass mobilization) were ranged against the land-reform cadres, the *cot can*, and sometimes the people who had shared in the distribution of

---

14. Ibid., 6 September 1956, p. 2; 19 October 1956, p. 2.

15. *Thoi Moi*, 21 November 1956, p. 1.

16. *Nhan Dan*, 19 March 1957, p. 2; 20 May 1957, p. 2.

17. Ibid., 8 September 1956, p. 2.

18. One such article appeared in *Thoi Moi* as late as 10 September. Since *Thoi Moi* was not a Party newspaper, it may not have heard immediately when the radicals lost power within the Party.

confiscated property. Land-reform cadres working on correction were naturally reluctant to admit, to themselves or to the public, that they had been wrong in expelling old cadres from the Party. Some tried to block reinstatement for old Party members even after authorities at higher levels had decided that the people in question were entitled to rejoin the Party. Land-reform cadres who did restore the Party membership of people who had been wrongly expelled during the land reform sometimes did so without explaining to the public why the people in question were no longer considered reactionaries. This omission undermined the morale and effectiveness of the newly reinstated Party members. On the other hand, as early as July *Nhan Dan* noted that some old Party members who had been expelled from the Party and then reinstated looked down on the new Party members.[19]

Once the radical line had been discredited at the national level, and its leading representatives had either abandoned it or lost the power to enforce it, the balance of power in the villages could shift. Those attacking the results of land reform were emboldened by Ho's statement of 18 August, and their ranks were soon swelled by substantial numbers of released prisoners. On 9 September the Office of the Prime Minister issued circular 3938/Pi, which concerned the release from prison both of people who had been jailed unjustly, and of people who had been guilty of minor offenses but were to be given clemency because their families had participated in the revolution. The release work was in full swing the same month, and over the next few months thousands regained their freedom.[20] The new cadres, conversely, faced increasing criticism and sometimes threats of physical violence. Before the end of September significant numbers of them were becoming so discouraged that they were thinking of resigning their posts.[21]

For Correction on a Broad Scale:
The Tenth Plenum and the Giap Report

At its Tenth (enlarged) Plenum, the Central Committee of the Lao Dong Party acknowledged the full extent of the land-reform errors. This plenum was held in September; given the difficulty of the issues involved, it probably lasted for most of the month. Its decisions were circulated within the Party, reaching the *xa* level in middle and late October, and then published on 30 October. The main communiqué said that the land-reform cadres generally had relied on the poor peasants and laborers, as was proper. But they had not held firmly to the Party's policy on class demarcation; in

---

19. *Nhan Dan*, 2 July 1956, p. 2; 9 July 1956, p. 2.
20. Ibid., 1 October 1956, p. 3; Tran Phuong, *Cach mang ruong dat*, p. 202.
21. *Nhan Dan*, 23 September 1956, p. 2; 30 September 1956.

some areas they had attacked too widely, relied on bad elements, and overestimated the area and productivity of land. Some poor peasants and laborers and many middle peasants had been harmed; rich peasants had been treated almost like landlords. Proper distinctions had not been made within the landlord class in favor of resistance landlords and those whose children had been cadres and soldiers. There had been places where attacks on the enemy had lost direction and had even struck within the ranks of the revolution. Village-level Party rectification had accomplished something in its early stages, but later, especially in Waves Seven and Eight of the rent reduction and Waves Four and Five of the land reform, errors had become serious and widespread and had caused severe damage to the local base of the Party. Rectification at the *huyen* and province levels, although only carried out in some areas before it was halted, had caused serious harm because policy and methods had both been wrong. The communiqué continued:

> The Central Committee Plenum recognized that the policy line of the Central Committee had basically been correct. But the reason why the errors mentioned above occurred was because there were shortcomings in the thinking of the leadership, and therefore some of the policies laid down were not concrete enough or not cautious enough....
> But the direct cause of the serious errors lay in shortcomings in the work of directing the implementation [of land reform] as follows:
> There were many deviations in ideological leadership. At first, when the movement was just being mobilized, the motto "oppose rightism and prevent 'leftism'" was correct. But later, when there were some "leftist" errors in the movement, the leadership not only did not expose these errors, but on the contrary one-sidedly emphasized opposing rightism and did not pay attention to preventing "leftism," and therefore the "leftist" errors became serious.
> Because of deviations in ideological leadership, many policies of the Central Committee were not understood thoroughly, or were misunderstood; there were even places that acted in contradiction to them. Responsible organs sometimes issued, on their own, incorrect directives on questions such as coordinating attacks on the enemy outside [our organizations] with attacks on the enemy within, the need thoroughly to dissolve enemy organizations within the Party, etc.
> The implementing organizations had many serious weaknesses. The land-reform agencies were organized into a separate system, from top to bottom, with excessively broad powers. In deploying the cadres, many areas assigned inexperienced cadres to lead cadres with much experience.... The subjective and self-satisfied thinking and the arbitrary and autocratic work styles of some land-reform cadres led to the phenomena of not carrying out correctly the policy line, not

respecting the principles and regulations of the Party and the laws of the nation, not listening to the ideas of the masses, becoming separated from reality, and becoming separated from the masses....

In general, *the errors in land reform and rectification of organizations were "leftist" errors.*[22]

When these errors had been exposed, the Politburo and the Central Committee had taken steps to correct them, but the situation in some areas was still complex. It was necessary to reclassify people who had been wrongly classified as landlords, rich peasants, or small renters, and to abolish completely the category "other exploiting elements." Those reclassified would enjoy political rights according to their corrected class status and would get appropriate[23] compensation for the economic losses they had suffered. People who had been wrongly *xu tri*[24] would have their honor and their work restored to them. Those who had died[25] as a result of having been wrongly *xu tri* would have their names cleared; their families would be cared for and comforted. The correction of errors would be carried out in a carefully planned manner. Party committees and local administrations at various levels would lead it directly; all elements in the National Front would participate.

The Central Committee recognized the need to strengthen democracy in the DRV; the people's role in government had to be increased. (The fact that this statement had to be made at this time is a sad commentary on the gap between the goals of the land reform and its actual results.) Elected bodies, including the National Assembly, were to be strengthened. New elections were to be held for people's assemblies and administrative committees at various levels. The democratic legal system, and in particular the laws on the political rights and personal freedoms of citizens, also would be strengthened.[26]

The Central Committee as a whole admitted that it had a responsibility for the errors that had been committed, but those of its members who had led the implementation of land reform had the most direct responsibility. These leaders had probably been

---

22. Communiqué of the Tenth (enlarged) Plenum of the Lao Dong Party Central Committee, *Nhan Dan*, 30 October 1956, p. 4.

23. Note the change in policy; the Party was no longer offering full compensation.

24. See discussion of this term on pp. 217–18, n. 31.

25. *Hy sinh,* literally, "sacrificed." This is the term formerly applied to people who had died in the struggle against the French.

26. Soon after this Vo Nguyen Giap said that the newspapers needed to criticize the mistakes of the government and the Party more than they had been doing, though they should not be permitted to exaggerate. *Nhan Dan*, 31 October 1956, p. 3.

engaged in self-criticism as early as July.[27] At the Tenth Plenum they were disciplined. Truong Chinh remained a member of the Politburo and the Central Committee Secretariat, but he resigned as general secretary of the Party and was replaced by Ho Chi Minh.[28] Ho Viet Thang, who had directly led the work of land reform, was removed from the Central Committee and reduced to an ordinary Party member; he was also dismissed as deputy minister of agriculture. Le Van Luong had been responsible for leading rectification of organizations, especially at the province and *huyen* levels. After discovering his errors he had been very energetic in helping to correct them, so although he was removed from his posts as deputy minister of the interior, chairman of the Party's Central Organization Committee, and member of the Politburo and the Central Committee Secretariat, he was permitted to remain an alternate member of the Central Committee.[29]

The Cabinet announced that the Central Land Reform Committee was being stripped of its powers; the decision to do this had probably been made by the Tenth Plenum. The committee continued to exist, but it was restricted to an advisory role.[30]

The day after the decisions of the Tenth Plenum were released, *Nhan Dan* published a very long report by General Vo Nguyen Giap, which went into greater detail on the causes of the land-reform errors and the means to be used in correcting them. The choice of Giap as spokesman for the correction of errors reflected the position of the army as the embodiment of nationalism, as contrasted to the exclusive focus of many land-reform cadres on issues of class struggle. There is no reason to assume that Giap was an opponent of land reform in the long run, but in the immediate disputes between the veteran cadres of the Resistance and the new cadres promoted during mass mobilization, Giap's personal and professional ties were with the former. Thus a few weeks later we find him attending a ceremony clearing the names of former Viet Minh soldiers, in a village of the Hanoi suburbs where five out of eight such veterans had come under unjust suspicion during land reform, and at least one had been imprisoned.[31] Statements on the correction of errors repeatedly stressed that the families of soldiers, many of whom had been attacked during land reform, should get special treatment.

Giap's report described how land-reform errors had harmed members of all classes. Exaggeration of the principle of relying on

---

27. *Nhan Dan*, 4 August 1956, p. 1.

28. There is some doubt as to how long Ho held either the functions or the title of general secretary. Le Duan replaced him at some time between 1957 and 1960.

29. *Nhan Dan*, 30 October 1956, p. 1; 2 November 1956, p. 1.

30. Ibid., 2 November 1956, p. 1; *Thoi Moi*, 19 December 1956, p. 1.

31. *Thoi Moi*, 21 December 1956, p. 2.

the poor peasants and laborers had kept the middle peasants from being given their proper political role, but at the same time some poor peasants had suffered when land-reform cadres attacked "old organizations," or when they set excessive figures for the area and productivity of land. Giap said:

> Because we did not do research, we thought the proportion of landlords in our society was rather high; because we did not hold firmly to the regulations for class demarcation and did not have the attitude [required by] policy, we committed many serious errors in the demarcation of classes. It was not just that in many areas some rich peasants or upper middle peasants were classified as landlords; there were even places where poor peasants and agricultural laborers were classified as landlords....
> Because of mechanically regarding all landlords as enemies, there were places where resistance landlords were also regarded as enemies. Because we did not distinguish the opposition activity of some diehard landlords from the tense situation caused by our incorrect application of policy, we went to the point of overestimating the enemy and thinking there were enemies everywhere. When suppressing [enemies], we emphasized decisiveness but did not emphasize caution, and we used illegal *truy buc*[32] methods. The policy of suppressing sabotage was incorrectly applied, and this further widened the area of struggle. The result was that many innocent people were arrested, *xu tri*, *quan che*, and *bao vay*....[33]
> Because we investigated too little and overemphasized class-ism in regard to the old organizations of the Party, the government, and the various people's organizations, we often slighted or denied accomplishments in the Resistance and only attached importance, in a distorted fashion, to accomplishments in the antilandlord struggle during the mass mobilization for rent reduction and the land reform. As a result we did not correctly evaluate the old organizations; there were even places where we thought that they were seriously complex, that there were enemy organizations within our organizations. Therefore, the deeper our attacks on the enemy went, the more they were misdirected; when we attacked the landlord

---

32. *Truy buc* might perhaps be translated "vigorous interrogation." It certainly included torture in some cases, but it also seems to have been used to describe interrogation of an unwilling subject by nonviolent means. These would probably have included threats, claims that it was the victim's patriotic duty to give the proper answers, and simply the constant repetition of questions and demands over a very long period.

33. For definitions of *quan che* and *bao vay*, see p. 214.

despots and saboteurs, we attacked within our own ranks at the same time. Some Party members and cadres who had worked with the Resistance, some families that had worked with the Resistance and the revolution, and many good [peasant] association members and [youth] league members... were regarded as reactionaries and *quan che, bao vay,* or *xu tri* illegally. The errors in the rectification of organizations were the most serious errors in the whole land reform.

Because of the incorrect treatment of people who were *xu tri,* and their families, and even of landlord families and their children, the livelihood of a number of people in the rural areas encountered many obstacles, and they became impoverished and wretched....

Since our society has been a colonial society, the political attitude of the landlord class is different at some points from that in countries that have not been colonized. The landlord class, considered as a class, is reactionary and must be overthrown. But looking closely at the political attitude of each individual landlord, [we see that] there are a number of small and medium landlords who, although economically they exploit by feudal means, politically have a certain degree of nationalist spirit.... *We must overthrow the landlord class but we must discriminate in our treatment* of each type of landlord; the fewer enemies the better....

The Vietnam Lao Dong Party is the Party of the working class, but it is developing in a country where the working class has not developed much; therefore, aside from aware workers, the Party must recruit outstanding elements of the peasantry, the petty bourgeoisie, and the revolutionary intellectuals, including some from bourgeois and landlord backgrounds who have participated enthusiastically in the revolution and accept the Party's education.... We must attach appropriate importance to class standing but absolutely *avoid falling into classism* and thinking that class standing determines everything....

The important and direct cause of the errors that occurred lay in serious shortcomings in the direction of implementation.

In the direction of implementation, if we review further, in regard to ideology there were "leftist" errors, mainly because things were not adequately founded on reality, and therefore there was not an adequate union between the theory of Marxism-Leninism and the reality of our country. The "leftist" errors in land reform and the rectification of organizations were expressed in the following problems:

a. Emphasizing satisfying the economic and political needs of the laboring peasants was correct, but the error lay in slighting the overall needs of the revolutionary task and in slighting the need to broaden the antifeudal front and the national united front.

Therefore, while carrying out the antifeudal task, we

slighted—there were even areas where the cadres denied—the achievements of the antiimperialist struggle. The land reform was separated from the Resistance and the revolution; there were even places where they were set in opposition to each other....

c. While mobilizing the masses to overthrow the landlord class, it was correct to emphasize decisively overthrowing the landlord class, but the error lay in attacking too widely, without carrying out the policy of discrimination—in not having consideration for the families of landlords who had worked with the revolution and for the families of landlords whose children had served as soldiers or cadres, in not having consideration for resistance landlords, and in not discriminating in the treatment of the landlords' children.

d. While carrying out attacks on the enemy, we overemphasized attacking decisively, did not attach importance to taking precautions against deviations, and did not emphasize the necessity for caution and for avoiding unjust punishment (*xu tri*) of innocent people; therefore we expanded the area of attack, attacked too broadly, and made widespread use of excessive repressive measures.

e. In carrying out land reform in areas with many religious people, we also expanded the area of struggle; we violated the policy of respecting the people's freedom of religion and worship....

In guiding the implementation [of land reform], *on the basis of incorrect ideological leadership as described above, many policies of the Party and government were more misunderstood the further down* [the chain of command] *they went....* Almost all supplementary policy measures aimed at broadening the antifeudal front or dividing the landlord class went unapplied or were inadequately applied. After peace was reestablished, policy emphasized restricting the area of struggle and using more administrative methods but in practice attack and struggle spread broadly; policy forbade *truy buc* but in practice *truy buc* became widespread.[34]

During Wave Five, the fundamental attitude of the land-reform cadres had generally been good, but most of them had been inexperienced, and their training had been inadequate and sometimes incorrect. As a result, they had gone seriously astray. In April 1956, when the errors began to be uncovered, the Politburo had issued a preliminary directive on correction. More recently a variety of actions had been taken, first of all the restoration of

---

34. Speech by Vo Nguyen Giap to a public meeting in Hanoi, 29 October 1956, in *Nhan Dan,* 31 October 1956, p. 2. All emphasis is in the original. Portions of the above, especially paragraph d, have sometimes been badly mistranslated.

freedom and honor to people who had been wrongly *xu tri*. These correction efforts had accomplished something, but the situation in many areas was still difficult and complex; the land-reform personnel had not been doing very well. The Central Committee had issued twelve points of policy for the correction of errors:

1. ...All Party members who have been wrongly *xu tri* must have their Party membership restored. Party members who belonged to the landlord and rich-peasant classes, and who met the standards for Party membership but were wrongly *xu tri* during land reform and rectification of organizations, should all have their Party membership restored.

2. Cadres and other people who have been wrongly *xu tri* shall all benefit from the correction. Politically, they shall have their civil rights, honor, and work restored. Those who have been wrongly imprisoned must all be freed. Economically, they must be given appropriate compensation and helped to make a living. All medals, honors, and titles that have been taken away must be restored.

3. The policy of special consideration for revolutionary soldiers, demobilized soldiers, the war wounded, the families of martyrs, the families of soldiers, and the families of democratic personalities must be carried out correctly.

4. Correct the classification of people who have been wrongly called landlords, rich peasants, and small renters. Abolish the category "other exploiting classes"; everyone so classified must be reclassified. Everyone whose class standing has been corrected shall enjoy political rights according to policy; economically, they shall receive appropriate compensation to [help] them make a living.

The question of giving back property to people who have been wrongly classified as landlords or wrongly *xu tri* should be discussed by the peasants so as to settle it on a basis of unity, compromise, negotiation, and mutual aid, so that they will have what they need to make a living; but in general one should not infringe upon the property rights distributed to the peasants in rent reduction and land reform.

5. Do not treat the rich peasants like landlords. Carry out correctly the policy of allying with the rich peasants.

Carry out correctly the provisions decided upon for the treatment of the landlords after the land reform. Resistance landlords must be treated like any other working person and not discriminated against in political, economic, cultural, and social matters. People classified as ordinary landlords, whose children are cadres or soldiers, shall be regarded as resistance landlords.

Now that the land reform is over, there must be broader provisions for the livelihood, movements, and change of class status of the landlords....

8. Wherever area and productivity have been measured

wrongly, they must be corrected so the people will feel secure in production and will pay their rightful shares. Wherever there is an error, it must be corrected; do not overcorrect.

9. It is urgent that we help people who, because of land-reform errors, are now seriously ill or have no way of making a living; emphasize helping old people and children of no matter what class.

10. Cancel all *quan che* of people wrongly labeled reactionaries or despots, no matter what class these people belong to; do not cancel *quan che* of [genuine] landlord despots not considered to deserve imprisonment, or of hooligans sentenced to *quan che* by a provincial court. Abolish all *bao vay*, even of people who are *quan che*....

11. As for cadres of the land reform and rectification of organizations who have committed errors, it is necessary primarily to criticize them and educate them to help them correct their errors. Correct cases in which people have been disciplined or commended incorrectly.[35]

The Development of Correction

At first the correction of errors was carried out piecemeal, with various problems being handled as they were discovered. Not until the end of 1956 was a coordinated three-step program of correction worked out and teams of correction cadres sent down to the villages. Even after this the campaign, while not free of commandism, did not attain the levels of order and uniformity that had been such prominent (and disastrous) characteristics of the land reform. The cadres sent down to the villages to work on correction had less power than those previously sent to work on land reform. They were sent to help local cadres carry out the correction, not to run things themselves. Also, there were only about three correction cadres sent to an average *xa*, of whom one or two might be former land-reform cadres.[36] During land reform there had been fifteen or twenty cadres sent to an average *xa*. The correction cadres had to get Party and government organs in the villages functioning reasonably well before they would be able to accomplish much else.

Step One, accomplished mainly during December 1956, attempted to restore order and calm to the villages, get local cadres back to working effectively, and prepare the way for full-scale correction. Correction policies were publicized. The Party, the non-Party cadres, and the people were invited to study the decisions of the Tenth Plenum and other key documents (though there is surprisingly little evidence that Giap's report was the subject of formal

---

35. Ibid., pp. 2–3.
36. *Thoi Moi*, 4 December 1956, p. 4; also 5 April 1957, p. 4.

study). The release of people wrongly imprisoned was almost completed, and a start was made on the correction of official figures for the area and productivity of land. There were also some people whose class status was corrected and who were paid compensation for the losses they had suffered in the land reform. The Party and government were reorganized at the village level, with many old cadres who had been expelled during land reform returning to key posts.

After Step One many cadres shifted their attention for several weeks to preparations for Tet, the Vietnamese New Year, which came at the beginning of February. This is a holiday for which families gather together in their homes, and with the correction of errors not yet completed, it presented enormous problems. For one thing, there were savage conflicts over possession of houses, as well as altars and other items necessary in the ceremonies of ancestor worship. Most families that had been classified as land-lords had had their houses and much of their other property confiscated and distributed to the poor peasants and laborers. Some of these families had been reclassified as peasants but had not yet received any property back; others expected to be reclas-sified, or said they did. They demanded that their homes be returned at once so they would be able to celebrate Tet properly. In some cases cadres were told to put people who had been wrongly classified as landlords back into their former homes *together with* the people to whom the houses had been distributed, to celebrate Tet together.[37] There must have been some rationale for this directive, but it looks like a recipe for disaster. In most cases houses were left for the moment in the hands of the peasants to whom they had been distributed, and families from whom they had been confiscated were told to stay where they were. (Large-scale reallocation of housing and the construction of new housing with government aid took place later in the year.) Around Tet the government distributed some food and clothing to ease the plight of those who had been wronged in land reform, and to ease tensions in the villages.

Another problem was that many soldiers and officials came home to visit their families over the Tet holiday. If they felt that their families had not been treated properly, they were likely to inter-vene very forcefully with local cadres, demanding justice. They had to be persuaded to let the correction of errors take its slow and very difficult course, and not to attack local cadres.

Step Two, the most important to the peasants, came after a reasonable degree of calm had been restored to the villages. Most of the correction of class standing took place during Step Two, and people who had been wrongly classified were given back part of the property that had been taken from them. It was divided into two substeps. The first, which consisted of handling some

---

37. *Nhan Dan*, 25 January 1957, pp. 1, 4.

problems left over from Step One and studying the policies on correction of class status and property compensation, occupied much of early 1957. The second, the actual reclassification and compensation, got started on a broad scale in May and lasted through most of the summer.

Step Three involved cleaning up loose ends, as well as completing the reorganization of political and administrative bodies in the villages. The bulk of the errors had been corrected by late 1957, but some of the more difficult cases seemed to drag on interminably. A Cabinet statement of June 1958 said that the correction of errors was basically complete, but even then some problems were still awaiting settlement.

Conflict in the Villages

The land-reform errors had sown hatred and fear in the villages; neither the victims nor the perpetrators of these errors could quickly forget the past and learn to work together again. A cadre investigating conditions in one *xa* of Thai binh recounted some striking vignettes. At a meeting to study correction policies, a demobilized soldier had brought a container of excrement to smear in the mouth of another person, who had made accusations against him during land reform. A man named Giang, after his release from prison, sharpened a knife and also took to carrying a staff with a sharp iron point everywhere he went. His neighbor Dao, who had made false accusations against him, fled the village and was not seen again for weeks.[38] Dao may have suspected that Giang could maim or kill him and get away with it. In another village of Thai binh, on the night of 8 October 1956, a group of men had darkened their faces, burst into the home of a 56-year-old woman whom they felt had wronged them in the land reform, and beaten her to death. The ringleader was the only member of the group sent to prison for this killing; the Appeals Court for the Left Bank Zone sentenced him to seven years. By way of contrast, when the same court heard the case of some men who had committed errors in the land reform, who had ambushed and killed one of their former victims who had taken an abusive and threatening attitude after his release from prison late in 1956, it gave prison sentences to four of the killers, for a total of nineteen years.[39] Clearly, justice was more friendly to the victims of land-reform errors than to the perpetrators.

The situation in T.N. *xa*, Hung yen, was very tense. Comrade Kiet was an agricultural laborer who had risen to command a platoon in the Resistance and then had spent the last two years of the war in a French prison. After the end of the war he was

---

38. *Thoi Moi*, 14 February 1957, pp. 1, 3.
39. Ibid., 13 March 1957, p. 4; 14 March 1957, p. 4.

released, and he returned home to become commander of the *xa* militia. Then the land-reform cadres came, branded him a counter-revolutionary (in defiance of the evidence and of public sentiment; see above, p. 231), and imprisoned him. His family got much less than a normal share in the distribution of landlord property and remained very poor. After his release from prison, his rage was maintained at a maximum by the sight of one of his close neighbors, who had served in the French armed forces up to the end of the war, returned to the village, became a *cot can* during land reform, and ended up living in comparative luxury in a fine large house confiscated from a landlord. Kiet used his prestige and leadership ability to organize assaults on the *cot can*. He was very systematic. Sometimes there would be incidents almost simultaneously in all three of the *thon* that made up T.N. *xa*. Kiet had a graded scale of punishments; a young woman who was regarded mainly with contempt got off with insults and slaps in the face, while the man who had been chief of police during the land reform (quoted above, p. 233) had to be hospitalized at least once for his injuries. This was not a brief outburst of violence; leading *cot can* were beaten over and over.[40] Although the victims included members of the Lao Dong Party, nobody even considered arresting Kiet for these beatings.

New cadres in many villages had been promoted too rapidly, without much training, to posts they could not handle. Le Van Luong, who had been the member of the Politburo most directly involved in Party reorganization during the land reform, had said explicitly that it was all right to promote people to posts for which they were not fully qualified, if they had the proper spirit.[41] This policy had led to a general decline in administrative efficiency; mass education and public health work may have suffered particularly. When public revelation of land-reform errors deprived the new cadres of even their moral authority, many *xa* were left almost leaderless. *Nhan Dan* reported: "In September and October of 1956, the situation was quite serious; there were chaotic phenomena in many areas, and leadership in the villages seemed almost paralyzed. In some places it was completely paralyzed."[42] When Ho's statement of 18 August reached one village where the actions and work style of the new cadres had been particularly bad, the masses, who had long disliked the new cadres, went out looking for them to attack them. The new cadres retreated into their homes and closed up like oysters, not daring to go anywhere or do anything. Almost all organization in the village collapsed.[43]

The development of labor-exchange teams suffered particular setbacks. In theory, there should have been a very vigorous

---

40. Xuan Chi, in *Thoi Moi*, 6, 8, 10, and 17 April 1957.
41. *Hoc Tap* 1, no. 3 (February 1956): 22.
42. *Nhan Dan*, 7 January 1957, p. 2.
43. Ibid., 8 February 1957.

development of labor exchange starting with the last stages of land reform. But many of the labor-exchange teams that had existed before land reform had collapsed when the old cadres who had organized them were purged. New teams had been formed under the auspices of the land-reform cadres and *cot can,* but they had been organized too hastily and many of the members had been coerced into joining them. Most of them fell apart when the *cot can* were discredited late in 1956. *Nhan Dan* said in December 1956 that 58 percent of all peasant households were in labor-exchange teams, but this was a purely theoretical figure, suspiciously close to the level of 60 percent that had been set as a target for the end of the year. It probably embraced all families that had been in teams either before or after land reform. The maximum proportion ever in labor-exchange teams at one time was probably less than 50 percent, and the number in functioning teams in December 1956 may have been less than 20 percent. Even at the end of 1957, after a year of recovery, less than 30 percent of the peasant households were in labor-exchange teams.[44]

The most pressing concrete task was to complete the release of people who had been wrongly imprisoned; they were freed in several stages. First came cadres and Party members who had been wrongly imprisoned; next came ordinary laboring peasants; finally came landlords who had not done anything that really merited imprisonment, and also some actual criminals who had committed comparatively minor crimes and were given clemency. Clemency was offered especially to members of the families of cadres, soldiers, and people who had died fighting the French. More than 12,000 people had been released by the beginning of December.[45] This figure probably included almost all the cadres and Party members wrongly imprisoned, plus a substantial portion of the ordinary peasants and a few landlords. The total number of cadres, Party members, and laboring peasants found innocent and released from prison was probably not much above 12,000. The release of substantial numbers of landlords, and persons considered actually to have committed crimes but given clemency, occurred mostly in the first half of 1957.

When old cadres were released from prison, they were not sent immediately home to their villages. Some needed a period of medical care and good food to restore their health, and all needed a considerable amount of indoctrination to persuade them not to seek revenge on those responsible for their imprisonment. When finally sent home, they were given something to live on while reestablishing themselves.[46] Once these people had returned to their villages,

---

44. Ibid., 5 December 1956, p. 1; 27 December 1956, p. 2; 18 May 1957, p. 2; 16 June 1957, p. 2; 28 November 1957, p. 1; 5 April 1958, p. 2; *Thoi Moi,* 27 June 1956, p. 1.

45. *Thoi Moi,* 4 December 1956, p. 1.

46. Provincial authorities in Nam dinh gave out 50 to 200 kilo-

they were entitled to positions in the Party and government. However, conflicts arose over their demands, which were often not granted, that they get back the particular posts they had held before the land reform.

There were, of course, disputes over who had really been imprisoned unjustly and who had not. Some people, including land-reform cadres afraid of losing face and *cot can* afraid of revenge by their former victims, but also people genuinely convinced that the land-reform victims would not have been convicted and imprisoned unless they were guilty, tried to prevent too many from being released. In Phu tho province it was argued that there had been serious errors only in Waves Four and Five, so no review of the cases of people imprisoned in Waves One and Two would be necessary. On the other hand, cadres in some areas, either reacting against the excesses of land reform or showing the tendency (previously mentioned in connection with the Chinese land reform) to carry out shifts in policy in an exaggerated fashion, released the innocent and guilty indiscriminately. This happened particularly in Hong Quang, Hung yen, Hai duong, and Ha dong.[47]

In the initial months of the correction, the *cot can* and their allies still had the upper hand in many villages. They were often reluctant to announce to the public that the comrades being released had been cleared of the crimes for which they had been imprisoned; they were also not eager to welcome them back into political and administrative bodies. But before the end of 1956, as repeated statements from Party and government spokesmen criticizing land-reform excesses took effect and as more old cadres returned to their villages, the new cadres were put on the defensive. It became accepted that most people *xu tri* had been wrongly *xu tri*.[48] In context, this meant both that most people expelled from the Party had been wrongly expelled and that most peasants and cadres imprisoned had been wrongly imprisoned.

Many of the old cadres returning from prison, despite the indoctrination they had received, were eager for revenge against the *cot can* who had wronged them. They were supported by land-reform victims who had not been imprisoned and also by some genuine landlords who saw the correction of errors as an opportunity to undo the land reform. There arose a widespread inclination to throw the new cadres out of all major village organizations. Some old Party members, when asked to meetings to discuss the decisions of the Tenth Plenum, said, "Give us back our Party membership and throw out all the new Party members; then we will come to the meeting."[49] The cadres responsible for the correction

grams of rice per person. Ibid., 15 November 1956, p. 1.

47. *Nhan Dan*, 8 December 1956, p. 2.
48. Ibid., 21 November 1956, p. 2.
49. Ibid., 8 April 1957, p. 2.

of errors often supported attacks on the new cadres. In an area of Nghe an where 1,839 people had been put onto *xa*-level Party committees during land reform, 1,163 had been removed by early 1957. All of the new members had been removed from the Party committees of thirty-two of the *xa* in this area.[50] In some areas female cadres were especially attacked, because the promotion of female cadres had become associated with the land reform. *Nhan Dan* explained: "Because of the tendency to throw everyone elected during the land reform off the [peasant-association] executive committees, and the wrong ideas that new cadres all lack ability and that women habitually made false accusations, are busy taking care of children, and cannot work, there were *xa* that did not keep a single new cadre; there were good women peasant-association secretaries, who had the confidence of the people, who were removed from the [peasant-association] executive committee."[51]

The old cadres had abilities and prestige that made them indispensable. However, the Party leadership also wanted to retain as many of the new cadres as possible. Some new cadres, who were too much hated, could no longer have any role in politics. Those who had committed excesses out of deliberate malice had to be punished. But the bulk of the new cadres had gone wrong simply by doing what the land-reform cadres had asked. They were, as a group, the political representatives of the policy promoting the interests of the poor peasants and laborers. This policy was vitally important; it could not be abandoned just because it had been so grievously misapplied. Some Party members argued that the land reform had gone wrong because of the policy of relying on the poor peasants and laborers; the people who held this opinion openly doubted that the poor had a greater revolutionary capacity than the other classes in the countryside. Some comrades cited the low proportion of poor peasants and laborers in the leadership of the Resistance, the errors committed by the poor-peasant and laborer *cot can*, and the poor performance of the new cadres since the correction of errors had begun.[52] These arguments struck at the heart of Party doctrine.

If the Party had permitted all the *cot can* who had committed errors in the land reform to be stripped of their positions, the principle of favoring the poor peasants and laborers might have been seriously compromised. The Party denied indignantly that it was defending the new cadres only because it had no choice, like a couple who wish they had not had a child but are forced to raise it,[53] but this was in fact a good description of some aspects of the

---

50. Ibid., 27 March 1957, p. 2.

51. Ibid., 16 January 1957, p. 3.

52. Ibid., 16 January 1957, p. 1; 7 February 1957, p. 2; 7 March 1957, p. 2.

53. Ibid., 25 November 1956, p. 2.

situation. The Party was stuck with the new cadres, in the short run, as representatives of their class.

The Party's defense of the new cadres was rather weak. It argued that they were poor peasants and were basically good, that the excesses they had committed had been primarily the fault of their superiors rather than themselves, and that they should be trained and helped to correct their mistakes. It did not try to deny that making false accusations against innocent people had been typical behavior for the new cadres during land reform; it only argued that their motives had not been malicious.

There were individual cases in which peasants who had made false accusations really did not deserve opprobrium. For example, a woman in Thai binh had become very nervous and had had trouble sleeping after both of her closest neighbors were arrested early in the land reform. Sure enough, she was hauled in one night to be questioned about them. The land-reform cadres alternated polite questions with shouted demands that she denounce her friends. She held out for three hours before they got her to agree that for one of her neighbors to have taught Chinese characters and classical Chinese literature meant that he had spread "propaganda of a corrupt and reactionary culture." From this other accusations followed. It was not really fair to brand this woman "the mother of false accusations"; she was a victim.[54] But the Party felt obliged to defend many peasants who had involved themselves in the land-reform errors far more deeply than this woman had, and under less compulsion.

Cadre morale was very low; both old and new cadres felt they had been subjected to denunciation and humiliation for actions that had been in accord with Party policy at the time they were committed. The old cadres were not satisfied simply to have been rehabilitated; with another change in policy they might be attacked again. The new cadres were not even certain they had really been forgiven; many suspected that after helping to restore order in Step One of the correction campaign, new Party members would be thrown out of the Party in Step Two. The families of both old and new cadres sometimes urged them to abandon politics; it had proven an unrewarding occupation in the recent past.

Both old and new Party members, even when asked to participate in Party activities, sometimes refused. T.N. *xa* may have been an extreme case; for a time none of the most important old Party members were willing to rejoin the Party. Three of them—Lan, Ton, and Kiet—formed a de facto government controlling all activities in their home *thon*, but they would not work together with the official government or Party organs of the *xa*. Comrade Lan's abilities and prestige were so great that he would be made both Party secretary and chairman of the *xa* administration when he became willing to accept these posts. But when the

---

54. *Thoi Moi*, 12 February 1957, p. 3.

correction cadres first approached him, he and his wife replied with bitter sarcasm that public affairs should be left to the *cot can*, who were better qualified and more "pure."[55]

One of the striking things about this period is the way *Nhan Dan* acknowledged the dichotomy between old and new cadres. The Party dearly wished to let bygones be bygones, but most of its statements accepted the idea that the new cadres as a group had committed errors during land reform, while the old cadres as a group had been attacked during land reform.

The Quynh luu Riots

In November 1956 severe rioting broke out among Catholic peasants in Quynh luu *huyen*, Nghe an province. The story of this incident presented in the standard histories by American scholars begins on 2 November, when a mobile team of the International Control Commission was traveling through Nghe an. A group of peasants tried to present petitions to the team, asking to go to the South, and when soldiers interfered the peasants attacked them. The riot quickly spread to become a revolt embracing the entire *huyen*, and large numbers of troops were required to suppress it. About a thousand peasants were killed or wounded, and several thousand were imprisoned.[56]

The version of these events given in the North Vietnamese press is less spectacular and does not mention the incident of 2 November. It begins on 5 November, when antigovernment elements from several *xa* in Quynh luu concentrated in Quynh yen *xa* and closed off the *xa*. This would have been a plausible sequel to the attempt to petition the ICC, if such an attempt was made. The instigators of the incident were reactionaries who had been plotting in secret for a long time; they were led by a man who had served the French as a paratrooper but had been pardoned by the DRV after the war. These reactionaries had obtained substantial public sympathy by exploiting the anger of Catholic peasants over the errors committed in land reform. When a delegation of cadres accompanied by soldiers came from the *huyen* capital to explain the government's policy and restore order, gangs composed mostly of peasant youths attacked them, injuring ten people and taking twenty-eight soldiers prisoner.[57]

---

55. Xuan Chi, in *Thoi Moi*, 6 April 1957, p. 3. Lan had been chairman of the *xa* administration before land reform. The pre-reform Party secretary does not seem to have been in the area during the correction of errors; he may have died during land reform.

56. Buttinger, *Vietnam*, 2:915–16, 1124–25. Fall, *The Two Vietnams*, pp. 156–57.

57. *Nhan Dan*, 18 November 1956, p. 3; 21 November 1956, p. 2;

On 13 November a large crowd, recruited from several places in the *huyen*, set out in a march on the *huyen* capital, armed with sticks, spears, and knives, and shouting antigovernment slogans. Soldiers met them on the road and tried to send them home. Members of the crowd attacked the soldiers. Some civilians living near the road came out to help the soldiers and attack the marchers. The soldiers were trying both to protect themselves against the marchers and to separate the marchers from the people who lived along the road. In the melee several people were killed, including one soldier. Finally, some of the marchers were arrested and the rest were dispersed. On the following day, soldiers came to Quynh yen *xa*, arrested the ringleaders of the affair, and dispersed the rest of the people gathered there.[58]

It seems likely that the second version of this story is much closer to the truth. It has as much internal consistency as can be expected in descriptions of such an affair.[59] The details seem plausible, except for one attempt to claim that the only Catholic killed had been one of the soldiers on the road on 13 November.[60] The story is in accord with the way the people involved might have been expected to behave under such circumstances. In particular, it is fully believable that civilians in this area would have come out to attack a crowd of antigovernment demonstrators. There were many poor peasants, especially *cot can*, suffering terrible humiliation over the false accusations they had made against fellow villagers during land reform. They must have been ecstatic at this opportunity to redeem their sins, in their own eyes and in those of the world, by assaulting some undeniably genuine reactionaries who were in the very act of attacking the government.

The version of events given by Buttinger and Fall appears to come from anonymous anti-Communist sources in Saigon. Certainly they did not have access to much accurate information about even the main outlines of events in the North in this period; both are under the impression that the correction-of-errors campaign was in large part a response to the "revolt" of November, and Buttinger even says that this revolt was what caused the DRV to halt the land-reform campaign.[61] If we accept their version of events and assume that what was published in *Nhan Dan* was deceptive, we

---

30 April 1957, p. 1.

58. Ibid., 18 November 1956, p. 3; see also *Thoi Moi*, 16 November 1956, p. 1.

59. *Nhan Dan*, 30 April 1957, p. 1, does not quite match 18 November 1956, p. 3. Also, for the "several" people reported killed in early accounts to have turned out finally to have been only two people (*Thoi Moi*, 26 November 1956, p. 3) is suspicious but not impossible.

60. *Nhan Dan*, 20 January 1957, p. 2.

61. Buttinger, *Vietnam*, 2:915.

will still have difficulty explaining the accounts in *Nhan Dan*. The most strongly held grudges in the countryside were those against the poor-peasant *cot can*; in any widespread revolt spurred by land-reform abuses, a number of *cot can* would certainly have been killed, and quite possibly some other poor peasants. If this had in fact occurred, it is very hard to see why the rebels would not have been accused of having killed a single peasant, either at the time of the incident or when the ringleaders were tried.[62]

There probably was no direct foreign involvement in the Quynh luu rioting. The ringleaders were referred to as lackeys of the Americans and of Ngo Dinh Diem, but this seems to have been meant only in a general sense; the DRV did not claim that the Americans, or Saigon, had helped plan the riots or had known about them in advance. Indeed, while *Nhan Dan* fulminated against people who were in a vague, spiritual sense "lackeys" of the United States or Diem, it had little to say about actual agents, less even than one would expect on the basis of American accounts of this period. *Nhan Dan* may not have wished to spread alarm by publicizing the activities of such agents, but one should also note that the American accounts may exaggerate the extent of external interference in the affairs of the DRV. Security personnel in Haiphong told Mieczyslaw Maneli that they believed that officials of the Saigon government had been writing falsified reports of infiltration of the North and pocketing the money that the CIA had given them to pay for the phony missions.[63] Those agents who actually did go to the North probably exaggerated the extent of their sabotage activities in their reports to Saigon.[64]

Reclassification

Some reclassification of people wrongly branded landlords or rich peasants had occurred as early as August 1956, and it continued on a piecemeal basis from that point onward. The first attempts were far too conservative. The national leadership of the DRV had not yet come out strongly against the land-reform errors, few of the old cadres who had been imprisoned in land reform had returned to their villages, and much of the reclassification was supposed to be carried out by the land-reform cadres and *cot can* who had committed the errors in the first place.

After the decisions of the Tenth Plenum were published, a substantial amount of reclassification occurred in some *xa*, especially in Hong Quang, Bac ninh, and Thai binh. The imprisoned cadres and peasants were just returning to their homes, feeling

---

62. *Nhan Dan*, 30 April 1957, p. 1; *Thoi Moi*, 4 May 1957, pp. 1, 3.

63. Mieczyslaw Maneli, interview, New York, 30 December 1975.

64. *Nhan Dan*, 21 March 1958, p. 4.

against land-reform errors was at its height, and the cadres responsible for reclassification did not yet have detailed directives from their superiors on how to carry it out. There was a tendency to lower the class status of a great many people, including some who really were landlords. In one *thon* of Bac ninh twelve families had been labeled as landlords during the land reform; three of these had been labeled as despots. A correction committee composed mostly of middle peasants, chaired by an old cadre who had been expelled from the Lao Dong Party during land reform and had not yet been readmitted, lowered eight of the families that had been called landlords, including all three of the despots, to the status of middle peasants. In one *xa* of Hong Quang where thirty-nine families had been called landlords and twenty-one called rich peasants, the correction left only five families landlords and four families rich peasants. Later checks showed that at least five of the families that had been lowered from landlord status really had been landlords. Hong Quang leaders took steps around mid December to prevent such overcorrection.[65]

Some supplementary directives on class demarcation appeared, clarifying the decrees that had been issued during land reform and making minor revisions.[66] In most *xa*, the peasants and cadres studied class-demarcation policy between February and April of 1957. The actual reclassification began to develop in broad areas in May. The people who had been classified as landlords during land reform would first be investigated by the *xa* reclassification committee and then have their cases discussed publicly at peasant meetings. Decisions on reclassification did not become final until approved by authorities above the *xa* level.

A new wave of conservatism, probably motivated by the immense problem of returning confiscated property to people whose class status was lowered, appeared in May and June. But in the end, more than half the people who had been classified as landlords during the land reform were reclassified.[67] The same was probably true of those who had been classified as rich peasants. Most of the people who had been wrongly classified turned out actually to have been middle peasants.[68] It is quite possible that if we excluded those wrongly classified as rich peasants and counted only those wrongly classified as landlords, a majority would still have been middle peasants.

Most of the reclassification was really what it claimed to be: a

---

65. Ibid., 13 February 1957, p. 2; 14 February 1957, p. 2; 13 August 1957, p. 2.

66. Decree 1196 TTg of 28 December 1956 on class demarcation in the countryside, text in ibid., 29 March 1957, p. 2; see also 1 April 1957, p. 2; 11 April 1957, p. 2; 15 April 1957, p. 2; 18 June 1957, p. 2.

67. Ibid., 18 April 1958, p. 2.

68. Ibid., 20 March 1957, p. 2; 2 June 1957, p. 2.

more correct application of the criteria that should have been applied during the land reform. There were some cases in which standards were altered and people were assigned a status to which they would not have been entitled under the regulations in force during land reform; the requirements for becoming a "resistance landlord" were loosened significantly. These cases, however, were a minority; most changes in class status represented correction of real errors.

The correction of class demarcation was plagued by partisanship on both sides. Those who had been victims of land-reform errors tended to sympathize with people wanting their class status to be lowered. Also, the friends and relatives of those classified as landlords helped to get their class status lowered. On the other side, the poor peasants in general would benefit if as few people as possible were reclassified, because they had been the beneficiaries when property confiscated in the land reform had been distributed. The *cot can* who had made the original classifications also had a natural desire to have their decisions confirmed. People who had no stake in either side often preferred to keep quiet even if they had clear opinions on the merits of a given case; recent events had suggested that unnecessary involvement in political decisions was most unwise. The Party was worried both that some real landlords would have their class status lowered and that some mistaken classifications would not be corrected. In the end, however, it decided the reclassification had been very satisfactory. In Son tay province, special checks were run in twelve *xa* where the number of families lowered from landlord status had been unusually large or small. Hardly any mistakes were found; these had simply been *xa* where the number of families wrongly classified had been unusually large or small.[69]

According to Table 12-1, after the correction of errors, about 1.8 percent of the households, or 2.3 percent of the rural population, were classified as landlords. Of the landlords, about 13 percent were considered despots and about 9 percent resistance landlords. Before the correction of errors, the total number of families classified as landlords had been more than twice as large; the proportion of the landlords classified as despots had probably been higher before the correction of errors and the proportion classified as resistance landlords much lower.

Up to the middle of 1956 there seem to have been few cases of people classified as landlords demanding their land and property back from the peasants after the land-reform cadres had left, probably fewer than in Central-South China. But by late 1956 substantial conflicts over property were breaking out. People who felt they had been wrongly classified sometimes demanded their property back from the peasants to whom it had been distributed

---

69. Ibid., 11 February 1957, p. 2; 13 February 1957, p. 2; 10 March 1957, p. 2; 18 July 1957, p. 2; 31 July 1957, p. 2.

Table 12-1—Class demarcation in the countryside, after the correction of errors

	Families		Persons	
	Number	Percent	Number	Percent
Landlords[a]	47,900	1.8	243,736	2.3
despots	6,220	0.2	34,861	0.3
ordinary landlords	37,411	1.4	185,399	1.7
resistance landlords	4,269	0.2	23,476	0.2
Rich peasants[a]	30,680	1.2	168,899	1.6
Middle peasants[b]		31.9		36.2
Poor peasants[b]		44.1		42.7
Laborers[b]		16.7		13.0
Others[b]		3.7		3.5
Total[c]	2,612,523		10,699,504	

a. Data from either 3,563 or 3,653 *xa*. Mazaev, *Agrarnaia reforma*, p. 103.

b. Data from 1,508 *xa*. Tran Phuong, *Cach mang ruong dat*, pp. 161–62.

c. Mazaev, *Agrarnaia reforma*, p. 87.

without waiting for formal reclassification. Some genuine landlords exploited the general discredit that had fallen on the land reform to "raise their heads" and try to get their property back. The Party repeatedly warned its cadres that they had to distinguish the legitimate demands of the peasants from the efforts of the landlords to raise their heads.[70] Problems were particularly great in Catholic areas, where the land reform had been in part an attack on the clerical and lay leadership of the church, and the landlords could claim that it was a religious duty for the peasants to renounce their gains.[71]

The Party wanted any restoration of property to its original owners to take place through formal channels, after formal reclassification. Persons who had been wrongly classified as landlords were not to get their land back directly from the people to whom it had been distributed, or even to negotiate a settlement with them and then ask the approval of village cadres.

When drawing up plans for the amount of property that was to be returned to reclassified families, the cadres faced almost insuperable obstacles. Most villages were so short of land that it was politically impossible to return all the land that had been taken from such families. Such a procedure would have meant taking too much away from the poor peasants and laborers and thus seriously compromising the Party's social and political goals. On the other hand, those who had been wrongly classified frequently demanded, with what appeared obvious justice, that what should never have been taken from them should be returned. When cadres tried to persuade one woman in Vinh linh to consider the Party's problems and accept less than the return of all her confiscated property, she said: "The Party didn't take anything of mine, and I am not making the Party pay compensation. Those people [peasants in her village] took my property, and they must give all of it back."[72]

Leaders at the national level abandoned the idea of full compensation as soon as they realized how many people had been wrongly classified. Cadres in some places where the reaction against the land-reform excesses was especially strong, notably Hong Quang, continued to support the idea of full compensation a bit longer. But local cadres usually had to negotiate with the people being reclassified to persuade them to accept something less than full compensation,[73] and had to use any possible method to get land to give them. One of the things that made compensation vital was that

---

70. Ibid., 18 January 1957, p. 2; 12 March 1957, p. 2.

71. See *Thoi Moi*, 24 February 1957, p. 2.

72. *Nhan Dan*, 22 June 1957, p. 2.

73. There were some cases in which families that had been wrongly classified were threatened that they would not be reclassified until they had promised to accept less than full compensation, but such cases do not seem to have been frequent. Ibid., 25 June 1957, p. 2; 13 August 1957, p. 2.

the people who had been wrongly classified as landlords had often lost considerably more of their property than should have been taken, under the land-reform law, even from landlords; their houses had been taken, and they had been left with less land than the amount being distributed to poor peasants living in the same area. Sometimes, therefore, the "compensation" only brought them up to the level of wealth they should have been permitted to retain if they really had been landlords. Even some genuine landlords had to be given something, if they had been so impoverished that they seemed in danger of starvation. The minimum compensation for those being reclassified was often described as "appropriate compensation to help them make a living."

By April 1958, about half the amount of land taken from people wrongly classified as landlords had been returned to them. Rich peasants wrongly classified as landlords had been given back less than half what they had lost, on the average; middle peasants had been given 63 percent, and other laboring classes had been given 89 percent; 64 percent of the people who had been wrongly classified as landlords had been given back their houses, and 17 percent had been given back part of the housing that had been taken from them.[74] The main source of the compensation was the property that had been distributed during the land reform. The cadres were not supposed to use commandist tactics to get the peasants to give up land; they were supposed to negotiate and persuade them to do so. Some people who had been correctly classified as rich peasants were offered reclassification as middle peasants if in return they would donate some land to be used as compensation for people wrongly classified.[75] Some land that had been set aside for athletic fields or other public uses was also given to reclassified peasants. Finally, as a last resort, the government paid for compensation in some cases where other arrangements were insufficient. The most important instances may have been government payment for the construction of new housing to end conflicts over confiscated homes. But as *Nhan Dan* pointed out, Vietnam was too poor for the government to be able to pay large amounts of compensation to the land-reform victims, and in any case it would all be coming from the peasants indirectly via taxes.[76]

The correction of errors had not gone very far in reversing the transfer of wealth that had occurred in the land reform. More than half of those who had been classified as landlords had been reclassified, but most of the land that had been redistributed had come from the truly rich, who really were landlords and had not been reclassified. The redistributed land, including communal land and land that had been taken from religious institutions and other

---

74. Ibid., 18 April 1958, p. 2.
75. Ibid., 6 May 1957, p. 1.
76. Ibid., 15 January 1957, p. 4; 20 March 1957, p. 2.

Table 12-2—Changes in land ownership and use, in hectares per person, from before the land reform to after the reform and the correction of errors

	Land Owned before Reform	Land Owned or Used before Reform	Land Owned after Reform
Middle peasants	.126	.168	.161
Poor peasants	.049	.101	.144
Laborers	.026	.081	.141

Source: Tran Phuong, *Cach mang ruong dat*, p. 212.

---

semipublic bodies, was still said to have been over 810,000 hectares, or something on the order of half the cultivated land in the area affected by land reform.[77] This figure seems slightly suspect, since it is no smaller than figures published before the correction of errors, but there may have been some shift in the categories used.

The shift in landownership patterns, as compared with the days before the revolution, was very substantial. It can be exaggerated if we look only at the amount of land owned by each class; the peasants obtained legal title during land reform to some land, notably communal land, which they had been able to use long before. Table 12-2 shows the changes in land use from before the land reform to after the correction of errors. The data come from a sample of 112 *xa* and 31 *thon*; it is not possible to tell how representative this sample was. The effective economic status of the middle peasants before land reform was higher than it would appear if we looked simply at the amount of land they owned. Land owned and used is a very good measure, given the rather strict definition of "used" in DRV statistics (counting rented land, on which rent is currently being paid, as being "used" by the owner rather than by the tenant). The middle peasants, on the average, would therefore have been slightly less well off after the land reform than they had been before it. They were probably still better off than they had been before the August Revolution.

---

77. Ibid., 18 April 1958, p. 2.

Taxation

North Vietnam had a system of progressive taxation on agricultural income much like that in China. It was based on figures for the area of each plot of land and its "normal" productivity. During the land reform these figures were recalculated; they were then supposed to remain unchanged for at least three years. When the government realized that many of them had been seriously exaggerated, it decided that correct figures had to be worked out before taxes could be collected on the 1956 autumn crop. It believed at first that the correction of area and productivity figures could be completed by the end of the year, but in fact these tasks stretched well into 1957, and the actual tax collection lasted until March and April.

One factor that was not much discussed in the press but that must have contributed to the delay was the problem of establishing the "normal" productivity of land just at the end of the dramatic postwar recovery of agricultural production. The government could argue that all crops before late 1955 should be discounted; it was the high yields that had been obtained in the 1955 autumn crop and in 1956 that would provide the best guide to probable future production. This was in fact perfectly correct. But the peasants, who could remember widespread death by starvation caused partly by excessive taxation in 1944–45, and serious hunger as recently as 1955, must have been disturbed (to say the least) by the idea of taking the largest harvests in recent memory as a standard by which to judge their future tax payments.[78]

To the extent that any pattern can be discerned in the changes of the official figures, it was the following: figures that were reasonably accurate at the beginning of 1956 were raised substantially during Wave Five of the land reform, then they were reduced to an unreasonably low level at the end of 1956, and then they were gradually raised again in 1957. Interzone III in general reduced tax quotas by at least 20 percent late in 1956, perhaps by as much as 40 percent. There was one extreme *xa* where the tax quota was reduced from 174 tons to 74 tons of rice in the first flush of the correction of errors; investigation in 1957 indicated that it should have been 118 tons. The fluctuations in the figures for the area of land were smaller than in those for the productivity, but even so we have two *xa* in Ha dong and Hong Quang where the total figure for area was 2,941 *mau* before land reform, 3,015 *mau* at the end of land reform, 2,614 *mau* at the end of 1956, and 2,864 *mau* by late 1957.[79] The agricultural tax was supposed to take, on the average, 17 percent of the crop. In April

---

78. Peasants subject to crop fluctuations tend to dislike fixed tax quotas in any case; see Scott, *The Moral Economy of the Peasant*.

79. *Thoi Moi*, 10 December 1956, p. 1; *Nhan Dan*, 25 February 1957, p. 2; 21 November 1957, p. 2.

1958 it was reported that the government was only getting 12–14 percent because of low figures for area and productivity. In Interzone III, the figures had at one point been so low the government was only getting 8.1 percent.[80]

The system used for setting figures, at all stages, was for the owner of the land to make an estimate that would then be discussed and criticized by other peasants and by the tax cadres. During land reform many peasants had been pressed to revise their initial figures upward. Late in 1956 when they were able to make new estimates, they reduced them to very low levels, whether out of the immemorial desire of peasants to evade all possible taxes, or because they feared the tax cadres would again bargain them upward from whatever figure they set at first. Their underestimates were often accepted in the first stages of the correction of errors; many cadres lacked the energy, the inclination, and the moral authority to criticize them. When these figures were challenged, the peasants protested: "The government said it would believe in the people."[81]

Recent Judgments

The DRV's evaluation of the land reform has remained about the same ever since 1956; it has emphasized that the campaign was basically successful while admitting that there were errors. The official history of the land reform, published in 1968, analyzes the nature, causes, and effects of the errors quite convincingly and at considerable length.[82]

Despite the claim that the land reform was basically successful, the way the land-reform errors were corrected and the way the Lao Dong Party has continued to admit the seriousness of those errors must be counted among the most remarkable examples of self-criticism in the history of Communism. The public repudiation of Stalinism in the Soviet Union and of the Cultural Revolution in China blamed errors on former rather than current leaders. Indeed, in China the attack on the Cultural Revolution and its excesses was led by people like Deng Xiaoping, for whom this represented self-justification rather than self-criticism. There is no true Chinese or Soviet parallel to the candid admissions by the Lao Dong Party Central Committee and by Ho Chi Minh as an individual[83] that they shared responsibility for the terrible injustices that had occurred.

---

80. *Nhan Dan*, 25 February 1957, p. 2; 24 April 1958, p. 2.

81. Ibid., 10 February 1957, p. 2.

82. Tran Phuong, *Cach mang ruong dat*, especially pp. 188–210.

83. *Thoi Moi*, 1 November 1956, p. 1.

13

Concluding Remarks

Land Tenure and Land Redistribution

Land reform could not by itself solve the basic causes of rural poverty, which were high population density and low productivity. The available wealth was not adequate no matter how it was distributed. Odd passages in a few Western works suggest either that a proper land reform really could have solved the land shortage or that the failure of the reform to cure the land problem made it a fraud, but few Communists had been foolish enough to suppose that redistribution alone would eliminate poverty.[1] They proposed collective agriculture and mechanization as long-range solutions.[2] The role of land reform was to create the conditions in which a transition to collective agriculture would be possible and to ameliorate the lives of the peasants for the interim until this could occur.

Land-reform planners had to deal with conflicting imperatives. On the one hand, they wanted to get as close as possible to equal distribution of land among the rural population. This would in their view be just, it would guarantee that under normal conditions no peasant would starve, it would ensure at least reasonably efficient use of the peasants' labor, and it would win the gratitude of the recipients of redistributed land (a majority of the population in most areas). On the other hand, land-reform planners did not want to expropriate too many people. To do so would make them a dangerous number of enemies and would cause both people who had been expropriated and people who feared future expropriation to lose their enthusiasm for agricultural production. The extent to

---

1. The main exception was in North China in the winter of 1947–48, when CCP leaders thought that the persistence of serious poverty must mean that the landlords' wealth had not been properly redistributed.

2. Liu Shaoqi, in the report of June 1950 that introduced the Agrarian Reform Law of 1950 to the Chinese people, openly referred to the organization of collective farms and the socialist reform of the countryside as the eventual goals of the CCP; *Xinhua yuebao*, July 1950, p. 494.

which these two considerations conflicted depended on the land-tenure situation in a given area.

If most of the land were owned by large landlords, there would be little difficulty. By expropriating a few wealthy individuals, the government could bring substantial benefits to a huge number of peasants. It would have no reason to attack well-to-do middle peasants. It could even show a certain lenience toward the land-lords and rich peasants and still provide large benefits to the poor. This is probably one reason why the CCP had so much diffi-culty persuading land-reform organizers in Guangdong, with its very concentrated landholding pattern, to attack the landlords and rich peasants vigorously.

If there were little or no land in the hands of very large land-lords, but much land in the hands of rich peasants and well-to-do middle peasants whose per capita landholdings were only moderately larger than the average for the rural population, then any land reform would face serious problems. If it did not expropriate these people, it would not be able to do much for the poor. But if it did take their land, it would be attacking a comparatively large number of people who, unlike most big landlords, made a real contribution to the economy, in order to extract from them an amount of land that still might only be adequate for a rather limited number of beneficiaries. This would be undesirable not only because few friends would be won for the revolution, but because if land reform benefited—and therefore was likely to involve—only a minor-ity of the poorest peasants, rather than the peasantry as a whole, it would be more likely to lead to leftist deviations and excessive violence; the poor might feel that they needed to make up by fierceness what they lacked in numbers.

Whenever any person owns more land than the average for his village, someone else must own less than the average. In a country in which the average was as low as in China or Vietnam, it was not desirable to leave anyone with significantly less than the average landholding. However, people whose landholdings are under twice the average, and most especially people whose holdings are under 1.5 times the average, make very unattractive targets for expropriation. They are not, and cannot plausibly be accused of being, pure parasites living off the labor of others. The ordi-nary peasant dreams of rising to their level and may become very uneasy when they are attacked. The amount of land that can be extracted from them is not very large, in relation to the political risks of antagonizing them. It is where these people are the only targets available for expropriation that one finds serious excesses in land redistribution. In these cases, land is taken from middle peasants, victims of expropriation are stripped down not just to equality with the poor but to absolute destitution, and the political base of land reform is restricted to the poor peasants and labor-ers. Such conditions are especially likely to occur where land reform comes only after a long period of patchy and informal class struggle in the villages. The early struggles will have eliminated most of the attractive candidates for expropriation, without having given wealth systematically to all the neediest peasants. North China in the 1940s provides the clearest such case.[3]

Land-reform authorities took surprisingly little open notice of the problems that could be posed by differences in tenure patterns. Central and southern China had, on the average, more concentrated landholdings than the areas of northern China where land reform was carried out in the 1940s. The land-reform law of 1950 was correspondingly lenient toward rich peasants; the 1948 law had shown them the harshness required by a situation in which hardly any land was owned by large landlords. However neither law, by itself, made much explicit allowance for local variations. The 1950 law provided for the requisitioning of land rented out by ordinary rich peasants in some areas and not in others, but the amount of land affected by this provision was very small. The special regulations for land reform in the *shatian* areas of Guangdong did not even mention the extraordinary concentration of landholdings there; they were simply concerned with the heavy investment in water control that was necessary to maintain productivity and that had traditionally been provided by the landlords.[4] Similarly, major reports on land reform in areas where the proportion of the population classified as landlords was unusually large, such as Sichuan and the mountainous regions of Zhejiang, do not mention any modification of the land-reform program to deal with this rather important difference in conditions. Both Chinese and Vietnamese land-reform planners felt that a single set of legislation could be applied to areas with a wide variation in tenure patterns. The central goals of the class struggle dealt with conditions that could be found almost anywhere. Every village possessed an elite, the members of which had more influence on village affairs than the average peasant. In almost every village the members of the elite were wealthier than the peasants, and at least some members of the elite used their wealth to avoid participating in physical labor. Land-reform planners wished to keep their programs as uniform as possible to ensure that the elite was overthrown in every village. Too much emphasis on the factors that differentiated villages, such as the exact degree of concentration of wealth, or whether the landlords were absentees, resident owners, or managers of clan land, would have given an opportunity for landlords or local cadres to say that their own villages did not have the specific characteristics that justified a radical land reform.

---

3. I have presented this argument in a longer and more mathematically rigorous form in "Radical, Moderate and Optimal Patterns of Land Reform," pp. 79–90. The diagrams in this article did not come out clearly; they were reprinted more legibly in the April 1978 issue, pp. 274–75.

4. Text in *Nanfang ribao*, 6 November 1950, trans. in *SCMP*, 31:28–30.

The Problem of Class

During land reform the Communists looked at the countryside in Manichaean terms; they saw a zero-sum game in which the good peasants were pitted against the evil landlords. They saw the landlords as a barrier to economic development in general, as a barrier to the advance of poor-peasant interests in particular, as an important part of the socioeconomic base for imperialist domination, and as a force overwhelmingly hostile to the revolution.

There was much truth in the picture of the landlords as enemies of the revolution, but there was also some exaggeration. Part of the exaggeration was a matter of interpretation; any action of the landlords that could by any stretch of the imagination be attributed to counterrevolutionary sentiments was so attributed. If the landlords obeyed the law, they could be charged with plotting to deceive the peasants and win their goodwill.[5] If they disobeyed the law, they would usually be accused of sabotage motivated by hostility to the peasants and the government, even in cases in which their behavior could much more plausibly have been seen as simple self-interest. By the time of the land reform, few landlords still counted on a victorious counterrevolution; what they wanted was to make the best accommodation they could to the new regime. This meant winning the goodwill of the peasants and local cadres and preserving their wealth to the maximum extent possible. The Communist parties of China and Vietnam had legitimate reasons for not wanting the landlords to succeed in these efforts, but it was a distortion to call them sabotage.

Aside from having their motives misinterpreted, some landlords were charged with things they simply had not done. This was most conspicuous in the late stages of the North Vietnamese reform, when people classified as landlords were routinely accused of having been much more hostile to the Anti-French Resistance than they actually had been. The extent of landlord exploitation was often overstated; generalizations about the rural areas frequently exaggerated both the proportion of the total crop area that was under landlord control and the amount of the crop taken as rent (usually by using a percentage of the main crop only).

In contrast, the poor peasants were continuously praised as the main force in the revolution and the great hope for the future. Again some of the greatest extremes were in Vietnam, where both before and after the revelation of the land-reform errors the fact that a person was a poor peasant, and thus inherently good, was considered adequate grounds for making that person a cadre in the absence of any demonstrated ability to perform the functions of the position in question.

This complex of attitudes became known as "classism" (the belief that social class determines, or should determine, everything). At

---

5. *Nanfang ribao*, 27 November 1950, p. 3.

its worst it could not only deprive the revolution of the services of good cadres who had come from the exploiting classes but could also cause trouble for laboring peasants. In the old society there were a variety of links between the rich and the poor—tenancy, wage labor, kinship ties, and assorted patron-client relationships. Land reform was supposed to weaken the kinship ties and break most of the other relationships. Cadres were trying to persuade the peasants that they had never had interests in common with the landlords and to inspire them to attack and overthrow their former masters.

The ease with which this could be done depended to a considerable extent on the nature of landlord-tenant relations before the revolution. The Communists regarded the tenancy relationship as inherently exploitative and almost always unjust. In some areas the peasants accepted this view quite readily. The landlords had seemed interested only in extracting wealth from the peasants, even if this threatened the peasants' minimum subsistence needs. When crops failed, peasants had been unable to obtain cancellation of rents. In the most extreme areas, "no landlord was willing to depart from convention on this score and treat his tenant with compassion for fear of losing face within his social class."[6] The peasants could probably be mobilized for a vigorous class struggle as soon as they were convinced that the revolutionary forces were strong enough to have some chance of protecting them against landlord reprisals.

But in other areas where the landlords had been more solicitous of their tenants' minimal needs, where patron-client relationships existed under which landlords provided significant services for their tenants, or where common membership in political, religious, or clan organizations had created a sense of solidarity cutting across class lines, many peasants were reluctant to believe that the landlords were their natural enemies. Most of them could still be persuaded to attack the landlords if they were sure that doing so would win them an improvement in their lives, but they needed strong guarantees that the attack was going to succeed, and even then the attack seldom had the power of great hatred behind it. Group discussion of whether it was the landlords who had supported the peasants or the peasants who had supported the landlords had to go on for a long time.

Conditions in the North China Plain had predisposed the peasants to hate the landlords. In Guangdong, the strong clan system and the existence of an adequate subsistence for most peasants had moderated class antagonisms. Even the land-reform apparatus reflected this fact; the result was considerable conflict between Guangdong cadres and their superiors in Peking. In North

---

6. Myers, *Chinese Peasant Economy*, p. 74, discussing peasant demands for the cancellation of rent arrears on mortgaged land in a village of central Hebei, 1937–41.

Vietnam, shared membership in the traditional village (much weakened under the French but not yet dead), the Viet Minh, and in some areas the Catholic church had likewise weakened the natural basis for class hatred in the villages, but moderate attitudes among the peasants were not reflected in the land-reform apparatus; the land-reform cadres were very strongly class-oriented. The difference between their attitude and that of the peasants helps to explain their extraordinary paranoia and their willingness to take a small group of *cot can* as representatives of the masses. They were operating in an environment permeated by attitudes of class accommodation that they had been taught were mystification, lies, and delusions spread by the landlords. They carried to extremes the tendency (also found among some of their Chinese counterparts) to become suspicious of poor peasants who were not as preoccupied with class as the land-reform cadres thought proper.

There were valid reasons for some of the exaggerations of classism. In societies where for generations the elite had been respected as the repositories of wisdom and the inevitable rulers of local affairs, cadres carrying out a social revolution had to push the opposite view as strongly as possible. They had to say that almost all peasants hated the landlords and that the poor were the legitimate rulers of rural society and the main driving force of the revolution. Saying it could indeed help to make it so. But this extreme view of the class nature of rural affairs sometimes went beyond the real interests of the revolution, and it often went beyond the bounds of objective truth.

Of all the figures involved in the land reform, it is the landlords—the principal victims—who appear least clearly. The scholar studying earlier centuries must search for information about the peasants in the documents and literature of the elite, but during the land reform it was the landlords who could not speak for themselves; they are visible to us now mostly through the writings of their enemies. We can discern the range of their possible responses to the revolution. Some—mainly landlords' children who had received modern educations and absorbed radical attitudes—abandoned the old order completely and gave their full allegiance to the revolution. Some tried to preserve family interests by cooperating with the new order. Some tried to evade programs for the redistribution of wealth by scattering family wealth to relatives, selling land for gold and burying the gold, etc. Some tried actually to oppose the revolution by spreading rumors, setting up phony peasant associations, and intimidating or attacking peasant activists. The antilandlord bias of the available sources makes it difficult to tell how common each of these responses may have been.[7]

---

7. A report on land reform in Hunan during the winter of 1950–51, published in *Changjiang Ribao*, 20 April 1951, p. 2, reported that ninety-three cadres had been murdered by landlords.

A Communist party needs the services of some people, especially intellectuals, who come from the exploiting classes, but allowing these people positions of power or privilege seems to violate the principles for which the party is struggling. This problem, which appears in some other contexts as the conflict of "Red versus expert," generates considerable emotional tension; many Communists have trouble dealing with it rationally. They may become a bit paranoid about the influence of those they consider members of the exploiting classes within the revolutionary ranks, or they may go to the opposite extreme and dodge the whole issue. In the aftermath of the extreme classism of land reform, when the Lao Dong Party was trying to justify the readmission to the party of old members who had been expelled during the reform because of unsatisfactory class backgrounds, it developed the interesting theory that it was a party of the working class, so that any person who joined it automatically became a person of the working class.[8] Of all types of statistics generated by a land-reform campaign, those on the proportion of landlords and rich peasants within the Communist party fluctuate the most wildly and must be considered the least reliable.

Law and Policy

Even when Communist leaders were advocating "legal struggle," they stressed that land reform could not be reduced to the simple matter of implementing a land-reform law.[9] The process of politicizing the peasants, undermining their respect for the landlords, and persuading them to take for themselves as much as possible of the initiative in land reform was not one that could readily be described in formal legislation. Land-reform cadres had to study long reports on correct policy and then try out this and that tactic in the villages to see how they actually worked before they could fully understand their tasks. Still, they needed some clear explanation of what types of property could be taken from what classes

---

Any effort to interpret such a figure requires considerable guesswork. It may have been inflated by revolutionary paranoia. Also, the article did not make clear just how large a portion of Hunan was covered by the figure given. However, it seems likely that this was supposed to be the number of cadres killed by landlords in an area with a population not much short of 14,000,000, in which we would expect to find somewhat over 100,000 adult male landlords. In other words, fewer than one landlord in a thousand killed a cadre. I am indebted to Vivienne Shue for this reference.

8. *Nhan Dan*, 15 January 1957, p. 4; 22 January 1957, p. 4; 7 February 1957, p. 2; 3 November 1957, p. 3.

9. *Changjiang ribao* editorial, 14 December 1950, reprinted in *Nanfang ribao*, 19 December 1950, p. 1.

of people, how those classes were to be defined, and who was to have the authority to make what types of decisions. It was appropriate that these things be laid down unambiguously in formal laws. The laws could not specify every detail of what was to happen; they left wide discretion to cadres and peasants. But they could explain, in clear and exact terms, how some important elements of the land reform were to be conducted.

The attention of the cadres had to be focused more on policy than on law, because political mobilization of the peasants, one of the most important parts of the land reform, could not be adequately described in laws. But it was demonstrated in Vietnam that a lack of respect for the formal legislation of rent reduction and land reform could also be disastrous.

DRV legislation was sometimes equipped with loopholes to keep it from restricting the flexible development of the class struggle. Thus the rent-reduction laws of 1949 and 1953 set a norm of 25 percent reduction but allowed local authorities to impose much greater reductions if they thought it appropriate, and after 1953 they all seem to have thought it appropriate. Class-demarcation laws in the DRV allowed people to be classified as landlords on political grounds, even if they did not have the economic role of landlords, and the result was that anyone down to an agricultural laborer could be classified as a landlord if the people doing the classifying were sufficiently irresponsible. On some occasions, formal legislation was simply disobeyed; thus the people branded as landlords lost far more of their property than they should have lost under the DRV Land Reform Law. Actual class demarcation was often at variance with the official decrees on the subject.

Statements of land-reform policy in both China and Vietnam usually seemed more radical than land-reform laws,[10] because it was the more orderly portions of the land-reform program that could be defined in laws. The laws should have placed limits on policy; in Vietnam they failed to do so. A *Nhan Dan* editorial later commented that mistakes had occurred because "we did not see that our laws are the people's laws, which protect peace and order in our new society."[11] The Vietnamese may have placed less value on their laws than the Chinese because they had not had to work so hard for them. Vietnamese legislation was not simply copied from Chinese models, but it borrowed heavily from them, without anything like the amount of trial and error through which the Chinese had had to go. The most extreme case was the Land Reform Law of 1953, which was adopted without so much as a single *xa* having undergone an experimental land reform first. The

---

10. Compare the land-reform laws of 1950 in China and 1953 in Vietnam with the reports by Liu Shaoqi and Truong Chinh, respectively, commenting on them.

11. *Nhan Dan*, 3 November 1956, p. 4.

careless haste with which the law was written may help to explain why the Vietnamese later felt free to treat it so casually.

Correct Policy and Errors

The formal regulations that were worked out to govern land reform in China and Vietnam were very similar. The Vietnamese could adopt Chinese models because the problems that land reform was supposed to solve were the same in both countries. A rural elite, differentiated from the peasants by wealth, power, and prestige but not by a formally defined system of hereditary status or caste, stood in the way of revolutionary change. Its position in society would have made it a barrier to the contact the Communists needed to form with the peasants, even if it could have been weaned away from active opposition to the revolution. Its wealth, considered in absolute terms, would when redistributed be a desperately needed first step in improving the conditions of the poor. Its wealth, considered in relative terms, would if not redistributed have represented a degree of inequality in village society that would have delayed or seriously distorted the development of cooperative agriculture.

Socioeconomic conditions were not exactly the same in China and in Vietnam. The process by which land was freed of customary claims and became the property of individuals who could and did buy and sell it at their convenience was further advanced in China than in Vietnam. French colonialism had made the landlord class weaker and less self-confident in Vietnam than in China. There were other more subtle differences. But the visible differences in economic and social patterns, cultural attitudes, and historical situations do not make the transfer of land-reform policies appear obviously unsuitable or explain why land reform gave so much less satisfactory results in Vietnam than in China.

Chinese land-reform errors, even in 1948, do not seem to have been quite as extreme as those in Vietnam. In Long Bow, which may have been unusually radical by the standards of 1948 (see Chapter 3), the suspicions raised against old cadres appear to have been comparable to those in an average *xa* of North Vietnam; they were not as bad as those in the worst *xa* of North Vietnam. But in Long Bow these suspicions were investigated slowly and carefully, and most of them were found to have been false or exaggerated before any decisive action had been taken. Of the four cadres arrested for crimes of which they were at least partially innocent, none was actually brought to trial. In Ten Mile Inn, which was probably closer than Long Bow to being typical, no old cadres were arrested, and the only one who came really close to being arrested was genuinely guilty of the charges against him. There also seem to have been differences in the types of errors committed in China and in Vietnam. The Chinese errors typically involved excessively harsh punishment for things that the people

in question really had done. In Vietnam there were more punishments for imaginary crimes. Indeed the plethora of false accusations in Vietnam may have led to a nominal leniency in the scale of
punishments; so many people were being accused of very serious
crimes that those accused of minor ones may have got off lightly.
In one rather incredible case, a landlord charged with having
beaten one peasant to death and having beaten another so badly
that he took a month to heal was classified as an "ordinary" landlord rather than a despot. [12]

The land-reform errors in China seemed slightly more connected
with efforts to benefit the poor peasants than did those in
Vietnam. Much of the attack on the old cadres was based on
charges that they had abused their positions to enrich themselves;
it was hoped that they could be made to cough up their illegitimate
wealth for distribution to the poor. [13] In Vietnam, old cadres were
more likely to be charged with being counterrevolutionaries. It was
assumed that purging them would benefit the poor peasants, but
the connection was less direct. Also, in China there were more
people who had land taken from them simply on the grounds that
they had a surplus, without their being classified as exploiters or
counterrevolutionaries. Although the CCP was concerned both to
help its friends and to harm its enemies, the ratio of the former to
the latter seemed higher than in Vietnam. Finally, in China the
errors were halted more quickly; the extreme period lasted only
about two months in the regions for which the best documentation
is available, and probably not much longer in other regions. In
Vietnam the extreme period lasted at least six months.

Many of the potential problems in land reform were not in the
outlines of the program, which were laid down in formal legislation,
but in the nuances of its execution and the perceptions of the
cadres. Was what the land-reform cadres expected to find when
they went out to the villages reasonably congruent with actual
conditions? Which way were borderline cases in class demarcation
decided? If a landlord were in danger of being classified as a
despot, or a party member in danger of being called a bad
element, how far into the past would the cadres go in searching
for crimes he had committed, how seriously would they treat
comparatively minor misdeeds, and how much evidence of repentance would they demand before forgiving him? How much evidence
would it take to convince them that he actually was guilty of any
given crime?

Mobilization of the masses presented very complex problems to
the leaders of the land reform. How much delay in the completion
of the reform could be tolerated in order to permit more thorough
mobilization and education of the peasants? What sort of compromise
should be made between the need for peasant activists to make

---

12. *Thoi Moi*, 11 January 1956, pp. 1, 3.
13. See Hinton, *Fanshen*, pp. 222–31, 326–49, and passim.

decisions themselves (rather than serving simply as fronts for the land-reform cadres) and the need to make them follow policy correctly? The base-level cadres needed to know how to identify peasants who would be good activists, and how to involve and educate such people.

Land reform was too complex and formidable a task ever to have been carried out in a perfect or even a near-perfect fashion. When Du Runsheng reported on land reform to the Central-South MAC in April 1951, the conditions were as good as anyone could have hoped for; the formal program had been perfected, and both higher leaders and the actual land-reform cadres had acquired extensive experience putting the program into effect. But all Du could promise was "continuous work, continuous commission of errors, continuous correction, and continuous advance."[14]

Three elements were required for anything even approaching correct action: a good formal program, a corps of cadres experienced in mass mobilization for class struggle, and a corps of higher-level leaders who could evaluate accurately reports coming up from the villages, detect any widespread and serious deviation, correct it without overreacting too badly, and help the land-reform cadres see and correct for themselves smaller and more localized deviations. The formal program could be borrowed from other areas, given a sufficient similarity of conditions, and prerevolutionary society in most areas of China and Vietnam was sufficiently uniform for free borrowing to be possible.[15] The second and third elements could be created only through experience; the people involved could no more have learned the necessary skills by hearing about others' experiences than they could have become successful surgeons by reading books on medicine.

In carrying out land reform, a country such as China or North Vietnam would be likely to attain a stable and satisfactory policy only after first committing a tremendous variety of errors and learning from experience how each type of problem arises and how it may best be prevented or solved. One can sometimes discern, in local conditions or in the attitudes of particular leaders, why certain problems occurred with particular severity or went uncorrected for an unusually long period in certain areas. Thus the penchant of the DRV leadership for planning major actions ahead of time, in detail, made it less flexible in land reform than another group might have been. The clan system made the development of class struggle exceptionally difficult in Guangdong. The small

---

14. *Changjiang ribao*, 18 April 1951, p. 2.

15. The earlier development of the revolution itself could create differences in conditions that would have to be reflected in major modifications of the program. An area where a prolonged Communist presence had already led to a substantial politicization of the peasantry and to partial equalization of landholdings had to be treated differently from a newly liberated area.

amount of land in the hand of the landlords and rich peasants in much of the North China Plain after 1945 contributed to the infringement of middle-peasant interests.

But the main reason why land reform was so much more successful overall in China than in North Vietnam had simply to do with the problem of experience. Chinese land-reform policy took its final shape in the winter of 1950–51, at a time when the reform had already been completed in areas with a total population of perhaps 150,000,000. It had not even approached final form until the middle of 1948, when it had already covered a population of about 100,000,000 and had gone through two periods of left deviation. North Vietnam, where the total population eligible for reform was less than 11,000,000, had not even had time to correct its first left deviation when it found the reform coming to an end. Probably less than half the people who served as land-reform cadres in North Vietnam ever had a chance to apply in a second *xa* the lessons they had learned in their first.

In North Vietnam there were less than three years between the beginning of the first experimental land reform and the completion of the program. In China there were more than twenty.

There is an apparent problem here. This book has shown a progression in land-reform policies from the self-conscious radicalism of the early years, with its paranoia about landlord influence and its preoccupation with revolutionary purity, to the calmer policies introduced from 1948 to 1950 in China and in 1956 in Vietnam. This progression has been traced essentially to the accumulation of experience; as the revolutionaries learned how to do things in an orderly and goal-directed fashion, they did so. The reader may ask, Is this not an argument that paranoia and a simplistic passion for revolutionary purity are restricted to the early stages of a revolution, and that China's Great Proletarian Cultural Revolution could not have happened? The answer is that what produces a calm attitude is not experience in itself but experience that has produced effective solutions to problems, solutions that can be applied calmly. Mao Zedong, years later, once commented on the relative unanimity party leaders had attained on the issue of land reform. Unanimity was possible because land reform involved problems for which there were good answers. A single set of policies had been devised that fitted Marxist doctrines of class struggle, the need to promote economic development, the genuine desire of many Communist leaders to promote the welfare of the peasants, and the party's need to consolidate its own power and destroy its political enemies. This policy could command the allegiance of everyone from Mao to Deng Xiaoping, despite the way their fundamental attitudes differed, because it simultaneously promoted all Communist goals. When such a policy is available, Communist leaders have little reason to dodge the issues and cast aspersions on one another's motives. All leaders can assume that reasoned argument will promote their own goals. Policy discussions can be expected to become steadily more rational over time as policy is perfected and people become accustomed to the benefits of rationality. A very good situation had been attained in China by 1950, and a fairly good one had been attained in Vietnam by the end of 1956.

No such generally satisfactory answers existed for the conflicts about egalitarianism that helped provoke the Cultural Revolution. The question of whether society needed to grant special power and special privileges to educated individuals (including technicians) provides a good example of the dilemmas the CCP faced in 1966. If highly educated people were denied special power and privileges, their morale would suffer and their authority to make the decisions that their education qualified them to make would be impaired. National development would be seriously hampered. Also, an attack on the educated elite would necessarily involve an attack on the power of the CCP, because most educated people either were Party members themselves or had been given an education by the Communist system in the belief that they would use their training in the service of the Party and the Party's programs for national development. On the other hand, giving special power and privileges to the educated would represent an abandonment of the egalitarian ideals of the revolution. Also, some of the educated would surely use their power to feather their own nests in ways not conducive to national development.

No satisfactory compromise was reached, nor was there any obvious way in which a satisfactory compromise could have been reached. Any policy involved substantial sacrifices of what were, from the Communist viewpoint, important goals. Anyone who admitted the importance of a goal that his favorite policy sacrificed had reason to be uncomfortable with a rational discussion of its merits, and anyone who denied the validity of the goals that he was sacrificing was regarded by his opponents as having in a sense deserted the revolution. The paranoia and fanaticism of the Cultural Revolution were also spurred by the involvement of many young people whose real political experience was negligible; one cannot assume that those active in politics in 1966 were more experienced than those active in 1950. But what was crucial was that there was no obvious rational solution to the problems of 1966 sufficiently attractive to lead all Party leaders toward that solution. Land reform in most areas of China and Vietnam, for all its difficulties, involved problems to which there were solutions almost all Communists could accept.

Glossary

Chinese Terms in the Text

bao (pao)	An administrative unit within the village (part of the *baojia* system).
baodian (pao tien)	A landlord who made a significant capital investment in the land he rented out.
baojia (pao chia)	A system of low-level officials in the countryside, involved in tax collection and other administrative matters. (In Chinese tradition, the *baojia* system was supposed to be a way of arranging the people in groups, and making the members of each group responsible for one another's behavior.)
baozhong (pao chung)	A landlord who made a significant capital investment in the land he rented out.
cun (ts'un)	The natural village.
dahui (ta hui)	Conference or assembly.
dajia (ta chia)	Everyone
erliuzi (er lui tzu)	The *erliuzi* and *liumang* were people who lived by irregular means: vagabonds, the rural lumpenproletariat, and so forth.
fanshen	Literally to turn oneself; in effect to alter one's life by acquiring the wealth and the self-confidence of an independent smallholder.
fenjia (fen chia)	Division of a household. Usually involves two or more sons splitting their father's property.
huiyi (hui yi)	Meeting or assembly.

283

jiji fenzi (*chi chi fen tzu*)	Activists.
liumang	See under *erliuzi*.
luan da luan sha (*luan ta luan sha*)	Indiscriminate (literally disorderly) beatings and indiscriminate killings.
moshou	Confiscate.
mou	A unit of area equal to about one sixth of an acre.
pingfen (*p'ing fen*)	Equal division (of land).
qu (*ch'u*)	An administrative unit intermediate between the *xian* and the administrative village.
shatian (*sha t'ien*)	The sandy lands of river deltas in Guangdong.
she	A subdivision of the natural village.
xian (*hsien*)	County.
xiang (*hsiang*)	The administrative village, usually including several natural villages.
zhengshou (*cheng shou*)	Requisition. (Requisitioning was simply a polite form of confiscation; there was no compensation involved.)
zili gengzhong zhi *tudi* (*tzy li keng* *chung chih t'u ti*)	Land cultivated by one's own labor.
zu (*tsu*)	Clan.

Vietnamese Terms in the Text

bao vây	A very severe form of house arrest involving total isolation of a person or family.
bắt rễ xâu chuỗi	"Getting roots and stringing beads" (recruiting activists among the peasants, and then sending them out to recruit further activists themselves).
bộ	The three units into which Vietnam was divided before 1954.
chi bộ	A base-level (usually village-level) branch of the Lao Dong Party.
chuỗi	"Bead" (a peasant activist recruited by another peasant native to the village, not by an outside land-reform cadre).
cốt cán	"Backbone element" (a peasant chosen by the land-reform cadres to become a village leader). The *cốt cán* had usually been *rễ*.
cụm	A grouping of several *đội* within a land-reform *đoàn*.
cưỡng ép dụ dỗ	To force and entice (phrase used to describe efforts to persuade people to leave North Vietnam in 1954–55).
đoàn	"Brigade." One *đoàn* of land-reform cadres was responsible for land reform in a considerable area, not necessarily limited to a single province.
đội	"Team." One *đội* of land-reform cadres was responsible for one administrative village.
huyện	An administrative unit intermediate between the province and the administrative village. Sometimes translated "canton." The *huyện* did not play as great a role in administration as did its Chinese equivalent, the *xian*.
hy sinh	"Sacrifice." To die, either in the struggle for independence or as a result of errors committed during land reform.

khu	Zone. Usually refers to a grouping of several provinces.
liên khu	Interzone. A grouping of several provinces.
lưu manh	Vagabond, person without regular means of support. Corresponds to the Chinese *liumang*.
mẫu	Unit of land measurement, ranging from 0.36 to 0.497 hectares.
nghiêm trị	"Severely punished." Sometimes used as a euphemism for "executed." Abbreviated form of *nghiêm trọng trừng trị*.
quản chế	A form of control sometimes amounting to house arrest.
rễ	"Root." A peasant recruited as an activist by a land-reform cadre.
sắc lệnh	Decree.
thăm nghèo hỏi khổ	To share poverty and inquire about sufferings. Procedure used by land-reform cadres to get to know individual peasants.
thôn	The natural village. Often translated "hamlet."
tịch thu	Confiscate.
truy bức	Vigorous interrogation. Often included the use of physical torture.
trưng mua	Compulsory purchase.
trưng thu	Requisition (confiscate without compensation, but politely).
trừng trị	Punish. Several euphemisms for "execute" were based on *trừng trị*.
ủy ban (kháng chiến) hành chính	(Resistance) adminstrative committee.
xã	Administrative village, sometimes translated "commune."

xóm   An administrative unit within the *xã*.

xủ' trí   "To deal with," in the sense of "to punish."
                         This term was never, so far as I have seen,
                         been used as a euphemism for "to execute."

xủ' tủ'   To sentence to death.

Bibliography

Serials

Changjiang ribao (Hankou).
Current Background (U.S. Consulate, Hong Kong).
For Your Information: *Yenan Broadcasts* (Shanghai: United States Information Service).
Hoc Tap (Hanoi).
Journal d'Extreme Orient (Saigon).
Nanfang ribao (Canton).
New York Times.
Nhan Dan (Hanoi).
Qunzhong (Hong Kong).
Renmin ribao (Wuan, 1947–48; Peking, 1949–).
Survey of the China Mainland Press (U.S. Consulate, Hong Kong).
Thoi Moi (Hanoi).
Times of Vietnam (Saigon).
Translations of Radio Broadcasts of Communist Hsin Hua Station, North Shensi (U.S. Consulate General, Peiping).
U.S. Foreign Broadcast Information Service *Daily Report* (*Area Editions*): *Far East*.
Washington Post.
Xinhua ribao (Chongqing).
Xinhua yuebao (Peking).

Books, Articles, and Pamphlets: Chinese

Jiefang she, ed. *Lun xin jiefang qu tudi zhengce* [On land policy in the New Liberated Areas]. Canton: Xinhua shudian, 1950.
Li Chengrui. *Zhonghua renmin gongheguo nongye shui shikao* [Draft history of agricultural taxation in the People's Republic of China]. Peking: Caizheng chubanshe, 1959.
Li Geng [pseudonym], ed. *Jiefang qu di tudi zhengce yu shishi* [Land policies and their implementation in the liberated areas]. Hong Kong: n.p., 1947.
Li Minghua, ed. *Zhonggong di tudi douzheng* [The land struggle of the Chinese Communists]. Taipei: Guoji guanxi yanjiu so, 1965.
Pingfen tudi shouce [Handbook for equal division of the land].

289

N.p.: Huabei xinhua shudian, 1948.

Qi Wu. *Yige geming genjudi di chengzhang* [The growth of a revolutionary base]. Peking: Renmin chubanshe, 1951.

Takeuchi Minoru et al., eds. *Mao Zedong ji* [Works of Mao Zedong]. 10 vols. Tokyo: Hokubosha, 1970–72.

Tudi gaige shouce [Land reform handbook]. Shanghai: Huadong zong fen dian, 1950.

Tudi zhengce faling huibian [Collected laws and decrees on land policy]. Shenyang: Dongbei renmin zhengfu nongcun bu, 1950.

Tudi zhengce zhongyao wenjian huiji [A collection of important documents on land policy]. N.p.: Zhongguo gongchandang, Jin-Cha-Ji Zhongyang ju xuanchuan bu, 1946.

Wei chunjie dang di zuzhi er douzheng [Struggle to purify the Party's ranks]. Hong Kong: Zhengbao she tushubu, 1948.

Yan Zhongping et al., eds. *Zhongguo jindai jingji shi tongji ziliao xuanji* [Selected statistics on modern Chinese economic history]. Peking: Kexue chubanshe, 1955.

Yuenan minzhu gongheguo tudi fa ji qi youguan wenjian [The land law and related documents of the Democratic Republic of Vietnam]. Peking: Shijie zhishi she, 1954.

Zhang Gensheng. "Zhongnan qu gesheng nongcun shehui jieji qingkuang yu zudian guanxi di chubu diaocha" [A preliminary study of social classes and rental relationships in the rural areas of the Central-South Region]. In *Xinqu tudi gaige qian di nongcun* [The rural areas of the New Liberated Areas before land reform]. Peking: Renmin chubanshe, 1951.

Zhang Youyi, ed. *Zhongguo jindai nongye shi ziliao* [Source materials on China's modern agricultural history]. 3 vols. Peking: Sanlian shudian, 1957.

Zhengfu gongzuo baogao huibian, 1950 [A compilation of government work reports, 1950]. Peking: Renmin chubanshe, 1951.

Zhongguo gongchandang yu tudi geming [The Chinese Communist Party and the land revolution]. Hong Kong: Zhengbao she, n.d.

Books, Articles, and Pamphlets: Vietnamese

Ban van dong thi dua ai quoc trung uong [Central Committee for the Patriotic Emulation Movement], ed. *Thi dua yeu nuoc* [Patriotic emulation]. N.p.: So Thong-tin Nam-bo, 1949.

Bon muoi lam nam hoat dong cua Dang lao dong Viet-nam [Forty-five years' activities of the Vietnam Workers' Party]. Hanoi: Su that, 1975.

Chong am-muu bat ep du do di dan cua de quoc My va be luu Ngo-dinh-diem [Oppose the plot of the American imperialists and the Ngo Dinh Diem clique to force and entice people to migrate]. [Haiphong?]: Ty tuyen truyen Hai-phong, 1955.

Cuoc khang chien than thanh cua nhan dan Viet-nam [The

magnificent resistance war of the Vietnamese people]. 4 vols. Hanoi: Su that, 1960.

Nguyen Kien Giang. *Phac qua tinh hinh ruong dat va doi song nong dan truoc cach mang thang tam* [Outline of the land situation and the life of the peasants before the August Revolution]. Hanoi: Su that, 1959.

Nguyen Ngoc Minh, ed. *Kinh te Viet nam tu cach mang thang tam den khang chien thang loi* [The economy of Vietnam from the August Revolution to the victory of the Resistance]. Hanoi: Nha xuat ban khoa hoc, 1966.

Nhung cai cach moi cua chinh phu [New reforms of the government]. Hanoi: Ty thong-tin Ha-noi, 1950.

Pham Van Dong. *Nha nuoc dan chu nhan dan Viet-nam* [The people's democratic nation of Vietnam]. Hanoi: Su that, 1964.

Tran Phuong, ed. *Cach mang ruong dat o Viet-nam* [The land revolution in Vietnam]. Hanoi: Nha xuat ban khoa hoc xa hoi, 1968.

Truong Chinh. *Tien len duoi la co cua dang* [Advance under the banner of the Party]. Hanoi: Su that, 1961.

Xuan Chi. "Sau nhung ngay song gio" [After the days of adversity]. Serialized in *Thoi Moi*, 5–20 April, 1957.

————. "Trong khong khi diu mat cua dem xuan" [In the cool air of spring nights]. Serialized in *Thoi Moi*, 7–23 May, 1957.

Books, Articles, and Pamphlets: Western Languages

Arturov, O. A., ed. *Demokraticheskaia Respublika V'etnam: konstitutsiia, zakonodatelnye akty, dokumenty* [The Democratic Republic of Vietnam: constitution, laws, and documents]. Moscow: Inlitizdat, 1955.

Ash, Robert. "Economic Aspects of Land Reform in Kiangsu, 1949–52." *China Quarterly*, no. 66 (June 1976): 261–92, and no. 67 (September 1976): 519–45.

Bays, Daniel. "Agrarian Reform in Kwangtung, 1950–1953." In *Early Communist China: Two Studies*. Michigan Papers in Chinese Studies, no. 4. Ann Arbor: Center for Chinese Studies, 1969.

Belden, Jack. *China Shakes the World*. New York: Monthly Review Press, 1970.

Buck, J. Lossing. *Land Utilization in China*. Vol. 3, *Statistics*. Nanjing: University of Nanking, 1937.

Burchett, Wilfred. *North of the Seventeenth Parallel*. Delhi: People's Publishing House, 1956.

Buttinger, Joseph. *Vietnam: A Dragon Embattled*. 2 vols. New York: Praeger, 1967.

Byrne [Moise], Rebecca. "Harmony and Violence in Classical China: A Study of the Battles in the *Tso-chuan*." Ph.D. dissertation, University of Chicago, 1974.

Chaliand, Gerard. *The Peasants of North Vietnam*. Harmondsworth:

Penguin, 1969.

Chen Han-seng. *Landlord and Peasant in China: A Study of the Agrarian Crisis in South China*. New York: International Publishers, 1936.

Cheung, Steven. *The Theory of Share Tenancy, with Special Application to Asian Agriculture and the First Phase of Taiwan Land Reform*. Chicago: University of Chicago Press, 1969.

Chou Li-po. *The Hurricane*. Peking: Foreign Languages Press, 1955.

Crook, Isabel, and Crook, David. *The First Years of Yangyi Commune*. New York: Humanities Press, 1966.

————. *Revolution in a Chinese Village: Ten Mile Inn*. London: Routledge & Kegan Paul, 1959.

————. *Ten Mile Inn: Mass Movement in a Chinese Village*. New York: Pantheon, 1979.

Dore, Ronald P. *Land Reform in Japan*. London: Oxford University Press, 1959.

Dorris, Carl E. "Peasant Mobilization in North China and the Origins of Yenan Communism." *China Quarterly*, no. 68 (December 1976): 697–719.

Esherick, Joseph. "Number Games: A Note on Land Distribution in Prerevolutionary China." *Modern China* 7, no. 4 (October 1981): 387–411.

————, ed. *Lost Chance in China: The World War II Despatches of John S. Service*. New York: Random House, 1974.

Eto Shinkichi. "Hai-lu-feng: The First Chinese Soviet Government." *China Quarterly*, no. 8 (October 1961): 160–83, and no. 9 (January 1962): 149–81.

Fall, Bernard B. *The Two Viet-Nams: A Political and Military Analysis*. Rev. ed. New York: Praeger, 1964.

————. *The Viet-Minh Regime: Government and Administration in the Democratic Republic of Vietnam*. Rev. and enl. ed. New York: Institute of Pacific Relations, 1956.

————. "Vietnam: The Agonizing Reappraisal." *Current History*, February 1956.

————, ed. *Ho Chi Minh on Revolution: Selected Writings, 1920–66*. New York: Praeger, 1967.

Foreign Relations of the United States, 1952–1954, vol. 16: *The Geneva Conference*. Washington: U.S. Government Printing Office, 1981.

Fourth Interim Report of the International Commission for Supervision and Control in Vietnam. London: H.M. Stationery Office, 1955.

Geertz, Clifford. *Agricultural Involution: The Processes of Ecological Change in Indonesia*. Berkeley: University of California Press, 1970.

Gittinger, J. Price. "Communist Land Policy in North Vietnam." *Far Eastern Survey* 28, no. 8 (August 1959): 113–26.

Goodwin, Richard. *Triumph or Tragedy: Reflections on Vietnam*. New York: Vintage, 1966.

Gourou, Pierre. *L'Utilization du sol en Indochine Française*. Paris: Centre d'Etudes de Politique Etrangere, 1940.

Government of the Republic of Vietnam. *Violations of the Geneva Agreements by the Viet-Minh Communists*. Saigon: 1959.

Henry, Yves. *Economie agricole de l'Indochine*. Hanoi: Inspection Generale de l'Agriculture, de l'Elevage et des Forets, 1932.

Hinton, William. *Fanshen: A Documentary of Revolution in a Chinese Village*. New York: Vintage, 1968.

Ho Chi Minh. *Selected Works*. 4 vols. Hanoi: Foreign Languages Publishing House, 1960–62.

Hoang Van Chi. *The Fate of the Last Viets*. Saigon: Hoa Mai, 1956.

———. *From Colonialism to Communism: A Case History of North Vietnam*. New York: Praeger, 1964.

———, ed. *The New Class in North Vietnam*. Saigon: Cong Dan, 1958.

Hsiao Tso-liang. *The Land Revolution in China, 1930–1934: A Study of Documents*. Seattle: University of Washington Press, 1969.

Hua Tse. "Left, Ultra-'Left' and Fake Left." *Peking Review* 21, no. 15 (14 April 1978): 6–10.

Huang, Philip C. C. "Analyzing the Twentieth-Century Chinese Countryside: Revolutionaries versus Western Scholarship." *Modern China* 1, no. 2 (April 1975): 132–60.

———. "Mao Tse-tung and the Middle Peasants, 1925–1928." *Modern China* 1, no. 3 (July 1975): 271–96.

Johnson, Chalmers. *Peasant Nationalism and Communist Power: The Emergence of Revolutionary China, 1937–1945*. Stanford: Stanford University Press, 1962.

Kataoka, Tetsuya. *Resistance and Revolution in China: The Communists and the Second United Front*. Berkeley: University of California Press, 1974.

Kim, Ilpyong J. *The Politics of Chinese Communism: Kiangsi under the Soviets*. Berkeley: University of California Press, 1973.

Kuo, Warren. *Analytical History of the Chinese Communist Party*. 4 vols. Taipei: Institute of International Relations, 1968–71.

Le Chau. *Le Viet Nam socialiste: une economie de transition*. Paris: Maspero, 1966.

Le Thanh Khoi. *Le Vietnam, histoire et civilization*. Paris: Minuit, 1955.

Lebar, Frank; Hickey, Gerald; and Musgrave, John. *Ethnic Groups of Mainland Southeast Asia*. New Haven: Human Relations Area Files Press, 1966.

Lee, Frank C. "Land Redistribution in Communist China." *Pacific Affairs* 21, no. 1 (March 1948): 20–32.

Lippit, Victor. *Land Reform and Economic Development in China: A Study of Institutional Change and Development Finance*. White Plains: International Arts and Sciences Press, 1974.

Liu Shao-ch'i. *Collected Works of Liu Shao-ch'i*. 3 vols. Hong Kong: Union Research Institute, 1968–69.

——. "The Confession of Liu Shao-ch'i." *Atlas*, April 1967.

Loh, Robert, and Evans, Humphrey. *Escape from Red China*. New York: Coward-McCann, 1962.

Lotveit, Trygve. *Chinese Communism 1931–1934: Experience in Civil Government*. Scandinavian Institute of Asian Studies, 1973.

Maneli, Mieczyslaw. *War of the Vanquished*. New York: Harper & Row, 1971.

Mao Tse-tung. *Selected Works of Mao Tse-tung*. 5 vols. Peking: Foreign Languages Press, 1961–65, 1977.

Marks, Robert. "The World Can Change! Guangdong Peasants in Revolution." *Modern China* 3, no. 1 (January 1977): 65–100.

Mazaev, Al'bert G. *Agrarnaia reforma v Demokraticheskoi Respublike V'etnam* [Agrarian reform in the Democratic Republic of Vietnam]. Moscow: Izdatel'stvo vostochnoi literatury, 1959.

Moise, Edwin E. "Downward Social Mobility in Pre-Revolutionary China." *Modern China* 3, no. 1 (January 1977): 3–31.

——. "Land Reform and Land Reform Errors in North Vietnam." *Pacific Affairs* 49, no. 1 (Spring 1976): 70–92.

——. "Land Reform in China and North Vietnam: Revolution at the Village Level." Ph.D. dissertation, University of Michigan, 1977.

——. "Radical, Moderate and Optimal Patterns of Land Reform." *Modern China* 4, no. 1 (January 1978): 79–90.

Murti, B. *Vietnam Divided*. New York: Asia Publishing House, 1964.

Myers, Ramon. *The Chinese Peasant Economy: Agricultural Development in Hopei and Shantung, 1890–1949*. Cambridge, Mass.: Harvard University Press, 1970.

Myrdal, Gunnar. *Asian Drama: An Inquiry into the Poverty of Nations*. 3 vols. New York: Pantheon, 1968.

Ngo Vinh Long. *Before the Revolution: The Vietnamese Peasants under the French*. Cambridge, Mass.: M.I.T. Press, 1973.

An Outline History of the Vietnam Workers' Party. Hanoi: Foreign Languages Publishing House, 1970.

Palmerlee, Albert E. "Viet Cong Political Geography." *Vietnam Documents and Research Notes*, no. 23. Saigon: United States Mission, 1968.

The Pentagon Papers: The Defense Department History of United States Decisionmaking on Vietnam. 4 vols. Boston: Beacon Press, 1971.

Pepper, Suzanne. *Civil War in China: The Political Struggle, 1945–1949*. Berkeley: University of California Press, 1978.

Pike, Douglas. *Viet Cong: The Organization and Techniques of the National Liberation Front of South Vietnam*. Cambridge, Mass.: M.I.T. Press, 1966.

Porter, D. Gareth. *The Myth of the Bloodbath: North Vietnam's Land Reform Reconsidered*. Ithaca: Cornell University IREA Project, 1972.

    A shorter but more reliable version of this paper appeared in *Bulletin of Concerned Asian Scholars* 5, no. 2 (September 1973):

2–15.

Race, Jeffrey. *War Comes to Long An*: *Revolutionary Conflict in a Vietnamese Province*. Berkeley: University of California Press, 1972.

Rue, John. *Mao Tse-tung in Opposition, 1927–1935*. Stanford: Stanford University Press, 1966.

Schram, Stuart. *Mao Tse-tung*. Harmondsworth: Penguin, 1966.

———, ed. *Chairman Mao Talks to the People*. New York: Pantheon, 1974.

Scott, James C. *The Moral Economy of the Peasant*: *Rebellion and Subsistence in Southeast Asia*. New Haven: Yale University Press, 1976.

Selden, Mark. *The Yenan Way in Revolutionary China*. Cambridge, Mass.: Harvard University Press, 1971.

Sergeyeva, N. "Liberated Vietnam." Part 2, "The Toilers of the Fields." *New Times* (Moscow), 7 July 1955.

Shue, Vivienne. *Peasant China in Transition*: *The Dynamics of Development toward Socialism, 1949–1956*. Berkeley: University of California Press, 1980.

Sixth Interim Report of the International Commission for Supervision and Control in Vietnam. Cmnd 31. London: H.M. Stationery Office, 1957.

Snow, Edgar. *The Battle for Asia*. New York: Random House, 1941.

———. *Red Star over China*. New York: Random House, 1944.

Solomon, Richard. *Mao's Revolution and the Chinese Political Culture*. Berkeley: University of California Press, 1971.

Tanaka Kyoko. "Mao and Liu in the 1947 Land Reform: Allies or Disputants?" *China Quarterly*, no. 75 (September 1978): 566–93.

Taylor, George. *The Struggle for North China*. New York: Institute of Pacific Relations, 1940.

Teiwes, Frederick. "The Origins of Rectification: Inner-Party Purges and Education before Liberation." *China Quarterly*, no. 65 (January 1976): 15–53.

Truong Chinh and Vo Nguyen Giap. *The Peasant Question (1937–1938)*. Translation and introduction by Christine Pelzer White. Southeast Asia Program Data Paper no. 5. Ithaca: Department of Asian Studies, Cornell University, 1974.

U.S. Operations Mission to Vietnam. *Activity Report, 30 June 1954 through 30 June 1956*. Saigon, 1956.

U.S. Senate Judiciary Committee. *The Human Cost of Communism in Vietnam*. Vol. 2. Washington, D.C.: The Committee, 1973.

Vo Nguyen Giap. *People's War, People's Army*. New York: Praeger, 1962.

Vogel, Ezra. *Canton under Communism*: *Programs and Politics in a Provincial Capital, 1949–1968*. Cambridge, Mass.: Harvard University Press, 1969.

White, Christine. "Agrarian Reform and National Liberation in the Vietnamese Revolution: 1920–1957." Ph.D. dissertation, Cornell University, 1981.

Wong, John. *Land Reform in the People's Republic of China: Institutional Transformation in Agriculture.* New York: Praeger, 1973.

Woodside, Alexander B. *Community and Revolution in Modern Vietnam.* Boston: Houghton Mifflin, 1976.

Yang, C. K. *A Chinese Village in Early Communist Transition.* Cambridge, Mass.: M.I.T. Press, 1959.

Yang Shang-kuei. *The Red Kiangsi-Kwangtung Border Region.* Peking: Foreign Languages Press, 1961.

Zelentsov, V. "Uspekhi demokraticheskoi respublike V'etnam v vosstanvlenii i razvitii narodnogo khozyaistva" [Progress of the Democratic Republic of Vietnam in restoring and developing the national economy]. *Voprosy Ekonomiki,* September 1957.

Index